The Practicum Companion for Social Work

The Practicum Companion for Social Work

Integrating Class and Field Work

Marla Berg-Weger
Saint Louis University

Julie Birkenmaier
Saint Louis University

Allyn and Bacon

Boston ■ London ■ Toronto ■ Sydney ■ Tokyo ■ Singapore

Senior Series Editor, Social Work and Family Therapy: *Judy Fifer*
Vice President, Social Sciences: *Karen Hanson*
Series Editorial Assistant: *Julianna M. Cancio*
Marketing Manager: *Jackie Aaron*
Production Editor: *Christopher H. Rawlings*
Editorial-Production Service: *Omegatype Typography, Inc.*
Composition and Prepress Buyer: *Linda Cox*
Manufacturing Buyer: *Julie McNeill*
Cover Administrator: *Jennifer Hart*
Electronic Composition: *Omegatype Typography, Inc.*

Copyright © 2000 by Allyn & Bacon
A Pearson Education Company
160 Gould Street
Needham Heights, MA 02494

Internet: www.abacon.com

Between the time Website information is gathered and then published, it is not unusual for some sites to have closed. Also, the transcription of URLs can result in unintended typographical errors. The publisher would appreciate notification where these occur so that they may be corrected in subsequent editions. Thank you.

Library of Congress Cataloging-in-Publication Data

Berg-Weger, Marla
    The practicum companion for social work : integrating class and
field work / Marla Berg-Weger, Julie Birkenmaier.
       p.   cm.
    Includes bibliographical references and index.
    ISBN 0-321-04519-X (alk. paper)
    1. Social work education.   2. Social service—Field work.
  I. Birkenmaier, Julie. II. Title.
  HV11.B44 2000
  361.3'2'071—dc21   99-16837
                                                CIP

Printed in the United States of America

10   9   8   7   6   5   4   3   2   1   04   03   02   01   00   99

To the social work field instructors and students who make all this possible.

CONTENTS

4   Making the Most of Your Practicum Supervision   69

9   Social Work Practice and the Legal System   203

PREFACE

New Beginnings

It's only the beginning now
A pathway yet unknown,
At times the sound of other steps
Sometimes we walk alone.

The best beginnings of our lives
May sometimes end in sorrow
But even on our darkest days
The sun will shine tomorrow.

So we must do our very best
Whatever life may bring
And look beyond the winter chill
To smell the breath of spring.

Into each life will always come
A time to start anew
A new beginning for each heart,
As fresh as morning dew.

—Angela Knight

Purpose of the Book

This book, *The Practicum Companion for Social Work: Integrating Class and Field Work*, is designed to accompany BSW or MSW social work practicum students through their initial experiences in the field component of the social work education process. This text will assist both BSW and MSW students within any practicum experience to integrate social work theory with practice and will provide guidance concerning practical issues that many students encounter. Discussion of "real-life" experiences and dilemmas involving a wide range of topics, clients, supervisors, staff, and other students at the agency will provide further guidance and knowledge in order to maximize the learning experience as well as to provide reassurance and support to the student.

Audience

This text is intended for social work students in undergraduate practica as well as for those in graduate-level field placements at any level. It may be used as a text in an integrative practice seminar, by students seeking further guidance and support without the aid of a field seminar, or by social work field instructors seeking further resources for their supervision of students. Those in other helping professions, such as psychology or counseling, may also find the material in this book applicable to their field practice. In addition, social work practicum field instructors may find it will help them in their roles as teachers and mentors.

Use of the Book

This book is divided into units rather than chapters so that the reader may progress through the topics in any order. Various options are available for the progression. Professors may wish to use the units in the order in which they are presented, to mix the order to suit the syllabi of their field seminars, or to utilize only a few units. Students and field instructors using this book independently may choose, rather than reading in unit order, to delve only into units that touch on timely issues in their experiences in practicum. Social work program field offices may consider providing copies of the book to all practicum sites or field instructors.

Use of Case Scenarios and Practice Applications

In addition to providing information on applying social work knowledge and skills in the field, each unit contains several case scenarios and practice applications. The case scenarios constitute situations relevant to the topic presented. Students may encounter similar situations in their field placements. Case scenarios end with discussion questions that lead into the topic.

The practice applications are discussion questions, role-plays, or exercises that will help students integrate the material covered in each unit and apply the material to their experiences. Both the case scenarios and the practice applications may be used to stimulate critical thinking and discussion in field supervision or the classroom.

Unique and Special Features of the Book

Student Profiles.   You will be able to follow the progression of four fictitious students—Ben, Cameron, Corina, and Lauren—through their practicum experiences. These students will encounter situations in their practica that may mirror your experiences or your classmates'. In addition, these students' stories will help other students apply the knowledge, skills, and issues presented in this text and help spur discussion. Postscripts to the scenarios are presented at the end of each unit.

The students are:

- **Corina,** a 22-year-old white female undergraduate student completing her BSW practicum with a public court system that works with family, domestic, and juvenile issues. This practicum is her first social work experience. As she begins her experience, she is confident about her choice to work with adolescents yet is intimidated by the teens' parents and somewhat fearful for her safety.
- **Cameron,** a 40-year-old white male undertaking his third MSW practicum in a chemical dependency treatment program. The facility offers both in- and outpatient therapy. Social work is a midlife career change for Cameron; he most recently earned a living as a painter. He is currently married to his second wife, is a recovering substance abuser, and attends AA meetings regularly. He is concerned about boundary issues and wonders whether he can separate his recovery experience from those of his clients.
- **Lauren,** a 30-year-old female who identifies herself as biracial (African American and white). She is a single parent of three young children. She will be completing her BSW practicum at a shelter for battered women and children. She is concerned about balancing work, school, and family life as well as about safety issues that accompany working in domestic violence.
- **Ben,** a 24-year-old Asian American graduate student. He will undertake his foundation practicum at a church-affiliated, community-based outreach program that works with youth and families. His undergraduate work was in biology, and he is still making the transition to this profession. He is concerned about potential cultural barriers between him and his clients.

Student Companion.   This book is designed to be utilized as students begin their practica. In contrast to other available field placement textbooks, this book assumes that the student has been placed in an organization and is ready to begin. Furthermore, the text's units follow the progression of issues as they arise for an "average" student in practicum.

Multidimensional Focus.   Social work practice is multidimensional: Social workers work at the micro, mezzo, and macro levels to address client needs. While avoiding duplication of content covered in practice theory courses, this text discusses practicum issues related to all three client system levels and provides context-sensitive suggestions to students.

Integration of Contemporary Issues Affecting Social Work Practice in the Field.   Social work practice does not exist in a vacuum. Just as social workers know that consideration of a client's environment is critical to the choice of an intervention for that person, social work students must consider the impact of contemporary issues on practice within their practicum organizations. Unit 5 discusses organizational issues that provide the context for the practicum, such as implications of working in a for-profit social service setting. Additionally, several units discuss the issues related to managed care, and Unit 8 considers the impact of welfare reform on practice.

Interwoven Ethical Dilemmas. The contexts within which ethical issues arise often dramatically affect the resolution of such conflicts. A number of ethical dilemmas are interwoven in each unit to mirror the realities of practice more closely. Ethical issues are also integrated into cases at the end of each unit. These issues raise critical reflection questions that students can discuss with other students, in class, or with their field instructors.

Practice Applications. Numerous practice applications appear throughout each unit. These practice applications, submitted by practitioners, field instructors, researchers, and teachers, include role-plays, case vignettes with questions, exercises to complete in or out of class, and journaling assignments. The practice applications are designed to further integrate the topics discussed with the practicum experience and to stimulate critical thinking and discussion. Situations that cover the spectrum from difficult supervision issues to troublesome safety settings will help assist students relate material presented to the nuances of practice within today's society.

Infusion and Discussion of Accreditation Standards for Field Education from the Council on Social Work Education. The Council on Social Work Education (CSWE) provides accreditation standards for social work programs. These standards explicate requirements for the social work field practicum. Units within the book make specific references to corresponding sections of these accreditation standards. Inclusion of the practicum requirements and links to the topics discussed focus students on their learning objectives in the field.

Supplements

Readers will find helpful resources in the appendices of this text:

Appendix A: Criteria for Determining the Best Graduate Program for You

Undergraduate students preparing for graduate studies often find the array of information about MSW programs dizzying. This checklist offers students specific criteria by which to evaluate the myriad graduate programs available.

Appendix B: Sample BSW Review Questions

Some social work programs require a comprehensive examination for graduating BSW students. Other students will take a licensing exam upon graduation. Sample review questions have been provided to help students assess their learning as well as to prepare them for a comprehensive examination.

Appendix C: Social Work: The Puzzling Profession

This crossword puzzle provides a fun and entertaining review of some major social work concepts.

Appendix D: NASW Social Work Code of Ethics

The National Association of Social Workers (NASW) Social Work *Code of Ethics* (1) is included in its entirety. Students will find this a handy reference for class as well as for practice questions.

Appendix E: Social Work Covenant

This covenant provides an inspirational guide for affirming social workers' commitment to their chosen profession.

Format

Each unit covers an issue pertinent to the social work field placement. Readers will find a logical progression of topics. Practice applications are woven throughout each unit to provide an avenue for student integration of the material into their practica. Each unit ends with a summary, student scenario postscripts, and one or more practice applications.

Unit 1: Getting Started on Your Social Work Practice Career

This unit provides guidance as students begin work at their practicum sites. Direction is given on such topics as developing relationships, defining one's learning style, expectations of all who are members of one's practicum team, developing one's learning plan, and maximizing one's integrative practice seminar experience.

Unit 2: Socialization into the Social Work Profession

Viewing oneself as a professional social worker is a challenge for many beginning social workers. This unit addresses establishing a professional identity, setting professional boundaries, self-care strategies to prevent burnout, and postpracticum career options.

Unit 3: Safety in Social Work Settings

Safety in the practicum setting is often a significant concern for students. Unit 3 covers such topics as the scope of safety risks in social work, guidelines for safe interaction with clients in the office and in the community, how to follow up when a crisis occurs, and sexual harassment.

Unit 4: Making the Most of Your Practicum Supervision

This unit answers the who, what, where, when, why, and how questions regarding supervision. Also discussed are ethical and interpersonal issues in supervision as well as strategies for maximizing the effectiveness of supervision.

Unit 5: Organizational Issues

Topics discussed in this unit include the impact of the organizational environment on practice as well as characteristics of and issues concerning government, for-profit, and nonprofit social service organizations.

Unit 6: Micro Social Work Practice in the Field

This unit focuses on both the "business" aspects (i.e., administrative, agency-related, and caseload-related issues) and the "process" aspects (i.e., the client-related issues) of micro social work practice.

Unit 7: Mezzo Social Work Practice in the Field

Issues related to group work examined include "business" aspects such as orientation, identifying oneself as a student to a group, and the role transition to group leader. "Process" topics discussed include theory/practice integration, marketing and recruitment of group members, and group dynamics. Strategies for working with nonclient groups are also provided.

Unit 8: Macro Social Work Practice in the Field

Macro issues are frequently one of the more difficult levels of practice for students to experience in practicum. Discussion of macro practice centers on both the "business" and "process" aspects of macro practice, and suggestions for incorporating macro practice into a practicum focused primarily on other client system levels are provided.

Unit 9: Social Work Practice and the Legal System

The interface of the social work profession and the legal system is discussed in this unit. Specific topics explored include grievance procedures and legal resources for clients, professional and student malpractice issues and liability, documentation as a legal record, and special issues in practicum.

Unit 10: Termination: The Beginning of an End (or the End of a Beginning?)

This unit considers both the emotional and the logistical issues related to the completion of the practicum. Topics include taking stock of the joys and frustrations of the practicum experience; the "nuts and bolts" of terminating with clients, the agency, the field instructor, and the social work program; and professional development issues.

Definition of Field Education Terms

1. *Field Placement* or *Practicum:* These terms are used interchangeably to describe the settings in which students complete the required agency-based experience

for their social work programs. A diversity of structures exists among social work programs in which students complete practicum requirements.

2. *Field Supervisor* or *Field Instructor:* These synonymous terms define the agency-based staff member who has responsibility for the student while the student is completing practicum requirements. This person may or may not be a degreed social worker, as social work programs have wide latitude to create requirements that suit their programs.

3. *Field Liaison, Faculty Liaison,* or *Field Advisor:* These terms are used to describe the social work faculty member who provides a direct link between the field experience and the social work program. This faculty member may be full- or part-time and may carry other responsibilities or focus solely on the delivery of the practicum curriculum. This person typically provides resources and oversight for the field experience.

4. *Field Integrative Practice Seminar:* In this book, a field seminar is a course designed as a companion to the practicum experience. Some social work programs may not offer a field seminar for students in practicum. The course may or may not be for credit and the structure of the seminar varies widely between programs.

5. *The Practicum Team:* This term is used throughout the book to refer to the social work program, the field supervisor/instructor, and the student.

6. *The Learning Agreement:* Synonyms for this term include *practicum contract, plan,* and *proposal.* Typically a written document, this agreement stipulates the expectations of the social work program, student, field placement agency, and field instructor for the practicum experience.

The Social Work Profession

The social work profession encompasses many different practice areas involving a continuum of client systems (individuals, families, groups, organizations, and communities). However, all social workers share a common purpose and professional identity. The National Association of Social Workers *Code of Ethics* (1) states that "a historic and defining feature of social work is the profession's focus on individual well-being in a social context and the well-being of society. Fundamental to social work is attention to the environmental forces that create, contribute to, and address problems in living." Social work differs from other helping professions (e.g., psychology, counseling, marriage and family therapy, sociology, criminal justice, human service, or guidance counseling) in the professional commitment to the core values of service, social justice, dignity and worth of the person, the importance of human relationships, integrity, and competence.

Further defining social work are the skills social work professionals offer to client systems. These include (adapted from 2):

100 Skills of the Professional Social Worker

Administration	Financial counseling	Political action
Activism	Fundraising	Post-discharge follow-up
Adoption	Gestalt therapy	Prevention
Advocacy	Goal setting	Problem evaluation
Applied research	Grantwriting	Problem-focused therapy
Assessment	Grass-roots organizing	Problem resolution
Basic skills training	Group therapy	Program administration
Behavior therapy	Health education	Program planning
Brief therapy	Health planning	Psychosocial assessment
Career counseling	Home studies	Public relations
Case management	Intake	Qualitative research
Child advocacy	Independent practice	Quantitative research
Client and family	Information and referral	Rational-emotive therapy
conferences	Interagency collaboration	Reality therapy
Client and family	Interdisciplinary	Recording
education	collaboration	Referring
Client screening	Interviewing	Residential treatment
Coaching	Intervention	Resource allocation
Coalition building	Legislative advocacy	Role playing
Cognitive therapy	Life skills education	Service contracting
Community organization	Lobbying	Service coordination
Conflict resolution	Mandated reporting	Short-term therapy
Conjoint therapy	Marital therapy	Social action
Consultation	Mediation	Social work education
Continuity of care	Mileau therapy	Staff development
Coping skills	Needs assessment	Supervision
Counseling	Negotiation	Support group
Crisis intervention	Networking	Task-centered casework
Data collection	Outcome evaluation	Teach coping skills
Direct practice	Outreach	Team player
Discharge planning	Parent training	Termination
Divorce therapy	Placement	Treatment planning
Empowerment	Planning	Utilization review
Expert witness	Policy analysis	
Family therapy	Policy development	

To the Students

It is our sincere hope that this book will differ widely from the other texts you have read for your social work courses. This text is not a practice, research, policy, human behavior, or social systems textbook, nor is it a book within which you will find a great deal of theoretical discussion. Rather, it is designed to assist you in your integration of theory with practice, where the "rubber hits the road." Some students report a wide chasm between the content covered within the social work program and their practicum experiences. We hope that this book serves as a companion on your journey and a bridge between the classroom and the real world.

Before You Head into the Field: A Prepracticum Guide

If you have not already received information from your social work program about practicum and prepared for the practicum placement/seeking process, the following guide can assist you as you make arrangements.

What Is Practicum?   Practicum (or field placement) is a social work internship served within an agency affiliated with your social work program that provides a type of social work service. The focus of practicum is gaining supervised social work experience in order to enhance the knowledge and skills gained from your coursework. The process by which students secure a practicum site varies widely.

Ask Yourself . . .   Questions to ask yourself as you begin the practicum placement/selection process include:

1. What client system(s) interest me (micro, mezzo, or macro)?
2. What type of clients interest me (children, elderly, teen mothers, etc.)?
3. What type of client issues interest me (homelessness, mental health, child abuse/neglect, troubled adolescents, etc.)?
4. What type of setting would I prefer (school, community-based health clinic, public child welfare, advocacy organization, etc.)?
5. What size agency would I prefer (large, midsized, or small)?
6. What skills do I want to gain as a result of this practicum experience?
7. What area of social work do I see myself involved in after I graduate?
8. What social work knowledge and skills do I need to achieve both my short-term and my long-term professional goals?

Reasonable Expectations for the Field Experience.   Although educational models of the field program vary widely across social work programs, there are general expectations of the field experience that stem from the accreditation standards issued by the CSWE (3). These include:

1. a field office consisting of a field director or coordinator as well as staff or faculty assigned to administer the placement/selection process as well as to monitor and evaluate your practicum experience
2. a structure that facilitates the integration of coursework with the experiences in the field. Models include a class taught on campus, periodic seminars taught in the classroom, and agency-based group learning experiences
3. a planned and structured learning experience with opportunities to provide services at the micro, mezzo, and macro system levels (4)
4. clear expectations for student learning responsibilities (3)
5. an orientation to the field agency, staff, and programs (4)
6. consistent, professional, educational, and timely supervision. Supervision should include constructive evaluative feedback on your work, support, resources, and any advocacy needed on your behalf (4)
7. a final evaluation process to provide comprehensive feedback on your work (4)

Tips for the Practicum Interview.   The extent to which students interview for a practicum position varies among social work programs. If you will interview with an agency representative, your preparation for the interview may include: (1) obtaining background information about the agency so that you can engage in a knowledgeable dialogue with the interviewer about the agency and (2) anticipating questions similar to those below and preparing answers.

Questions That May Be Asked of You at the Interview

1. Why are you interested in working with this particular population/agency/field supervisor?
2. What courses have you completed that may be relevant to this setting/work?
3. What are your strengths related to social work skills and knowledge? Your weaknesses?
4. What are your strengths related to professional work habits? Your weaknesses?
5. What are your career goals? Goals for this practicum? How could this practicum help you achieve your long-term goals?
6. Under what type of supervision do you learn best?
7. What is the most effective way in which you learn (by watching and modeling others, by listening to others talk about their work, by jumping in and learning from your mistakes, etc.)?
8. What experience/interest/skills do you have that set you apart from other candidates for this practicum slot?

An interview often includes time for questions to be asked of an agency representative.

Questions to Consider Asking an Agency Representative

1. What is the history of the organization?
2. What has the range of learning experiences been for previous students at this agency?
3. What are some possible tasks/activities with which I will be involved?
4. What style of supervision is used by the field instructor?
5. Does the agency have a formal training procedure/orientation for students?
6. What are the expectations of the field instructor regarding logistics (i.e., hours at the practicum, flexibility of hours, availability of the student to clients, expected dress, meetings, parking, travel, etc.)?
7. Will other students be working in the agency during my practicum?
8. Will the person interviewing me become my field instructor?
9. Will I have the opportunity to have contact with all aspects of the agency and learn more about the overall functioning of the agency?
10. Will the work entail any health or safety risks? Will I need any health tests or immunizations to work at the agency?
11. Does the work at the agency pose any legal liability risks? Do I need to arrange for my own professional liability coverage, or would the agency policy also cover me?

Acknowledgments

We would like to recognize the valuable input made to this book by the following reviewers, contributors, and supporters: Gary Behrman, MSW, LCSW, Saint Louis University School of Social Service; Ellen Burkemper, Ph.D., LCSW, MFT, Private Practitioner, Consultant, Adjunct Instructor, Saint Louis University School of Social Service, Lecturer, George Warren Brown, School of Social Work, Washington University; Melford Fergusen, MSW, ARCHES, St. Louis, MO; Jason Garay, BSSW Student, Saint Louis University School of Social Service; Janelle George, MSW, Project Respond, St. Louis, MO; Marian Hartung, MSW, Saint Louis University School of Social Service; Pam Huggins, MSW, University of Indiana, Bloomington, IN; Heidi Jaeger, MSW, Private Practitioner, Minneapolis, MN; Dana Klar, MSW, JD, Kathy J. Weinman Children's Advocacy Centre, St. Louis, MO; Lisa Knapp, BSSW Student, Saint Louis University School of Social Service; Suzanne LeLaurin, MSW, PLCSW, International Institute, St. Louis, MO; Donald Linhorst, Ph.D., Saint Louis University School of Social Service; Claire McCown, Ph.D., Saint Louis University Department of Education; Jan McGillick, MA, Alzheimers Association, St. Louis, MO; William Padberg, DSW, Saint Louis University School of Social Service; Carole Price, MSW, LCSW, Saint Louis University School of Social Service; Robert Sontag, LCSW, St. Louis Veterans Administration Medical Center & Delmar Gardens, St. Louis, MO; Susan Tebb, Ph.D., Saint Louis University School of Social Service; Cheryl Waites, Ph.D., MSW, North Carolina State University, Social Work Program, Raleigh, NC; Stephen Wernet, Ph.D., Saint Louis University School of Social Service; Doris Westfall, MSW, LCSW, St. Louis Society for the Blind and Visually Impaired, St. Louis, MO; Janice Wiggins, formerly of Addison Wesley Longman Publishers; Jan Wilson, MSW, LCSW, Saint Louis University School of Social Service.

We would also like to thank the reviewers of this edition: Sally Alonzo Bell, Azusa Pacific University; Cynthia Leonard Bishop, Meredith College; Arlene Kaplan Brown, Florida International University; Mary M. Gress, University of Southern California; Wanda Whittlesey-Jerome, Texas A&M University—Commerce; and Pamela Potter Ratliff, Benedict College.

M. B.-W.

J. B.

REFERENCES

1. National Association of Social Workers. *Code of ethics.* Washington, DC: NASW Press. 1996.
2. Board of Directors, Missouri Chapter, National Association of Social Workers. 1998.
3. Council on Social Work Education. *Handbook of accreditation standards and procedures.* Alexandria, VA: Author. 1994.
4. Schneck, D. What social work students should know. . . . *The New Social Worker.* 1994, 1(2):10–11, 24.

The Practicum Companion
for Social Work

1

Getting Started on Your Social Work Practice Career

For the things we have to learn before we can do them, we learn by doing them.
—Aristotle

That long-awaited point in every student's social work training has finally arrived. The semester in which you begin practicum has begun. The hours that you, your practicum site, and the social work program faculty spent in developing practicum plans have resulted in a placement. Everyone is ready to begin. "The field practicum is an integral component of the curriculum in social work education. It engages the student in supervised social work practice and provides opportunities to apply classroom learning in the field setting" (1).

The field practicum experience is the integration of the theoretical knowledge you have gained in the classroom with the skills you will learn in the field. It is viewed as a necessary and dependent complement to the didactic classroom experience (1). You will obtain supervised practice experience in which you can apply the knowledge, skills, values, and ethics that you have learned in the classroom to "enhance the well-being of people and work toward the amelioration of environmental conditions that affect people adversely" (2). The practicum experience is the factor shown to have the strongest impact on a social worker's development of practice (3). It also provides an opportunity for you to explore the numerous and varied areas of the social work profession you may wish to pursue (4). The practicum will be unlike any other academic experience you have had to date, as you are required to apply your learning through practice, develop and maintain professional autonomy, and represent yourself as a social work professional. While you continue to be a "consumer" of learning, the practicum enables you to be a "provider" of social work services.

The readings, exams, role-plays, case vignettes, and videotaping you completed as preparation for social work practice will be put to the test in the next

weeks and months. These areas of preparation provide you with the strategies you will need to engage in the development of your self-awareness in areas of social work knowledge, skills, and values clarification (4). This text is intended to help, guide, and support you through this exciting, stimulating, and sometimes challenging learning experience. This unit will address the issues to consider when beginning your practicum—developing relationships, learning styles, expectations for the practicum, and the integrative practice field seminar.

Getting Started in Your Practicum

> *Cameron has accepted a practicum at a substance abuse treatment facility. He has completed the orientation and is contemplating his first day of practicum. He has begun to question his choice of a practicum site because he is unsure if he can separate his role as a social worker from his status as a recovering person and Alcoholics Anonymous sponsor. He is concerned about the stresses that this practicum may create for him and wonders if he may be tempted to begin drinking again. Should he raise these issues and fears with his field instructor?*

Cameron's dilemma is not an uncommon one. Many social workers have had life experiences that strengthen them as social work professionals but have concerns that these same experiences will impede their ability to be competent practitioners. As in Cameron's situation, the dilemma focuses on the student's ability to blend the personal with the professional. These are important issues to consider as you begin to plan for your first day at practicum.

Following the all-important self-reflection process and the negotiation of your practicum arrangements—start date, schedule, and supervisory assignment—the real work begins. You must begin by preparing emotionally and practically for your field experience. Areas for you to consider in anticipating the practicum include:

- developing relationships with your field instructor, staff, and clients
- identifying and finding your "niche" within the agency
- identifying and understanding expectations for the experience
- identifying (and developing a relationship with) the agency or social work program person(s) to turn to with questions, problems, and crises
- developing a plan for and managing your time to avoid overload and conflicts
- identifying your learning style and role
- beginning to consider the amount and type of personal disclosure you may want to share with your field instructor and staff (helping professionals are not uncommonly personally familiar with life traumas; if this is the case for you, consider whether you feel it appropriate to share your life experiences—and how much).

Developing Relationships at Your Practicum Site

Building relationships is essential to a successful and meaningful learning experience during your practicum. Relationships with coworkers, field instructors, and fellow practicum students that begin in the practicum may become lifelong personal and professional associations. Many social workers go on to work, collaborate, and become friends with colleagues met during practicum. Social workers report that the practicum experience is the most critical course completed and that the student–field instructor relationship is the strongest, most meaningful symbol of their social work educational experience (5). One of the essential factors associated with student satisfaction with the field experience is the relationship with the field instructor (6).

The relationships that emerge as meaningful for you may evolve for a variety of reasons. Even the student–field instructor relationship, though rooted in a formal mentoring structure, may result in a sharing of common interests, goals, and mutual learning. You may also establish relationships with staff because you share mutual interests and experiences. However, you should not assume that all meaningful, even powerful, learning need be based on positive experiences. You may find that skills and knowledge can be gained from relations with agency staff, even clients, that are not always pleasant; the most memorable and valuable learning may result from the most difficult, challenging, and (what seemed at the time) unsuccessful encounters that you experience. You should therefore remain open to all potential relationships and consider each encounter an opportunity for learning. Do you recall any memorable learning that did not at the time feel valuable?

In the development of relationships within the practicum setting, you can call upon skills learned in your prerequisite coursework. For example, applying the rapport-building skills practiced through role-plays can be a first step toward integrating oneself into the "community" of the agency. You are encouraged to employ such additional engagement skills as initiating contact with others by introducing yourself, using others' names, and inquiring about staff roles and responsibilities and agency culture, history, and tradition.

The Adult Learner—What Is It and Am I One?

Social work education is based on the assumption that each student brings a lifetime of experiences to the practicum learning process and assumes responsibility for optimizing the learning potential of the classroom and field experiences. This is known as the adult learner model of education (7). Adult learners use their life experiences to motivate themselves to gain further knowledge and skill building (7).

The social work practicum serves as an excellent opportunity for you to develop and utilize the adult learner model. By taking responsibility for your own professional growth and development in social work practice, you can explore and deepen your knowledge and skills for future practice. Moreover, this approach enables you to build on the strengths previously developed through employment, volunteer/community service, coursework, other educational experiences, and life in general. Finally, incorporating the adult learner concepts into your practicum experience will prepare you for future social work employment, in which you will have to function autonomously and professionally.

Three areas affect the adult learner's ability to gain from the learning environment (8): (1) personal characteristics, (2) cognitive development, and (3) learning style. You and your teacher-mentor must be aware of and identify your individual traits and patterns in each of these areas. Personal characteristics (e.g., gender, age, ethnicity) influence the way in which you will perceive the learning experience. Your phase of cognitive development determines your capabilities for learning. Also, each student possesses a unique learning style. Your learning style determines your ability to perceive and process information and to translate that information into behavior. Identification of your learning style is particularly relevant for you and your field instructor as you develop the tasks and activities required for the learning agreement (the learning plan/contract that you negotiate with your field instructor) and the strategies for implementing and evaluating these activities. Although there are numerous frameworks available for identifying your learning style, you may opt simply to consider your learning style, communicate your assessment to your field instructor, identify the field instructor's teaching style, and discuss the fit between the two. Awareness of these teacher–learner styles enables you and your field instructor to make the most of the supervisory relationship by increasing each person's ability to be flexible and creative and by reducing conflict (9). Your ability to assert your educational needs is enhanced by heightened understanding of your informational processing styles (9).

What Kind of Learner Am I?

Corina knows from her practicum orientation that the social work program expects her to be an "adult learner," but she is unsure exactly what this means in terms of her behaviors and performance at her practicum. She is feeling lost, overwhelmed, and intimidated by the staff and clients at the detention facility. She feels that she needs more direction than her field instructor seems to want to provide. She senses that her field instructor expects immediate independence. Corina is unsure if other students feel this way, and she is reluctant to raise her fears with others. Should she ignore her feelings and dive into her work, or should she voice her anxiety to others (if so, to whom)?

Corina's fears are not unusual, particularly for students in their first practicum experiences. Think of other new ventures on which you have embarked during your life. Until you have had the opportunity to familiarize yourself with the setting, the expectations, and the people involved, you naturally question your decisions and abilities.

Characteristics of the adult learner are many and varied, but they emphasize several themes, including: (1) adults often gain as much from informal learning as from structured, planned experiences; (2) adults need to participate in structuring their learning experiences; and (3) adult learners must be challenged beyond their existing capabilities (10). Learner styles have been conceptualized from various perspectives, but one framework holds particular relevance for the social work student-learner. Walter and Sadtler (9)—building on the models developed by Fox and Guild (11); Kolb, Rubin, and McIntyre (12); and Webb (13)—describe and operationalize learning styles as belonging to three categories:

1. *Intellectual/cognitive:* uses abstract thinking skills to process information and develop a response
2. *Intuitive/experiential:* uses the ability to sense and feel a situation and then engage in the situation experientially
3. *Incremental/step-by-step:* uses the tendency for concrete thinking to process information and then execute a plan in a step-by-step manner (engage in a behavior and repeat)

PRACTICE APPLICATION **1.1**

Learning and Teaching Style Exercise

Which of the learning styles described above best describes you? Using these categories, take a few moments and talk with your field instructor regarding your individual learning style. You may use the table provided as a trigger for your discussion. Once you have addressed this question, consider the learning style of your field instructor. Ask your field instructor how he or she perceives him- or herself as (1) a learner, (2) a teacher (and how his or her learning style influences his or her approach to teaching), and (3) a supervisor. A related issue to remember is that most of us will adapt our learning styles to create our approach to teaching; your field instructor's teaching style may therefore be simply an extension of his or her approach to learning.

(continued)

PRACTICE APPLICATION **1.1**   Continued

How is the fit between your learning styles and how can the two of you negotiate the inevitable differences? Patience, creativity, and respect will be the keys to a successful negotiation.

Learning Style	Student	Field Instructor (as a learner)	Field Instructor (as a teacher)
Intellectual/Cognitive			
Intuitive/Experiential			
Incremental/Step-by-Step			

When problems arise in practicum between students and their field instructors, they may be rooted in the interaction of the students' and instructors' learning styles. Should you encounter a problem in your practicum experience, consider reevaluating the fit between the learning–teaching styles of you and your field instructor. When you have reconsidered the learning style issues, you may want to describe your perception of your learning style and needs to your field instructor.

You may find yourself learning differently at different points in your life and professional development. Students and field instructors often prefer learning through concrete experience because students can actively engage in the experience, which then provides the basis for discussion and processing of that experience (14). However, there is no one right learning style. The key is to gain awareness of your individual style and then build on its characteristics as strengths. Despite the fact that your specific learning style will not determine a successful or unsuccessful practicum outcome, the optimal learning situation occurs when you and your field instructor adapt your teacher–learner styles for maximum fit.

Whether you consider yourself a new or a seasoned adult learner, the field practicum experience provides you an excellent opportunity to assume responsibility for the application of your previous and ongoing social work learning. You cannot assume, however, that knowledge gained from coursework will automatically and easily integrate into your new practicum setting (3). Therefore, as an adult learner, you must take the initiative to optimize your learning experience by integrating your existing knowledge and skill with newly learned skills in order to prepare for social work practice. The following discussion provides some suggestions that you may consider when using the adult learner model to enhance your practicum learning.

What Is My Role as a Student Learner?

Embedded in developing relationships in the field site are the critical tasks of determining your role and integrating yourself into the overall functioning of the agency. The practicum may be some students' first professional experience. It may be others' first time in a social work setting. For still others, it may be just one of many experiences in a social service setting. No matter where you are in your personal or professional life, the practicum is a new beginning. This is the first time you have functioned as an undergraduate or graduate level social worker. Such a new beginning requires you to devote time and attention to gaining a clear understanding of your role within the unit/department, agency, and community.

PRACTICE APPLICATION **1.2**

Self-Assessment: What Do I Know and What Do I Need to Know?

In developing an understanding of your "place" as a student-learner within this practicum experience, you can engage in a thorough self-assessment prior to its onset. This self-assessment can become a practice that continues throughout the entire learning experience and beyond. Your self-assessment should include consideration of such issues as:

- What do I know about this agency—mission, services, population/community served, policies, and funding?
- What is the "dominant culture" of the organization (i.e., what discipline and service are the primary focus of the setting)?
- What knowledge, skills, and values do I bring to this experience?
- What knowledge and skills do I want to acquire from this experience?
- What are my strengths, particularly as they relate to the mission and services of this agency or organization?
- What role have students traditionally had at this site? If I am the first practicum student at this site, what do I think the student role might entail?

Think about other questions you would like to add to this list, and then share it with your field instructor. Beginning the process of role identification by raising these questions brings you to consider the area of expectations. The following discussion will focus on the many and varied expectations that will be imposed on you as you move through this field experience.

What Can I Expect from My Practicum?

Because the practicum is an interactive and structured learning process, numerous expectations will be placed on you. The social work program will communicate educational expectations for students, agencies, and field instructors. However, as an adult learner, you, too, must develop expectations for your agency and your field instructor. Establishing a clear understanding of mutual expectations will enhance your ability to determine your goals, roles, and performance standards.

Depending on your level of training and experience, the first two to three weeks of your practicum may begin with more passive learning activities, such as attending orientation, observing others, and reading manuals and literature. You may find this passive learner role somewhat frustrating and stifling to your enthusiasm for beginning practice social work. The normal progression of learning social work practice is to move from the passive to the active learning mode. While reading and observing others are essential components of your learning, you should begin engaging in more active learning activities within the first month of your practicum (depending on your previous experience and current knowledge and skill level). Guided by ongoing assessment of your skills and comfort level, you and your field instructor should consistently infuse challenges into your work. Specifically, you should transition from the passive learner role to an active learner role by engaging in such activities as assuming responsibility for another worker's case, cofacilitating a group or meeting, and being observed by others. Your ultimate goal is to progress to a higher level of autonomy at which you are solely responsible for cases/projects and group/meeting facilitation.

You will begin your practicum with a wide range of learning needs and goals. In addition to accepting the objectives established by the social work program, you are encouraged to identify your individual educational agenda for supervision. For example, are you interested in learning general social work skills to be used with a broad population or in developing expertise in a specific area (e.g., working with sexually abused children, grantwriting, or group facilitation)? Graduating social work students have offered these guidelines for you and your field instructor to consider as you develop and negotiate your practicum experience (15):

- Observe the work of others.
- Gain exposure to specialized cases and practice approaches.
- Engage in collaborative cofacilitation activities.
- Invite and accept feedback and critiques of your work.
- Request more direct supervision.
- Develop more self-awareness.
- Welcome support and encouragement.
- Obtain training in group work.
- Improve diagnostic skills.

What Will the Social Work Program Expect from Me?

Each accredited social work program must adhere to the requirements set forth by the Council on Social Work Education for accreditation (2). However, the program has flexibility in determining how best to deliver the practicum curriculum. The program will inform you and your fellow students of the expectations for fulfilling the field component of the social work degree.

In general, each student must fulfill a number of administrative and curricular requirements to initiate and finalize arrangements for the completion of the field experience. As an adult learner, you are responsible for ensuring full aware-ness of all program requirements, which may include:

- completion of practicum forms
- verification of your health status and completion of any health-related requirements (e.g., immunizations, physical examination, and tuberculosis skin test)
- verification of malpractice coverage
- completion of criminal background and child abuse and neglect checks

The Learning Plan

In Ben's practicum orientation, the social work program faculty described the completion of the learning plan as a process mutually negotiated between the field instructor and the student. Ben approached his field instructor, stating that they needed to develop his learning plan. The field instructor responded by asking Ben what he wanted to do in his practicum. She further suggested that Ben complete the learning plan and she would sign off on it. What do you think Ben should do at this point?

Although Ben's experience is, one hopes, unusual and unfortunate, his situa-tion presents him with an opportunity to begin to assert himself as an adult learner and advocate (for himself!). Ben should not accept sole responsibility for complet-ing the learning plan and he can legitimately protest.

You can expect that the social work program will provide a structure and for-mat for developing educational outcomes for the field experience and that it will communicate learning and performance expectations (16). The resulting final doc-ument should be the collaborative effort of your practicum "team"—your social work program, the agency, and you. The completed learning plan then serves as a contract among all parties for the learning experience.

The development of the learning contract should occur in a stepwise pro-gression. As an adult learner, you are responsible for the initiation and coordina-tion of the learning contract development process. Figure 1.1 outlines a general plan you can follow to complete your learning contract. The development of your learning contract may have begun to evolve during the interviewing and place-ment process, possibly even before you or the agency made a commitment to the specific practicum arrangement. After you have confirmed your practicum site, give further consideration to your expectations for learning at the agency. You should begin by reviewing the agency's mission and services and engage in dis-cussion(s) with the field instructor regarding specific practicum roles and respon-sibilities. At this point, you can develop a list of potential tasks and activities to be completed throughout the practicum. You should then consider how the potential tasks and activities would fulfill the educational objectives mandated by the social work program.

FIGURE 1.1   **Steps in Completing Your Practicum Learning Plan**

Step 1: Conceptualization ("The Big Picture") Stage
- Identify goals for social work program.
- Identify goals for agency and field instructor.
- Identify goals for yourself.
- Identify actual learning opportunities available and possible at the practicum site.

Step 2: Developing Activities Stage
- Using the social work program expectations as a guide, you and your field instructor can develop a list of potential tasks and activities for inclusion in the learning plan.

Step 3: Draft Stage
- Develop a draft of planned tasks and activities (using format/form provided by the social work program) identifying:
  - specific tasks and activities
  - timeframe
  - evaluative criteria for each task and activity
  - persons and resources required for each task and activity

Step 4: Draft Review Stage
- All relevant persons (field instructor, task instructor, other staff who will be responsible for any of your activities, faculty liaison, and, of course, you) should review the draft of the learning plan.

Step 5: Revision Stage
- Using the input obtained from the review, revise your learning plan.

Step 6: Finalization Stage
- Complete a final version and submit (by the social work program's due date!).

Step 7: Integration Stage
- Regularly integrate your learning plan into your supervisory session as a checklist for progress and evaluation.

After the development of the practicum learning plan and activities, continue to invite ideas for new learning and consider tasks, activities, and roles to include in the learning contract. As the development of this document is a collaborative process, you can engage in ongoing discussion and negotiation with your field instructor and faculty liaison in anticipation of its finalization.

The learning agreement should delineate a plan that will fulfill the practicum goals established by the social work program. This plan should articulate student roles, tasks, and activities planned for the practicum along with the evaluation criteria by which your progress and performance will be assessed. In order for the learning contract to be an effective tool for your growth, the tasks and activities outlined within the contract should be specific; challenging; relevant; appropriate to your level of experience, interests, and goals; appropriate to the setting; and measurable. You and your field instructor should determine items for inclusion that are realistically achievable given your schedule, timeframe, skill level, and access to supervision and resources.

Students often feel ill prepared to assert themselves in the development of specific tasks and responsibilities to be completed in the practicum. Using the adult learner philosophy as a guide, you are responsible for conveying to your field instructor and practicum faculty your skills, interests, and goals. Although the agency, field instructor, and social work program may have far more experience with developing learning contracts, the document becomes individualized only with the input provided by your unique perspective as a student-learner. You are able to "own" the educational experience if you feel invested through active participation in the process.

However, keep in mind the possibility that your goals and interests may not always mesh with the structure and limitations of the practicum site. The agency may have conflicting policies, inadequate resources, and other constraints that will prohibit you from engaging in all potential learning experiences. The learning plan should also serve as a mechanism to ensure that you are learning social work skills as opposed to fulfilling a needed role at the agency (e.g., typing, filing, childcare, or transportation). Should either of these situations arise, you are encouraged to discuss with your field instructor the possibility of gaining the desired experiences outside your practicum agency. For instance, if you are interested in developing your group work skills in a way the agency cannot accommodate, you may want to explore group opportunities in a related agency setting. If you feel your self-advocacy efforts have been unsuccessful in negotiating with your field instructor, you may consider discussing the issues with your faculty liaison.

A key facet of the development of the learning agreement/contract is the evaluative component. Students and field instructors should always be vigilant about the primary purpose of the practicum—you are working at the agency to learn skills that will enable you to be an effective social work practitioner. Your goal is to acquire and learn social work skills that are transferable to your future as a social worker. Although you should be intent on learning to be a competent practicum student and, eventually, an effective employee, these are not the only aims of this experience. Therefore, you should initiate each task, activity, role, and responsibility by considering its learning value the evaluation criteria to be used.

Integrating evaluation into the beginning phase of the practicum experience provides you and your field instructor the opportunity to engage in an ongoing evaluative process throughout the duration of the learning experience. Having clear and diverse strategies for measuring each task and activity enables you and your field instructor not only to engage in assessment but also to modify the learning contract, as needed, to reflect your growth, progress, and agency realities accurately. Actively use the learning contract to guide discussions with your field instructor *throughout* the practicum experience so that you can integrate intermediate benchmarks and feedback. Do not wait for all assessments to be made and conveyed at the end of the practicum.

Using a range of evaluative techniques will provide you and your field instructor with the most comprehensive and helpful feedback regarding your learning and performance. These techniques include direct observation by your field instructor or other staff of you performing your practicum tasks and activities, review of written work, audio- or videotaping of you in action, process/summary recording of your encounters with clients, group supervision/case conferences in which you present and discuss your work, and maintaining a daily log of how you spend your time.

PRACTICE APPLICATION 1.3
Watch Your Body

Electronically recording your social work practice can be a valuable experience (if a somewhat painful one, at least in the beginning!). When possible, audio- or videotape yourself engaged in your practicum activities. If you have the opportunity to videotape yourself, review the recording, then rewind the tape and review again—this time with the audio muted. Critically examine your body language and nonverbal behavior and the client's body language and nonverbal behavior in reaction to *your* behavior. Do you see things during this review that you did not see before? Record your perceptions in a journal entry and share them with a member of your practicum team.

Developed by Ellen Burkemper, Ph.D., LCSW, MFT

When the time comes for the formal evaluation forms to be completed, you and your field instructor will have ample data from which to evaluate your progress and performance. Additionally, incorporating evaluative standards into the learning agreement phase maintains your and your field instructor's focus on the goals of the field experience and establishes the basis for supervisory sessions over the course of the practicum. Further, thinking forward to the evaluation of your experience provides you and your field instructor with an opportunity to discuss the "legacy" that you hope to leave the agency as a result of the time you have spent there. Your legacy might be a project you completed, a program you developed and/or implemented, a grant proposal you wrote, a resource directory you compiled, or a practicum student orientation you created. Finally, emphasizing evaluation as part of the learning environment provides an appropriate and valuable indoctrination for you to the real world of contemporary social work practice, in which considerable attention is paid to evaluation and outcomes.

What Can I Expect from My Practicum Site?

Individual field instructors and agencies develop and maintain differing standards of professional social work behavior and practice for practicum students. Agency and supervisor expectations may range from well defined and structured to open-ended and informal. As an adult learner, you are responsible for ensuring that you have a thorough knowledge and understanding of both agency and field instructor expectations.

You can expect that your field instructor will initiate and facilitate a thorough orientation at the outset of the practicum experience. Some agencies provide students the opportunity to participate in new employee orientation, while other agencies develop orientations specific to practicum students. However, some agencies do not provide formal orientations but instead engage in an informal orientation process with each student. You should inquire about the type of orientation process your agency makes available. Regardless of the type of orientation format, you should obtain information regarding the agency's and field instructor's expectations of you and clarify your expectations of the agency and the field instructor. Some general guidelines for agency orientation include:

- completion of required agreements with the social work program regarding practicum expectations, precautions, and opportunities
- complete tour and introduction of key staff
- introduction to office space available to you
- clarification of rules for use of office space (e.g., is it to be shared, used for client interviews, locked?)
- information regarding agency procedures (e.g., schedule, time cards/clocks, parking, breaks [times, locations, restrictions], identification, credentials, sick/vacation leave, confidentiality, and management of client/case information)
- information concerning location of equipment (e.g., telephone, fax, computer), clarification regarding student use of equipment, and instructions for use (to include passwords and codes)
- information concerning the communication system, including e-mail, mail boxes, telephone messages, and regular meetings
- identification of staff with whom you will have contact and staff roles as they relate to you as a practicum student
- information about policies regarding reimbursement for practicum-related expenses (e.g., personal vehicle mileage incurred as a result of practicum-related travel)
- information concerning your responsibilities for after-hour emergencies involving your clients
- safety information—procedures to follow within the agency, with clients, in the community, and on home visits

What Can I Expect from My Field Instructor?

"Students should expect their instructors to create learning environments in which they are challenged by ideas just far enough beyond their grasp that they must struggle to learn, but not so far that they become frustrated and disillusioned" (17).

You should feel that your field instructor is pushing the limits of your abilities but supporting your growth in the process. In addition to facilitating your orientation to the agency, your field instructor may undertake the following tasks during your practicum:

- convey a commitment to your educational growth and development
- serve as a mentor
- demonstrate respect and fair treatment (17)
- provide balanced feedback on a continual basis throughout the practicum in which he or she provides you with information regarding your strengths and areas for growth
- clarify his or her approach to practicum supervision to include:
  - ◆ teaching style
  - ◆ performance expectations
  - ◆ formal and informal availability
  - ◆ identify a contact/resources person available in the case of his or her non-availability
  - ◆ formal supervision sessions (time, format, and student responsibility)
  - ◆ evaluation philosophy
- provide support in developing a plan for learning, to include:
  - ◆ orientation approach (schedule, activities, staff involvement, and student preparation)
  - ◆ opportunities for observation ("shadowing") of field instructor, other staff, and other students
  - ◆ case/project assignments
  - ◆ staff/student collaborations
- share information regarding practicum student roles in such areas as:
  - ◆ practicum structure and parameters
  - ◆ agency and field instructor history with practicum students
  - ◆ the organization's formal or informal strategic plan (i.e., the plan that guides the work of the staff)
  - ◆ flexibility regarding agency "culture," learning plan, and timeframe
  - ◆ student role as distinct from that of a volunteer or staff or board member
- clarify physical and emotional boundaries as they relate to the practicum experience
- provide information you need to learn about and function as a practicum student within the department, agency, and community, including:
  - ◆ agency/professional information and resources—policy/procedure manuals, resource directories, readings, and staff orientation materials
  - ◆ administrative/logistical information—attendance policy, parking, and identification of self as a student
- provide resource information regarding community resources (e.g., referral/referring groups, provision of information for referrals, and contact information)
- inform you of key dates or schedules that afford special learning opportunities (e.g., annual meetings, conferences, fundraising events, or lobby days)

- provide information regarding appropriate behavior, dress, and role with clients, staff, administration, and community professionals, including information regarding such activities as identifying yourself as a student, seeking out assignments from the field instructor and other staff, reading during practicum hours, completing homework during practicum hours, and collaboration with staff and community professionals

What Can I Expect from My Faculty Liaison?

Your social work program practicum faculty can be a valuable resource as you plan and complete your field experience. While the role of the practicum faculty member assigned as your resource or liaison person varies from program to program, you can generally expect the faculty member to provide the following support:

- serving as a link between the faculty and administration of the social work program and the agency, field instructor, and you to promote and monitor the completion of a quality field experience (1)
- providing orientation to the practicum process and social work program expectations of you, the field instructor, and the agency
- offering information and assistance in the development of the learning agreement/contract, including suggestions for tasks and activities, evaluation criteria, and outcomes
- providing support regarding practicum issues by responding to questions, mediating conflicts, implementing changes, and advocating as needed on your behalf
- serving as a consultant to practicum agencies and field instructors in the establishment and evaluation of practicum arrangements, plans, and structures and providing assistance and support to field instructors in their roles as teachers and mentors (1)
- monitoring the practicum experience to ensure that you and your field instructor are meeting the goals established by you and the social work program (Note: Most social work practicum faculty will conduct at least one on-site visit each semester to the practicum site to meet with you and your field instructor to discuss tasks, activities, progress toward goals, and any problems or concerns.)
- being available throughout the practicum experience to assess and reassess your interests, goals, skill development, and professional aspirations
- being available to provide you with a "safe space" to process your practicum experiences and challenges

What Should I Expect from Myself?

You should establish high standards of performance and learning for yourself as you move into and through the practicum experience. Valuable learning occurs as a result of constantly challenging your abilities and limits. However, be realistic regarding your knowledge, skills, and potential achievements (18). The list below offers guidelines for self-expectations (18, 19, 20).

- Take responsibility for your own learning by:
  - seeking out new and challenging experiences/feedback
  - exploring and becoming familiar with the agency and surrounding community
  - familiarizing yourself thoroughly with:
    - the NASW *Code of Ethics* (see Appendix D) to gain understanding about the ethical philosophy of the social work profession as it relates to your practicum site and service delivery system
    - agency safety, emergency, and restraint policies
    - agency, social work program, and professional liability issues and risks
  - asking questions, observing, and participating in as many diverse activities as possible (e.g., case staffing, staff meetings, continuing education activities, fundraising events, grantwriting activities, board meetings, and volunteer activities)
  - offering thoughtful input and feedback when relevant and beneficial
- Conduct a thorough and ongoing self-assessment to determine:
  - your personal and professional goals and interests
  - the manner in which you receive feedback and how you measure your successes
  - your comfort areas regarding issues of diversity (age, gender, race, ethnicity, and sexual orientation)
  - your strengths and areas for growth and development
- Engage in ongoing self-reflection and growth using such strategies as:
  - personal or professional journaling[1]
  - creation of your professional social work portfolio (composed of selected materials from your practicum experience, which may include but will not be limited to assessments, evaluations, samples of your written and oral work, and your resume)
  - development of a personal resource directory/file
- Commit to leaving a "legacy" for the agency by completing a needed project or resource.
- Utilize field instructor (and other staff) supervision and mentoring to the fullest extent possible by being prepared for your supervision sessions, soliciting feedback (both positive and negative), and following up with field instructor and staff suggestions.
- Learn to advocate for yourself and clients appropriately.
- Approach the social work faculty and field instructor as an adult learner by being able to distinguish between personal and professional conflicts (18).

---

1. Journaling may be required by your field instructor or faculty liaison. If it is not, you are strongly urged to maintain your own journal in which you include a summary of your learning activities, your thoughts and reactions to your learning, progress toward goals, challenges faced within the practicum, and questions for your field instructor, faculty, and yourself.

- Invest in your own self-care (e.g., stress and time management and finding a balance between personal and professional obligations).
- Take advantage of all resources offered by the social work program, the agency, friends, and family.
- Have fun and learn!

Integrative Practice Field Seminar

Through the accreditation of social work programs, the Council on Social Work Education (2) mandates that social work programs ensure the integration of social work theory and practice. "The need for integration of classroom and field learning is inherent in social work education" (21). The integration of theory with social work practice has been an emphasis of social work educators since the beginning of formalized social work education. Historically, however, a lack of clarity exists regarding the definition and operationalization of theory–practice integration and how to determine the success or failure of such an endeavor. Focusing on the integration of theoretical knowledge with the application of social work practice further enables you to maintain a perspective on the evolution of our profession and to link contemporary field instruction issues to the social work profession's historical development.

The integration of theory with the application of social work skills requires you, the student, to engage in a "reformulation of theoretical knowledge, self-knowledge and critical analysis" (22). To facilitate the integration process, you must develop an ability to absorb conceptual information; translate that knowledge into concrete, interventive strategies; and apply the strategies through the practice of social work. Although such an integration is the desired goal of professional social work education, social work educators, field instructors, and students find the process challenging. Therefore, the process of effectively integrating theory and

practice demands that all members of your social work practicum team work together collaboratively. Each member of your team contributes a unique and valuable perspective that promotes the desired integration—the educator provides the substantive theory; the field instructor brings the practice wisdom; and you, the student, possess the ability to reflect and critically analyze the information received and to act on it. Your practicum team must develop strategies for implementing the integration plan.

One strategy for facilitating this integration process is the integrative practice field seminar. All social work baccalaureate programs and an increasing number of graduate programs require students to complete an integrative practice field seminar concurrently with the field experience. There is wide variation in the structure, format, and delivery of this practicum-related curriculum. The following discussion offers insights and suggestions for maximizing the learning potential of the integrative practice field seminar.

What Can I Expect from the Integrative Practice Field Seminar?

A field seminar provides you an opportunity for individual and group reflection on the application of classroom and field learning (16). The integration of social work theory and practice is most likely to occur through use of a structured format that involves focused group exercises and case presentations with group discussions (21). Social work educators also recognize the value and learning potential of the unstructured opportunity to share and engage in mutual support and problem solving. Thus, the integrative practice field seminar is typically a mixture of structured and unstructured activities aimed at supporting you and your colleagues while providing the opportunity for theoretical frameworks to be applied to actual social work practice. Students and instructors find a range of diverse activities to be most valuable, particularly when the structured group activities are instructor- or student-led group exercises and the unstructured group sharing emphasizes processing and problem solving (to include discussion of practice dilemmas and successes) (21). Focusing on the common experiences and concerns of the students can create an environment truly suited to stimulation and integration.

The seminar can serve as an environment in which you can test and refine ideas and experiment with the application of new skills (23). You should be challenged to translate and apply the theoretical concepts and knowledge you have learned into behavioral social work practice skills. Such a transformation will require you to engage regularly and frequently in in-depth self-assessment, risk taking regarding new ideas and practice techniques, and ongoing evaluation of your knowledge, skills, and values.

Derived from the experience of the authors and others, general objectives appropriate for an integrative practice field seminar include (21):

- integration of content on social work issues (history, policy, human behavior, diversity, practice, research, and evaluation) with the practicum experiences
- networking and processing with your peers and instructor

- professional and peer support
- development of your knowledge of the community and its resources
- exploration of your values, beliefs, attitudes, and competencies
- professional socialization and a deepening of your knowledge of the breadth of the social work profession
- creation of a safe environment for the development of your own self-awareness
- exploration of treatment issues, particularly regarding the use of self in your social work practice
- inventory and comparison of diverse social work settings and "cultures" within which social work practice occurs
- discussion of organizational and policy issues

What Can I Expect from My Seminar Instructor?

The integrative practice field seminar may be unlike any other course you have completed during your academic career. In the seminar, the instructor will utilize a variety of teaching techniques but will serve primarily as a "facilitator" for your learning. Generally, you should anticipate that the seminar instructor will:

- create an environment that promotes open, respectful, and meaningful discussion for you and your colleagues (24);
- communicate clearly his or her expectations for the course, students, and the practicum sites;
- stimulate discussions focused on peer support, values, and ethically related issues and dilemmas;
- facilitate discussion of social work practice issues, the social work practice community, and professional development issues;
- emphasize the importance of maintaining confidentiality;
- consult with students and practicum sites regarding practicum questions, concerns, and dilemmas; and
- challenge students in areas of practice skills and issues.

What Can I Expect from the Other Students?

Because of the emphasis on process and peer support, each student should approach the integrative practice field seminar with high expectations of his or her fellow students. Often, the most valuable learning results from input from other students with facilitation provided by the seminar instructor. Therefore, you should expect the following from your seminar classmates:

- *Attendance.* Because of the ongoing nature of information processing, students should be in regular attendance so that other students feel respected and valued and do not have to repeat information and so that each contributor's input is relevant and consistent.

- *Active preparation and participation.* Because mutual and reciprocal interaction is the goal, all students must be able and willing to engage actively in seminar discussion.
- *Respect.* Because students will be taking risks in presenting and exploring ideas, values, and newly acquired skills, students must respect each other's right to take such risks in practicum and to articulate opinions, fears, frustrations, and experiments. Students must also offer support for each other's willingness to share and must respect each other's right to reject input or suggestions.
- *Confidentiality.* Due to the potentially confidential nature of the information shared in the seminar, all students must adhere rigidly to a high standard of confidentiality.
- *Balanced feedback.* As students provide input to colleagues, each should try to provide positive, strengths-based ideas along with comments on areas for growth and change.

What Should I Expect from Myself?

Each student, within the concept of the adult learner model, is relevant in optimizing the learning potential of the integrative practice field seminar. You should maintain expectations of yourself that mirror those noted in the previous discussion regarding your expectations of other students. You should also:

- commit to learning through constant challenging of your knowledge, skills, and values;
- commit to the learning of others through the modeling of strengths-based interactions;
- actively interact with other students and the instructor through ongoing exchanges and explorations of issues;
- be willing to challenge, question, and take risks;
- invest in the value of the input of others; and
- be willing to follow up on viable suggestions, questions, and areas of concern.

PRACTICE APPLICATION 1.4
Seeing My Practicum Site with Different Eyes

On your third or fourth visit to your practicum site following your initial orientation, approach the setting visualizing yourself as a client of this agency. When you arrive on the premises and enter the building as a client, identify and assess the following facets of your experience:

- Do your perceptions of the agency and staff change? If your perceptions do change, how do they change?

- What are your first impressions in terms of the sights, sounds, smells, client–client interactions, client–staff interactions, and staff–staff interactions, and agency "culture"?
- How do your impressions make you feel about the agency? Yourself? Your profession?

Following completion of this exercise, reflect on your experience through journaling of your impressions and explanations for your feelings. You may then want to share your reflections with your field instructor and fellow students.

You may want to repeat this exercise later in your practicum and record how, if at all, your perceptions and observations have changed and the reasons for these changes. This can provide an opportunity for you to discuss your impressions and any recommendations regarding the agency with your field instructor.

Developed by Jan McGillick, MA

PRACTICE APPLICATION **1.5**

Seeing My Field Instructor with Different Eyes

During one of your early supervisory sessions with your field instructor, take the opportunity to learn more about the professional socialization that your field instructor experienced. The following questions can serve as a springboard for this discussion:

- Where did you complete your practicum (practica)?
- What do you recall about the experience(s)—positive, negative, and meaningful aspects?
- What was most helpful/least helpful about your field instructor's teaching style?
- Regarding your experiences as a field instructor, what have been your most/least successful experiences with students (without disclosing confidential/specific information)?

A discussion centered around these and other related issues can serve to open a dialogue between your field instructor and you about values, work styles, and expectations. You can also learn about your field instructor's perception of supervision and accountability. From this discussion, develop with your field instructor a list of at least three strategies for structuring your practicum to optimize the benefit for you (as a learner), your field instructor (as a teacher), and your practicum site.

Developed by Jan McGillick, MA

Summary

This first unit has established the foundation for the remainder of this book. We encourage you to consider yourself an adult learner in the practicum setting, in the integrative practice field seminar, and in the use of this text as a learning tool. This unit has addressed the beginning phases of the practicum experience, enabling you to move from the first days of the practicum and the first seminar meeting to the orientation and, finally, to the development of the learning agreement/ contract. While the social work faculty, seminar instructor, and other students are there to support and guide you, you have the opportunity and responsibility to embrace the challenges that lie ahead in your practicum, the seminar, and beyond.

STUDENT SCENARIO POSTSCRIPTS

Cameron discussed his concerns with his practicum liaison. His liaison recognized the validity of his fears and acknowledged that these issues are normative for students with Cameron's life experiences. The liaison encouraged him to consider that the stresses of beginning a practicum and transitioning from a consumer of services to a provider of services may have heightened his vulnerabilities regarding his own recovery process. Second, with the liaison's urging, Cameron initiated a discussion with his field instructor. His field instructor ensured him that his response to the situation was normal, stating that many new substance abuse treatment professionals question their ability to work effectively with abusers/addicts while maintaining their own abstinence and recovery. The field instructor suggested that Cameron pay particular attention in the upcoming weeks to his feelings and reactions to client situations and identify any situations/remarks that raise unresolved issues for him. Further, the field instructor asked that Cameron maintain a journal, focusing particularly on his ongoing feelings about working with a recovering population, and raise the issue during supervision sessions as he felt necessary.

Corina raised the issue of autonomy (and her fears about not having attained autonomy yet) in her integrative practice field seminar. With the support of the seminar instructor and fellow students, she chose to approach her field instructor with her concerns. Her field instructor had no idea that Corina was feeling the way she was and commended her for taking responsibility for confronting the autonomy issue. The field instructor then initiated a discussion of his expectations regarding her performance, during which he recognized that he may have been pushing Corina too hard and fast given her comfort level. They agreed to check in with each other at each supervisory meeting to determine Corina's status. This situation could easily have evolved into a less satisfactory outcome, but Corina's willingness to take the initiative in her learning experience led to a positive one.

Ben confronted his field instructor at a supervision session, stating that he felt that she was not interested in his learning, as evidenced by her cavalier attitude toward his learning plan. The interaction was quite strained and resulted in both Ben and the field instructor independently contacting the social work program faculty to state that they did not believe the practicum would work out. The practicum liaison initiated a three-way meeting to discuss the problem. Both Ben and the field instructor had the opportunity to present their perspectives on the situation and, with negotiation facilitated by the liaison, they agreed to continue the practicum. The field instructor agreed to commit more time and energy to Ben's learning, and the three discussed ways in which Ben could handle difficult situations in a calmer, more diplomatic manner.

REFERENCES

1. Brownstein, C., Smith, H. Y. & Faria, G. The liaison role: A three phase study of the schools, the field, the faculty. In Schneck, D., Grossman, B. & Glassman, U. *Field education in social work: Contemporary issues and trends* (pp. 237–248). Dubuque, IA: Kendall/Hunt. 1991.

2. Council on Social Work Education. *Handbook of accreditation standards and procedures.* Alexandria, VA: Author. 1994.

3. Tolson, E. R. & Kopp, J. The practicum: Clients, problems, interventions and influences on student practice. *Journal of Social Work Education.* 1988, 24(2):123–134.

4. Ross, S. T. Field placement: A building block to your career. *The New Social Worker.* 1997, 4(1):16–17.

5. Kissman, K. & Van Tran, T. Perceived quality of field placement education among graduate social work students. *Journal of Continuing Social Work Education.* 1990, 5(2):27–30.

6. Fortune, A. E., Feathers, C. E., Rook, S. R., Scrimenti, R. M., Smollen, P., Stemerman, B. & Tucker, E. L. Student satisfaction with field placement. *Journal of Social Work Education.* 1985, 3:92–104.

7. Knowles, M. S. *The adult learner: A neglected species* (3rd ed.). Houston: Gulf. 1984.

8. Memmott, J. & Brennan, E. M. Learner-learning environment fit: An adult learning model for social work education. *Journal of Teaching in Social Work.* 1998, 16(1/2):75–98.

9. Walter, C. A. & Sadtler, L. C. The role of the field liaison in identifying learning/teaching styles to facilitate student learning. *Areté.* 1997, 21(2):50–60.

10. Wilson, S. J. *Field instruction: Techniques for supervisors.* New York: Free Press. 1981.

11. Fox, R. & Guild, P. Learning styles: Their relevance to clinical supervision. *The Clinical Supervisor.* 1987, 5(3):65–77.

12. Kolb, D. A., Rubin, I. M. & McIntyre, J. M. *Organizational psychology.* Englewood Cliffs, NJ: Prentice-Hall. 1974.

13. Webb, N. The role of the field instructor in the socialization of students. *Social Casework.* 1988, 69(1):35–40.

14. Van Soest, D. & Kruzich, J. The influence of learning styles on student and field instructor perceptions of field placement success. *Journal of Teaching in Social Work.* 1994, 9:49–69.

15. Munson, C. E. *Clinical social work supervision* (2nd ed.). New York: Haworth Press. 1993.

16. Schneck, D. What social work students should know about field instruction. *The New Social Worker.* 1994, 1(2):10–11, 24.

17. Groccia, J. E. The student as customer versus the student as learner. *About Campus.* 1997, 31–32.

18. Fogel, S. My practicum: Why do I hate it so? *The New Social Worker.* 1996, 3(1):12–13.

19. Ligon, J. & Ward, J. Ten tips for a successful field placement. *The New Social Worker.* 1998, 5(2):20.

20. Simon, S. & Schatz, M. S. The portfolio approach for BSW generalist social work students. *The New Social Worker.* 1998, 5(1):12–14.

21. Mary, N. L. & Herse, M. H. What do field seminars accomplish? Student and instructor perspectives. *Journal of Teaching in Social Work.* 1992, 6(2):59–73.

22. Vayda, E. & Bogo, M. A teaching model to unite classroom and field. *Journal of Social Work Education.* 1991, 27(3):271–278.

23. Walden, T. & Brown, L. N. The integration seminar: A vehicle for joining theory and practice. *Journal of Social Work Education.* 1985, 21(1):13–19.

24. Moxley, D. P. & Thrasher, S. P. The intervention design seminar: Structure, content and process. *Journal of Teaching in Social Work.* 1996, 13(1/2):73–92.

UNIT

2

Socialization into the Social Work Profession

Social work is not something you do but something you become.

—Julie Birkenmaier

Socialization is a concept often discussed in terms of establishing one's identity within a particular group. Socialization can be considered as "the process by which you learn all that you need to know in order to get along in the world in which you live" (1). Through your socialization into a group, you informally, and possibly formally, learn the rules, roles, norms, customs, traditions, and value and philosophical bases of that group. If you opt to continue as a member of the group, you determine which of the group's qualities and characteristics you accept and which you reject. In the final analysis, you establish your identity within and affiliation to that group.

The practicum is but one phase of your socialization as a social work professional. The decision to become a social worker began your socialization process. You may have had an experience with a social worker or have a family member or friend who is a social worker. Think for a moment about your decision to become a member of the social work profession.

Now that you have reflected on your initial decision to join the social work profession, consider how your socialization process has evolved thus far. You have completed part of the required coursework, and you may even have had volunteer or paid social work–related experiences. The coursework and volunteer or employment experience you have gained was the beginning of your formal socialization as a social worker. You have learned of our profession's history, achievement, challenges, values, and ethical stances. You have learned that some social workers emphasize a generalist approach and that others, building on the generalist perspective, develop specialized expertise in a particular area of practice. As you have learned, social work is a discipline comprising an extremely diverse membership. The profession includes differences on many fronts—political views, religion, and ethnicity, to name a few. In fact, social work is a profession that prides itself on acceptance of diversity, both that of those we serve as well as that of our own members. Therefore, socialization into this profession can and should be an individualized process unique to each person that takes into account his or her culture and ethnicity, personal and professional experiences, and personality.

"The vitality and coherence of any profession is enhanced by the presence of a common core of agreed-on beliefs, values and interests among its members, in other words, a professional identity" (2). Part of your socialization process requires you, as a new social worker, to find your niche within the profession. Because the social work profession is a broad, demanding, and complex occupation, you must learn to juggle and balance the many and diverse demands placed on you in virtually any setting in which you practice social work. You are required to maintain objectivity while staying committed to the profession. You are required to exhibit empathy—but not sympathy—and you must confront the ethical dilemmas that will surely arise. While aspects of these issues are skill-based, much of your competence in these areas will emerge through your socialization into the profession.

Your professional socialization process will never end. You will find that you change, grow, and evolve throughout your life and learn new knowledge, skills, and competencies as you progress through your social work career.

There are two (often concurrent) avenues of socialization that will occur as you develop your social work identity. First, you will become socialized into the social work profession, in general. This phase of socialization involves learning the knowledge, skills, and values of the profession as a whole. Second, your basic social work socialization process will be enhanced by the knowledge, skills, and values gained that are specific to your area(s) of interest, field of practice, and practice setting. For example, you will develop your identity as a social worker, but you

may also identify yourself as having particular interest and expertise in one area, such as domestic violence or health. Your challenge is to blend and balance these two potentially conflicting processes.

This unit will aid you in identifying yourself as a social work practitioner; learning to balance the multiple, often conflicting, roles you will assume as a social worker; establishing professional and personal boundaries; managing the inevitable stressors that emerge; and anticipating the transitions that will occur as you move through your life as a social worker. We hope that you will use this information to enhance your socialization experience and to contribute to the positive image of the social work profession.

Me? A Social Worker?

Ben was certain about his decision to change his career plans from medicine to social work—that is, he was until he had completed the coursework that precedes practicum. During class discussions, Ben frequently felt as though he was missing something. He marveled at his fellow classmates who seemed to understand intuitively the subtleties of a client situation. He found that these nuances often escaped him. He is growing increasingly concerned about his ability to be a member of the social work profession, particularly now that he has started his first practicum. He knows he wants to work with people but wonders if his "missing it" is what prevents him from being as intuitive as his peers. He questions whether this is due to his innate skills, his upbringing, his Asian heritage, being male, or being a biology major. What do you think about Ben's perceived dilemma? Are his fears realistic? What would you suggest he do?

Many social work students find themselves in the dilemma that Ben is facing and ask themselves, "How can I possibly understand the clients' problems and be helpful to them?" Students often become intimidated when observing more experienced social work students, practitioners, and field instructors, questioning whether they will ever be that skillful and effective. Beginning to define oneself as a social work professional is one step toward achieving the "practice wisdom" that is so critical to the competent practice of social work. Klein and Bloom (3) define the concept of practice wisdom as "a system of personal and value-driven knowledge emerging out of the transaction between the phenomenological experience of the client situation and the use of scientific information." Practice wisdom encompasses all the aspects of a social worker's socialization into the profession—knowledge, values, principles, and experiences. The practicum experience signals the beginning of the development of practice wisdom as a part of the social worker's repertoire of knowledge and skills. This developmental process then continues throughout one's career.

PRACTICE APPLICATION **2.1**
Often-Asked Client Questions

Clients make a significant contribution to your ability to perceive yourself as a professional social worker—both positive and negative. Role play with your field instructor or other seasoned social work professional the following scenarios, in which clients present you with such situations as:

1. "You're just a student. I want a *real* professional (or social worker)."
2. "Do *you* have children?"
3. "What is the *success* rate with treating _____?"
4. "I'm here today because I don't know where to turn. What can you do for me?"
5. "You know, it's really hard for me to be here, but here I am. What do I have to do to get through this, and how can you [just a student] help me?"
6. "It's hard to describe my situation because, very frankly, I don't understand how it happened. It seems like this situation has taken on a life of it's own. You're an expert, so I know you'll know what to do."

Process your thoughts and feelings regarding these potential situations with your field instructor. Can you think of other questions or situations that might jar your confidence?

Developed by Ellen Burkemper, Ph.D., LCSW, MFT

Strategies for Your Socialization as a Social Worker

We have defined professional socialization and emphasized the necessity for the process. The questions that need to be addressed now are: How does professional socialization happen? Who is responsible for it happening? And will it occur if you are passive and reactive? These issues should become an intregal part of your field experience. Yes, your socialization may happen "to" you, but, as with any endeavor, you will likely have a richer, more meaningful experience if you are proactive and take responsibility for initiating your socialization into your new profession. Although it is important for all individuals to approach new ventures at their own paces and in their own styles, we have compiled the following suggestions for you and the other members of your practicum team to consider as you begin your journey into social work:

Student-Initiated Strategies
- Join professional social work organizations at your school and in the community. Be an active participant in these organizations (e.g., run for office, attend conferences, and volunteer for committees).

- Join and invest energy into an existing professional or student organization.
- Start a student social work organization if one does not exist in your social work program, or establish a special-interest group with other students who share your interests.
- Become involved with your school's alumni activities through such programs as career mentoring, student recruitment, and continuing education events.
- Volunteer or seek part- or full-time employment in a social service setting while you are a student.
- Identify your field instructor, faculty, and yourself as the learning team that is responsible for your professional socialization.
- Identify a social worker to serve as your mentor. This person may be a faculty member, field instructor, or other social work practitioner whose expertise you value and respect.
- Seek out as many and varied practicum-related experiences as you can to broaden your social work horizons and skills.
- Develop your professional social work portfolio, including your resume and examples of your work.
- Read social work–related literature (e.g., *NASW News*, topic specific journals and books) and peruse the social work journals on a regular basis for articles in your areas of interest.
- Form or join a peer/professional support group, which may focus on supervision, licensure examination preparation, and common interests and concerns.
- Participate in your community's social, cultural, and political activities even if you do not plan to remain in the area following graduation.
- Seek opportunities to practice defining a social worker to others (friends, family, and clients).
- Put yourself in situations in which you represent the profession to non–social work professionals and community groups (there is no better way to gain confidence in your professional identity than to portray your profession to others!).

We have encouraged you to be proactive in your socialization process. You are not, however, solely responsible for covering every aspect of your orientation and immersion into social work. Another member of your learning team, your field instructor, can be an invaluable resource, guide, and mentor as you grow and develop as a professional social worker. Field instructors can model what a professional "is" and "does" (4). We offer the following ideas about how your field instructor (or other social work practitioner) can support you in your professional development. Although your field instructor may naturally assume the role of mentor and guide, do not hesitate to ask or suggest that he or she facilitate these experiences for and with you.

Field Instructor-Initiated Strategies
- invite you to participate in social work activities (e.g., case conferences, staff meetings, in-service training sessions, continuing education events, professional meetings, events, lectures, and seminars)

- assign or suggest relevant readings and discuss the material with you in terms of the implications for your practice
- be a mentor or connect you to a mentor
- connect you to other social workers to broaden your perception and definition of social work
- require you to maintain a professional journal or log, read the log, and provide you with regular feedback regarding your growth as a social worker
- in supervision sessions, raise issues related to the profession of social work—in other words, take supervision beyond the technical/clinical realm and help you to think *automatically* from the social work perspective
- refer to him- or herself, you, and other staff as social workers to solidify your perception of yourself and others as professional social workers (versus counselors, case workers, or therapists) (2)
- suggest items for and help you to develop your professional portfolio
- routinely raise issues of self-care as a normative expectation for the profession

You have now had the opportunity to consider your own socialization into the social work field. Where do you think you are in the process? What have you achieved? What do you want to achieve in the future? How can you approach your goals?

A significant part of any socialization process is gaining an understanding of the group to which one is being socialized. As a practicum student, you strive to understand not only the social work profession but also your practicum site. You can begin your socialization to your practicum site by considering the relationship between your socialization and the organization's norms and controls (1). Norms are the informal operationalization of the organization's rules, while controls are put into place to ensure compliance with the rules and the norms (1). Gaining insight into the dynamics of the organization's norms and controls can aid you in identifying the way in which you and the staff are socialized into that organization.

PRACTICE APPLICATION **2.2**

Social Work from Your Own Perspective

Prepare a written statement describing your

- definition and philosophy of social work and
- perception of the role of the social work professional in your practicum site.

Interview representatives of as many of the disciplines represented in your practicum agency as possible. Ask each person to describe social work in general, to define the role of social work in the agency, and to compare and contrast social work with his or her own discipline's philosophical and theoretical stances. Using your prepared statement, share with the person you are interviewing your own perspective of social work and discuss the similarities and differences between your respective views of social work.

(continued)

| PRACTICE APPLICATION **2.2**　Continued

Summarize your findings, and share them with your field instructor, agency staff, fellow students, and your integrative field practice seminar. Consider the following questions:

- Have your perceptions of social work changed?
- If so, how have they changed?
- Who was instrumental in contributing to this changed perception?
- If your perceptions are not changed, have they been strengthened by this exercise?

If you find that your perceptions have, in fact, been altered as a result of this exercise, rewrite your original prepared statement on social work and use it in your discussions with others. Be certain to save your statement(s) so that you can reference them as you move through your professional development.

PRACTICE APPLICATION **2.3**
Social Work from Many Perspectives

The following practice application is designed to strengthen your identity as a social worker as well as to aid you in understanding the professional perspectives of other disciplines. You may use the case presented here or refer to a situation that has arisen at your practicum site that involved at least three different disciplinary perspectives. You may also opt to complete this exercise as a group activity (another opportunity to gain learning from multiple perspectives). After reading the case, follow these steps.

- Identify the disciplines most critical to the intervention, and determine who should be in attendance at the upcoming meeting.
- Identify the issues you consider most relevant in developing an intervention.
- Develop a list of questions you would pose to a representative of each discipline.
- Locate a representative from each of the disciplines identified in your assessment. (These may be employees at your practicum site, colleagues of agency staff, and faculty members at your university or college.)
- Ask each representative to read the case and respond to the list of questions that you have developed from the perspective of his or her discipline.
- Summarize your findings for presentation to your field instructor or integrative field practice seminar.

The Case
You are a social work practicum student in an elementary school. You were assigned by your field instructor to work with Danielle and her family. Danielle is a 12-year-old female who is in the sixth grade, having been retained in the third grade for poor academic performance. Her mother recently died, and Danielle is living with her stepfather and her younger half-sister from her mother's marriage to Danielle's stepfather.

Danielle receives special education services based on the recommendation of the Multidisciplinary Conference (MDC). In addition to a poor academic performance history, Danielle has been diagnosed with attention deficit disorder (ADD) and reads and comprehends several levels below her grade level. You are preparing for Danielle's upcoming Individual Education Plan (IEP), an annual review of the educational and behavioral goals established by the MDC when Danielle's eligibility for special education services was determined.

The Disciplines

Teacher: Danielle's teacher made the original referral to the school guidance counselor based on several concerns, including: poor academic performance, reading deficits, truancy, and behavioral problems in the classroom (difficulty focusing on the tasks assigned, excessive talking, and difficulty staying seated). Even after Danielle began taking Ritalin for her ADD, the teacher finds her a behavioral problem in the classroom. The teacher will be reporting on Danielle's current academic performance and classroom behavior.

Guidance Counselor: Upon receiving the referral from the teacher, the guidance counselor initiated referrals to the school psychologist (for educational testing) and social worker (for truancy). The guidance counselor is the coordinator of the school's IEP process and will be facilitating this meeting.

Psychologist: The psychologist has completed educational testing with Danielle and will be reporting on the findings at the IEP.

Resource Room Teacher (i.e., Reading Specialist): The reading teacher has been working with Danielle for several months and will be reporting on the reading problems identified in the MDC's initial eligibility determination, type of reading problems, and Danielle's progress in meeting her goals.

School Social Worker: Upon receiving a referral for social work services, you have completed a home visit to Danielle's family. You found the home itself to be unclean and in a state of disarray and the home situation to be chaotic. You have determined that Danielle's stepfather is immobilized by his grief over the loss of his wife, unable to provide adequate care or monitoring for either of the children, and not at all attached to Danielle. He appears to have appropriate parental feelings about his biological child, but he said to you that if Danielle had "anywhere else to go, she'd have been shipped there as soon as the funeral was over."

As a part of the MDC to determine eligibility for special education services, you were involved in the completion of the social developmental study that included a family history, classroom observation, and behavioral analysis. As a result of your assessment, referrals were made for Danielle to receive services from the resource room teacher and a psychiatric evaluation to determine the presence of an attention disorder diagnosis (resulting in the prescribing of Ritalin).

Public Child Welfare Worker: A protective service investigation was completed based on an anonymous report to the protective service agency that included the following information: Danielle does not attend school regularly, is out late at night with older males (may be involved in alcohol and drug use), and is left unsupervised for several days at a time. The protective service worker reported to you in an earlier telephone conversation that the stepfather wants to "get rid of her as soon as somebody will take her."

The Perspectives

Obtain the perspectives of each of the disciplines, and compare and contrast your findings.

Pulling It All Together: How Can I Juggle All the Roles?

Your professional social work socialization can be considered a slate on which you and others write the social work knowledge, skills, and values that you gain during your educational experiences. This slate is not blank: You bring to the social work profession your personal and professional life experiences. Once you have begun to fill up your professional slate, the next step for you, as a new professional, is to take the concepts from your slate and internalize them as part of your professional social work personality. The slate will become filled very quickly, and you will begin to question how you can manage all the knowledge, roles, and interests that have taken a place on it.

The process of filling your slate may be guided by a number of different and varied persons with whom you interact during your training. Your field instructor and social work program faculty will probably have the most influence on your socialization. As a part of developing your social work personality, you and your mentor may choose to focus on certain tasks and discussions to increase your self-awareness and self-control (4). Increasing your self-awareness in the areas of your interests, goals, styles, frustrations, and needs can be key to gaining a viable balance in your social work career. Issues and tasks that seemed paramount in the beginning may recede once you have considered the realistic capabilities of your agency, your client, and, most important, yourself.

While increasing your self-awareness and ability to balance your emotions may seem awkward and uncomfortable in the beginning, you can rely on the social work values that you have learned to maintain a realistic perspective (5). The Council on Social Work Education stipulates that the practicum experience should result in a heightened awareness of oneself in the process of intervention (6). Again, your mentor can be a resource for challenging you to delve into issues of self-insight. "Self-awareness—and strategies to cope with it—can't be 'taught' in schools" (7). Therefore, while in the field, you must push yourself to explore and challenge your feelings, history, stereotypes, and attitudes in order to deepen your understanding of yourself and your place within the social work profession. Your mentor has the advantage of having more social work experience than you have at this point in your career. He or she can teach you the skills necessary for prioritizing the demands on you and the roles to which you have been assigned or you have chosen for yourself.

Some issues to consider as you contemplate how you can effectively juggle the many and varied roles that you want and need to fulfill and the emotions that accompany them are:

- *Balance, balance, balance:* No one part of your professional or personal life should dominate the others to the detriment of other responsibilities and interests.
- If you are able, build on your capacity to multitask (to complete more than one activity at a time), but do not impose this expectation on yourself if you are not comfortable with it.

- To the extent possible, arrange your schedule so that you are at your best when you are faced with the most difficult aspects of your learning (i.e., schedule your most challenging tasks and activities for the mornings if you consider yourself a morning person).
- Gain insight into your work style and patterns and build on those strengths.
- Ensure that you regularly leave your office or building for breaks, lunch, or home visits.
- Pace yourself—spread your obligations out so that you will have time for unplanned events and demands.
- To the extent possible, diversify your work activities to provide variety in your daily routine.

To enhance your ability to manage your workload, additional strategies that you may want to consider include (8, 9):

- Do not assume that just because you are actively engaged in an activity you are being productive.
- Devote yourself to managing and planning your workload (every hour spent in planning can result in a savings of three to four hours of actual work). Have a daily work plan in which you note tasks to be completed today, tasks to begin today, or tasks that can wait until later. To identify strategies for increasing your efficiency, consider documenting the way in which you spend your day.
- Assume that events that you did not expect will, in fact, occur often and build in time to respond to these unexpected disruptions (i.e., do not procrastinate on meeting deadlines so that you do not have time, energy, and resources to handle the unplanned occurrences).
- Learn to use technological resources to your advantage (e.g., telephone, voice mail, fax, computer programs, e-mail, Internet, and databases) to increase your efficiency and effectiveness.

Setting Professional Boundaries

Cameron had been concerned about potential overlapping conflicts that could occur as a result of his roles as a recovering person and an AA sponsor. Despite his heightened self-awareness regarding this issue and previous discussions with his sponsor and practicum team, his worst fears are being realized. He is encountering clients from his practicum at his own AA meetings, and they are approaching him before and after the meetings to discuss their recovery struggles, asking if they should reenter the treatment program and even if he would see them for individual sessions. Despite being flattered by their confidence in him, several dilemmas have emerged for Cameron: (1) How can he separate himself from his professional role when he is attending an AA meeting? (2) How can he set limits with former clients without the client feeling rejected? (3) How can he be certain what his student role should be? What suggestions do you have for Cameron's situation?

Cameron's particular dilemma may be unique, but this type of dilemma is not an uncommon one for social workers. Although we may try to leave our professional lives at the office, our families, friends, neighbors, and communities may not make this an easy task for us. Social workers, in general, and new social workers, in particular, may have difficulty setting limits—that is, saying no—when people ask for our help. Like many social workers, you probably joined this profession because you are a compassionate person who wants to contribute to improving others' quality of life. However, without limit setting, you may find yourself in the helping mode around the clock.

Boundaries distinguish the professional relationship from the social/personal relationship (10). Further, establishing clear-cut limitations with your clients aids the client–worker relationship by: maintaining both client and worker focus on the goals of the professional relationship; ensuring confidentiality; balancing the power differential that can occur between you and the client; and preventing any inappropriate or "dual" relationship from emerging (10).

The line between professional and nonprofessional behavior and activities can become blurred. One type of dual relationship is present in Cameron's situation. Fellow group members view him as a professional social worker in a situation in which he is attempting to function as a participating member of a self-help group. Dual relationships can also be social (i.e., friends or sexual partners), business, or financial and can occur before, during, or after the professional relationship (10). While engaging in a nonprofessional relationship with a client may seem natural and comfortable because of mutual interests or issues, such a relationship can be disastrous for both the worker and the client. Problems can arise in terms of client progress, worker competence, confidentiality, and mutually unrealistic expectations (10).

The NASW *Code of Ethics* (11) clearly states that social workers should not be in situations in which conflicts of interest, dual relationships, exploitation, or violation of confidentiality can occur. The *Code of Ethics* also addresses the propriety of having a dual relationship with a former client following the termination of the professional relationship: the general consensus is that a posttermination relationship is not ethical due to potentially conflicting expectations and unmet needs (10).

An issue related to Cameron's situation and boundary setting, in particular, is that of self-disclosure. The question of how much information to self-disclose can become a dilemma—too much self-disclosure can lead to a role reversal with the client, while too little can result in feeling a lack of connection with the client (12). Many beginning social workers find that working with certain populations or issues can bring to life past and traumatic issues and memories (12). Should this dilemma occur for you, consult with your field instructor and other seasoned practitioners. You may find that processing the issues will enable you to put them in perspective and will guide your self-disclosure choices, but you may also find that you need to seek additional support to address your past.

Engaging in appropriate interactions with clients and colleagues can be an emotional and frustrating one for helping professionals. Should you experience discomfort from your own feelings or from verbal or nonverbal messages sent by your client, immediately seek out your field instructor or a faculty member. These are issues that you do not have to confront on your own.

Stress: Bane or Boon?

All helping professionals encounter professionally related stress on a regular basis. This is part of the territory that comes with being in a discipline that is intimately involved in the ongoing crises of individual, family, and community life. There are three avenues for responding to inevitable stressors:

1. negative response—intimidation, feelings of being overwhelmed, immobilization, and, ultimately, burn-out
2. positive response—reframe the stressor as a challenge or a valuable learning experience
3. combination of the previous two responses—begin on one avenue and move to the other, or vacillate back and forth between the two

Although learning is not usually a painful experience, powerful learning experiences are not always perceived as positive!

Generally, *stress* is considered to be a response to a positive or negative event in which one's usual coping mechanisms do not adequately address the stimulus. Even positive events (e.g., marriage, the birth of a child, or a new job) can produce stressful reactions. Social work students experience a combination of positive and negative stressors. Embarking on a new career and being in class and field work can be exciting and stimulating, but juggling a weekly average of 16 hours of coursework and 20 hours of practicum, possibly coupled with employment and family life, can create a high level of stress (12). Stress can occur when you have high and/or unrealistic expectations for yourself and others or when your values come into conflict with those of your client, agency, or community and can be further exacerbated by denying that you are experiencing a negative response (13). The latter is an occupational hazard particularly for helping professionals because we may feel that we should be able to handle more than the average person due to our training and knowledge; we may believe that we should be able to treat or counsel ourselves.

Stressors can originate at the societal, community, agency, or individual levels. At the societal level, our profession has changed dramatically in recent years with the increase of family and community violence, the advent of HIV/AIDS, and the changes brought on by welfare reform and managed care. These changes have filtered down to the community level, resulting in a disintegration of neighborhoods in some communities. At the agency level, changes have resulted in decreasing resources, increasing workloads, and workers being responsible for tasks for which they are not adequately trained (5, 14, 15). These changes can certainly create— particularly for the new social worker—a disillusionment with the profession and "the system" and a perceived conflict with social work values (5). At the individual level, we must recognize that even we, as social workers, are not immune to the stressors that befall others. Just because we develop heightened self-awareness and have the knowledge and skills needed to respond appropriately to life's stresses, we are not guaranteed the ability to stave off the effects of life events. Social work students report that interactions with clients create, by far, the most stress for them during the practicum experience, followed by staff/agency/field instructor problems and the field process (14).

PRACTICE APPLICATION 2.4
How Well Is Your Well-Being?

A well-being checklist (Figures 2.1 and 2.2) is provided here for you to use as an exercise to determine your level of well-being at this phase of your personal and professional life. The well-being scale (16) is built using a health-strengths model (17, 18) that de-emphasizes the psychopathology typically associated with stress scales and emphasizes the individual's assets, resources, and supports. Take a few moments to complete this checklist by taking into acount your life over the past three months. To score, add together the value of each item circled. A score of 60 or greater on Part I (Activities of Living) and a score of 64 or greater on Part II (Basic Needs) (Figure 2.2) indicates that you may want to explore your well-being further and consider strategies for enhancing your day-to-day activities and stressors. Share your results in your integrative practice seminar class. You may want to use this scale to check your well-being status as you move through your social work practicum and career. We have found this scale to be a useful tool in identifying the positive and negative areas of our lives.

The following section identifies some common signs and symptoms associated with social work-related stress that may emerge during your practicum experience. This list of indicators of stress is not exhaustive, but it may aid you in gaining insight into the ways in which you respond to stressful stimuli. Following this section is a discussion of strategies you can employ to engage in appropriate and necessary self-care.

Stress is typically manifested in terms of a physical or psychosocial response. You should consider that you are experiencing a stress reaction if you note a change in your usual behaviors, thoughts, or feelings. These insights require that you are "in tune" with your physical and mental states. Some physical indicators that you may experience when confronted with acute or ongoing stress include:

- being more clumsy or awkward than usual
- increase in frequency or severity of physical illnesses (e.g., colds, flu, and headaches) that may result in increased absences from work, school, or social events

FIGURE 2.1   Well-Being Scale

Part I: Well-Being—Activities of Living
For each activity listed, think over the past three months. With what frequency has each activity been completed using the following scale: **1. Almost always; 2. Often, frequent; 3. Sometimes; 4. Seldom, on occasion; or 5. Never, almost never:**

	Almost always	Often, frequent	Some-times	Seldom, on occasion	Never, almost never
1. Buying food	1 ☐	2 ☐	3 ☐	4 ☐	5 ☐
2. Preparing meals	1 ☐	2 ☐	3 ☐	4 ☐	5 ☐
3. Getting the housework done	1 ☐	2 ☐	3 ☐	4 ☐	5 ☐
4. Getting the yard work done	1 ☐	2 ☐	3 ☐	4 ☐	5 ☐
5. Getting home maintenance done	1 ☐	2 ☐	3 ☐	4 ☐	5 ☐
6. Having adequate transportation	1 ☐	2 ☐	3 ☐	4 ☐	5 ☐
7. Purchasing	1 ☐	2 ☐	3 ☐	4 ☐	5 ☐
8. Washing and caring for clothing	1 ☐	2 ☐	3 ☐	4 ☐	5 ☐
9. Relaxing	1 ☐	2 ☐	3 ☐	4 ☐	5 ☐
10. Exercising	1 ☐	2 ☐	3 ☐	4 ☐	5 ☐
11. Enjoying a hobby	1 ☐	2 ☐	3 ☐	4 ☐	5 ☐
12. Starting a new interest or hobby	1 ☐	2 ☐	3 ☐	4 ☐	5 ☐
13. Attending social events	1 ☐	2 ☐	3 ☐	4 ☐	5 ☐
14. Time for reflective thinking	1 ☐	2 ☐	3 ☐	4 ☐	5 ☐
15. Having time for inspirational or spiritual interests	1 ☐	2 ☐	3 ☐	4 ☐	5 ☐
16. Noticing the wonderment of things around you	1 ☐	2 ☐	3 ☐	4 ☐	5 ☐
17. Asking for support from your friends or family	1 ☐	2 ☐	3 ☐	4 ☐	5 ☐
18. Getting support from your friends or family	1 ☐	2 ☐	3 ☐	4 ☐	5 ☐
19. Laughing	1 ☐	2 ☐	3 ☐	4 ☐	5 ☐
20. Treating or rewarding yourself	1 ☐	2 ☐	3 ☐	4 ☐	5 ☐
21. Maintaining employment	1 ☐	2 ☐	3 ☐	4 ☐	5 ☐
22. Taking time for personal hygiene and appearance	1 ☐	2 ☐	3 ☐	4 ☐	5 ☐
23. Taking time to have fun with family or friends	1 ☐	2 ☐	3 ☐	4 ☐	5 ☐

FIGURE 2.2

Part II: Well-Being—Basic Needs

For each need listed, think about your life over the past three months. During this period of time, indicate to what extent you think each need has been met by responding to the same scale as on the last scale: **1. Almost always; 2. Often, frequent; 3. Sometimes; 4. Seldom, on occasion; or 5. Never, almost never.**

	Almost always	Often, frequent	Some-times	Seldom, on occasion	Never, almost never
24. Having enough money	1 ☐	2 ☐	3 ☐	4 ☐	5 ☐
25. Eating a well-balanced diet	1 ☐	2 ☐	3 ☐	4 ☐	5 ☐
26. Getting enough sleep	1 ☐	2 ☐	3 ☐	4 ☐	5 ☐
27. Attending to your medical and dental needs	1 ☐	2 ☐	3 ☐	4 ☐	5 ☐
28. Having time for recreation	1 ☐	2 ☐	3 ☐	4 ☐	5 ☐
29. Feeling loved	1 ☐	2 ☐	3 ☐	4 ☐	5 ☐
30. Expressing love	1 ☐	2 ☐	3 ☐	4 ☐	5 ☐
31. Expressing laughter and joy	1 ☐	2 ☐	3 ☐	4 ☐	5 ☐
32. Expressing sadness	1 ☐	2 ☐	3 ☐	4 ☐	5 ☐
33. Enjoying sexual intimacy	1 ☐	2 ☐	3 ☐	4 ☐	5 ☐
34. Learning new skills	1 ☐	2 ☐	3 ☐	4 ☐	5 ☐
35. Feeling worthwhile	1 ☐	2 ☐	3 ☐	4 ☐	5 ☐
36. Feeling appreciated by others	1 ☐	2 ☐	3 ☐	4 ☐	5 ☐
37. Feeling good about family	1 ☐	2 ☐	3 ☐	4 ☐	5 ☐
38. Feeling good about yourself	1 ☐	2 ☐	3 ☐	4 ☐	5 ☐
39. Feeling secure about the future	1 ☐	2 ☐	3 ☐	4 ☐	5 ☐
40. Having close friendships	1 ☐	2 ☐	3 ☐	4 ☐	5 ☐
41. Having a home	1 ☐	2 ☐	3 ☐	4 ☐	5 ☐
42. Making plans about the future	1 ☐	2 ☐	3 ☐	4 ☐	5 ☐
43. Having people who think highly of you	1 ☐	2 ☐	3 ☐	4 ☐	5 ☐
44. Having meaning in your life	1 ☐	2 ☐	3 ☐	4 ☐	5 ☐
45. Expressing anger	1 ☐	2 ☐	3 ☐	4 ☐	5 ☐

- increase in frequency or intensity of crying, particularly if you find that you are crying more often than usual or that crying is triggered more easily than usual
- regression to former, broken, or unhealthy habits (e.g., smoking, substance use/abuse, and over/undereating)
- significant changes in eating or sleeping patterns

Stress can also present itself in less concrete ways, as evidenced by changes in your emotional status. Should you find yourself experiencing one or more of the reactions included in the list below, you may want to evaluate your life situation and investigate ways to decrease your stress levels.

- withdrawal from or avoidance of usually enjoyable social or professional activities
- denial that stress exists in your life or denial that you may not be coping well with the stressors in your life
- missing deadlines, meetings, and appointments or being consistently late
- procrastination
- increase in the number of items that you lose or misplace
- variability of your affect
- feeling that you are out of control
- changes in your usual organizational patterns (you may be less organized or overly organized)
- feelings of hopelessness and helplessness
- inappropriate emotional outbursts (e.g., anger, dismay, or hysteria)
- frequent or constant complaining with no follow-up action to rectify the situation about which you are complaining
- persistent anger that may be inappropriate, frequent, or misdirected
- responses that are inappropriate to the situation (e.g., over- or underreaction)
- overwhelming desire to flee the situation, your practicum/job, or your life in general
- decrease in your efficiency or effectiveness, particularly regarding professional or academic performance
- feedback from others that you seem tired, stressed, burned out, or unhappy
- negative change in your interactions with those close to you

Consider the ways in which you respond to stressors: Do you know your "red flags" (those reactions or behaviors that prompt a negative response in your life) and what they mean when they occur? Are your stressors different based on your being in the early, middle, or late stage of the crisis situation? Think back to a particularly stressful period or event in your life, and consider these questions:

1. How did you know that the event/period was stressful?
2. What were the physical or psychosocial indicators that you were experiencing stress?
3. How did you respond to the stress? Was your response positive or negative?
4. Was your response effective in resolving the stressful situation?
5. Would you respond to future stresses in the same way, or would you choose a different response? If the latter, what strategy(ies) would you use to handle the stress more effectively?

Stress can lead to burn-out, even at the beginning of your career. Burn-out is "excessive stress combined with alienation" (19). In cases in which the stress has become severe or chronic, you may begin to experience symptoms of clinical depression, anxiety, or physical illness. In the event that you do not feel able to cope adequately with the stressors in your life, do not delay in raising the issue with your field instructor or contacting a mental health professional. Social workers are human and can periodically benefit from the very services that they provide to others. Your field instructor or social work program faculty can be excellent resources should you choose to pursue treatment options. In addition to consulting with their field instructors, faculty, or staff, other strategies used by social work students in confronting acute stress include positive self-talk and taking professional action (20).

Self-Care as Professional Development

What did you think of as you read the heading of this section? What does *self-care* mean to you? Take a few moments to consider the meaning of this concept and ways in which you do or do not engage in self-care. *Self-care* can be defined as the self-initiated, proactive behaviors that are intended to maintain your physical, emotional, and social health.

Promoting self-care is a common strategy that social workers encourage their clients and patients to incorporate into their lives to prevent illness, maintain their physical and emotional health and well-being, and reduce stress. As social workers, we should be willing and able to integrate this practice into our lives as well so that we may:

1. act as role models for those we urge to accept the concept of self-care;
2. empower others to care for themselves;
3. understand the challenges that come with taking care of ourselves so we may empathize with others; and
4. be healthy, balanced care providers for others.

You have seen that in your role as a social work student, you will likely be confronted with numerous demands, often simultaneously. These demands may often be overlapping and conflicting. Self-care therefore becomes a necessity, as opposed to a luxury, if you are to meet these demands without paying too great a price in terms of your health, well-being, and effectiveness.

Strategies for balancing your myriad roles appeared earlier in this unit. The list provided here includes a sampling of self-care strategies that can be used to supplement your efforts to maintain a personal–professional balance. You may already be familiar with or use some of the suggestions included on this list. If not, you may wish to consider adding them to your repertoire of self-care techniques. A healthy person often has a wide and diverse range of self-care strategies that are used alternately or for specific situations. Our list includes:

- Acknowledge self-care as a priority and a part of your lifestyle. You may even wish to add an addendum to your learning plan that includes your plans for self-care during your practicum.

- Attend faithfully to your physical and mental health well-being.
- Acknowledge your emotions, particularly your reactions to your work—it is sometimes necessary to allow yourself to feel anger, grief, and elation concerning your clients, your work, and social issues.
- Develop and use both a personal and a professional support system. But you are cautioned not to exploit or overuse your support network, particularly not to engage with your field instructor, faculty, or fellow students as if they are your therapist.
- Join personal and professional groups that you enjoy and that stimulate you.
- Develop a student peer support group at your site or at your school.
- Ask for help if you need to from your field instructor, faculty, fellow students, family, or formal university and community services.
- Build into your regular schedule nonoverlapping time for completing your practicum hours, school work, fun activities, and down time.
- Stay tuned into yourself at the mind and body levels and conduct reality checks on a regular basis (you may even want to ask others to reality check with you).
- Develop relationships with significant others who can challenge you, if needed.
- Know and heed the signals that tell you that you are becoming stressed.
- Ask others to share their strategies for ensuring their emotional and physical health.
- If one self-care strategy does not seem to be effective for you, try something different.
- Have attainable personal and professional goals, monitor your progress in reaching them, and reevaluate these goals on a regular basis.
- Although you want to challenge and stretch yourself consistently, do not push yourself beyond your limits over a long period. You may be able to overextend yourself successfully in the short term, but you can suffer if you push yourself over the long term.
- Use considerable caution in resorting to artificial means to maintain your energy (e.g., drugs, alcohol, diet aids, excessive caffeine, and stimulants).
- Do not expect others to take care of you—they may raise issues, but you are ultimately responsible for taking action.
- Use humor as much as you can to keep the work and your issues in perspective (19).
- Work to your strengths and know your limitations, changing what you can.
- Avoid procrastination—the crisis of a last-minute deadline can create even more stress.
- When you elect to confront a stressor or injustice, choose your battle carefully— your energy may be more effectively directed to another area at that time.

Do you have any strategies that you can add to this list? You may want to use this list as a springboard for class or supervisory discussions. You can never have too many tools and techniques for caring for yourself.

The Transitions of Professional Socialization

The final area to consider as we discuss your socialization as a social worker is the transitions that you have experienced and will experience as you continue on your professional journey. Transitioning from one phase of an experience to the next provides the opportunity to evaluate, reevaluate, and plan for the future. There are several natural transitions that will occur as you move into and through your social work career. Beginning with your practicum, we will highlight these transitions here and focus on issues for you to consider while you are a student. Your social work socialization includes transitions that can be categorized as:

1. Coursework   to   Practicum
   a. Beginning of first practicum or first semester of practicum   to   Middle phase
   b. Middle phase of first practicum   to   Termination phase
2. Subsequent practica or second semester of practicum   to   Graduation
3. Practicum student   to   Professional social worker

Coursework to Practicum

The transition from theory to practice is intregal to your socialization as a social worker and begins with the planning of your first practicum. As you have learned, social work education emphasizes the integration of the theoretical and conceptual frameworks with the application of social work skills attained through experiential field work. During this phase of your development, you move from the classroom setting in which you gained theoretical and conceptual knowledge to the skills-based field experience.

You may or may not have entered your social work program with an idea of the type/area of social work in which you are interested. Moreover, by the time you began to plan your first practicum, you may have continued, focused, or changed those interests as a result of faculty/peer influence, readings, class exercises, or guest lecturers. Despite the way in which your interests and planning process are evolving, you are making or have made the transition from classroom to field during this phase of your professionalization.

The key issues to grasp during this phase may seem basic, but they are key to your social work development. During this stage, you must consider such questions as:

- With which population(s), settings, and areas of social work do I want to develop my skills?
- Have I conducted an inventory of my knowledge and skills to determine what I know and what I do not know?
- Do I have a grounding in basic social work-related theory and how to begin to apply those theories to actual practice situations?

Do not be dismayed if you do not have the answers to these questions. You have hundreds of hours of field experience before you during which you can work on the answers.

Beginning to Middle Phase

The issues raised in the previous section may seem rudimentary. But the issues that occur in this phase are perhaps the most abstract and difficult ones you will encounter throughout your social work journey. The issues that emerge here may make you feel overwhelmed at times, and you may vacillate between thoughts of self-doubt and jubilation regarding your career choice. Here are some thoughts to consider as you move through the beginning phase of your practicum.

- Identify your skill level at the onset and ending of the beginning of your practicum.
- Identify your goals for this phase as well as those of your field instructor and social work program. (Know where you want to be at termination.)
- Periodically review your goals, and evaluate and plan the direction for the next phase of your practicum experience.
- Engage in mutual feedback with your field instructor regarding this phase of the experience.

Middle Phase to Termination Phase

By the middle phase of your first practicum, you have survived the beginning of this new experience. You have gained a working knowledge of the agency's function and operations. You have been implementing the goals, tasks, and activities outlined in your learning plan; you have been assigned a workload (cases and projects); and you are comfortably entrenched in the daily routine of your practicum organization. Now is the time to begin *actively* planning for your termination from this practicum. Some areas for you to think about and discuss with your field instructor include:

- strategies and timeframes for termination of practicum responsibilities (e.g., case transfers and final reports);
- areas of gain (knowledge and skills growth and values clarification);
- areas for continued growth (for the remainder of this practicum and beyond);
- a plan for the targeted areas for growth;
- your feelings regarding your termination from your clients, groups, coworkers, and field instructor;
- mutual feedback regarding your practicum experience; and
- the plan for completion of the evaluation.

Subsequent Practica or Second Semester of Practicum to Graduation

Once you have successfully completed your first practicum experience, the subsequent semester(s) in which you complete practicum builds on familiar practicum activities and developing new learning opportunities that enhance earlier learning objectives. In some instances, you may find that you could easily function on automatic pilot regarding your practicum experiences, particularly if you continue to work in the same or similar setting or with a comparable population. You can optimize your learning by seeking out new and challenging levels of responsibility, activities, and experiences to extend your capabilities and limits. Some key strategies to consider as you move along this segment of the social work path include:

- continuing to engage in an ongoing evaluation of your goals, skill level, strengths, and areas for growth (you may want to use your learning plan as a tool for monitoring your progress);
- developing strategies for addressing those issues identified above;
- identifying new experiences desired that may or may not be required by your social work program;
- utilizing available resources to help you identify future career, employment, and training directions;
- integrating, as much as possible, your practicum experiences into your course work;
- engaging in discussion with your field instructor and social work program faculty regarding their willingness to provide a reference for you (some agencies and individuals exercise caution regarding references and have a no–reference letter policy); and
- Ensuring that your evaluation or reference letter will hold no surprises.

Practicum Student to Professional Social Worker

A phenomenon that often occurs during this phase of a social worker's professional development is akin to a panic—one suddenly realizes how little one knows, school loans may be coming due, and the job market looms ahead. This experience may not become a reality for you or may be gradual or may come and go. Regardless of how you experience this milestone, there are a number of issues to consider as you move out of the role of student and into the role of professional social worker. Some strategies for easing this transition include:

- Identify your goals for the next chapter of your life—another degree, additional training, employment, or long-term volunteer service (e.g., Peace Corps)?
- Develop your résumé using your school's career service office. This office may offer résumé development services, employment workshops, employment listings, and the opportunity to conduct practice employment interviews.
- Establish your goals and criteria for employment.
- Determine the realities for your transition—economic, geographic, and skill preparation.
- Keep your options open, particularly as you consider your first social work position at your current level.
- Maintain contact with faculty—many have extensive community and professional contacts.
- Be visible—regardless of whether you have chosen to continue your training or to become employed, use your networking skills to maintain and develop your ties to the social work community.
- Once in the new position, explore the organizational norms, identify any potential conflicts, and use these to grow and change as a professional (1).

Good luck—you have embarked on what promises to be a challenging, seldom dull, and rewarding career!

PRACTICE APPLICATION **2.5**

A Day in the Life of a Social Worker

This exercise focuses on gaining further understanding and insight into the roles and responsibilities, overall job requirements, and client and agency expectations in a "typical" day in the work life of a social worker. You will be able to analyze and potentially change how your time is actually spent. This exercise will prove most helpful if performed in the middle or termination phase of your practicum experience, when you are working somewhat autonomously.

Exercise Instructions
Select a "typical" day at your practicum. Prior to arrival at your practicum site, take a piece of paper and, on the left side, write down every half-hour time slot, beginning with

(continued)

PRACTICE APPLICATION 2.5   Continued

your start time (i.e., 8:00 A.M., 8:30 A.M., etc.) and going through to your expected ending time. Divide the rest of the paper into two columns. In the left column, write down in each half-hour slot, the activities that you plan or anticipate for the day. Include the vast array of activities in which you are typically engaged, such as reading mail, collaborating with other professionals, meeting with clients (e.g., counseling, intake, and services), making telephone calls, recording assessments/notes, attending staffings, meeting with your field instructor, making a home visit (include travel time), presenting at a community meeting, and so on. Do not forget to write in breaks and lunch. Keep this list handy throughout the day and write in the *actual* activities that occurred. In small student seminar groups or with your field instructor, review the completed planned and actual activity lists. Then consider these questions:

1. What was accomplished and what was not accomplished?
2. What activities took longer or shorter time spans than expected?
3. How were priorities met or unmet?
4. How were expectations and needs of clients, your agency, community contacts, and your field instructor met or not met?
5. How did recording via computer, handwritten notes, or dictating fit into the day?
6. What happened when there was a client crisis?
7. Were you surprised, pleased, or satisfied with your results?
8. Where do you need to allocate more or less time to meet the job requirements for the day?
9. Did you spend time on activities when, in fact, you wished you were spending time on other activities?

Debriefing

As professionally trained social workers, our days are often very busy and unpredictable. Our work requires frequent communications and collaborations and the ability to change tasks continually, from answering telephone calls, to being a therapist, to collaborating with other professionals, to traveling in the community, to responding to a grieving family, to numerous other activities. Our services may be needed for longer than could be predicted. Some experienced social workers reflect that there is no typical day. Instead, their day flows with a sense of the priorities among their responsibilities and the services they provide. As many modern-day professionals remark, there is not enough time in the day to complete their work, and social work is no different.

This exercise is designed to provide insight into how you spend your time, what time may be needed to perform your professional responsibilities, and where you may want to take an active approach to managing time for your overall effectiveness and performance as a social worker. For example, finding the time to record assessments or case management goals and progress notes is often put off, and before you know it, this job has become overwhelming. Where can this fit in your day? Your field instructor will help you evaluate and plan for this situation and any others that become apparent as a result of this exercise. Near the end of your practicum, try this exercise again.

Developed by Pamela Huggins, LCSW

PRACTICE APPLICATION **2.6**
Thinking Like a Social Worker

This exercise uses a case vignette to aid you in strengthening your responses to social work practice situations. You will be better able to integrate generalist social work knowledge and skills by focusing on the strengths and empowerment orientation.

Exercise Instructions
This exercise is most helpful if completed in large groups (i.e., integrative practice field seminar) because many ideas can be expressed. Information on the case is provided in small increments and builds into a larger case scenario. This offers several opportunities to think like a social worker. Following the completion of each section, the group is asked to share their responses to these questions:

1. What are your thoughts and impressions?
2. What questions or responses would you have in relation to assessment?
3. What micro, mezzo, and macro interventions (including therapeutic responses) would you suggest?

Case Vignette
- A 35-year-old woman comes to your office stating that she is "depressed." She tells you that her two children have been placed in foster care because the family's water and electricity were shut off due to nonpayment and neighbors are no longer willing to help with food.
  Group Sharing (see above questions)

- The client is ineligible for public assistance because her husband works erratically as a day laborer, thus generating income for the family.
  Group Sharing (see above questions)

- Her husband is not currently working due to active alcohol dependence and past work history.
  Group Sharing (see above questions)

- The client and her family were unable to gain admittance to either a homeless shelter or a transitional housing unit because both were full and had waiting lists. This resulted in her inability to keep the children with her.
  Group Sharing (see above questions)

- The community believes that poor people are responsible for their own plight.
  Group Sharing (see above questions)

Debriefing
1. How would you evaluate your ability to think in terms of a strength practice approach versus by focusing on "problems" and "dysfunction"? Were you aware of automatic "judgmental" or "blaming the victim" thoughts?
2. In what ways were you aware of "empowering" approaches? In what ways do you support the client's efforts to assume responsibility and gain a sense of competence, confidence, and control?

(continued)

P R A C T I C E   A P P L I C A T I O N   **2.6**   Continued

> 3. What social problems, policies, or programs can you identify that would be appropriate in this case?
> 4. What micro, mezzo, and macro interventions did you identify?
> 5. Were there aspects of this case about which you need more information in order to be effective (e.g., alcohol dependence, legislative impact on welfare programs)? Specify the area(s) in which you required more information. How can you obtain this information?
>
> This case illustrates the social work profession's unique generalist approach to helping others and impacting systems. Many of our interdisciplinary colleagues are very skilled helpers, particularly in the area of treating this client's depression. Our helping orientation, however, prepares us to understand and work effectively with individuals, families, groups, and the community. This means that we approach this case by providing social services for this woman, including individual support and assistance. Other services focus on her environment (i.e., multiple systems—family, friends, religious and cultural affiliations, community, government programs, health care, economic opportunities, societal attitudes, and discrimination).
>
> Developed by Pamela Huggins, LCSW

Summary

This unit has focused on a wide range of issues, all related to your social work journey. You are well on your way to becoming socialized as a professionally degreed social work practitioner. We have emphasized the need for a proactive approach to your socialization experience, ongoing attention to your professional goals and needs, anticipating the possible pitfalls that may occur along the way, strategies for addressing stresses, and awareness about the transitions that occur.

STUDENT SCENARIO POSTSCRIPTS

Ben's fears about the profession he has chosen almost succeeded in immobilizing him. For several weeks (even after he began his practicum), he thought daily about the possibility of withdrawing from the MSW program. Because he had been too fearful about his concerns to talk with anyone, the anxiety had mounted. The turning point for Ben was a question posed to him by his field instructor during supervision. He sat down in his field instructor's office for their weekly session, and his field instructor said, "Ben, how's it going?" Wanting desperately to talk with someone about his almost paralyzing fears, Ben immediately began to pour out his story to his field instructor. Fortunately, Ben's field instructor was able to validate and normalize his experience. The supervisor shared with Ben a similar experience (which most of us have had at some point in our social work careers) that enabled Ben to put his fears into perspective and understand that learning to practice social work is not all about intuition, but about learning knowledge and skills.

Cameron considered the three dilemmas that faced him regarding the distinction between his role as a social work student and his role as a recovering person. Once he was able to realize that feeling flattered by the former clients/AA members' attention was not helpful to him or the AA members, he began to process the information from a professional standpoint. Although Cameron recognized that he had to convey to the AA members that his roles as a practicum student and fellow AA member could not overlap, he found that implementing his realization was an entirely different issue. On several future occasions, Cameron found himself literally cornered by former clients/AA members who were asking for his "professional" opinion. Cameron felt at a loss as to how to extricate himself from this dual and overlapping role. He tried several strategies:

1. *Avoidance.* He stopped attending that particular meeting and went to a meeting farther from home. (This just made him angry at the others and himself.)
2. *"Turfing."* He persistently attempted to refer the AA members to other professionals. (This was not successful.)
3. *Confrontation.* Cameron finally simply told them that he was uncomfortable with his dual role and that he would not be able to discuss their individual treatment issues with them further. This worked.

REFERENCES

1. Russo, R. *Serving and surviving as a human service worker.* Prospect Heights, IL: Waveland Press. 1993.
2. Bogo, M., Raphael, D. & Roberts, R. Interests, activities and self-identification among social work students: Toward a definition of social work identity. *Journal of Social Work Education.* 1993, 29(3):279–292.
3. Klein, W. C. & Bloom, M. Practice wisdom. *Social Work.* 1995, 40(16):799–808.
4. Collins, P. The interpersonal vicissitudes of mentorship: An exploratory study of the field supervisor-student relationship. *The Clinical Supervisor.* 1993, 11(1):121–135.
5. Embrescia, E. Thoughts of a social worker becoming less green. *The New Social Worker.* 1997, 4(3):6–7.
6. Council on Social Work Education. *Handbook of accreditation standards and procedures.* Alexandria, VA: Author. 1994.
7. Linsley, J. Stressed out by self-awareness: Looking at yourself. *The New Social Worker.* 1997, 4(3):4–5.
8. Sheafor, B. W., Horejsi, C. R. & Horejsi, G. A. *Techniques and guidelines for social work practice* (2nd ed.). Boston: Allyn & Bacon. 1988.
9. Sheafor, B. W., Horejsi, C. R. & Horejsi, G. A. *Techniques and guidelines for social work practice* (4th ed.). Boston: Allyn & Bacon. 1997.
10. Strom-Gottfried, K. & Dunlap, K. M. How to keep boundary issues from compromising your practice. *The New Social Worker.* 1998, 5(2):10–13.
11. National Association of Social Workers. *Code of ethics.* Washington, DC: NASW Press. 1996.
12. DiGuilio, J. F. Concerns in the field placement. *The New Social Worker.* 1998, 5(1):19–20.
13. Munson, C. E. *Clinical social work supervision* (2nd ed.). New York: Haworth Press. 1993.

14.   Rubio, D. M., Birkenmaier, J. & Berg-Weger, M. (1998). Human service nonprofit agencies: Studying the impact of policy changes. Unpublished manuscript.

15.   Rubio, D. M., Birkenmaier, J. & Berg-Weger, M. (1999). Social policy changes and social work practice. Under review, *Advances in Social Work Practice.*

16.   Tebb, S. S. An aid to empowerment: A caregiver well-being scale. *Health and Social Work.* 1995, *20*(2):87–92.

17.   Weick, A. N. The philosophical context of a health model of social work. *Social Casework.* 1986, *67*:551–559.

18.   Weick, A. N. & Freeman, E. *Developing a health model for social work.* Unpublished manuscript, School of Social Welfare, University of Kansas. 1983.

19.   Furman, R. Flying with the winds of change. Six ways to prevent burn-out in times of transition and change in social work practice. *The New Social Worker.* 1998, *5*(1):10–11.

20.   Cochrane, S. & Thornton, S. *Dimensions of adjustment in field placement: Implications for social work education.* Paper presented at Midwest Biennial Social Work Education Conference, Utica, IL, April, 1990.

3 Safety in Social Work Settings

Life is either a daring adventure or nothing. Security does not exist in nature, nor do the children of men as a whole experience it. Avoiding danger is no safer in the long run than exposure.

—Adapted from Helen Keller

Have you wondered about your physical safety at your practicum site? Does the thought of home visits stir feelings of anxiety? Have family members worried about your choice of profession because of safety issues? Have you heard other students and faculty discuss agency safety issues?

Many students, especially beginning students, have concerns about safety and security and struggle with the decision to voice their concerns to their professors, other students, and their field instructors. Students may be reluctant to discuss safety fears and concerns with others for fear of being viewed as uncommitted to the profession or to clients. Other students may assume that the role of the social worker is viewed as strictly one of helper and enabler and cannot fathom being viewed as a threat. However, the practice of social work typically does involve some degree of risk. If not addressed, concerns about personal safety can significantly affect learning opportunities in the field placement. This unit will address safety concerns associated with social work and provide guidelines that can assist you in minimizing the risk of harm.

The Scope of Personal Safety Risks in Social Work

On her first day of practicum, Corina was given a tour of the detention facility, introduced to all of the staff, oriented to the various systems, and provided with agency manuals and policy guidelines. She began shadowing other social workers and sat in on their group therapy sessions. On the third day, she remembered to ask about the unusual name of the unit in which she would be completing her practicum. She was told it was named after a staff member who had been shot to death by a client in the office a year ago. She was shocked. She had no idea that this practicum could pose a threat to her well-being. Are her fears real? What would you do?

Faced with this kind of information, most students would be concerned about working within the agency. Some might even contemplate requesting a transfer to another agency. Other students might consider the likelihood of this kind of incident occurring twice to be very small and so disregard safety as a serious matter. Should safety be a concern for students in practicum? According to recent research findings and anecdotal information, concern over personal safety issues in social work is warranted. The number and lethality of safety risk incidents on the job has increased for social workers (1). Social workers are second only to police officers in terms of the risk of having work-related violence directed at them (2). On an annual basis, 1 of every 10 child welfare workers is either physically or psychologically assaulted by one or more clients (3). Physical assaults include minor attacks (e.g., hitting or shoving) as well as lethal injuries (e.g., shooting) (3). Approximately one fourth of social work field instructors have been physically attacked by clients and 62 percent have been verbally assaulted by clients (4). One third of school social workers report that they experience fear for their safety approximately once per month, and 35 percent have been physically assaulted or threatened during the past year (5).

Several factors have merged in recent decades to increase the level of danger faced by social workers. These include (6)

- a shift to a more law-enforcement (versus psychosocial) approach with the passage of child abuse acts, the expansion of child protective services, passage of adult and elder protective laws, and increased efforts to collect child support on the federal government level;
- increased public awareness of and expectations that social workers will solve violent family situations;
- an increase in the involvement of court systems in the lives of families; and
- the increasing complexity of cases correlating to greater societal violence and an increase in the number of families with few available supports.

Safety in the Practicum Setting

Social work practitioners and students are increasingly subject to threats in the workplace. Students are well advised to consider safety and liability issues when considering practicum sites and learning activities. The anxiety felt by many students regarding safety is justified by the experience of previous students. Although most students never experience any personal risk (7), approximately one fourth of MSW and BSW practicum students have experienced some form of violence in the field placement, the majority of cases occurring within the practicum agency (4). Approximately one third of schools of social work have been affected by violence,

directed toward either students or alumni (8). More than half of students in one study were verbally or physically threatened by a client at least once during their practica (7). The most common form of threat to a practicum student is a verbal threat from clients, paraprofessionals, or other professionals (4, 9, 10).

The Council on Social Work Education (CSWE) policy standards (11) do not address physical safety, assessment of potentially dangerous clients, or strategies for ensuring safety in the workplace (10). Social work programs vary widely in their knowledge of and approach to safety concerns. Thirty-five percent of social work programs report that they rely on the university or practicum site safety policies or well-defined school or practicum program policies or the inclusion of safety training and discussion in the curriculum (10). Those programs whose students have experienced assaults or threats in the field are not more likely to offer safety programs (10).

Reasonable Concerns and Caution

Social workers often work in neighborhoods, in communities, and with groups and clients that others may deem "unsafe." Social work practitioners often work with the impoverished in high-crime areas. Although being careful is always important, you should strive to separate stereotypes and myths from reality. You must have a realistic portrayal of your risks in order to be effective. If not addressed, the beginning anxiety that you may feel can impede a willingness to draft ambitious and valuable learning plans. Talking with other students currently in practicum at your site, other current and former practicum students at the agency, and your field instructor can help you determine the level of risk involved in conducting specific tasks and your comfort level in completing those tasks. You must ensure your safety and avoid allowing unfounded fears or inexperience to become impediments to the delivery of effective services.

The type of agency setting can significantly influence the level of perceived risk to the staff. If you are working in a residential setting (e.g., a children's residential facility, hospital, substance abuse treatment facility, domestic violence facility, or a correctional facility), you will likely encounter a highly structured setting with specific procedures regarding some or all of the following:

- locks
- confidentiality regarding location
- client restraints
- situations in which staff must work in teams to ensure safety
- standard precautions (e.g., universal precautions) for avoiding exposure to illnesses such as HIV/AIDS, hepatitis, and tuberculosis (12)
- the completion of safety and violence response workshops in which you are trained to respond to violent aggression by clients and are expected to intervene physically with clients

On the other end of the continuum, if you are working in a community-based agency, you may encounter a more flexible agency setting with fewer (if any) protocols and safety guidelines. Situations posing physical threats to social workers can occur in any setting, and students are well advised to exercise due caution regardless of the perceived risk.

Under optimal circumstances, your field instructor will discuss safety matters with you during the interview process for the practicum so that you have a realistic view of risk prior to your commitment to the agency. Whether or not this occurred prior to the start of your practicum, completing the following practice applications can help you gain a realistic perception of the safety risks in your setting and implement agency safety policies.

PRACTICE APPLICATION 3.1
Gathering Information

The use of this exercise will enable you to gather pertinent, current, and accurate information about the safety risks, resources, and protocols associated with social work practice in your practicum site as well as the safety resources and protocols of your social work program.

At Your Practicum Site
- Inquire about the number of recent incidents of physical or verbal abuse, sexual harassment, or other violence that staff have experienced inside or outside the agency.
- If not included in the orientation, inquire about agency safety protocols (e.g., telephone number for emergency assistance, location of the first aid kit, emergency exit procedures for the building, and location of fire extinguishers).

- Request a tour of the surrounding neighborhood, particularly if you will be conducting home visits.
- Ask whether certain neighborhoods or areas are avoided or approached with more caution than usual by staff members for safety reasons, and be prepared to follow suit when working independently.
- Observe safety protocols implemented by staff members conducting similar duties to those you have planned for the practicum both inside and outside the agency.

Within Your Social Work Program
- Ask how many students have experienced problems related to safety in practicum in recent years.
- Research the safety protocols of your social work program, if any.
- Take advantage of safety resources available from your social work program, or ask the faculty for assistance in obtaining resources such as safety training, seminars, videos, handouts, and discussions.

After you have gathered all the information noted above, demonstrate the knowledge you have gained through a discussion with your field instructor, a reflection paper for your integrative seminar class, or a journal entry.

PRACTICE APPLICATION **3.2**

Gaining Skills

Ask to be observed by a staff member as you are making the transition to independent work with clients, and ask for feedback regarding safety risks and the implementation of safety guidelines. Journal about these early experiences related to safety issues as well as safety precautions utilized and not utilized by you or by staff.

PRACTICE APPLICATION **3.3**

Assessment and Reflection

Discuss and critique the following with a member of your practicum team:

- information gathered regarding safety issues in the practicum site
- skills you are developing related to the implementation of safety guidelines
- the safety protocols of the both the agency and your social work program (were the protocols sufficient? reasonable?)
- your apprehensions or fears concerning your safety while conducting practicum activities (Are your apprehensions based on reality and experience? How much of a factor could myths, stereotypes, inexperience, or bias be playing in your fears?)

Assessment of Potentially Violent Clients

Due to the increased safety risks faced by social workers in many settings, the ability to assess potential risk accurately is critical. Although you will not always be able to determine risk accurately in advance of an actual threat to your safety, you should be aware that certain factors may increase the risk of harm (see Box 3.1). Caution should be exercised when working with certain client groups under the following circumstances:

- young male clients with criminal records or histories of substance abuse, weapons possession, or violent behavior (13)
- mentally ill clients with specific risk factors and symptoms (i.e., paranoid delusions, command hallucinations, and syndromes such as mania, paranoid schizophrenia, and panic) (13)
- a history of weapons possession (14)
- a history of violence, substance abuse, or ritualistic or cult practices (14)
- pending or actual removal of a family member (14)
- geographic location that may pose danger (i.e., rural, isolated, or high crime area) (14);
- working into the evening hours (14)
- the presence of animals in the home that may pose a threat (14)

Specific Guidelines for Safety within the Office

Many students will meet with their clients in an office setting and encounter few problems. However, even in the most structured setting, the office setting cannot guarantee complete safety. The following suggestions can reduce the chances of experiencing physical harm in the office:

- Follow agency safety policies to the letter.
- When possible, study the case files of all clients before interacting with them to ascertain the risk involved in working with them (14).
- Ask another staff member to accompany you when working with a client with a violent history or one who exhibits behaviors that may pose a threat (14).
- Remove all objects from your desk (pens, staplers, and paper weights) that could be used as weapons (14).
- Leave a client who is becoming belligerent or threatening and seek help from a colleague (15).
- If there is not one in place, develop a system whereby you can discreetly signal another staff member that you need assistance. As an example, you might develop a system by which you will call another staff member, state the name of the client, and say that you need "the progress folder" (14).
- Arrange the furniture so that you are closest to the door (14).

BOX **3.1**

History is often the best prediction of risk. Increased caution should be exercised when working with clients who (14):

1. have severely violent behavior;
2. have a history of remorseless parental brutality;
3. have a history of fighting and school problems;
4. have difficulty getting along with others and authority figures;
5. have a history of overt parental seductiveness;
6. have a familiarity with weapons;
7. are currently under the influence of drugs or alcohol;
8. are currently under severe stress and are feeling overwhelmed or hopeless;
9. currently verbalize being upset and angry or will not communicate with you;
10. are currently threatening to you either verbally or physically;
11. are currently involved in illegal activities;
12. have erupted verbally or physically in the last 30 to 40 minutes;
13. are unable to sit still or are pacing; or
14. are currently suicidal.

- When possible, develop relationships with those who are charged with ensuring your safety. Let them know when you will be working late and ask the guards/safety patrol officers to escort you to your car after work when needed.
- Maintain a confidential, locked location for your valuables while at the agency (16).
- If clients have access to the office in which you are working, lock it whenever you leave (16).

While all violence cannot be prevented, these steps represent the efforts that you can make to help ensure your safety in the office setting. If safety is an issue within the practicum office and some of the aforementioned suggestions are not being utilized, consider suggesting some of the procedures. It is important to take safety issues seriously within an office setting.

Interacting with Clients within the Home and the Community

Ben was unsure about the contents of the long case in the client's hand. The client walked quickly, put the case in the back seat, and joined Ben in the front seat. As Ben greeted him and reiterated the need for the trip to the office, the client began to ramble incoherently. However, Ben was able to understand that the client wished to go first to a different location to pick up a check. When Ben objected, the client referred to the shotgun he had placed in the back seat. Furthermore, the client made disparaging remarks about Ben's obvious Asian heritage. Frightened and unclear about what he "should" do, Ben drove to the office the client requested and then drove him home. As Ben debriefed later with his field instructor, he found himself shaking and short of breath. Did he do the right thing in this situation? How did diversity issues affect the interaction?

As Ben discovered, stepping into the community to serve clients entails leaving the structured environment of the office setting. Working with clients outside an office setting can also, as in Ben's case, leave a practitioner wondering which course of action is best as an interaction with a client unfolds in the "real" world. Home visits and encountering clients in the community can offer the opportunity to gather a rich array of information about the client that is not available from a meeting in the office. The home visit enhances the delivery of services to clients in their natural setting. While interacting with clients outside of the agency can be intimidating for a new professional, the delivery of professional services on the "home turf" of the client can be essential to the success of the intervention.

In recent decades, a rapid expansion of home-based services has occurred, evidenced in part by such organizations as the U.S. General Accounting Office (17) recommending the delivery of services to the home. Social workers can expect this trend to continue. Although not every home visit will pose a safety risk, following the suggestions below on a routine basis can significantly decrease the potential for harm.

Preparation
Preparing for work with clients outside of the agency can minimize your risk of physical harm and liability.

Transportation
If you will be transporting clients in a car, check the following (15):

- The ages of any children you may be transporting. Make arrangements for car seats for young children.
- The number and condition of seat belts.
- The travel resources in your car. Have a current street map of the metro area and practice using the map prior to independent home/community visits.
- Whether your car is equipped for emergencies. Equipment that may be needed includes a spare tire (and the necessary changing equipment), ample fuel, and battery cables. If your work will involve extensive travel, consider obtaining emergency roadside assistance coverage.
- Insurance coverage. Adjustments may be needed to ensure coverage for clients transported in your personal vehicle. Before using an agency vehicle, verify that students and volunteers are covered by the policy carried by the agency.
- Keep only necessary keys on your key ring. Consider obtaining a two-part key ring that allows you to detach a portion that contains your car keys.

Other

The following precautions may minimize your risk in the community (14, 15, 18):

- Before leaving for a home visit, review the case file at the agency to assess any known risks. Note how many individuals live at the home and whether there is a history of violence in the family.
- Leave a schedule with someone at the agency with the addresses of the clients you plan to visit, your expected route, and your expected arrival time back at the agency. If you suspect a potential for danger, arrange for someone to call you during your visit, and, if possible, take another staff member with you.
- Take only materials that are absolutely necessary for the home visit and leave valuables (e.g., extra cash, unneeded credit cards, and jewelry) at the agency or at home.
- Schedule home visits in the morning when possible. Neighborhoods and homes tend to be calmer during the morning hours than at any other time of day.
- If you have reason to exercise caution, visit new clients during the day or in the evening at a neutral (public) site.
- If cellular phones or beepers are standard for other staff in the field, consider asking for a loan of this equipment during your practicum. Also, know that they can be tempting for thieves. If not available from the agency, consider obtaining your own cellular phone. Plan to keep it concealed but turned on during your visits so that you can use it at a moment's notice.
- Prominently display forms of identification to the client (e.g., agency name badge, business card, or logo on the agency vehicle).
- Pattern your dress after the other field staff. Some agencies will prefer a professional look in the field, while others promote a casual dress style. Limit your jewelry to the bare essentials.
- Have clear written directions to the home location. Allow extra time if you are unfamiliar with the area. If you get lost, retrace your route. If you must ask for directions, go to a public place to do so. Do not ask directions from persons on the street, and *never* allow anyone to get into your car to show you the way to your destination.
- Listen to and trust your instincts. If the situation seems uncomfortable and you sense the possibility for trouble, reschedule the appointment or make alternative arrangements.

During the Visit

Adhering to the following suggestions can ensure safety during home visits (14, 15, 18):

- Park your car as close to the client's home as possible and store unnecessary belongings in the trunk (e.g., large bags, backpacks, coats, a purse, or items to be delivered to another client).
- Lock all car doors and keep your keys in a place in which you have quick, easy access to them (e.g., pocket, on your clipboard).

■ Note the presence of any animals on the property and ask the client for assistance with any unleashed animals.

■ Avoid walking through a group of unknown individuals when attempting to enter the house (you may wish to leave and call to reschedule).

■ Take note of individuals present in the home and ask the client about strangers. If you are uncomfortable in the presence of others in the home, ask if you can meet with the client alone or somewhere quiet. Encourage the client to keep confidential the information you will be discussing by asking others to leave the home.

■ If possible, sit with your back to a wall on a hard chair so that you can leave quickly if necessary.

■ Take note of all exits as you enter the house.

■ Avoid talking with a client in the bedroom or in the kitchen as weapons are frequently stored in these rooms.

■ Leave the home immediately if weapons or drugs are visible.

■ After the visit, move your car to another location to complete the paperwork. Avoid sitting in a car in front of a client's home after a home visit. Document any risks associated with your visit.

PRACTICE APPLICATION **3.4**

Role-Play: Off-Site Safety Rules

Review and role play the physical safety protocols practiced by your agency for off-site work with your field instructor. Situations to role play include: (1) leaving the agency, (2) arriving at the home, (3) interactions within a home, (4) leaving a home, and (5) returning to the agency. In the role-plays, include such details as:

1. making an appointment with a client;
2. obtaining directions to the home;
3. time of day of visit;
4. ensuring that the vehicle is in optimum working order;
5. appropriate personal and professional items to take and safe methods of transporting and carrying them;
6. appropriate attire;
7. appropriate locations to stand/sit in the home;
8. greeting the client with a review of the purpose of the meeting;
9. ending the visit and leaving;
10. documentation and follow-up with the field instructor; and
11. appropriate responses for various situations that warrant caution (e.g., walking past a crowd on the front porch, presence of a dog, presence of unknown individuals, a loud argument occurring in the house, or vague reference to weapons nearby by the client).

Developed by Ellen Burkemper, Ph.D., LCSW

Working with Angry, Resistant, or Aggressive Clients

Despite the best planning, preparation, and adherence to protocol, you may find yourself in a situation with an angry, resistant, or aggressive client. Ideally, you would be able to leave a situation or attempt to get help. If this is not an option, consider the following strategies (14, 18):

- Maintain a quiet, calm, and firm demeanor. Avoid exhibiting any alarm, hostility, distress, or defensiveness. Talk to the client with simple, direct sentences.
- Offer positive choices to the client (e.g., "Would you like to move over to my desk so that we can sit and discuss this?").
- Attempt to slow down the pace of the interaction so that the client has time to ventilate, calm down, and think.
- Avoid any physical contact with the client.
- Attempt to engage verbally with a client upon the first outward signs of agitation to allow for ventilation at the earliest possible point.
- Allow ample room between the two of you (more than one arm's length) to give the client plenty of personal space.
- Make every effort to seat the client. If it is not feasible to sit, allow ample room between the two of you and stand off center to the client to give yourself plenty of room to maneuver.
- Use minimal force if attacked. Apply only the amount of force needed to restrain the person or to free yourself and move to another location for assistance.

Working with agitated clients requires a calm, professional demeanor and preparation. If you are presented with a risky situation in the office or in the field, these suggestions can serve to defuse a potentially dangerous interaction.

Follow-Up to Crises

Even with the best preparation and planning, crises still occur. If you are involved in an incident, report the incident to your field instructor in a manner that is in accordance with the policy of your agency. Your field instructor should communicate with agency administration and provide you with the support and guidance you need. Agencies should thoroughly review an incident and support those who are involved in and those who are affected by a serious incident. Such efforts might include filing a police report, holding debriefing sessions, making changes to staff schedules and suggested routes, and identifying resources and protocols to ensure staff safety in the future (6).

Regardless of the response of your field instructor and agency, take advantage of the peer support networks available at your agency and within your social work program as well as your personal support system. If the incident involved a high degree of risk or you are finding that you have been deeply affected by the situation, you may wish to consider contacting a mental health practitioner to process and work through the incident.

Dilemmas Involving Safety Issues

What should I do if my agency physically restrains clients and I hold a personal philosophy against this? How do I decide whether to carry out activities in my practicum that my family or friends have asked me not to do? What should I do if I observe another staff member not following agency safety procedures? What should I do if I am required to conduct a home visit even after I discuss my uneasiness about the arrangements with my field instructor? What will I do if I am required to work at night even though I feel uncomfortable doing so? These questions are evidence that, even under the best circumstances with clear guidelines, students sometimes encounter situations that demand difficult decisions.

At times, difficult situations involving conflict between your personal beliefs, agency protocols, and client interests may emerge. At the practicum site, you may be asked to carry out activities to which you are personally opposed. In addition, you may be asked to conduct practicum activities under circumstances about which you feel uneasy. Although the NASW *Code of Ethics* (19) is silent on the matter of safety, the primacy of client interests is clear (Section 1.01: "In general, clients' interests are primary". . .). Furthermore, the *Code of Ethics* discusses the obligation social workers have to carry out the work of their employers in good faith (Section 3.09: "Social workers generally should adhere to commitments made to employers and employing organizations"); however, the *Code* does not explicitly require social workers to follow agency policies and procedures. This can leave you in a quandary when determining the best course of action in a situation that involves conflict between your beliefs and comfort level, agency procedures, and client interests.

Ideally, you were informed of the need for the activities in question prior to your commitment to the agency and you either made a decision to allow the interests of the agency and the clients to supersede your feelings or negotiated different arrangements prior to your commitment. However, if expectations or arrangements related to safety emerge after your commitment, you may decide to:

1. negotiate your involvement with activities about which you feel strongly with your field instructor/agency after you begin the practicum;
2. make a decision to engage in the activities in question regardless of your feelings;
3. process and explore your feelings to determine whether your fears are founded;
4. discuss your experiences and feeling in integrative seminar in order to determine a course of action;
5. discuss the situation with your faculty liaison; or
6. attempt to switch to another practicum site if you are unable to resolve the conflict.

Although guidelines outlined in this unit serve as suggestions, situations are rarely clear-cut, and students are often left to their own best judgments to discern a course of action. Indeed, students often struggle with the same dilemmas faced by seasoned social workers. As social workers strive to deliver quality services under increasingly volatile circumstances, the struggle to integrate personal feelings with professional demands and to resolve safety dilemmas becomes more difficult and more common.

Sexual Harassment

An openly homosexual female staff member has asked Lauren out several times for drinks after work. Despite Lauren's repeated refusals, she continues to ask. She seems to create reasons for contact with Lauren and brings her small gifts of food. Lauren surmises that the staff member perceives that she is also lesbian. The field instructor and staff member are good friends. In discussions with her family about the situation, Lauren has been pressured to end the problem by involving administrators or outside agencies. Is she being harassed? What should she do?

Situations such as this call for careful thought, tact, and a judgment call. It may be very difficult to distinguish between friendliness and harassment. It is important to note that an additional form of violence that occurs to social work practitioners is sexual harassment. Armed with good intentions, the NASW *Code of Ethics*, and some social work professional work experience, many students conclude that sexual harassment will not be an issue for them. Given the value base and humanist orientation of the profession, you might think that the social work workplace would be free of sexual harassment. However, social workers do encounter sexual harassment in their workplaces (20, 21, 22, 23). Approximately one third of female social workers experience sexual harassment (21, 22), and one third of social work students encounter at least one instance of harassment (24, 25). Social work practicum students can expect to encounter sexual harassment as frequently as do social work practitioners.

Sexual harassment "exists on a widespread basis in human service agencies, despite the commonly held view that it is largely confined to the public sector" (21). Although the majority of those experiencing sexual harassment are female, male workers are not immune. One-seventh of male social workers report a previous experience of sexual harassment by coworkers, clients, supervisors, or administrators (22). Over half of social work programs experience problems with sexual harassment, and one fourth of the complaints target field supervisors (26).

Defining Features of Harassment

Sexual harassment occurs in many forms, ranging from jokes involving sexual themes to sexual intercourse. Early studies of the issue focused solely on behaviors and verbalizations, such as provocative jokes, asking for unwanted dates, and unwanted touching (20, 21, 22). Later work in this area defines sexual harassment more broadly. Sexual harassment is currently defined as verbal (pressure for sexual activity, comments about the female or male body, sexual boasting, and sexist and homophobic comments); nonverbal (looking up dresses or down shirts, obscene gestures, and suggestive sounds); physical contact (touching, patting, pinching, kissing, etc.); or environmental (sexually offensive literature, pictures, or music). Verbal harassment is the most common form of harassment (20, 22).

Agencies are compelled by law to address the issue of sexual harassment by ". . . seek[ing] solutions to such work-related abuse through programs of prevention, clear policies, and effective mediation and discipline" (23). In response to increasing awareness and complaints, Title VII of the 1964 Civil Rights Act provides legal protection against sexual harassment (20) and the Equal Employment Opportunity Commission (EEOC) issued guidelines in 1980 to provide guidance to agencies on the matter (21). In addition, the NASW *Code of Ethics* (19) drives the social work profession's response to this issue. The *Code* requires social workers to reject sexual activities with clients under all circumstances, to renounce all forms of discrimination, and to avoid relationships that pose a conflict of interest as well as to maintain a clear interest in social justice and to preserve human dignity. Both your field instructor and your agency have a clear interest in maintaining an atmosphere that is free of harassment.

Intervention

What should you do if you encounter sexual harassment at the practicum? The circumstances of the harassment will assist to fashion the response. Consider the following steps:

- Document the circumstances of the harassment, including dates, times, quotations, other details of the interaction/situation, and verification from any witnesses (27).
- Document your work accomplishments and maintain copies of evaluations. This documentation may be critical if your work performance becomes an issue when you taking action against the harassment.
- Seek other victims of harassment and consider taking action as a group.
- Confront the harasser in person or in written form. Include the facts, your feelings, and a clear directive to stop the harassment (27).
- If appropriate, report the experience(s) to your field instructor at the agency and your faculty liaison with your social work program.
- Explore the complaint process available at the agency as well as within your social work program and consider filing a formal complaint.
- Consult with other social work students. Take advantage of field seminars or other mechanisms to consult with and receive support from other students (27).
- If a complaint process does not exist, consider advocating for one. A formal complaint system within agencies appears to deter sexual harassment activities more effectively than does an organizational policy (21).

- Consider contacting outside resources. You may wish to contact an attorney or a local, state, or federal agency charged with addressing complaints of harassment (e.g., the Federal Equal Employment Opportunity Commission), a nonprofit organization (e.g., NAACP), or another resource (27) (addresses and contact information for these organizations can often be found in the telephone book).

Regardless of the order in which you take the actions suggested above, it is important to take action if confronted with this problem. Victims of sexual harassment must take action to address this serious issue. It is important that all victims of this type of harassment advocate for themselves, use the resources that are available, and seek support from others.

PRACTICE APPLICATION **3.5**
Safety: Your Comfort Zone

To increase your comfort zone, role play the following situation with your field instructor:

- During a routine office visit, one of your clients begins to share her despondency over her life situation. She has just broken up with her abusive boyfriend and discusses her suicidal thoughts with you. She mentions that she has a gun and is tempted to "do it" now and "get it over with." In her rambling, she talks about how no one, not even you, has been able to help her, and she is angry. As she continues to talk about killing herself, she mentions "taking you with her."

Should you take the threat seriously? What should you do?

PRACTICE APPLICATION **3.6**
Role-Play: Sexual Harassment

Read the two vignettes presented here and select one for role playing with your field instructor, colleague, or classmate:

1. You are a female social worker. You are preparing to take some clients of the day treatment center for the chronically mentally ill on an outing. A male client of a different ethnicity has approached you as you climb into the agency vehicle. This client has made several remarks to you in the past that have been of a sexual nature. He has also commented that he thinks you will not date him because he is of a different ethnicity. When you discussed the situation with your field supervisor, she suggested that you confront the client. While obviously leering at you, he comments, "Boy, you have a great set of wheels there! Will you take me for a ride?"

(continued)

PRACTICE APPLICATION **3.6**   Continued

2. You are a male social worker. You have been uncomfortable working around an older, recently divorced, female staff member at work. She has dropped by your desk several times without reason, has asked many questions about your personal life, and has exhibited flirting behavior in several encounters. Other staff are beginning to tease you about this staff member. She is in the administration of the agency and a friend of your field instructor; therefore, you have a fair amount of interaction with her. You are uncomfortable with her behavior and are contemplating how to approach a discussion with your field instructor about this issue. Other issues involved in the situation are: (1) you would like a job at this agency when you graduate and wish to maintain good relationships with the staff; (2) you are questioning whether her behaviors constitute sexual harassment; (3) you are contemplating whether to use the agency grievance procedure about her behavior; and (4) you wonder whether your field instructor will take the situation seriously. As you engage in a dialogue with your field instructor about this, you would like to role play a confrontation with the staff member.

Summary

This unit addressed the issue of safety in the social work setting. Topics discussed included the scope of personal safety risks in social work; safety in the practicum setting; reasonable concerns and caution; assessment of potentially violent clients; specific guidelines for safety within the office and the community; safety suggestions for home/community visits; working with angry, resistant, or aggressive clients; follow-up to crises; dilemmas involving safety issues; and sexual harassment. In your capacity as a social work student, you are well advised to explore the topics of safety risks and safety procedures with your field supervisor. Know the risks, implement safety procedures, use the resources at hand, and serve your clients well.

Raising the issue of safety with faculty, other students, and your field instructor is an important facet of your practicum experience as it enables you to take the appropriate precautions when working with clients. After all, many dangerous situations can be avoided if the practitioner requests assistance from a colleague (13). Practitioners and students are well advised to trust their gut instincts about their safety and to seek support whenever needed. Indeed, you cannot adequately serve your clients in a state of significant mental or physical impairment. Your safety is imperative to the effectiveness of your work and, ultimately, to the benefit of your clients.

STUDENT SCENARIO POSTSCRIPTS

Corina's fear after hearing of a homicide of a worker at the site immobilized her for the remainder of the day. She realized that she could not function without addressing her concerns. In her supervision session with her field instructor the next day, she inquired about the incident. Although she had been informed about security procedures during orientation, she raised questions regarding:

- the security procedures that had been in place at the time of the incident;
- the changes in security procedures that had been implemented since this incident; and
- the prevalence of dangerous encounters with clients in the office.

To increase her comfort level, she also role played a dangerous situation with her field instructor. Are there any other reasonable steps that she could take to ensure her safety?

Ben shared with his field instructor that he responded to the client's rambling about the shotgun in the back seat only out of fear and that he never considered the safety of the client while in the interaction. In their discussion, the field instructor allowed him to ventilate his feelings, then began to problem solve with him. Other options for a response they discussed included:

- confronting the client while in the car, thereby risking agitating the client (and harm);
- getting out of the car immediately and fleeing the scene;
- driving to the office over the objections of the client; and
- driving to the location the client preferred, following the client inside the office, and placing a phone call to the authorities.

Can you think of other alternatives? What response would you have made? Why?

Lauren decided that she must do something about the staff member who has made uncomfortable overtures to her. The next time she asked Lauren to drinks after work, Lauren decided to confront the situation. She began by thanking the staff member for the invitation and commented on the friendliness of the staff at the shelter. She informed her that, due to a demanding work, practicum, school, and family schedule, she had decided to eliminate most of her social life for the semester and is turning down all invitations. Therefore, she will be unable to join the staff at any social occasions but appreciates the offer.

Did she confront the situation? How would you handle the situation?

REFERENCES

1. Landers, S. Social workers combat on-the-job attacks. *NASW News*. February 1993, 3.
2. Kipper, W. Violence and the social worker. *New Society*. September 26, 1986, 7–8.
3. Horeji, C., Garthwait, C. & Rolando, J. A survey of threats and violence directed against child protective workers in a rural state. *Child Welfare*. 1994, 73:173–179.

4. Tully, C. T., Kropt, N. P. & Price, J. L. Is field a hard hat area? A study of violence in field placements. *Journal of Social Work Education.* 1993, *29*(2):191–199.

5. Astor, R. A., Behre, W. J., Wallace, J. M. & Fravil, K. A. School social workers and school violence: Personal safety, training and violence programs. *Social Work.* 1998, *43*(3):223–232.

6. Griffin, W. V. Social worker and agency safety. In R. L. Edwards (Ed.), *Encyclopedia of Social Work* (19th ed.) (pp. 2293–2304). Washington, DC: NASW Press. 1995.

7. Knight, C. A study of BSW students' perceptions of and experiences with risks to their personal safety in the field practicum. *The Journal of Baccalaureate Social Work.* 1996, *2*(1):91–108.

8. Wayne, J. & Raskin, M. S. Attitudes and practices of field education directors toward student safety concerns. *Areté.* 1996, *21*(1):1–12.

9. Ellison, M. L. Field can be hazardous to your well-being: Fact or fiction? *The Journal of Baccalaureate Social Work.* 1996, *2*(1):79–89.

10. Reeser, L. C. & Wertkin, R. A. Danger: Field placements may be hazardous to your health. Paper presented at the Council on Social Work Education Annual Program Meeting, San Diego, California. 1995.

11. Council on Social Work Education. *Handbook of accreditation standards and procedures.* Alexandria, VA: Author. 1994.

12. Deaconess Health System. *Blood borne pathogens and tuberculosis: Self-study packet.* St. Louis, MO: Author. 1998.

13. Newhill, C. E. Client violence toward social workers: A practice and policy concern for the 1990s. *Social Work.* 1995, *40*(5):631–636.

14. Griffin, W. V., Montsinger, J. & Carter, N. *Personal safety handbook.* Durham, NC: Brendan Associates and ILR. 1995.

15. Versen, G. Be careful, it's a jungle out there: A look at risks in field placement. *The New Social Worker.* 1995, *2*(1):7–8.

16. Deaconess Health System. *Annual packet: A review of safety and other topics vital to Deaconess Health System employees.* St. Louis, MO: Author. 1998.

17. U.S. General Accounting Office. *Home visiting: A promising early intervention strategy for at-risk families.* Washington, DC: Author. 1990.

18. Whitehead, D. Personal communication. September 16, 1997.

19. National Association of Social Workers. *NASW code of ethics.* Washington, DC: NASW Press. 1996.

20. Dhooper, S. S., Huff, M. B. & Schultz, C. M. Social work and sexual harassment. *Journal of Sociology and Social Welfare.* 1989, *16*(3):125–138.

21. Judd, P., Block, S. R. & Calkin, C. I. Sexual harassment among social workers in human service agencies. *Areté.* 1995, *10*(1):12–21.

22. Maypole, D. E. Sexual harassment of social workers at work: Injustice within? *Social Work.* 1986, *31*:29–34.

23. Singer, T. L. Sexual harassment. In R. L. Edwards (Ed.), *Encyclopedia of Social Work* (19th ed.) (pp. 2148–2156). Washington, DC: NASW Press. 1995.

24. Fogel, S. J. & Ellison, M. L. Sexual harassment of BSW field placement students: Is it a problem? *The Journal of Baccalaureate Social Work.* 1998, *3*(2):17–29.

25. McNeece, C. A., DiNitto, D. M., DeWeaver, K. L. & Johnson, P. H. Social work education: No sexual harassment here? *Human Service Education.* 1987, *8*(2):20–28.

26. Singer, T. L. (1989). Sexual harassment in graduate schools of social work: Provocative dilemmas. *Journal of Social Work Education.* 1989, *25*(1):68–76.

27. Sheafor, B. W., Horejsi, C. R. & Horejsi G. A. *Techniques and guidelines for social work practice* (4th ed.). Boston: Allyn & Bacon. 1997.

4 Making the Most of Your Practicum Supervision

The mediocre teacher tells.
The good teacher explains.
The superior teacher demonstrates.
The best teacher inspires.

—William Arthur Ward

What is practicum supervision and why is it important? Social work educators and practitioners place considerable emphasis on the provision and receipt of supervision, in general, and on the field training experience, in particular. Because of the intense and complex nature of social work practice, multiple perspectives are essential to the provision of high-quality services. A major component of the social work curriculum is delivered through a real-life, experiential field practicum in which you work directly with clients, client systems, community resources, and governmental bodies. For this reason, access to a seasoned social work practitioner who can serve as a teacher and guide to challenge and support you through the social work learning and socialization process is essential. Regardless of whether this person is referred to as a practicum/field supervisor or field instructor, he or she will play an important role in your social work education.

Supervision within the social work field experience is considered an educationally focused teaching relationship that is authority based and has periods of closeness and distance [1, 2]. The field instructor–student relationship is typically implemented through an individualized, one-on-one teaching arrangement based in a community agency [3]. Along with supervising practicum tasks and activities, the field instructor can (but may not always) become a mentor for you. The mentoring relationship can be described as "a close interpersonal 'helping relationship' between two individuals who are at different stages in their professional development" [4]. The mentoring relationship can continue when your practicum experience is completed and maintain a prominent place in your professional growth and development. Even if the mentoring relationship dissipates over time, the experience may still hold a significant place in your development as a social work professional.

What Is Practicum Supervision?

The Council on Social Work Education requires accredited social work programs (4) to ensure and monitor that social work students are placed in practicum situations that include opportunities for supervised practice in the application of social work knowledge, values, and ethics (4). However, each social work program establishes individualized criteria and policies for the specific implementation of field instruction by the agency and the field instructor. Thus, individual agencies and field instructors determine the teaching approach to be used.

An important distinction to make when describing practicum supervision is to note what is not included in the definition. First, practicum supervision should be distinguishable from employment supervision. The focus of practicum supervision is on the teacher–learner relationship, in which the learner grows and develops personally and professionally. Employment supervision, on the other hand, emphasizes the supervision of the employee in the implementation of the duties for which he or she has been hired by the organization. Often, the employee learns and grows and the supervisor may become a mentor, but the primary mission is the delivery of social services by the employee. Second, supervision is not comparable to professional consultation. Consultation is considered as input/feedback that is intended to be suggestive or in recommendation form. Consultation may be provided by a supervisor or colleagues and may be provided individually or in a group setting, such as a staff meeting.

Who Provides Practicum Supervision?

Because social work programs have the discretion to approve supervisory arrangements that meet the educational interests of the practicum student, supervision can be provided by a graduate-level social worker, a baccalaureate-level social worker, or a non–social worker. Social work educators recognize that valuable learning can be facilitated by professionals from a variety of disciplines. Under rare circumstances, most social work programs will approve a field instructor who does not possess a social work degree. In fact, practicum students placed in agencies that do not employ social workers may have the opportunity to gain a nontraditional social work experience and learn interdisciplinary collaboration skills. However, most social work educators agree that non–social work supervision is not the optimal educational situation. Although a professional of a different discipline can enrich the student's learning, being socialized into the profession by a social worker is considered the ideal learning environment in which to train. Specific attention should be given to matching the student with the site and the field instructor, taking the student's developmental level and the agency culture into consideration (5).

In the case of a student being supervised by a non–social work supervisor, the social work program is, nonetheless, obligated to ensure that the student is provided with the social work perspective (4). Each social work program has a policy for monitoring the provision of this perspective. The social work perspective may be provided by a degreed social worker employed elsewhere within the practicum agency, a volunteer with the organization, or a social work program faculty member. To ensure optimal learning and to limit confusion regarding supervision, you should have a clear understanding of the parameters of a nontraditional supervisory arrangement and adhere to them.

Students may also have the opportunity to complete their practica at the sites in which they are employed. A place-of-employment practicum can create opportunies for flexibility, providing service to your agency, learning different aspects of your agency, preparing for a new position, financial benefits, and expanded supervision (6). You should exercise caution if you are completing or considering this practicum arrangement because potential pitfalls include a diminished quality of learning, inadequate monitoring, confusion of your dual roles and relationships, and conflicting agency demands (6). Additional requirements may be in place for you should you opt to complete a place-of-employment experience. Although a place-of-employment placement can be rewarding and can reduce the stress of balancing school, work, and practicum, you must call upon your adult learner skills to ensure that you have a high-quality learning experience.

The Practicum Supervision Approach

The supervisor–supervisee relationship is an extremely important aspect of the social work student's educational experience and is possibly the most important and powerful (7). You may come to admire and respect your field instructor for his or her knowledge, abilities, competence as a practitioner, and willingness to serve as a mentor. However, the field instructor–student relationship can also elicit such charged reactions from the student as dependency, threats to autonomy, ignorance, failure, submissiveness, and competition, as well as pleasure (8). For the field instructor, emotions may range from fear of authority and hostility to nurturance (8). Therefore, it is essential that both you and your field instructor are committed, knowledgeable, and clear regarding the parameters and expectations of the supervisory relationship. Attaining the optimal teacher–learner fit can be a goal for the student and field instructor as well as a part of the learning experience. Achieving an effective and meaningful relationship with your field instructor will enable you to take advantage of his or her knowledge and skills and to apply that experience to your current learning situation. Learning to negotiate and function effectively in a supervisory relationship can provide you with a foundation for future supervisory relationships in which you may be either a supervisee or a supervisor.

As an adult learner, you are responsible for identifying your learning style along with the teaching style of your field instructor. Routinely engaging in discussion about each other's styles will enable you and your supervisor to continue to understand how the other processes and utilizes information. The insights gained from identifying your field instructor's supervision style will serve as a guide for your field instructor in assigning tasks and activities, teaching knowledge and skills, and evaluating your performance and progress.

Supervision style can be defined as the way your field instructor shares his or her theoretical orientation and practice and supervisory philosophies (9). The field instructor style may be generally categorized as (1) active—problem oriented, directive, and interpretive—or (2) reactive—process oriented, indirect, and noninterpretive (9). Which style of supervision does your field instructor use? How does this fit with your previously identified learning style?

Gaining awareness of teacher–learner styles does not guarantee a match of styles. An examination of the two individual styles may reveal that your field instructor's style is dissimilar to your learning style. Learning of such a mismatch need not predict supervisory relationship outcome. In fact, a teacher–learner style difference can serve as an opportunity for new learning for both the teacher and the student. Each of you can use the situation to explore different methods of interacting with someone who perceives the practicum experience with a different method of information processing. You can apply this experience to work with your clients, coworkers, agencies, and the community, who frequently perceive situations in a different light.

Regardless of field instructor–student style congruence, you may initially be unsure of and uncomfortable with this new relationship. Unless you have completed previous practica, your relationship with the field instructor will be unfamiliar. Initially, you will legitimately feel a greater sense of dependence on your field instructor and a heightened sense of vulnerability, thus creating a desire for increased structure and more directive supervision (10). You are cautioned to resist the temptation to allow your learning style to be folded into the teaching style of your field instructor (9). Supervisees, often eager to learn and please the field instructor, may subjugate individuality to "enhance" the supervisory relationship. To normalize and allay such concerns, you should pay particular attention to preparing for your new role as a supervisee and consumer of social work supervision.

What Can I Expect from Practicum Supervision?

After reflection regarding his concerns about boundary issues in his practicum site (delineating his social work role from his role as a recovering person and an AA sponsor), Cameron discussed the issues with his field instructor. The field instructor validated Cameron's concerns and shared that other students and staff struggle with similar challenges. The field instructor suggested that both of them make a concerted effort to address proactively boundary issues and Cameron's concerns on an ongoing basis. What would you suggest to Cameron if his field instructor (1) had not been so supportive or (2) does not follow through with this commitment?

Cameron's situation is not uncommon in that students often have concerns about personal or professional issues that they need and want to raise with their field instructors but feel uncomfortable because they are unsure of what to expect from the supervisory relationship. When you begin your practicum, you should engage in exploration and self-reflection to gain clarity regarding your expectations of your field instructor, the supervisory relationship, and yourself. The field instructor–student relationship may be unlike any relationship you have previously experienced because your field instructor is responsible for monitoring the completion of tangible duties as well as for mentoring, teaching, and socializing you as a member of the social work profession and for evaluating and awarding or recommending a grade for the practicum. Moreover, your field instructor assumes a legal obligation when he or she agrees to serve as a field instructor for your social work program. By virtue of the fact that your field instructor is providing supervision during your practicum, he or she is, in ssence, legally liable for your actions. Therefore, you should enter the supervisory relationship with an understanding as clear as possible of the expectations of your field instructor and yourself.

You may want to begin preparation for supervision by considering the reasons that a practitioner is motivated to serve as a field instructor. Gaining insight into your field instructor's motivations for supervising you may enable you to understand how your supervisor approaches and carries out the task. This role is voluntary, in most cases, and is sometimes completed above and beyond the field instructor's normal workload. Field instructors are intrinsically motivated to seek out the opportunity to mentor a new social work professional, but they may be unable to continue in this role on a long-term basis due to organizational or personal conflicts (11). Some social workers may also view serving as a field instructor as a way to return the gift of supervision and mentoring received earlier in their social work careers (1). Still others may view teaching through field instruction as a mechanism for honing their own social work skills (12). Unfortunately, some field instructors may be fulfilling an employment obligation and may therefore perceive the student as an additional staff resource. Regardless of the motivation, your field instructor makes a significant investment in your professional training by his or her willingness to serve as your field instructor.

What Can I Expect from My Field Instructor?

Each member of your practicum team—the social work program, the agency, your field instructor, and you—will have similar, but possibly differing, perspectives on the implementation of the practicum and the structure and format of the student–field instructor relationship. Depending on the experience of all parties, the perspectives may range from the rigidly defined to the seemingly undefined. Although you are responsible for understanding the expectations placed on you, the social work program is responsible for conveying expectations and information to the agency, your field instructor, and you. Moreover, the agency and field instructor are responsible for providing you and the social work program with information relevant for your placement and functioning within your practicum setting.

The supervisory relationship is often a balancing act for your supervisor. The field instructor must balance his or her role as a worker, supervisor, or administrator with the added role as a field supervisor/teacher/mentor. If student supervision is a new role for your field instructor, he or she may be unsure of the expectations and responsibilities required of the role. Social work programs routinely provide a general orientation for new field instructors; however, there are nuances and aspects of field instruction that evolve as the practicum develops or that are unique to the specific agency setting.

Regardless of the field instructor's longevity as a practicum supervisor, you and the field instructor must develop your own relationship with each other. Initially, you may have only your past experiences as a supervisee (or supervisor) on which to rely, while the field instructor may have a wide repertoire of experiences on which to draw. The field instructor, however, is responsible for initiating the relationship and setting the stage for the future of supervision (13). In general, you can expect that your field instructor will assume the following responsibilities (2, 9, 10, 14, 15, 16):

- demonstrate commitment to your learning by creating a safe and trusting environment and culture that are conducive to optimizing your professional growth and development
- transmit knowledge that integrates theory and practice activity and apply research knowledge and methodology to practice
- provide a clear structure and format for the supervisory relationship, in general, and the supervisory sessions, in particular, that includes
  - boundary limitations;
  - expectations and goals of supervision;
  - times and location of supervision sessions;
  - format for supervision, including opportunities for alternative forms of supervision (group, interdisciplinary, or off-site); and
  - mutual preparation expected for supervision sessions (e.g., written agendas, case/project presentations, or topics identified for discussion)
- serve as a professional role model by engaging in ethical, competent social work practice

- utilize, as possible, a variety of supervisory techniques and strategies that may be implemented through individual, group, or interdisciplinary supervision formats
- possess a supervisory style that is flexible and responsive to your needs and stage(s) of development
- commit to the supervisory arrangement by ensuring regularity and consistency of time of supervision, location, privacy, and absence of interruptions and by taking the initiative to make alternative arrangements when scheduling conflicts arise
- adhere to the social work program–agency training agreement regarding provision of supervision, learning opportunities, information, liability coverage, and safety precautions
- commit to the creation and maintenance of an effective supervisory style that enhances student learning
- assign appropriate tasks and activities based on your level of experience, training, interests, and goals; these assignments should be clearly stated and include your participation in their development
- establish and maintain an appropriate professional supervisor–supervisee relationship, which includes boundary setting (understanding behavior appropriate to a professional relationship) and in most cases precludes the development of mutual/dual relationships with you (*dual relationships*, in this instance, refers to those relationships that are social, therapeutic, or financial/business in nature);
- be sensitive to your feelings and appropriately ask you about your feelings and discuss your concerns
- provide frequent, ongoing, and balanced feedback regarding your performance and progress toward practicum and personal goals
- embrace the role of teacher and have a positive attitude when expected to answer questions and explain actions

PRACTICE APPLICATION **4.1**

Forewarned Is Forearmed

Within the first two weeks of your practicum (and before any differences of opinion have to be negotiated), ask your field instructor the following questions:

1. How would you would like me to address any concerns or differences of opinion that may arise during my practicum?
2. How have you handled differences in the past?

Should a difference of opinion occur during your practicum, be mindful of keeping the discussion at the cognitive level. Strategies to employ include using "I" statements and avoiding references to feeling words (i.e., "I think . . ." versus "I feel . . .").

Developed by Ellen Burkemper, Ph.D., LCSW, MFT

What Should I Expect from Myself?

The supervisory relationship is a mutual and interactive process. Your field instructor is responsible for facilitating your application of theories and knowledge, learning of agency policies and procedures, and professional socialization. While you are considering the contributions that your field instructor will make to your learning, you should also be contemplating the responsibility that you will assume for the learning experience. Your expectations of yourself should be similar to those that you have of your field instructor and should include the following rules:

- Demonstrate a commitment to your own learning by being
  - open to new learning and experiences;
  - motivated;
  - flexible in your personal, theoretical, and practice ideas;
  - interpersonally curious;
  - minimally defensive; and
  - introspective (10).
- Clearly communicate your expectations of learning to your field instructor, including the tasks, and activities that you wish to undertake and client populations and client issues that you would like to experience.
- Understand the philosophical orientation of the social work program regarding the field experience (2).
- Develop your knowledge of the social work program's practicum policies and procedures for students and field instructors.
- Commit to your supervisory arrangement by ensuring preparation, regularity, and consistency of time of supervision, location, privacy, and absence of interruptions.
- Adhere to the social work program–agency agreement regarding
  - student responsibility for participation in and compliance with supervision requirements and arrangements,
  - completion of practicum-related forms,
  - learning opportunities,
  - agency policies and procedures,
  - your responsibility for liability coverage, and
  - safety precautions.
- Commit to the creation and maintenance of an effective supervisory arrangement that enhances your learning (15).
- Actively participate in the development of your educational/learning plan and utilize the plan as a working document to monitor your progress through the field experience.
- Clearly understand the evaluative criteria and ensure that the learning agreement matches the evaluation and that tasks and activities are moving you toward the goal of achievement and competence.
- Maintain an appropriate professional supervisor–supervisee relationship, which, in most cases, precludes development of mutual/dual relationships with your field instructor (2).

- Be willing to take risks and discuss your fears and anxieties regarding your practicum as well as controversial, uncomfortable issues with which you are confronted during your practicum experience.
- Be willing to provide feedback to your field instructor regarding his or her supervisory style.

An issue that may arise for you as you work with your field instructor is related to personal disclosure—both yours and your field instructor's. There may be issues or experiences that you bring to the practicum experience that are relevant to share with your field instructor. For example, if you received services from a social worker earlier in your life and that experience influenced your decision to become a social worker, you may choose to share that experience. However, you may not feel comfortable sharing the issues that brought you into contact with a social worker unless they have direct relevance to your practicum responsibilities. Sharing personal information and experiences is usually voluntary and done to enhance the supervisory experience. If you have personal information or experiences that are pertinent to your ability to deliver services, you should inform your field instructor of that part of your history. You may be required to share information with the agency if a criminal record, child abuse/neglect, or physical health check is required. If you are unsure about the appropriateness of sharing historical or current information about yourself (e.g., mental/physical illness, addiction, sexual assault/molestation, or criminal record), discuss this issue with your faculty liaison. As a general rule, sharing the information is preferred as it can often enhance the quality of your learning experience.

PRACTICE APPLICATION 4.2
Supervision from the Other Side of the Desk

This practice application will help you gain insight into the field instructor's experience. It will enable you to assume the posture of a supervisory social worker. Read the following case and, using the list of questions provided, develop a plan of intervention *from the field instructor's perspective.* Following your completion of the questions, consider discussing or role playing this case with your field instructor, with your fellow students, or in integrative practice field seminar.

The Case
Your practicum student has come to you in a very agitated and emotional state. She has just learned from another staff member that a support staff member who lives in the student's community has begun telling the agency's staff that she (the student) is a lesbian. The support staff person is in your department but does not report to you. While the information is, in fact, accurate, the student had purposefully not yet shared her sexual orientation with her family, other students, faculty, or practicum agency staff because she had not yet felt comfortable presenting herself as lesbian.

(continued)

- As the field instructor, what do you do?
- What do you say to the student?
- How do you support the student?
- Is it appropriate for the support staff person to reveal this information without first approaching the student?
- What is your responsibility regarding the handling of the support staff person's behavior?

Ethical and Interpersonal Issues in Supervision

Lauren identifies equally with both of her racial and ethnic backgrounds (European and African). Her new field instructor is extremely Afrocentric and feels adamant that anyone of African heritage should identify primarily with that heritage. Lauren is concerned that this issue may interfere with her practicum experience and could even affect her grade. What do you think she should or could do in this situation?

Although not every student will share Lauren's experience, you may encounter areas in which you and your field instructor differ. These differences may be related to personal (as in Lauren's case), philosophical, political, or work style issues. Having differences does not necessitate a negative experience and can create a powerful learning opportunity.

Despite the fact that most practica are relatively free of problems, occasional problems can occur. The nature of these problems can range from administrative to interpersonal to ethical. Such situations can create personal and professional dilemmas for you, your agency, and the social work program. But if the problem is addressed appropriately, valuable learning can result for all involved.

Some dilemmas can result from a lack of clear communication or understanding of philosophy, policy, or requirements. The field instructor is responsible for articulating and clarifying his or her ethical and value-related stances as well as those of the agency and the profession (9). The NASW *Code of Ethics* (17) should be integrated into your supervisory sessions as a tool for interpreting and applying the profession's ethical standards. The *Code of Ethics* is an essential facet of contemporary social work practice because it serves as a guide for practice and a resource when an ethical dilemma arises (and more than common sense is needed) (9). The *Code* is available in Appendix D of this text.

Regardless of your awareness of and sensitivity to ethical practice issues, situations may arise in which a problem becomes insurmountable and the practicum experience or site must be terminated. This situation should not continue without the involvement of the social work program faculty, whose responsibility it is to provide consultation, to intervene, and to mediate, if necessary.

Dilemmas that may arise for you may be categorized as problems with the field instructor–student relationship, with the agency, or with professional behavior/practice. Field instructor–student problems may include the following:

- student perception that field instructor is not:
  - assigning appropriate number or type of assignments
  - providing adequate supervision
  - clear regarding expectations, boundaries, or procedures (15)
  - fulfilling the expectations set out in the learning plan regarding type and location of learning experiences
  - adequately ensuring that personal conflicts do not affect the professional relationship
- inadequate communication between field instructor and other staff regarding your performance on tasks and activities supervised by those other staff members (18)
- your perception that the midterm or final practicum evaluation is not an accurate reflection of your actual performance
- your feelings of isolation, alienation, and lack of support from the field instructor, agency staff, or social work program faculty (15)

Agency problems may include the following:

- your perception that you are not accepted by the
  - staff due to lack of acceptance of students or social workers, lack of clarity regarding the student role, or perceived competition from the student
  - client system(s) or community due to your status as a student or clients' lack of clarity regarding the student role and capabilities
- lack of adequate resources, space, or equipment available for your use
- lack of availability of assignments for you due to decreased client census, inadequate funding, or inadequate administrative support for student involvement

Professional behavior/practice problems may include the following:

- your perception that your field instructor or staff are behaving in an unprofessional or unethical manner in the areas of
  - client–worker interactions
  - dual relationships
  - resource management, or
  - field instructor–student relationship (e.g., sexual harassment, dual relationship, misuse of authority or power, and incompetent supervision)

Of particular relevance to the field instructor–student relationship is the issue of a sexual relationship developing between student and field instructor. Not only can a sexual relationship be detrimental to a student's learning experience and self-esteem but also such a relationship can be an abuse of power on the part of the field instructor and creates considerable role conflict (19). Moreover, the supervisory relationship is a critical aspect of student learning and future practice as it can establish the student's perspective on interactions, therapeutic relationships, and ethical behavior (19).

Students are often fearful of raising potential issues with their field instructors. This is particularly true when the problem is sensitive or controversial and when the field instructor is involved. You may even be reticent about asking for more supervision and assignments than the field instructor has provided (18). To maintain your silence about a problem heightens the problem and the potentially dysfunctional nature of the relationship by creating a secretive element, which results in missed learning opportunities and potential abuses of the student (20). Therefore, it is critical that you, your field instructor, and social work program faculty be able and willing to raise and intervene in potential or actual problems at the point at which they first arise.

Should you become concerned about a potential problem within your supervisory relationship, you should consider the following (20):

1. Do you have feelings about your field instructor that make you uncomfortable?
2. Are you are uncomfortable with your field instructor's supervision?
3. Do you interact differently with your field instructor because of uncomfortable feelings?
4. Is your field instructor unavailable to you?
5. Do you feel your field instructor is judgmental or biased about you?
6. Do you feel blamed by your field instructor in a problem situation?
7. Do you feel exploited by your field instructor?
8. Has your field instructor informed you that you should maintain confidentiality regarding the supervisory interactions?

In essence, are there any problems or issues that are creating a negative impact on your learning? Should you have any concerns regarding your relationship with your field instructor, the practicum faculty should be contacted immediately. The following discussion addresses proactive strategies that may serve to prevent a conflict from occurring.

PRACTICE APPLICATION 4.3

What Are You Saying and What Are You *Really* Saying to Your Field Instructor?

Monitoring your interactions with your field instructor is a helpful way to gain insight into your interpersonal skills and behaviors. For each of the following statements, consider the response that you would offer to address (1) the *content* (i.e., the substance or factual information) of the statement being presented to you and (2) the *process* (i.e., the dynamics between you, and the field instructor) of the interpersonal interaction.

Field Instructor to Student

1. "I am quite concerned about whether or not I should have you see this particular client."
2. "The manual asks you to do it this way, but I'm thinking it might be better to approach it this other way."
3. "I am having a little bit of difficulty understanding how you are dealing with this client."
4. "I am concerned that you are taking on too much responsibility."

After you have developed responses from both the content and the process perspectives to these statements, discuss each with your field instructor and fellow students to gain additional outlooks on these potentially conflictual interpersonal encounters.

Developed by Ellen Burkemper, Ph.D., LCSW, MFT

Strategies for Maximizing the Effectiveness of Your Practicum Supervision

The practicum experience is intended to be a challenging and rewarding experience, but you can enhance it further by developing a repertoire of techniques and strategies designed to allow you to take full advantage of the learning opportunities. Although not exhaustive, the following list suggests areas in which you can take further responsibility for your learning.

- Prepare for supervisory sessions by developing a written agenda and sharing it with your field instructor prior to the meeting so that he or she can be prepared with the appropriate information or materials.
- Develop and maintain reasonable and realistic expectations of your supervisor regarding his or her time, availability, knowledge, and patience.
- Engage in professional behavior by being on time for all agency activities and supervisory sessions.
- Use self in the supervisory sessions, noting issues that arise during the discussion of cases, projects, and client and staff interactions (2).
- Document the supervision sessions (issues discussed, assignments, recommendations, and responsibilities) and share the notes with your field instructor (2).
- Initiate or be open to creative techniques for supervision, including audio/videotaping, process recording, journaling, shadowing, role playing, live supervision/observation, and case presentation (2)
- Maintain open communication with your field instructor (18).
- Negotiate and renegotiate, as needed, your learning agreement, and supervisory plan (18).
- Utilize the learning agreement regularly as a tool for monitoring your learning and progress made toward your practicum, personal, and professional goals.
- Conduct meetings with your field instructor and any other staff members with whom you have worked during the practicum to discuss your performance evaluation (18).

- Assert yourself in communicating with your field instructor regarding training needs and supervision issues or assignment of tasks and activities, particularly if you feel the assignment is inappropriate for your level of training, experience, and goals.
- Invite your faculty liaison to take a more integrated role in practicum through observation of your practicum activities, participation in case presentations/staffings, and an increased number of on-site agency visits. Having a third, knowledgeable member of the supervision team can enhance your learning potential (21).
- In the case of a problem or conflict with the field instructor or practicum setting, utilize any and all available resources provided by the social work program, university, agency, and professional social work organizations as soon as possible.
- When you and your field instructor have exhausted all perceived possibilities, request consultative or interventive support from social work practicum faculty to renegotiate your learning agreement and your supervisory arrangement or to discuss conflicts.

PRACTICE APPLICATION 4.4

Supervision: Expectations and Assessment

Independent of each other, both you and your field instructor should develop a list of expectations and assessment criteria for the supervisory relationship from both perspectives. Specifically, you should develop a list of expectations for yourself and your field instructor, and the field instructor should develop a list of expectations for him- or herself as well as for you. Compare and contrast the completed lists and develop a mutually agreed-upon set of expectations of each other regarding supervision. Examples of areas to consider in developing your lists include (use the additional spaces to add your own expectations):

Expectations of Self (List specific expectations of yourself)	Assessment Criteria (List measurable outcomes used to determine whether expectations are achieved)
Use of supervision	
Preparedness for supervision	
Follow-up to supervisory recommendations	
Demonstration of adult learning	
Demonstration of assertiveness	

Expectations of Field Instructor *(List specific expectations you have for your field instructor)*	Assessment Criteria *(List measurable outcomes used to determine whether expectations are achieved)*
Preparedness for supervision	
Facilitation/stimulation of student learning opportunities	
Follow-up to student requests for information or resources	

PRACTICE APPLICATION **4.5**

Use of Self—Finding Trends in Interactions?

To help you optimize your use of your practicum supervision, this practice application will help you explore your ongoing interactions with your field instructor. Develop a journal (or journal within your practicum journal) that specifically addresses your supervisory interactions. Spend approximately five minutes following each supervision session documenting your reactions to the session and your field instructor, paying special attention to your (1) cognitive reactions (i.e., what you are *thinking*), (2) affective reactions (i.e., what you are *feeling*), and (3) behavioral reactions (i.e., what you *do* as a result of what you were thinking and feeling). Identify the trends in each category.

Developed by Ellen Burkemper, Ph.D., LCSW, MFT

PRACTICE APPLICATION **4.6**

Questions to Consider

This practice application is designed to help you explore your perceptions of practicum supervision. Develop responses to the following questions and include discussion of your responses in an upcoming supervisory session with your field instructor and peers.

1. What is practicum supervision, and how does it differ from other types of supervision?
2. Identify four characteristics of
   a. a practicum supervisor who would fit your learning style and of
   b. a difficult practicum supervision relationship.
   Explain the reasoning behind each of the characteristics you identified.
3. What emotions do you think you will (or did) experience at the beginning of your practicum related to supervision? Why? How have you reacted in the past to any

(continued)

PRACTICE APPLICATION **4.6**   **Continued**

> other type of supervisory experiences, and how may these reactions and experiences influence your current/future supervisory experiences?
> 4. Identify four learning experiences that you would like to receive from a practicum. What kinds of supervisory activities would facilitate the accomplishment of these goals?

Developed by Doris Westfall, LCSW

PRACTICE APPLICATION **4.7**
A Student's Worst Fear

In this practice application, you have the opportunity to examine a challenging situation from a dual perspective—your own and your field instructor's. Read the following scenario, and respond to the questions that follow. Share this exercise with your field instructor, and ask him or her to share his or her reactions to the scenario.

The Scenario
During a group therapy session, a student strongly confronts a client regarding the client's interpersonal behaviors with other family members. As a result of the confrontation, the client writes an unflattering evaluation of both the program and the student.

Discussion Questions
1. If you were this student, how would you feel, and how might you respond to this situation, particularly as you discuss the evaluation in supervision?
2. If you were the student's practicum instructor, how would you respond to the situation, and what might you say to the student during supervision?

Developed by Doris Westfall, LCSW

Summary

The field instructor–practicum student relationship is a unique and powerful part of your professional development as a social worker. As discussed in this unit, an important facet of a successful supervisor–supervisee association lies with the negotiation and communication that occurs throughout the learning process. The primary factor that predicts your perception of your field instructor is the field instructor's skill and the quality of the experience created by the field instructor (22). As you move through your practicum, you have the opportunity to be mentored by an experienced social work professional, to learn skills necessary for social work, practice, and to gain insights into your thoughts, feelings, and values.

STUDENT SCENARIO POSTSCRIPTS

Cameron demonstrated the skills of an adult learner by sharing his concerns with his field instructor regarding his worries about his potentially conflicting roles. He took a risk that his field instructor would suggest that a substance abuse treatment facility is not an appropriate practicum for someone who clearly has not resolved his own addiction issues. Fortunately, the field instructor validated Cameron's concerns and shared that other students and staff struggle with similar challenges. Cameron's field instructor suggests that both of them make a concerted effort to address proactively boundary issues and Cameron's concerns on an ongoing basis. Had the field instructor not been supportive of Cameron's concerns, he would be faced with two choices.

1. He could have stated his "case" to his field instructor and asked for the opportunity to forge on with his practicum. He may have experienced difficulty, however, as he would be both struggling with his own recovery issues and working in an environment in which he may now not feel comfortable.
2. He could have opted to leave his practicum.

Fortunately, Cameron continued in his practicum and in his journey toward his own recovery.

Had Cameron's field instructor initially conveyed support and then not provided it, Cameron would be faced with choices similar to those described above. However, Cameron is an adult learner who assumes responsibility for his own learning. Therefore, he would feel capable of confronting his field instructor regarding the lack of follow-up.

Lauren has identified an issue (racial and ethnic identification) that may significantly impact her practicum experience, particularly if she does not feel that she can address her concerns adequately. After considerable reflection and discussions with her fellow students and a trusted faculty member, Lauren elected to raise the issue with her field instructor in a supervisory session. Initially, the field instructor exhibited a defensive posture and inquired whether Lauren was accusing her of being discriminatory. At that moment, Lauren's worst fears were realized—her field instructor's response was the "worst case" scenario that Lauren had anticipated but had hoped would not occur. She wanted to run out of the room. But, with professionalism, Lauren stated that she was not suggesting this but was concerned that the field instructor might have negative feelings toward Lauren because she does identify equally with both her European and African heritages. Because Lauren was calm and mature, the field instructor was eventually able to "hear" Lauren's concerns and engage in dialogue that ended up being extremely helpful for Lauren (who had little experience with an extreme Afrocentric perspective). As a result of this discussion, Lauren gained insight into the contribution that an Afrocentric perspective can offer in empowerment work with clients. In addition, Lauren and her field instructor were able to discuss issues of diversity openly in a meaningful way.

REFERENCES

1. Collins, P. The interpersonal vicissitudes of mentorship: An exploratory study of the field supervisor-student relationship. *The Clinical Supervisor.* 1993, *11*(1):121–135.

2. Floyd, C. Preparing for supervision. *The New Social Worker.* 1995, *2*(2):8–9.

3. Walter, C. A. & Sadtler, L. C. The role of the field liaison in identifying learning/teaching styles to facilitate student learning. *Areté.* 1997, *21*(2):50–60.

4. Council on Social Work Education. *Handbook of accreditation standards and procedures.* Alexandria, VA: Author. 1994.

5. Abram, F. Y., Hartung, M. R. & Wernet, S. P. (1998). The NonMSW task supervisor, MSW field instructor, and the practicum student: A triad for high quality field education. In press, *Journal of Teaching in Social Work.*

6. Berg-Weger, M. & Huggins, P. J. Can I do my practicum where I work? *The New Social Worker.* 1996, *3*(2):16–18.

7. Kissman, K. & Van Tran, T. Perceived quality of field placement education among graduate social work students. *Journal of Continuing Social Work Education.* 1990, *5*(2):27–30.

8. Mordock, J. B. The new supervisor: Awareness of problems experienced and some suggestions for problem resolution through supervisory training. *The Clinical Supervisor.* 1990, *8*(1):81–92.

9. Munson, C. E. *Clinical social work supervision* (2nd ed.). New York: Haworth Press. 1993.

10. Berger, S. S. & Buchholz, E. S. On becoming a supervisee: Preparation for learning in a supervisory relationship. *Psychotherapy.* 1993, *30*(1):86–92.

11. Raskin, M. S. The Delphi study in field instruction revisited: Expert consensus on issues and research priorities. *Journal of Social Work Education.* 1994, *30*(1):75–89.

12. Rubio, D. M., Birkenmaier, J. & Berg-Weger, M. (1998). Human service non-profit agencies: Studying the impact of policy changes. Unpublished manuscript.

13. Bogo, M. The student/field instructor relationship: The critical factor in field education. *The Clinical Supervisor.* 1993, *11*(2):23–36.

14. Gelman, S. R. The crafting of fieldwork training agreements. *Journal of Social Work Education.* 1990, *26*(1):65–75.

15. Fogel, S. My practicum: Why do I hate it so? *The New Social Worker.* 1996, *3*(2):12–13.

16. Caspi, J. & Reid, W. J. The task-centered model for field instruction: An innovative approach. *Journal of Social Work Education.* 1998, *34*(1):55–70.

17. National Association of Social Workers. *Code of ethics.* Washington, DC: NASW Press. 1996.

18. DiGuilio, J. F. Concerns in the field placement. *The New Social Worker.* 1998, *5*(1):19–20.

19. Bonosky, N. Boundary violations in social work supervision: Clinical, educational, and legal implications. *The Clinical Supervisor.* 1995, *13*(2):79–95.

20. Jacobs, C. Violations of the supervisory relationship: An ethical and educational blind spot. *Social Work.* 1991, *36*(2):130–135.

21. Weinzettle, R. Observing students in the field. *The New Social Worker.* 1997, *4*(3):20–21.

22. Knight, C. A study of MSW and BSW students' perceptions of their field instructors. *Journal of Social Work Education.* 1996, *32*(3):399–414.

UNIT

5

Organizational Issues

Organizations are like a puzzle
Little pieces everywhere
Every piece is symbolic
Pieces of fate and pieces of care

Each puts his piece together and when they are set
A single effort is what we get
Together all the pieces make one whole
United in one goal

—Adapted from "The Missing Piece" (Jason Garay)

The feedback from Ben's supervisor about his first few weeks of practicum at the community-based outreach program was mixed. He was told that, although he was performing adequately with clients, he needed to be more independent and to take more initiative to do things on his own. Coworkers had complained that he was too hesitant to carry out his work autonomously and constantly asked others for guidance and permission to conduct activities with which he should have been comfortable at this point. Ben agrees with the assessment. He is confused about which staff member to turn to with questions, the limits of his autonomy to carry out work on his own, and how to work well within the agency. Ben feels that his previous work experience in a publicly funded research institution has not prepared him for work in this setting. How can Ben gain the knowledge he needs to succeed in this organization? What does he need to know? What are some of the differences between public and nonprofit agencies?

Many social work students are enthralled with the idea that they are finally going to be able to work with individuals and families in their practica. But, like Ben, you may find that your previous work experience has not prepared you to work in your practicum setting. Expectations differ widely from setting to setting—a work style that works well at one organization may not fit the expectations of another organization. You may be puzzled in the early weeks about your inability to serve clients to the extent needed. Like Ben, you may be so busy learning about the logistics of service delivery in the first few weeks of practicum that you may not have the time to gather information about the organization.

However, accredited social work programs must establish standards for field practicum settings within the guidelines of the Council on Social Work Education's (CSWE) accreditation standards (1). Therefore, your social work program has considered the context of your practicum agency and approved it as a site. Furthermore, programs are required to provide students with the opportunities to implement, critically assess, and evaluate agency policy (1). Your analysis of your agency context is a critical element of your field learning experience.

Ben has come to realize that understanding the context in which services are delivered in his agency is important to his performance and to the quality of services he is able to deliver. He is struggling with both his knowledge of the context of the services delivered and his socialization into the agency. As you begin to work with clients, you will begin to discover the importance of the agency context. The image you create within the organization—your behaviors, relationships, and methods of interacting with others—can be critical to your practicum success and satisfaction. The professional working style you develop in the early part of your practicum may have ramifications for you throughout the duration of your practicum and its effects may be key to your future career path (2). Your supervisor and other staff may make decisions about your practicum activities and level of responsibility based on your performance of duties early in the practicum. Furthermore, striving to go above and beyond minimum requirements to learn thoroughly about and become a part of the agency may enable you to be viewed as a desirable future employee. Being perceived as a student who is willing to go above and beyond requirements can also be helpful in your future employment searches, because it will be noted in job references made by your field instructor and other staff.

This unit will focus on the importance of understanding the organization within which you will complete your practicum, the essential elements of an organization, strategies to uncover the needed information about the agency, and the process of becoming socialized into an organization. Nonprofit, for-profit, and public organizations are defined; differences between them are explained; and the positive and negative factors of working within each type of organization are debated. Finally, the impact of various leadership theories on organizations is discussed and the role of social work within organizations is defined.

The Importance of Organizational Knowledge

Many students find the early weeks of practicum to be a series of emotional highs and lows. Beginning a professional role within an agency and serving clients can be exhilarating. More complex, however, can be gaining insight into the culture and function of your practicum agency. Organizations can be very complicated; mastering an understanding of the agency can take time and the persistence needed to work through early mistakes.

Most social work practice takes place within the parameters of an agency's philosophy, values, and resources. Very few social workers practice completely autonomously. The reality is that most social workers have a structure around and limits on their service delivery (3). Just as you consider the environment of your clients as pivotal to their social functioning, so, too, must the framework of your sponsoring organization be considered a defining influence on your social work practice.

You may find your role as a practicum student within your practicum agency to be clearly defined, your role well understood by agency staff and administrators, and mechanisms established whereby you are easily able to glean the important information about the agency. However, many students find their positions within their agencies to be nebulous, misunderstood by others, and unclear even to them. Are you a staff member? Volunteer? Is your role as practicum student clearly delineated? Where can students get needed information about agency administrative issues? For many students, accessing information about the agency's structure and administration and the students' role is akin to a scavenger hunt. If you find yourself in the latter situation and unclear about what to do with the clues you may have been provided, be persistent and willing to work through the unknown. As a social worker, your understanding of how your agency works becomes the backdrop and basis for your work with clients. Agency philosophy, policy, goals, and restrictions directly affect the work you can and cannot do with clients. Later in this unit, suggestions for uncovering administrative information are provided.

Internal Elements of an Organization

Organizations can be defined as "collectives of individuals gathered together to serve a particular purpose" (4). Whether you are completing your practicum in a for-profit, nonprofit, or public agency or within a large, medium, or small agency, your practicum organization was established to serve a purpose that would be impossible to accomplish well by one individual. Your practicum site is an entity that has many features that make it distinct from any other agency, including a history, culture, goals, structured administrative and service delivery system(s), and identifiable boundaries (5). In addition, as a type of organization, social service agencies have problems that differ from those of other organizations you may have worked in (see Box 5.1). As you begin to examine your practicum organization and observe its characteristics and administrative style, a brief discussion of types of organizations may assist you.

Governmental (Public) Organizations

Public organizations are characterized by two unique factors.

1. Funding is derived exclusively through tax revenue (federal, state, county, or local government funds) (3).
2. Statute or executive order provides the legal basis for the existence of the agency (4).

BOX **5.1**

Common Problems of Social Service Organizations

The following are several categories of problems common to social service agencies but that private businesses rarely encounter. Many problems stem from the complexity of working with human beings, including (5):

1. *Unstable environment:* Funding sources, social policy, accreditation standards, and affiliated organizations are in constant flux.
2. *Oversight difficulties:* The nonstandardization of human services makes oversight inherently difficult.
3. *Lack of clear, measurable organizational goals of service delivery:* Evaluating the effectiveness of services is difficult without quantifiable performance goals.
4. *Goal displacement:* The shift from an original goal of the agency to meet an identified human need to the goal of organizational survival can alter service delivery.
5. *Impersonal behavior:* Individuals both inside and outside the organization can attribute the motive behind an action to a personal response to them.
6. *Lack of rewards and recognition:* Social service organizations often lack a system of positive, public feedback to employees.

Other characteristics of a public agency can include large quantities of paperwork, complex rules and procedures, a relatively rigid bureaucratic structure, and a conservative administrative philosophy (3, 6). Within governmental agencies, a high degree of control is vested within top layers of administration (7). Last, stigma is often attached to those receiving services from a public agency (8).

Several advantages exist for those working within public agencies. Compared to working within the private (i.e., nonprofit and for-profit) sector (6), needed services can be offered to clients with less consideration given to cost-effectiveness. Furthermore, social workers within public agencies tend to enjoy relative predictability and job security due to a fairly stable funding source (3), as well as enjoy higher salaries than in the nonprofit sector (6). Last, clients served are typically those without many alternatives; therefore, they tend to be those with few resources. Social workers within these agencies are carrying out social work's historical preference for working on behalf of the poor.

The future for public agencies, however, may force significant changes. Since the 1980s, services traditionally delivered by government agencies are increasingly being delivered by the private sector under the presumption that the private sector can deliver services in a more efficient and effective manner than can large government bureaucracies (4). Predictions are that this trend will continue and that the role of government will continue to shift from service provider to supervisor of services delivered by private agencies (9).

Examples of government agencies commonly used as practicum sites include public child welfare agencies, aging services, and corrections institutions. A practicum within a public setting can offer the opportunity to gain knowledge about the public social service system that can prove invaluable whether you stay within a public setting or move to a private setting after graduation. Additionally, students in these settings work with a wide range of client issues and with clients presenting complex problems because governmental agencies tend to be the resource of last resort for clients (4). Providing services to clients with complicated or chronic problems can challenge your social work abilities and provide you with excellent experience.

For-Profit Organizations

The number of for-profit social service agencies has grown, and social work programs are increasingly utilizing these agencies as practicum sites (10, 11). In contrast to nonprofit organizations, the driving goal of for-profit (or proprietary) agencies is to produce a profit for their shareholders (owners). A for-profit agency may be a small, one-agency business (such as a private practice) or part of large, centralized, diversified national corporations (such as a health maintenance organization). The capitalistic, free-enterprise economic system in the United States has been the catalyst for the growth of for-profit social service agencies as, under this system, business has looked to new, expanding markets for growth (10). Social services have provided an opportunity for for-profit agencies to expand into a growing sector. For-profit agencies have expanded into many areas of social services, particularly nursing homes, medical and psychiatric hospitals, long-term care for disabled people, home health services, health maintenance organizations, and child welfare services (4, 11). The most common for-profit practicum sites are hospitals, nursing homes, and outpatient health care agencies (11). One third of social work programs use private practice settings for practica (10).

There can be obvious advantages to completing a practicum in a for-profit setting. Many social workers expect ultimately to practice in for-profit agencies or private practice settings; therefore, completing a practicum in a for-profit setting can help prepare you for the "real world" of practice within the type of setting in which you might hope to find employment. In addition, students in for-profits typically enjoy a more comfortable physical setting than in public or nonprofit agencies (12). Students in a proprietary setting can also help the agency carry out the goals of client-centered human services and help to ensure the fulfillment of for-profits' moral and legal obligations to serve the community (13). Because the mission is earning a profit in for-profit settings, social workers in these settings may find it necessary to advocate for client-centered services such that the provision of needed services to individual clients and the community is the primary concern of service delivery.

If you are working in a for-profit setting, you may find more resources available to assist you in your work, the use of more cutting-edge interventions and treatment modalities, and higher expectations of efficiency and effectiveness than in a nonprofit or public setting. Additionally, you may experience more diversity in clients because increasing numbers of low-, middle-, and upper-income clients are now seeking health and mental health services from the same for-profit providers (14). You may also observe little dissention concerning salaries, as professionals tend to be paid higher wages in for-profit settings than in nonprofit and public organizations (3). Finally, the agency may be more flexible and receptive to innovations and change than are other types of agencies (10). All of this can lead to an exhilarating learning experience.

However, many social work field coordinators are apprehensive about placing students in for-profit agencies (10). Unique and formidable barriers to the successful achievement of learning objectives can exist in the for-profit setting, where profit motive is the driving factor behind service delivery and the highest degree of control is exercised over types of clients served and eligibility criteria (4). Social work has historically had an uneasy relationship with for-profit organizations. The approval given to private practice as a legitimate area of social work practice at the 1962 National Association of Social Workers' Delegate Assembly was coupled with a statement affirming socially sponsored organizational structures as the primary avenue for implementation of the practice of the profession (10). Field work coordinators are concerned about the socialization aspect of the practicum and note that "the introduction of profit is seen as straining our perception of social work as a profession driven by altruism and a service mission" (10). For-profit settings may pose unique challenges for students who need exposure to the implementation of the value commitments of service and social justice. Furthermore, the common corporate concern to reduce costs may result in reduced social work staff and very high workloads (12).

Nonprofit Organizations

Currently, a wide range of nonprofit social service agencies exists. Private nonprofit organizations can be sectarian (affiliated with an organized church) or non-denominational (freestanding, without ties to the government or to an organized church) (3). Unlike for-profit organizations, many nonprofit social service organizations have historical commitments to serve the poor (4). Nonprofit social service organizations also vary considerably in size, from one-staff-member advocacy organizations to several-thousand-staff-member hospitals. Nationally, 47.6 percent of social workers are employed by nonprofit organizations (15).

Nonprofit organizations tend to have diverse funding bases. Possible sources include government funding (e.g., contracts, grants, fee-for-service agreements, and matching funds); direct client payments; fundraising appeals and events; grants from private foundations; donations from individuals; a religious denominational sponsor; endowments; investments; third-party payers (i.e., insurance companies); indirect contributions (e.g., United Way); memberships; and a for-profit unit of the agency. Additionally, nonprofit organizations also benefit from in-kind sources of revenue such as volunteer time and tax benefits. Non-profit agencies classified as 501c(3) organizations are exempt from paying most federal taxes, and most contributions to them are tax deductible to the contributor (3, 4). Nonprofits tend to aspire to a very diverse funding base to ensure autonomy and flexibility. With a diverse funding base, the loss of one source would not risk the existence of an organization (4). However, on a national scale, nonprofit organizations rely on government sources for 50 percent of their funding (16). Therefore, governmental policy changes can dramatically affect the work of most nonprofit organizations. Due to declining government resources for social services, many nonprofits have increased fundraising activities (3) and have taken on the habits of the corporate sector (6). Still, social workers employed within nonprofit organizations tend to be paid less than their counterparts in the public and for-profit sectors (6).

Nonprofit organizations tend to employ heavy use of volunteers for a variety of purposes. Most of these agencies have all-volunteer boards of directors, while others involve volunteers directly in the operations of the agency through fundraising, public relations efforts, and even service delivery.

Practicum experiences within nonprofit social service organizations vary considerably due to the range of size of agencies and the scope of services delivered. Although resources may be more constrained in a nonprofit than in a for-profit organization, you will likely find that the agency readily serves vulnerable and disenfranchised populations. Additionally, both nonprofit organizations and staff within nonprofits tend to have the ability to respond with more creativity and flexibility to client needs and can offer more flexibility than can those in public agencies. If you find that flexibility, creativity, and innovation are important to you, you may find that a nonprofit agency is well suited to your style.

Agency Size

In addition to type of agency, the size of an organization can also affect the practice of social work. In particular, very large and very small agencies can offer unique opportunities and challenges.

Large Agencies

Large agencies tend to have formal structures with organizational charts, formal channels of communication, and lines of authority specified in writing. Public, private, and nonprofit organizations can be large, bureaucratic agencies (see Box 5.2). Although some attribute large organizations with more ability to deliver efficient and effective services, others believe that the highly specialized units, close supervision, and minimal independent functioning characterizing large agencies actually impede efficiency and effectiveness (5). As a practicum student, you may find that working within a large organization requires considerable knowledge of forms, procedures, and the lines of authority under which your activities are approved. However, large organizations can offer opportunities to learn a variety of social work skills within a variety of programs and services.

Large systems can pose formidable challenges for the delivery of human services. Value conflicts can occur between social workers and their employing organizations. While the primary interest of helping professionals is the interests of the clients, large agencies typically consider agency survival and growth as the primary concerns. This tension between the social worker's and the employing organization's primary concerns can cause value conflicts. Although large organizations typically resist innovation and change, social workers within them often tailor services to meet needs of clients (5).

Small Agencies

Small private for-profit and nonprofit agencies usually offer worker discretion and a wide variety of possible experiences (5). These agencies are somewhat decentralized, having less formal structure than larger agencies. Students in these settings are often required to exercise more autonomy, independence, and initiative than in large agencies because smaller agencies often have little structure in place for employees and students. If you are completing a practicum within a small-agency setting, you may find that you are quickly able to assume a great deal of responsibility. Often, fluidity exists between the job responsibilities for the staff. Students in these settings are often required to become autonomous quickly, to be able to work in informal settings, and to pitch in and do whatever it takes to get the task completed.

PRACTICE APPLICATION 5.1
Reflections on Practice Context

To gain a clearer perspective on the type of agency in which you are completing your practicum, follow this list:

1. Define your practicum site as a nonprofit, for-profit, or public entity.
2. Categorize it as a small, medium, or large agency.
3. With a member of your practicum team, discuss the characteristics of your agency relative to
   a. the source and amount of funding,
   b. the number and type of clients served,
   c. community perception of the agency,
   d. personnel issues (e.g., turnover, job security, salaries), and
   e. the amount and type of bureaucracy.

Compare and contrast your practicum setting and experience within the setting with those of other students in your program.

BOX **5.2**

How to Survive in a Bureaucracy

In addition to the tips outlined in Unit 2 and Unit 4, the following tips may help you thrive in a practicum within a large, bureaucratic organization (17):

1. Treat administrators with the same respect with which you would treat clients. Administrators are human beings with feelings. Resolve conflict without resorting to dehumanizing the opposing party.

2. Avoid extreme adversarial situations with bureaucracies. Systems will find a way to weed out individuals with which they are at war. Seek to identify and build on the strengths of the system.

3. Realize that, as a practicum student, you are in the role of learner. This role may preclude you from attempting any change within the organization.

4. If your needs or those of your clients are not being met, talk with your supervisor. Seek permission to use the problem-solving approach to attempt to address the need (i.e., [a] identify the unmet needs within the bureaucracy or service delivery; [b] generate a wide range of options for meeting the needs; [c] evaluate the positive and negative merits of each option; [d] select a solution; [e] implement the solution; and [f] evaluate the solution).

5. If you do not receive permission to make any changes, realize that you are a short-term "guest" in the environment. You may not fully understand the context, history, or current efforts being made to address unmet needs. Recommit to your learner role and strive to learn all you can about the difficulties in the system as well as efforts that have already been made and those currently being made to address problems.

6. Develop and maintain a support system with your colleagues at the practicum. Use the informal system of the agency as much as possible.

7. If you receive permission to work toward a change, focus on an area(s) over which you have some control. Dismiss the illusion that you can change everything and spend your energies on those areas that you have a reasonable chance of influencing. Start small and build to larger problems.

8. Interact with the bureaucracy with neutral emotions. Control counterproductive emotions (i.e., angry outbursts) and learn to channel and deal with stress in appropriate ways.

9. Seek opportunities to interact with the administrators in informal settings. Sit with your supervisor and other administrators at lunch or attend occasional weekend social gatherings. Socializing prevents isolation and can provide you with a glimpse of administrative issues at the agency.

10. Seek self-actualization and meaning in life through other pursuits. Bureaucracies (and practica!) cannot provide this.

11. On a periodic basis, assess whether your career goals can be achieved through the bureaucratic system in which you are placed. If they cannot, consider pursuing employment in a different bureaucracy or a position at a smaller agency upon graduation.

Management Theory

You may notice that part of the uniqueness of your practicum site is the style in which the organization is administered. Knowledge of some leadership theories may serve to frame your experience within your site and provide some perspective on ways in which other organizations are led. As you become settled in your practicum, notice the process and methods by which your practicum agency is administered. You may find that understanding the theory(ies) by which the organization is led demystifies and depersonalizes the administrative process. While the style and personality of an administrator does affect the ways in which an organization is managed, the theory by which an organization is administered also plays a large role in the process.

Although there are many theories about the ways in which organizations function, scholars of management theory often place theories into one of four categories, (1) classical scientific management, (2) human relations, (3) structuralist, and (4) systems (18).

Classical Scientific Management Theories

Classical scientific management theories are often used in traditional bureaucracies (18). These theories emphasize efficiency, quantifiable performance (i.e., explicit, specific performance expectations), minimal input from and discretion among employees, and a high degree of supervision and control. The structure of an organization using these theories is formal and rigid (5).

Human Relations Theories

Human relations theories are concerned primarily with the emotional well-being and morale of the workforce. Cooperative work and group decision making are encouraged, and employee input regarding policy and procedures is sought (5). A defining influence in this school of thought has been Douglas McGregor's theories of leadership, that is, Theory X and Theory Y. A core assumption of Theory X is that individuals must be forced to work under threats (19). Theory Y, however, assumes that people seek opportunities for self-direction, autonomy, and growth; therefore, coercive force is unnecessary. This theory assumes that people will work to their capacity under optimal circumstances (19). Effective leadership according to the human relations theories is democratic and employee centered (20).

Structuralist Theories

The effect of structure on organization behavior is the focus of structuralist theories (18). Concepts considered by structural theories include:

- the effects of technological change on organizational variables (21),
- matrix design structures (i.e., specialists from units work with teams to perform common tasks) (22), and
- the limitations on rational decision making in organizations (23).

Systems Theories

Systems theories emphasize the importance of the environment and the influence of other systems on the organization. According to these theories, spontaneous interaction between the organization and members of its environment require constant assessment and adaptation (5).

Does it appear that the administrative style of your organization is described by one of these theories? No one leadership theory is the best fit for all organizations. However, general agreement exists that agencies that use a model of joint decision making and broad delegation of responsibility are more likely to keep competent, satisfied professional staff (3). Do you see evidence of joint decision making and delegation of responsibility in the administrative functions of your practicum site? Discussing with your field instructor the way in which the agency is administered may provide new insights into the internal processes of the agency.

The Role of Social Work within the Organization

Social work settings can be classified as belonging to one of two types: primary and secondary settings. Primary settings are those in which social work is the main or primary profession represented within the organization. The advantage of this type of setting for the employees is shared values and perspectives emanating from similar education and training. The roles, responsibilities, and abilities of social workers are understood throughout the organization (5). Examples of primary settings are child welfare agencies, domestic violence shelters and counseling, and mental health and family service agencies. If your practicum is in a primary social work setting, you may notice a high level of camaraderie among the staff. There may be a shared vision and agreement among the staff regarding the

services needed by clients. However, due to the lack of professional diversity within the setting, staff may experience greater difficulty with interdisciplinary collaborative projects, which require skill in working and negotiating across various disciplines.

Secondary (or host) settings are those settings in which there is a variety of professional staff, such as health care organizations, correctional facilities, and schools. Secondary settings can be challenging for social workers because they must learn the language of other disciplines. Additionally, social work values and perspectives can clash with those of other professionals (5). In these settings, social workers often find themselves possessing little power to make or carry out decisions that involve other professionals. Role ambiguity can become a problem if the goal of meeting client needs clashes with the mandate to reinforce agency norms (24). For example, role ambiguity can occur in a correctional facility, where social workers perceive a tension between the goals of punishment and rehabilitation.

If you are in a secondary setting, you may find the field instructor providing detailed instructions regarding collaborative work with a group of professionals or describing the history of relationships between social workers and other staff. Working in a less powerful position within an organization usually requires increased assertiveness, tact, and awareness of the role of power within relationships. Take the opportunity to notice the topics and activities around which perspectives diverge between members of the professional staff and the method by which such conflicts are resolved. You may notice that after working within a secondary setting, you are easily able to articulate the role of professional social work as related to other disciplines, have gained assertiveness skills, and possess a higher level of negotiation skills.

PRACTICE APPLICATION 5.2

Gathering Information

To begin your exploration of your practicum site's organizational makeup, gather the following specific information and discuss it with a member of your practicum team or in integrative practice field seminar.

- agency mission, goals, and objectives (What is the purpose and intention of the agency?)
- agency history (Why was the agency started? What need did it intend to meet?)
- agency philosophy and value system (What is important to the administration? On what basis does the agency make resource and procedural decisions?)
- programs and services provided (What does the agency do?)
- types of clients served and eligibility requirements (Whom does the agency intend to serve? Who is served?)
- funding base of the agency (What entities supply monetary resources for the agency? Any changes in funding planned? Any sources in danger of being lost? New possible sources?)

- organizational structure and context (What are the hierarchy of and qualifications for staff positions? What diversity is represented among the staff and administration? What are the compensation ranges for the various staff and administration positions? What are the procedures for filling vacant positions?)
- important organizations in the environment of the agency (What agencies serve as referral sources to the agency? To whom does the agency refer clients? Is the agency accredited and by whom? With what agency(ies) does the organization collaborate to deliver services? With what organizations does the agency network?)
- the current issues for the agency. (With what is the agency most struggling? Upon what strengths is the agency attempting to build?)
- the future directions of the agency. (Where is the agency headed?)
- characteristics of oversight entity (What body or person(s) oversees the work of the agency? How does the person/group make decisions? What diversity is represented by the oversight entity? What are the professional and other affiliations of the board of directors/supervisors?)

Sources of the above information for your practicum agency may include the following (4):

- recent annual reports
- policy and procedure manual
- articles of incorporation (for-profit or nonprofit) or executive order or statute (public)
- by-laws
- minutes of recent board of directors meetings as well as of various committees of the board
- agency brochures/marketing materials
- list of members of the board and various committees, which may ascertain professional affiliations and background
- agency mission statement
- list and description of programs and services provided
- programs' goals and objectives
- copies of recent program evaluation reports
- organizational chart
- personnel guidelines and job descriptions for staff and administrators
- interviews with administrators and other representatives of various disciplines within the organization (e.g., CEO, executive director, teachers, physical therapists, counselors, other program staff, accountants)
- interviews with members of the board of directors or entity to which staff and administration are accountable
- recent newspaper and magazine clippings or publicity videos
- recent budget information (agency budget, governmental appropriations, and grant proposals/reports)
- copies of recent (funded and unfunded) private and government grants and purchase of service contracts
- notes of recent meetings regarding agency collaborative projects, community task forces, and other interagency efforts
- needs assessment surveys
- case records
- human resources plan, including affirmative action/equal employment opportunity plans

(continued)

P R A C T I C E   A P P L I C A T I O N   **5.2**   **Continued**

- personnel recruitment and selection procedures
- performance evaluation forms
- statistics on absenteeism, turnover, and usage of sick leave
- grievances and complaints filed with the human resources department
- financial audit reports

The Informal Organization

Lauren was scheduled to work at her practicum on Wednesdays. During her fifth week of practicum, she awoke on Wednesday morning and discovered that her car would not start. She dutifully called her field instructor and left a message that she was unable to come in that day due to car problems, but she was confident that she would be in Friday, her next regularly scheduled day for practicum. On Friday, she was pulled aside by Cathy, the program director, and reminded that she needed to call in when she was unable to come to practicum. When she explained that she had called her field instructor, she was told that "everyone" knows that, when unable to come in, staff should call Cathy, as she is the one who makes the staff schedule. Cathy chastised Lauren, stating that the shelter had been short staffed on Wednesday and that she should have made more efforts to make personal contact with someone or should have called Cathy directly. Lauren feels terrible about the confusion and the hardship she created for the other staff. Should she have known about the correct procedure? Was Cathy right to admonish Lauren for the effects of her behavior?

Beginning work in any organization is a challenge. Equally important as learning the formal structure of an organization is learning the informal structure or the processes unique to an organization that may not appear in its official documents. Lauren, in the above scenario, is learning the hard way about the informal structure and rules of her practicum agency. Informal structures and rules of organizations are often uncovered by talking to more experienced workers or by unintentionally violating an unwritten rule.

Assume responsibility for learning the informal organization that exists in every agency. The informal, or shadow, organization is the result of groups of people who work together. It consists of "understandings and unwritten rules that produce an influence flow and a control system" (25) (see Box 5.3). These relationships, understandings, and unwritten rules can profoundly effect the day-to-day work of an organization (25). They can be considered the "grease" that allows tasks to be completed (26). Knowledge of this system can be acquired through observation: Who gives information to whom? Who supervises others? Who helps whom? Who is really in charge of decisions? What priorities does the agency emphasize to staff versus the kinds of activities that are actually rewarded? Time and experience (and possibly mistakes) will assist you in this effort.

BOX **5.3**

Examples of Explicit and Implicit Organization Rules (27)

Explicit Rules	Implicit Rules
Do what is best for the clients.	Do what is best for the agency.
Take all concerns to the administrator.	The administrator's door is always closed.
Treat clients with respect and individualized attention.	See as many clients as possible so that we'll look good for funding.
Everyone's voice should be heard in decision making.	Voicing dissenting opinions runs the risk of hurting someone's feelings.
Multiple opportunities exist for student participation and projects.	Students should handle low-level work so that staff can do "real" work.
Feel comfortable about approaching staff and discussing your needs.	Staff have better things to do than bother with students' petty concerns.

Although this system does not appear on the organizational hierarchical chart, informal processes and implicit rules have a powerful influence on decision making within an organization (25). More important, learning the formal and informal rules can help you recognize the constraints under which you are operating and make you less likely to operate under misunderstandings in the practicum site, which may reduce the stress you might otherwise feel as a new worker within the agency (27).

PRACTICE APPLICATION **5.3**

Reflection on Explicit and Implicit Rules

Review the chart in Box 5.3 and reflect on your experiences at your practicum site. Journal on your reflections. In your entry, discuss the following questions:

1. Which (if any) of the explicit and implicit rules listed match with those at your practicum site?
2. What other conflicting explicit and implicit rules are implemented at your practicum site?
3. How does the implementation of implicit rules affect the work of the agency? the staff?

Share your reflections with your field instructor or in integrative practice field seminar.

Socialization into the
Social Service Organization

The process of socialization into the social service organization is dependent on many factors, including your prior socialization to both the profession of social work and a work environment. If you arrived at the organization with values and work behaviors that are congruent with the organization, the socialization process may be smoother than if this is your first experience in such an organization. If, however, your personal values and norms are not consistent with or affirmed by the organization as you anticipated, a successful socialization process must first involve a detachment of your former values and norms before a new definition of your professional self can occur (28). This process can be unpleasant and involve a great deal of time and commitment.

As you become grounded in your practicum, you may develop ideas about ways in which programs and services might be operated more smoothly or better serve clients. Unless you are asked for new ideas and feedback, resist the temptation to make major contributions or to share ideas until you have earned acceptance from others at the agency and have a clear understanding of the organization. Approaching the organization and assigned tasks as a learner and being willing to share your lack of knowledge and experience may be the optimal strategy for learning. (For some tips, see Box 5.4.) Agency staff often enjoy sharing their expertise, knowledge, and experience. Seize opportunities to learn the agency's culture and politics. Investigate the expectations staff have of you as a student, discover the work ethic and social norms, and find ways to blend in with others in the organization. Although you may not always be comfortable as a new "employee," the learner approach will lay the groundwork for learning the proce-

---

BOX **5.4**

Laying the Groundwork for a Positive Experience within an Organization (2)

- Adopt the right attitude.
- Adjust your expectations.
- Master breaking-in skills.
- Manage the impressions you make.
- Build effective relationships.
- Become a good follower.
- Understand your organization's culture.
- Develop organizational savvy.
- Understand your new-hire role.
- Develop work savvy.
- Master the tasks of your job.
- Acquire needed knowledge, skills, and abilities.

dures of the organization and being accepted by others. Once you have gained the respect and acceptance of your peers, you will likely be more productive because you are "in the know," valued, and connected. Additionally, you will then also be in a position to assert yourself and to share your suggestions.

Last, realize that socialization into an organization can take considerable effort. A supportive work group can be pivotal to your socialization effort. A peer group of other students or staff members is often a buffer between you and the more unpleasant aspects of working within an organization. Use a peer group to provide additional feedback regarding your performance and the subtleties of agency functioning. Although the values of a peer group can be partially out of sync with the organization as a whole (28), a supportive group can offer an appropriate mechanism for releasing tension. Without a thorough socialization, the prospects for a successful practicum experience are slim.

PRACTICE APPLICATION 5.4

Reflections on Your Organizational Socialization

Discuss your socialization into your practicum site with a member of your practicum team. Topics and questions to discuss include:

- personal values and norms of which you have become more aware since beginning the practicum and any conflicts of these with those of the organization;
- the work behaviors/ethics that you expected of staff within the organization and any differences of which you have become aware since beginning the practicum;
- your observations of the culture and politics of the agency;
- your perception of the expectations others (staff and administration) have of you as a student;
- your feelings about being a "newcomer" in the organization;
- your field instructor's perception of your socialization process; and
- your overall perception of your socialization process.

Uncovering Staff Violations

Through hands-on work in an agency, you may stumble across staff violations of policy, procedure, or even the law. Violations can range from taking small items home from the agency without approval to fraud and extorting funds. You may wonder whether to report a violation that you witness. A decision to report a violation can be difficult and complicated. Should you find yourself in such a situation, consider:

1. your length of service to the agency;
2. your reputation and relationship with the administration;

3. the nature, seriousness, and effects of the violation;
4. the length of service to the agency of the staff member in question and his or her reputation;
5. your relationship with the staff member; and
6. the possibility that you have misinterpreted an action due to lack of knowledge or experience.

Reporting a staff infraction can be risky and can cause damage to your reputation and relationships with others (25). Before taking any official action, consult with your field instructor and possibly other staff members. Consider the following questions:

- Does the infraction seriously affect clients or the viability of the agency?
- Is there a pattern of infractions?
- Are you willing to risk the potential consequences of reporting an infraction?

Answering yes to one or more of these questions may provide you with the basis needed to make the decision to report. Otherwise, reporting an infraction could result in more harm than good.

PRACTICE APPLICATION **5.5**

Reflections on the Organization

The following activities will help you acquire knowledge about your practicum site and critique various aspects (e.g., mission, diversity, and effect of change(s)) of the organization:

- Read the agency mission statement and review the agency organizational chart. Are the staff positions well suited to carrying out the mission statement of the agency?
- Review the diversity (i.e., racial, ethnic, sexual orientation, and gender) of the agency's staff members. Talk with your field instructor about the diversity represented by the staff. How well does the staff reflect the diversity of the local community? What efforts are being made to recruit and maintain a diverse staff?
- Ask your field instructor about any recent changes (personnel, administrative, structural, or funding source) that the agency has undergone. What was the impetus for the change(s)? What effects have the change(s) had on client services? the mission of the agency? staff? the community?

Discuss your findings with a member of your practicum team or in integrative practice field seminar.

Developed by Jan McGillick, MA

PRACTICE APPLICATION 5.6
Reflection through Illustration

This exercise will assist you in the process of learning about external entities with which your practicum site has relationships and the types of relationships that exist.

Create an agency eco-map and include the following:

1. all entities external to the organization with which the organization interfaces (e.g., governmental entities, other social agencies, businesses, community organizations, and religious institutions)
2. a graphic description of the relationships between the organization and these entities using different types of connections (e.g., broken lines, thin lines, thick lines, and curving lines)
3. a legend/key that explains the types of connections

Explain and discuss your eco-map with a member of your practicum team or in integrative practice field seminar.

PRACTICE APPLICATION 5.7
Learning about Agency Structure through the Lens of Service Area/Client Issue

An important aspect of learning about your practicum site is comparing and contrasting the organizational structure with agencies that provide similar services. In addition, the process of making career choices within social work also entails determining your organizational fit with agencies that provide the type of services in which you are interested. This exercise will help you learn about another agency that provides services in which you are interested.

Select a service area/client issue about which you would like to learn more (e.g., play or art therapy, attention deficit disorder (ADD), or school social work). This may be a client issue addressed by or a service provided by your practicum site. Working with three to four students, select at least one agency to visit (other than your practicum site) that provides the service or works with the client issue of interest. Request approval from the agency and coordinate a group visit. Develop a list of questions to ask during the visit, including questions about the funding, philosophy, staffing, service delivery, and agency responses to current social policy changes as well as the past, present, and future role of social work within the agency. If possible, try to contact a social worker at the site. After the visit, discuss your experiences in your integrative practice field seminar. Compare and contrast agencies relative to client issues and service area(s).

PRACTICE APPLICATION 5.8

Tying Together the Agency and Social Work Values and Principles

Social workers implement the social work *Code of Ethics* (29) in their work within a wide variety of contexts. An important aspect of your learning is linking your work to the profession. This exercise will contribute toward explicating the goodness of fit between the service delivery of the agency and social work values and principles.

Obtain a copy of the agency mission statement and policy and procedures manual. Using these documents and drawing upon your experiences thus far in the practicum, engage your field instructor in a dialogue concerning the service delivery of the agency relative to the social work values and principles articulated in the *Code of Ethics*. Discuss whether the agency does/does not operationalize the following values and principles (29):

- Service—"Social workers' primary goal is to help people in need and to address social problems."
- Social justice—"Social workers challenge social injustice."
- Dignity and worth of the person—"Social workers respect the inherent dignity and worth of the person."
- Importance of human relationships—"Social workers recognize the central importance of human relationships."
- Integrity—"Social workers behave in a trustworthy manner."
- Competence—"Social workers practice within their areas of competence and develop and enhance their professional expertise."

Developed by Ellen Burkemper, Ph.D., LCSW

Summary

This unit focused on the importance of understanding the organization within which you will complete your practicum, the essential elements of an organization, strategies to use to uncover the needed information about the agency, and the process of becoming socialized into an organization. Nonprofit, for-profit, and public organizations were defined, differences between them were explained, and the positive and negative factors of working within each type of organization were debated. Finally, the impacts of various leadership theories on organizations were discussed, the role of social work within organizations was defined, and tips for gathering needed organizational information were provided.

Knowledge of organizations is crucial to the success of your practicum. Just as knowledge of clients' environments is central to understanding the issues clients present, knowledge of organizational matters is essential to understanding the parameters of service delivery in an organization. Learning the methods by which to serve clients within your organization and the organizational framework for those services should occur simultaneously.

STUDENT SCENARIO POSTSCRIPTS

Ben shared with his field instructor his insights regarding his hesitance to be more independent and to take more initiative in his work at the practicum. He discussed his experiences working at large publicly funded institutions, explained that he had been rewarded for work behaviors that included taking little initiative in work assignments, and had become accustomed to a high degree of structure and bureaucracy. His field instructor explained that he was now in a loosely structured organization with an expectation that staff would take a great deal of initiative and exercise flexibility in their work environments. He was encouraged to "jump in and make mistakes" rather than to wait until someone gave specific instructions. As the semester went on, Ben became more comfortable with the structure, yet he realized that he felt more comfortable with a higher level of structure and would probably seek employment in a large nonprofit or a public agency upon graduation.

Lauren called her field instructor immediately after she finished talking with Cathy. She explained to her field instructor that, although she had called the agency to report her absence in a timely manner, she had not known that she was to call Cathy and she felt terrible that the shelter had been short staffed because of her lack of knowledge. Lauren's field instructor apologized, stating that she should have told Lauren about the informal rules of the shelter and said that she would talk with Cathy and take the responsibility. Lauren then asked her field instructor to tell her explicitly about other informal rules so that she could avoid duplicating the mistake. Although Lauren felt that Cathy could have handled the situation better, she chalked it up as a lesson learned about the informal rules of organizations—a lesson learned the hard way.

REFERENCES

1. Council on Social Work Education. *Handbook of accreditation standards and procedures.* Alexandria, VA: Author. 1994.

2. Holton, E. The critical first year on the job. *Planning job choices: 1996.* Bethlehem, PA: National Association of Colleges and Employers. 1995.

3. McInnis-Dittrich, K. *Integrative social welfare policy and social work practice.* Pacific Grove, CA: Brooks/Cole. 1994.

4. Netting, F. E., Kettner, P. M. & McMurtry, S. L. *Social work macro practice* (2nd ed.). New York: Addison Wesley Longman. 1998.

5. Kirst-Ashman, K. K. & Hull, G. H. *Generalist practice with organizations and communities.* Chicago: Nelson-Hall. 1997.

6. Fine, S. H. *Social marketing: Promoting the causes of public and nonprofit agencies.* Boston: Allyn & Bacon. 1990.

7. Gummer, B. Reinventing, restructuring and the big bang theory of organizational change. *Administration in Social Work.* 1995, *19*(3):83–97.

8. Johnson, L. & Schwartz, C. L. *Social welfare: A response to human need* (2nd ed.). Boston: Allyn & Bacon. 1991.

9. Menefee, D. Strategic administration of nonprofit human service organizations: A model for executive success in turbulent times. *Administration in Social Work.* 1997, *21*(2):1–20.

10. Beckerman, A. & Fontana, L. Fieldwork in proprietary agencies and private practice settings: The perceptions of fieldwork coordinators in graduate social work programs. *Journal of Teaching in Social Work.* 1993, *7*(2):113–128.

11. Hancock, T. U. Field placements in for-profit organizations: Policies and practices of graduate programs. *Journal of Social Work Education.* 1992, *28*(3):330–340.

12. Stoesz, D. Corporate health care and social welfare. *Health and Social Work.* 1986, *11*(3):165–172.

13. Stoesz, D. Corporate welfare: The third stage of welfare in the United States. *Social Work.* 1986, *31*(4):245–249.

14. Ortiz, E. T. For-profit social service and social work education: Rapid change and slow response. *Journal of Independent Social Work.* 1987, *2*(1):19–32.

15. Gibelman, M. & Schervish, P. H. *What we earn: 1993 NASW salary survey.* Washington, DC: NASW Press. 1993.

16. Independent Sector. *Nonprofit almanac: Dimensions of the independent sector.* San Francisco: Jossey-Bass. 1997.

17. Knopf, R. *Surviving the BS (Bureaucratic System).* Wilmington, NC: Mandala Press. 1979.

18. Wernet, S. P. A case study of adaptation in a nonprofit human service organization. *Journal of Community Practice.* 1994, *1*(3):93–112.

19. McGregor, D. *The human side of enterprise.* New York: McGraw-Hill. 1960/85.

20. Perrow, C. *Complex organizations: A critical essay* (2nd ed.). Glenview, IL: Scott, Foresman. 1979.

21. Lawrence, P. R. & Lorsch, J. W. *Organizations and environment: Managing differentiation and integration.* Cambridge, MA: Harvard University Press. 1967.

22. Galbraith, J. *Designing complex organizations.* Reading, MA: Addison-Wesley. 1973.

23. March, J. & Simon, H. *Organizations.* New York: John Wiley & Sons. 1958.

24. Dane, B. O. & Simon, B. L. Resident guests: Social workers in host settings. *Social Work.* 1991, *36*(3):208–213.

25. Russo, J. R. *Serving and surviving as a human service worker.* Prospect, IL: Waveland Press. 1993.

26. Gitterman, A. & Miller, I. The influence of the organization on clinical practice. *Clinical Social Work Journal.* 1989, *17*(2):151–164.

27. Um, M. Y. & Brown-Standridge, M. D. Discovering organizational "rules" that contribute to student stress in social work field placements. *The Journal of Applied Social Sciences.* 1993, *17*(2):157–177.

28. Kolb, D. A., Rubin, I. M. & McIntrye, J. M. *Organizational psychology: A book of readings.* Engelwood Cliffs, NJ: Prentice-Hall. 1971.

29. National Association of Social Workers. *Code of ethics.* Washington, DC: NASW Press. 1996.

6 Micro Social Work Practice in the Field

Don't be afraid to take a big step if one is indicated. You can't cross a chasm in two small jumps.

—David Lloyd George

The opportunity to work one-on-one in direct practice with adults and children is the impetus for many students and practitioners to pursue social work as a career. While micro-oriented social work practice may be the motivation for entering the profession, you have learned by now through coursework that an effective generalist social work practitioner develops competence at all three levels of social work practice—micro, mezzo, and macro. In fact, the National Association of Social Workers (NASW) *Code of Ethics* (1) mandates that all social workers develop and practice a range of social work skills to ensure effective delivery of social work services.

Although each social work program has the autonomy to define and operationalize the teaching of generalist social work practice consistent with the program's mission and philosophy (2), a general definition of the concept has been adopted by the social work community (3). Generalist social work practice is typically considered to be multimethod, multilevel, theoretically eclectic, and dual focused (private and social justice issues), with an emphasis on problem solving and empowerment (3).

The focus of this unit, micro-level social work practice, is but one facet of the generalist practice perspective. Micro practice is generally considered to be those "professional activities that are designed to help solve the problems faced primarily by individuals, families and small groups" (4). Micro social work practice places a strong emphasis on the development of assessment and intervention skills. However, the practice of micro-focused interventions can be far ranging.

Expectations for Student Learning in Micro Practice

Historically, micro practice learning has emphasized the application of systemic-focused theory and development of skills, knowledge, and techniques conducted with professionalism (6). For example, the range of micro tasks and activities is broad and can include operating a food pantry in a community-based center, conducting intake assessments for a mental health center, providing family preservation services for a religiously affiliated family service agency, and providing discharge planning services in a hospital setting.

Recent work has advanced the profession's perception and knowledge of those areas deemed essential for micro social work practice. In general, social work programs and field instructors expect that students engaged in micro practice will (1) explore factual information, (2) engage clients in problem identification, (3) address issues of diversity, and (4) collect, organize, and analyze information through development of strategies for data collection, assessment, intervention, and collaboration (7).

Dore, Epstein, and Herrerias (6) identify eight specific areas for skill, knowledge, and value development critical for micro practice learning.

1. specific micro practice skills (e.g., engagement of client system, exploration of problems and feelings, goal setting, contracting, termination, and application of appropriate treatment strategies)
2. capability for critical thinking (e.g., conceptual understanding and integration of values and theory)
3. capacity for self-directed learning (e.g., management of dependencies and ability to seek and accept new knowledge)
4. professional competency (e.g., flexibility, self-initiative, and risk taking)
5. leadership ability (e.g., communication, advocacy, and commitment to social change)
6. caseload management (e.g., knowledge of community resources and time management skills)
7. interpersonal skills (e.g., use of self in the helping relationship, relational capacities, and ability to engage in effective collaboration with and on behalf of the client)
8. administrative skills (e.g., case preparation and presentation and self-evaluation)

These skill areas are intentionally broad and may seem vague. You have the opportunity to work closely with your field instructor to identify specific tasks and activities that will enable you to develop and refine your skills in these areas for your present experience. Although you may identify areas specific to your current practicum setting, the value of micro practice competence is that each of the skills identified and developed can be transferred to almost any other setting and population.

As you have learned through your prepracticum coursework and experiences, micro practice includes such skills as relationship building, empathy, cultural competence, assessment, intervention, termination, and evaluation. Moreover, you are now well schooled in the philosophy that these skills are essential at *all* levels of social work practice. The aim of this unit is not to review the micro practice content that you have covered in your social work practice courses but rather to aid you in integrating theory and practice, to understand the parameters of micro practice

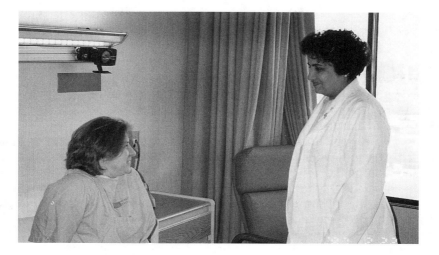

learning, and to establish a foundation for the following two units, which address learning mezzo and macro practice in the field. This unit will specifically address two primary areas on which your practicum team can focus to direct your learning of micro social work practice: (1) the "business" of micro practice—the administrative, agency-related, and caseload-related issues of micro practice; and (2) the "process" of micro practice—client-related issues of micro practice.

Learning the "Business" of Micro Practice

Direct social work practice intervention skills are central to the overall delivery of social work services regardless of the type and level of practice or the setting in which social workers work. Practicum settings and field instructors therefore place considerable emphasis on the development of these skills. Applying knowledge and gaining the skills needed to interact effectively with clients are the major, but not only, aspects of learning necessary for competent micro practice. Learning to function within the social service setting and the community are essential achievements to be made during your practicum experience. This discussion will focus on the areas to be covered in your micro practice learning, including: orientation, caseload assignment, identifying yourself as a student, role transition, charging for services, confidentiality, documentation, seeking answers, coverage, and collaboration. Although many of the issues presented here apply across all levels of social work practice, this discussion will focus on the relationship of each area to micro practice.

Orientation

You may be in the midst of the formal orientation to your practicum or you may have completed the formal orientation process. However, there are additional facets of the practicum learning experience that will continue throughout the entirety of your time in this setting. Regarding your micro-focused practice learning, you will continually be oriented to agency rules, policies, cultures, traditions, and even clients well known to the agency. You and the agency have a mutual responsibility to clarify such organizational issues related to micro practice as professional functioning within the agency and the community; workload management; expectations for problem identification, assessment, and interventions; learning; and professional development (7).

A concern often voiced by students in the early phases of the practicum experience is the issue of the orientation. Some students find the orientation process to be too long, while others fear that the orientation is not long enough to prepare them adequately for actual social work practice. Out of a fear of making mistakes and appearing incompetent, students have wished for or actually prolonged the orientation process. Your own reaction is probably dependent on several factors—your learning style, your previous social work-related experiences, and your comfort level within the practicum setting. Are you eager to jump in and get started with learning, or do you prefer to absorb all you possibly can about the situation before launching into the experience? Take a few moments and recall your insights regarding your learning style (refer to Practice Application 1.1, p. 5) and think also about the related issues of experience and comfort. This exercise may help you evaluate your feelings regarding the orientation process.

Caseload Assignment

Regardless of the fears and anxieties related to practicum, students are usually eager to receive their case assignments. A number of questions arise, however, regarding case assignments. Such questions might include:

- What is an appropriate, manageable number of cases for the beginning, middle, and end phases of my practicum?
- Am I going to "shadow" my field instructor (or other worker(s)) before I am assigned my own caseload? If I am shadowing another worker, when will I be able to assume responsibility?
- Will I have sole responsibility for my cases?
- What types of cases will I be assigned—clients new to the agency, clients who have been with the agency previously, or clients who are typically assigned to the practicum students?
- Are there only certain categories of clients to whom I can be assigned because of restrictions regarding third-party reimbursement or legal issues?
- Will I have a balance in my caseload (e.g., will the cases all be "easy" or "hard," or will there be a balance of both types)?
- What is my role with my clients—do I have the authority to make decisions with the clients, or does that have to be approved by my field instructor?
- Will I have a lighter caseload than workers and will I be taken seriously by other workers if I am not carrying a full caseload?

■ Will I be able to work with clients from the intake through the termination process, or will I enter the helping relationship after another worker has established a relationship? If I am receiving a transfer case, what were the circumstances of the previous worker's termination with the case and will the client be able and willing to accept me?

Have these questions arisen for you? What other questions do you anticipate as you receive your case assignments? Rest assured that most practicum students contemplate these questions at some point. You are encouraged to raise and discuss any and all questions regarding case assignment with your field instructor. Moreover, you should be comfortable in sharing any thoughts and feelings about the case assignment process with your field instructor as well. Despite the fact that your field instructor may not "unassign" a case because you voice anxiety, you are obligated to raise your concerns and welcome the opportunity to process your feelings and develop a plan for handling the situation.

> *Lauren has been shadowing and observing her field instructor and other social work staff for the first several weeks of her practicum at the battered women's shelter. She has now been assigned her first client—a battered woman who has been sheltered at this site a number of times. Lauren has read the client's file, has discussed the case with her field instructor, and feels anxious but ready to get involved. Upon meeting the client the day after her arrival at the shelter, Lauren introduces herself to the woman. Due to her "first-client encounter jitters," Lauren forgets to identify herself as a student. The client does not recognize Lauren from her previous stays at the shelter and asks her about her qualifications, experience in domestic violence, and success rate with treating battered women. The client tells Lauren that she has been to every agency in town (and this shelter eight times) but no one can help her. The client states that she sure hopes Lauren can help her because no one else has. Lauren now remembers to inform the client that she is a student. The client becomes upset, stating that if the others could not help her, how could a student? The client then declares that she does not want to work with Lauren. What are the micro practice issues that arise for Lauren? How might Lauren have handled this situation differently? How might she handle the situation at this point?*

Identifying Yourself as a Student

The issue of your role as a practicum student may have been addressed during the social work program or agency practicum orientation. You may wish, however, to clarify with your field instructor the manner in which the agency and your field instructor would like you to introduce and identify yourself to clients. Although some students may be issued nametags or badges that identify them as students or volunteers, others are not so readily identified as nonemployees. Despite the fact that you may be acutely aware of your "rookie" status, most clients, in all likelihood, will not be. Students may feel uncomfortable or inadequate informing clients of their status, feeling that the client will feel short-changed by being assigned to "just a student." In actuality, being assigned to a practicum student provides the client with not only your expertise but also that of your field instructor, agency staff, and possibly faculty at your social work program. Moreover, because of your role as a practicum student, you will likely be able to spend more time with clients, unlike your colleagues, who probably have more extensive and demanding responsibilities. If you are unsure about the way in which you will approach this issue, you may want to rehearse with your field instructor or fellow students alternatives for introducing yourself to your clients. Then, when the opportunity presents itself (and it will!), you will feel comfortable and confident in your role.

In the preceding scenario, Lauren experiences a negative client reaction to her student status. You have considered the issues and Lauren's potential responses to the client's comments. First and foremost, Lauren should not become defensive or apologetic regarding her status as a student. She can inform the client that, while she is a learner, she has developed knowledge and skills regarding domestic violence and, with the help of her field instructor and other staff, she believes that she can competently serve the client. Further, Lauren can acknowledge to the client that she does not have the experience of domestic violence and ask the client to share that experience with her. Not only does this potentially defuse the client's anger and frustration but also such a strategy can serve as the entry into the relationship-building and intervention process. Should the client be unwilling to work with Lauren at this point, Lauren has the opportunity to discuss with the client the client's feelings regarding being assigned to a student. Last, Lauren and her field instructor may determine that being assigned to work with this client may not be in Lauren's best educational interests or in the best interests of the client.

Role Transition

Most field instructors and students believe that the optimal approach to learning micro practice skills is for the student first to observe seasoned professionals modeling appropriate skills. As with the orientation process, the length of time for which you function in the observer role can be determined through a negotiation between you and your field instructor. The process for this negotiation should occur at the onset of your practicum and should center on the question of whether your field instructor expects that you will let him or her know when you are ready for the transition or whether your field instructor will determine when you are ready to make the transition. Do you have the option of assuming partial responsibility for a case and gradually moving toward assuming more or full responsibility? Being clear about your mutual thoughts regarding this shift can prevent the possibility of unmet expectations in the future.

You may find yourself in an agency in which practicum students are not allowed to assume sole responsibility for cases. Should this happen to you, how can you maximize your learning despite not being able to have the experience of handling a case on your own? Again, negotiating with your field instructor can shed light on this issue. Clarifying the extent of the role you can assume, ensuring that you have access to as much information as possible about the progress of each case, and being assigned responsibility for a portion of the case are three strategies for optimizing your learning.

Charging for Services

Student-generated revenue can present a dilemma for students, agencies, and social work programs. With the advent of managed care and decreasing revenues for agencies, more nonprofit agencies are concerned with generating revenue (8). Increasing numbers of students may find practicum agencies exploring or expanding client-generated fees. The issue of charging for student-provided services can be problematic. Some agencies have rigid policies regarding charging or not charging for student-provided services. At the same time, your social work program may have a clear-cut policy regarding this matter. Should your agency operate within the philosophy that all clients should pay at least a minimal amount for services, does that mean that students are expected to charge for services provided?

The important task for you, as the practicum student, is to obtain clarity regarding both the agency and the social work program policies regarding student-generated revenue. Should a conflict occur (e.g., your agency wants to charge, but your social work program prohibits charging for student-provided services), involve your faculty liaison immediately. If you are completing a practicum in which the agency will receive income from services provided by you, you will need clarification regarding the liability issues related to charging for services.

The task of informing clients about fees and, in some cases, actually collecting the money can be awkward for students. You may even wonder if charging for services (particularly a student charging for services) is unethical social work practice (i.e., does charging for services conflict with the social work/agency mission to serve underserved and oppressed groups?). However, this activity may certainly have implications for your future practice and can be a valued learning experience.

An issue related to charging for student-provided services is the practicum that is completed in a managed care setting. Some practicum sites have been eliminated because of the student's inability to charge for services or the practitioner's need to spend all his or her time in "billable" activities (which would not include field instruction). Social work programs are seeking ways to work with managed care companies because students need training in social work practice within managed care settings in order to gain proficiency in such areas of contemporary social work practice as documentation, cost-benefit analysis, mediation, and contracting (9). A possible strategy is to create opportunities for students to provide services to those clients who might not otherwise be eligible to receive services (e.g., pro bono practice) (9).

Confidentiality

You have heard, learned, and discussed much about the issue of confidentiality throughout your social work education. As you know at this point, client confidentiality is considered sacred and is fiercely protected by social work professionals. Despite the strong emphasis on the preservation of client confidentiality, practicum students are often unsure of how the concept is defined and practiced in their field settings. You will want to have a clear understanding of these issues before you experience your first client encounter.

Because the issue of confidentiality has been emphasized so strongly during social work coursework, students are often concerned about violating confidential information regarding a client. A breach of confidentiality can be defined as "disclosing identifying information or confidences revealed by clients without the client's consent, when compelling professional reasons did not exist" (10). Compelling reasons can include, but are not limited to, supervision, responding to a subpoena, or providing information regarding a mandated child or adult abuse or neglect report (10). As a practicum student, you are responsible for ensuring that you understand the parameters of confidentiality and strategies for preventing the violation of clients' confidential information.

Questions to pose to your field instructor to ensure your understanding of confidentiality might include:

- What information is appropriate to know about the client prior to the first contact?
- What questions can I ask and of whom can I ask them prior to the first client contact?
- What information is recorded in the client's chart/file?
- How do I treat information received unsolicited about the client from another person(s)?
- What client information can I share with others? What steps do I take to share that information?
- Can I talk freely about the client with agency staff?
- Under what circumstances can I discuss the client in my classes?
- Where is it appropriate to discuss the client (e.g., lunch/break room, hallway, or behind closed doors only)?
- How do I approach discussions with the client's family members? What information can I share?
- What information can I share with professionals to whom I might be referring the client?
- What can I share with the person(s) who referred this client to this agency?

Although other legal issues related to confidentiality will be further discussed in Unit 9, the questions presented here are important to consider as you begin to build relationships with your clients and to engage in micro practice.

Documentation

Why do you need micro practice writing skills? Contemporary social work practitioners, by necessity, are required to demonstrate professional writing skills for several reasons. The ability to provide social work services is a result of agency funding, and program funding is often linked to providers' documentation of services provided and needed (11). In fact, approximately 30 percent of a social service practitioner's time is spent documenting the way in which he or she delivers services (11).

In general, writing is used to impart information, identify feelings, and convey recommendations (12). Micro practice documentation can be conceptualized as descriptive or analytical writing. Practice skills required for describing a person, an experience, or an interaction require reflection, detail, ability to bring clients to life, observation, values, and respect, while analytic writing involves the ability to think critically (12). The Council on Social Work Education requires that students have the opportunity in the field experience to learn oral and written professional communications that are representative of the agency and the profession (2).

Documentation is critical to agency survival. On the aggregate level, client information is used for compiling data on services delivered and not delivered, identifying gaps in the service delivery system, justifying funding needs, and supporting or rejecting legislative actions related to the passage of laws. On the individual level, client records are critical documents for treatment planning, case management, court actions, referrals to intra- and interagency services, and internal and external utilization reviews (particularly for program accreditation).

The "business" of recording social work activities with clients has been referred to as "the good, the bad, the ugly" (13). Documentation skills are frequently not learned in the coursework that precedes the practicum experience. The actual writing skills required for documentation of social work activities are probably unlike any writing that you have produced to date. Social work practice writing includes facets similar to general academic writing (e.g., conciseness, clarity, and appropriate presentation of information [grammar, spelling, and punctuation]). However, micro practice writing, which is focused exclusively on the client, is intended to achieve accountability, to protect client privacy, and to promote efficiency (13). Moreover, the client record is a vehicle for identifying and monitoring client progress throughout the service delivery process. Your progress notes should describe the "measurable" changes experienced by the client (12). Specifically, documented goals and objectives should predict successful outcomes (14).

The "good" of documentation referred to above addresses the characteristics of well-kept records. Specifically, the records are accurate, organized, current, and based on sound social work practice ethics and methods (13). The "bad" encompasses the characteristics of poorly kept records—lacking accountability, incomplete, inefficient, or poorly written. The "ugly" of documentation refers to the actual content of the records themselves—poor grammar and punctuation, irrelevant or inappropriate client information, judgmental or speculative observations, or lack of focus (13). Much can be learned by considering what a record should and should not contain.

Each agency/organization that provides direct services to clients has specialized documentation policies, practices, and requirements. Your field instructor or other agency staff will instruct you regarding the concrete documentation requirements—that is the easy part! The challenge is condensing and organizing the wealth of client information you will possess into a useful, efficient, and easily readable document. Your field instructor may ask you to review records written by other workers. You will want to review client files compiled by several different workers so that you can learn various styles and approaches to documentation.

Regardless of the particular documentation style, format, or system that your practicum site utilizes, there is consensus within the social work community regarding the general content appropriate for client record keeping. Essentially, agencies strive to develop a "record of service" (15). Such a record should include *pertinent* client information and demonstrate a clear rationale for worker decisions, actions, and interventions (15). Kagle (15) provides the following general guidelines for the content to be included in client records, while we offer examples of appropriate and inappropriate documentation.

- **characteristics of the client relevant to the service(s) being delivered**

  The wrong way: Ms. Jones, a 53-year-old overweight, never-married female requested energy assistance service because she could not pay her utility bill this month.

  The right way: Ms. Jones requests energy assistance.

- **means and reasons for initiating service**

  The wrong way: Ms. Jones could not pay her utility bill because she took a trip to see her sister and her car broke down on the way home and then she went to her church, which could not help her but sent her to this program.

  The right way: Ms. Jones was referred to the energy assistance program by her minister.

- **descriptions of the past and current client situation**

  The wrong way: Ms. Jones goes to visit her sister in Florida every Christmas and then cannot pay her electric bill because she lets her grandchildren stay in the house while she's gone and they party round-the-clock and run the electricity bills up so that she can't pay them in January.

  The right way: Ms. Jones has applied for energy assistance each January for the past three years.

- **resources and barriers**

  The wrong way: Ms. Jones's family should be a resource for her, but I think they're actually a barrier because they seem to abuse her.

  The right way: Ms. Jones agrees to talk with her grandchildren about two issues: (1) contributing to the utility bills and (2) limiting their use of electricity during her absence. The client also believes that she could ask other family members to check on the grandchildren while she is away in Florida and possibly to lend her money to pay the utility bills.

- **assessment**

  The wrong way: Ms. Jones's grandchildren are taking advantage of her generosity and she shouldn't let them get away with this.

The right way: Ms. Jones appears to have established a pattern of need. Each January, she applies for energy assistance because, by her report, she cannot pay her December electric bill. It appears that the cause of this need can be linked to Ms. Jones's grandchildren using excess electricity during her two-week absence from the house.

- **purpose of service**

The wrong way: Keep client from asking for help every winter.

The right way: Assist client in identifying the reason for her need and develop a plan with the client to address the present need and prevent future need in this area.

- **plan of service**

The wrong way: Told client to get level payment plan and demand that family help her.

The right way: In collaboration with client, developed a plan to prevent future energy assistance needs: (1) Enroll in the electric company's level payment plan to create a fixed bill amount per month. (2) Ask grandchildren to decrease electricity usage during her absence and to contribute financial support for household bills. (3) Ask three adult children (particularly the parents of the two teenage grandchildren who live with client) if they would ever be able or willing to contribute financial support in an emergency situation. (4) Worker will follow up with client in two to three months.

- **service reviews**

The wrong way: Called client—no answer.

The right way: Telephone call to client on 3/1—no answer. Telephone call to client on 3/3—she has not yet applied for level payment plan or talked with her family. Discussed with client her questions regarding the level payment plan application and strategies for approaching her family about these difficult issues.

- **means and reasons for ending service**

The wrong way: Maxed out.

The right way: The client has received maximum financial assistance from the program as well as guidance in developing a plan to prevent future need in this area.

- **summary of service activities and outcomes**

The wrong way: Level plan, talk with others.

The right way: During the two visits Ms. Jones made to the agency, the following plan was developed and implemented: (1) Contact electric company to enroll in level payment plan. (2) Talk with grandchildren regarding decreased electricity usage and making financial contributions to the household bills. (3) Talk with her three adult children about their willingness and ability to provide occasional financial support.

■ **follow-up**

The wrong way: (No entry made)

The right way: 3/16—Telephone call made to Ms. Jones, who reports that she has followed through with the plan and has (1) enrolled for the level payment plan; (2) talked with her grandchildren about electricity use and contributing financially to the bill; and (3) talked with her three adult children, who agreed to provide financial support if they could.

As you begin to document your own service activities, you are encouraged to discuss with your field instructor his or her expectations for content *and* process for documentation. First, ask your field instructor to clarify for you the format, language, and information to be included in the client's record. Second, consider these three questions related to the completion of the client record:

1. What is the agency timeframe for completion of records?
2. Does your practicum agency require that student documentation be approved and cosigned by a field instructor or other staff member (this may impact the deadlines for submitting documentation)?
3. What are your field instructor's expectations regarding your initial and later recording responsibilities (e.g., you complete a draft, he or she reviews the draft, and you edit the draft before formally entering the information into the client record)?

Are there other questions that you have regarding the documentation process? If so, be sure to include them on your supervision session agenda.

If your practicum site's policy regarding official documentation precludes you from having sole responsibility for recording client encounters in the file, you may want to record your thoughts and impressions simultaneously with the official record keeper. You can then use this "mirrored" record as a mechanism for identifying your strengths and areas for growth in record keeping. Overall, an important skill to have regarding your social work writing skills is *be willing to ask for feedback.*

PRACTICE APPLICATION 6.1
Documentation: Your Turn

There are four key concepts—the four Cs—to consider when trying to document social work information effectively. These four Cs are (1) centralization—identify your central point in the opening paragraph/statement; (2) clarification—provide further clarity of the central point if needed; (3) confirmation—support your central point; and (4) closing—provide a summary of your central point (16).

Read the following example of a social worker's documentation of an activity. Using the four Cs, read the following two paragraphs and rewrite the entry. Discuss your rewritten entry with a member of your practicum team.

Ms. Jones is a 32-year-old, African American woman. Although she is not certain which gender child she would like to adopt, Ms. Jones has said that she would like the child to be under the age of five. Ms. Jones would not want a child who has severe emotional or behavior challenges because she is a single parent.

She recently moved into a three-bedroom, two-bathroom home with her eight-year-old daughter, Jackie, from a previous relationship. Currently, Ms. Jones has worked for the state department of corrections as a parole officer for two years, where she makes a little over $32,000 a year. She became interested in adopting a child after seeing a profile of a little girl available for adoption, "Kimberly," in the local newspaper two years ago. At that time, Ms. Jones had just begun her new job and wanted to wait until she was settled.

Developed by Janelle George, MSW

(Note: For our suggested revisions, see the Practice Application 6.1 Follow-Up at the end of this unit).

Seeking Answers

On the one hand, in the early weeks of your practicum, you are highly motivated to provide efficient and effective client services; but you may be unsure of your ability to do so autonomously. On the other hand, you are striving to attain independence as a competent social work professional and do not want to appear dependent on your field instructor. Students often struggle with the tension between feeling that they want and need to ask questions but not wanting to appear unsure, incompetent, or overly "needy" (or to jeopardize their practicum grade).

This issue is best addressed by openly raising your concerns with your field instructor. Again, you may wish to consider the type of learner you are along with the type of teacher your field instructor is as you and your field instructor anticipate how you will approach your journey to independence. Discuss with your field instructor his or her preferences for:

- the types of questions that are appropriate;
- the questions to be directed to him or her and the questions appropriate for other staff;
- how and when questions should be presented (any time, any place, or saved for weekly supervision sessions);
- person(s) to consult in his or her absence;
- when or at what developmental phase you should be functioning with some level of autonomy; and
- how to define autonomy—this concept may have different definitions and operationalizations depending on the individual field instructor or agency.

Coverage

Students often have the opportunity to provide coverage for their field instructors or other workers who are away from the agency. Although this situation can result in valuable learning for you, you should consider several related issues. First, does providing coverage for another worker meet your educational needs and goals or just fill a personnel need for the agency? Second, are you qualified to provide coverage for others whose cases may be different from those with which you have become familiar? Third, will covering for another worker create excessive work for you? Last, if you provide coverage for a worker other than your field instructor, will your field instructor have the authority to supervise your work or does that need to be negotiated with agency administration?

Should the opportunity present itself for you to take responsibility for another worker's cases, clarification of several issues is important.

1. the duration of coverage
2. expectations for involvement (i.e., monitoring, actual intervention, or responding to requests on an as-needed basis)
3. the process for transition from the other worker to you—will you be able to review client information, ensure that the client(s) is told that you are available and told the extent of your role, verify your contact information, and meet the client prior to the transition?
4. the process for transition from you back to the original worker

The issue of coverage for your caseload when you must be absent is one to consider as well. First, you should have a clear understanding with your field instructor regarding planned absences (e.g., does a university holiday excuse you from practicum, and do official agency holidays count toward practicum hours?).

Because practicum students are not typically in the agency on a full-time basis, determining the way in which your clients can and will be served on those days you are not available is essential. Your field instructor or other worker may be available to respond to client needs, but your clients must know when you are not available and the person(s) to contact should a need arise. Additionally, you will want to discuss with your field instructor the plan for coverage when you are away from your practicum for longer periods of time (e.g., semester breaks, university holidays, and vacations).

Collaboration

Working with other professionals is a part of every social worker's responsibility, regardless of the type of social work practiced or the setting. The ever-changing world of social service delivery has created both opportunities and challenges for social workers engaging in intra- and interdisciplinary collaboration activities. Micro practice social workers, in particular, routinely collaborate with other social workers, other disciplines, and community groups on such issues as individual client treatment and management planning, client advocacy, resource development, program planning, and coalition building.

Practitioners who receive training on collaboration early in their careers tend to feel more positive and open about incorporating collaboration in their practice (14). However, learning effective collaboration skills can prove challenging. Encountering such disciplinary issues as jargon, professional socialization, and lack of clarity regarding roles and expertise can dampen the enthusiasm of even a motivated collaborator (17, 18). The more opportunities you can seek out to gain familiarity and comfort with and knowledge of effective collaboration, the better able you will be to represent your clients and your profession.

How does intra- and interdisciplinary collaboration fit into your practicum experience, in general, and into learning micro practice, specifically? You can begin to answer this question by asking your field instructor about his or her experiences with intra- and interagency collaborations, your practicum agency's philosophy about and attitude toward collaborations, and opportunities to observe and engage in collaborative relationships. Examples of ways in which you may be able to collaborate with other agency staff on individual client issues include one-on-one consultations, case presentations/staffings, referrals, and group supervision sessions.

Agency collaboration may provide the opportunity for both intra- and interdisciplinary collaboration, depending on the staff composition of your practicum agency. Interagency collaborations can also present the opportunity for both intra- and interdisciplinary collaboration, but they provide a different experience. Not only are you able to observe and engage in collaboration between disciplines but also you must learn to negotiate between cultures, agencies (e.g., public versus private and large versus small), and communities (19). Collaboration can be a stimulating learning experience, but not always an easy one.

Ongoing Evaluation

A discussion of evaluation is typically considered an "ending" activity, whether at the end of a course, workshop, book, or practicum. However, evaluation of your growth and development as a micro practitioner should be integrated into your practicum experience from the outset. As you develop your learning plan, identify ways in which your performance will be evaluated. You can then use these checks and balances as a mechanism for monitoring your progress in completing the learning objectives and becoming a competent practitioner.

Your field instructor may have established a routine for ongoing evaluation. For instance, your field instructor or other staff member(s) may regularly observe your encounters with your clients. Although observation is possibly the most convenient evaluative technique, other strategies include audio- or videotaping and, of course, process recording. Videotaping of client sessions is not always possible or feasible, particularly if equipment is not available or if the nature of the agency's work does not lend itself to taping. Although videotaping is an excellent tool for assessing and monitoring the development of micro-focused practice skills, other techniques can be just as effective. Audiotaping, for instance, is a useful way to "listen" to yourself as you engage with clients. You do not have the opportunity to observe your nonverbal communication, but having only the audio portion of the encounter available eliminates the potential distraction created by the picture and allows you to listen critically to the exchange. Finally, process recording, while not as frequently used now as in the past, can be valuable for processing and analyzing your client encounters and discussing your observations during supervision.

Employing a variety of evaluative strategies and evaluators is beneficial for your learning experience. The key, however, is to structure the process for ongoing evaluation formally and to incorporate the structure into your daily practicum activities and regular supervisory meetings. Evaluation, although often perceived as a burdensome task, need not be a negative experience. In fact, creatively approaching the evaluation process can provide you and your field instructor with data helpful to assessing your strengths and guiding the areas for growth and development during the remainder of your practicum experience. What other evaluative methods do your field instructor, agency, or fellow students use? You may want to broach this issue with others to share ideas.

In sum, while this discussion of the "business" of micro practice has not been exhaustive, you have had the opportunity to anticipate a number of issues that may occur during your field experience. Building on the theoretical frameworks and life experiences that you bring to your practice learning, the issues presented here can serve to allay some of your anxieties, raise new questions, and aid you in preparing for learning the "process" of micro practice.

Learning the "Process" of Micro Practice

Providing social work services to individuals and families is the most eagerly awaited aspect of most students' social work training. However, providing social work services to individuals and families can also create the most anxiety for students (20). Students' self-doubts regarding their ability to meet clients' needs and serve their agencies are the most frequently cited concern regarding practicum (20). The following discussion will highlight issues and concerns that are typical and normal for beginning social work professionals in micro practice.

Corina is in the midst of her first practicum site visit with her field instructor and faculty liaison. She and her field instructor have given the faculty liaison a tour of the detention facility, have highlighted her practicum activities, and are discussing her progress in completing the learning objectives. The faculty liaison inquires about the theories that Corina is using to guide her interventions with the clients and their families. The liaison then asks Corina to describe the way in which she integrates the theories with her social work practice. Corina does not know how to respond to these questions. She and her field instructor have not discussed theoretical approaches to practice in the family court. Several issues emerge: (1) How can Corina handle the liaison's questions? (2) How can Corina ensure that the theory–practice integration issue is addressed in her practicum? (3) What strategies can help Corina facilitate the integration of theory with social work practice?

Theory–Practice Integration

Controversy has long surrounded the integration of theory with social work practice and is particularly relevant in this era of increased accountability (21). In general, the social work profession is committed to the "idea that sound theory and good practice are inseparable partners" (21). Social workers are being called on to identify measurable problems and attainable solutions that are grounded in a proven method (22). Such a requirement compels the profession to determine a rationale for integration, to define theory–practice integration, and to devise strategies for achieving and evaluating integration (both for the classroom and the field).

Integration occurs when you apply a broad, theoretical perspective along with a worldview and use the two to guide professional activity (5). Although the application of theory to practice may be difficult to define, teach, learn, and implement, theory should have value beyond being "an analytic academic exercise and be essential for understanding and guiding direct practice activities" (5). Students (and social work programs) rely on field instructors to facilitate the process of learning ways in which to utilize theory in social work practice (23). However, the responsibility for facilitating this process is jointly shared by the social work program's faculty, your field instructor, and you.

In the student profile above, either Corina has not adequately considered this issue or she may not be aware that she and her field instructor have, in fact, discussed the issue. Corina can inform the faculty member that she and her field instructor have not yet addressed this issue. This creates the opportunity for Corina, her field instructor, and the faculty liaison to discuss the applicable theories used in this setting (possibly enlightening Corina to the fact that theoretical frameworks are indeed considered and applied) and to strategize about ways in which learning experiences can be designed to meet her educational need. Although the profession places considerable importance on the integration of theory and practice, the realities of daily social work demands in the field sometimes do not permit in-depth discussions of theory. Moreover, social workers may at times find themselves in the role of "theory-developers"—utilizing a strengths-based perspective to create understanding and explanation of the client situation within the context of the client's situation and the worker's theoretical knowledge base (21). If Corina's field instructor has in fact neglected to address theory–practice integration, Corina can take the responsibility for initiating this aspect of her learning experience.

Bogo and Vayda (24, 25) present a model by which the integration of theory with practice can be both understood and achieved. The Integration of Theory and Practice (ITP) Loop suggests a process in which you:

1. initially obtain information regarding the practice situation;
2. reflect on the retrieved information and examine your personal associations and feelings regarding the information presented to you by the client system, which then leads to an objective and sensitive assessment;
3. identify and utilize your knowledge to explain both the retrieved information and your reflection on the information; and
4. analyze the information to formulate a professional response from which a plan is developed.

PRACTICE APPLICATION **6.2**
Application of Theory to Practice: Testing Your Knowledge

The following scenarios can serve as triggers for your thought and discussion regarding the application of four commonly used theoretical approaches to typical practicum situations.

Corina is working with a 16-year-old female remanded to the detention facility for truancy and running away with her 22-year-old boyfriend. The teen's behavior toward Corina and the other staff is extremely belligerent. The client has no actively involved social support system. Corina and her field instructor believe that cognitive-behavioral theory has merit for application in this case. What strategies can Corina employ to integrate this theory?

Ben is working with a family of four who live in the neighborhood served by his community center practicum site. The 33-year-old mother, recently diagnosed as HIV-positive, appears depressed, as evidenced by her unkempt appearance, weight loss, lethargy, and withdrawal from center activities. Her boyfriend's interest in and involvement with her and her children appear to have decreased significantly. The 10-year-old son is failing fourth grade and has been involved in a number of fights at school and on the bus. The mother suspects that her 15-year-old daughter is sexually active and may be involved in a gang. The clients' house is in a serious state of disrepair. Ben wants to incorporate a systems theory approach. What strategies can he consider?

Lauren is working with a 20-year-old woman and her two children, who are residents of the battered women's shelter. This is the client's third admission to the shelter, and she states that she is certain that she wants to leave the abusive relationship this time. If Lauren uses a problem-solving approach to guide her intervention with this client, what issues arise for Lauren and her client? How can Lauren implement an intervention?

Cameron is working with a 64-year-old retired male corporate executive being treated for alcohol addiction. Cameron feels unfamiliar with the issues that this client is experiencing and realizes that he needs to employ an intervention based in ethnic-sensitive theory. Where does Cameron begin in his implementation of this theoretical framework? How might he work effectively with this client while maintaining ethnic sensitivity? How will Cameron know if he has or has not responded appropriately to ethnic and cultural differences?

Regarding the application of various theoretical approaches, do you find that you are comfortable with the scenarios described above? If you are able to identify and determine possible intervention strategies, you can feel assured that you have, indeed, grasped the complex concept of theory–practice integration. If you are uncertain or at a loss regarding possible applications of theory to practice in these situations, you may benefit from reviewing theories used in social work practice, consulting with your field instructor or social work program faculty, and raising the issue for discussion in your integrative practice field seminar.

The identification of appropriate theory-based methodologies lends itself to the operationalization of the integration. The field experience, in general, and the supervisory relationship, in particular, are viable mechanisms for experimenting with this complex learning objective (21). During your practicum and in supervision, you can safely contemplate, discuss and "try on" new explanations and approaches to your micro practice skills and behaviors (23). The setting and the supervisory relationship, however, must be established and secure enough to allow both the student and the field instructor to give and receive feedback to facilitate this practice learning, which differs significantly from traditional learning. Once achieved, this relationship can serve as the springboard for empowering you as you develop your practice competence and your ability to give and receive feedback (23).

From the theoretical–practice foundation established by you and your field instructor for your micro-focused practice can flow the learning related to your practicum activities. Areas related to learning the "process" of micro practice to be highlighted in the following discussion include working with "difficult" clients, unique micro practice challenges, developing appropriate expectations for yourself and your clients, and use of self in micro practice.

Working with "Difficult" Clients

During the learning process, students often feel a lack of confidence about working with any and all clients. Working with violent, suicidal or homicidal, resistive, dependent, or inappropriate clients can, however, prompt a unique set of anxieties. Although not all practicum sites serve client populations that are typically considered "difficult," all social service agencies serve clients who can present challenges for social workers. Moreover, what constitutes "difficult" for one worker or agency may not be perceived as challenging at all by others. Most of us consider openly hostile or violent clients difficult, but do you consider the overly dependent client who constantly asks your advice and opinions on life matters difficult? What about the client who seems too familiar or friendly? This client may ask you numerous personal questions, bring you gifts, or ask for your home telephone number. What about the client who is persistently late or misses appointments or who does not follow through with agreed-upon tasks? What about the client who appears to be under the influence of alcohol or other drugs? Do you confront the client, refuse to see him or her at that time, ignore the issue unless the client exhibits blatantly obvious signs of inebriation or altered state? Working with the client behaviors described here can pose considerable challenges for all helping professionals, not just practicum students. Interacting with "difficult" client issues can cause students to feel overwhelmed, mistrustful, a lack of confidence, naïve, and unable to balance the client's right to self-determination with issues of safety and health (26).

Based on your experiences and your knowledge of yourself (your personality and interactional style), what client issues have been or will be difficult for you? Take the opportunity to talk with your field instructor about this issue and learn about his or her challenging experiences and strategies for confronting the difficulties. Then, consider the responses that may be most effective for you. Although each scenario will require an individualized response, suggestions for dealing with difficult client situations include the following:

- Be able and willing to recognize when a client situation makes you feel uncomfortable (e.g., are you feeling anxious, frightened, or manipulated?).

- Do not minimize or discount your feelings. Instead, conduct a reality check for yourself by talking with your field instructor or other staff member(s). The "reality" may be that this client's behavior has affected other workers in a similar way. You may simply need an opportunity to process your feelings and develop a pro-active response. Or something about your encounter(s) with this client may have triggered a memory or past experience for you. Or, in an extreme case, you may need to terminate your relationship with the client.
- Consider setting clear-cut time, access, and interactional boundaries for yourself with the client in order to minimize the challenging behaviors.
- In the case of a client suspected of being under the influence of alcohol or other drugs, be certain you know the agency's policy regarding contact with such clients and rehearse with your field instructor ways in which you can confront the client in this situation.

Regardless of the client issue that triggered your reaction to the situation, working with challenging client behaviors can result in powerful learning. Often, the most difficult experiences are those that provide the most knowledge, skills, and values clarification needed for your professional growth and development. Even when confronted with a difficult case situation, you have the opportunity to learn (1) valuable micro practice skills and (2) about the resources available to support and promote that learning.

Unique Micro Practice Challenges

Although we cannot cover all potential practice situations and responses here, several client issues that may arise for you in your practicum include (1) personal knowledge of or connection to the client, (2) encountering the client outside the agency, (3) conflict with the client, (4) sexual attraction to or from the client, and (5) suspected system abuse of or by the client.

Personal Knowledge of or Connection to the Client. Not infrequently, practicum students find that a friend, acquaintance, or even family member is receiving services from the agency in which the student is completing his or her field requirement. You may realize that you have knowledge of a client that has bearing on the relationship to the agency (e.g., service eligibility, legal standing, or relationship with an affiliated agency). Particularly in smaller communities having fewer service delivery agencies, you may encounter a familiar face in the lobby, intake office, or on a home visit; review the chart of a friend; or hear about someone you know in a case staffing meeting. This can, in fact, occur in any size setting or community.

Several questions arise in these situations—do you acknowledge the client, accept the assignment, read the chart, share the information you have, or participate in the case discussion? First, discuss the situation with your field instructor and inquire about the agency's policy or tradition regarding workers having personal knowledge of a client. Depending on the agency setting in which you are placed, services provided, and the community, working with persons you know may be routine *or* may be completely unacceptable. Second, you must also consider your own feelings about the situation. Are you comfortable working with a casual acquaintance from high school around the intense issues of spousal violence, for instance? Can you work with your parents' friend to place her mother in a nursing home?

In determining how you can respond to such dilemmas, you should consider not only agency culture but also your ability to work with such a client as well as the client's feelings about working with you or knowing that you are familiar with his or her case. Your response should be based on the individual situation and take into account your skill level in helping the client to make a decision (26).

Encountering the Client Outside the Agency.   You may find that you will meet your clients outside the practicum setting at the grocery store, mall, or even a social event. Do you acknowledge or ignore the client? A general rule of thumb is to wait for the client to acknowledge you. Some clients may be comfortable meeting and talking with you outside the agency setting, while others will be mortified, particularly if they are with family or friends who do not know that they are receiving services from your agency. Some clients are so comfortable that they will introduce you to their companions or attempt to engage at length with you about their cases. Although you can certainly be friendly when this occurs, it is prudent to keep the encounter brief and superficial, leaving case-related discussions for a more appropriate time and location.

Conflict with the Client.   What should you do if you find either that you do not "like" the client or that the client does not "like" you? *Like* can mean many different things to each person. You may find the client's philosophy, attitudes, personality, behaviors, language, or lifestyle so foreign or offensive to you that you feel you cannot be an effective practitioner. Differences can range from the client's beliefs regarding abortion to his or her practice of discriminatory behaviors to his or her inflicting physical harm on others.

What can you do should this challenge arise in your practice learning or later in your career? It presents you with the opportunity to examine your own feelings about diversity and to explore your ability to be a competent social worker when you do not agree with a client's beliefs or choices. You may have considered your thoughts and feelings about diversity during earlier social work courses or in your volunteer/work experience. However, until you find yourself face-to-face with an individual who espouses a belief or behavior that contradicts your own *and* you must provide services to to him or her, you may not have fully considered the implications of such a situation.

Because you will respond both positively and negatively to clients, you must incorporate your emotional and subjective reactions into your learning and practice experiences (23). An in-depth examination of your own beliefs, your commitment to social work values, and your ability to identify self-worth and strengths in all people can guide you in developing the skills needed to confront this difficult practice issue. Seek out these challenging situations to help clarify your values, confront issues of diversity, and, through experience, identify those populations with which you may *not* be as effective. Effective techniques for identifying and overcoming your negative experiences with clients may include engaging in the observation of other professionals working with similar clients, journaling your thoughts and feelings about yourself and the client, audio/videotaping or completing process recordings of these client encounters, and role playing challenging client encounters with other students or professionals (27).

The client may find your presentation of yourself equally offensive. Ideally, the client should have very limited information regarding your personal situation but may, based on physical evidence and assumptions, decide that he or she cannot relate to you in a productive manner. Important learning can occur for both you and the client in this situation. By addressing the client's resistance and openly confronting his or her perceptions of you and of your abilities, you and the client can learn to overcome the negative feelings and to work together effectively.

Sexual Attraction to or from the Client. Sexual attraction directed from or toward clients is not unheard of in the helping professions. When humans share intimate details of their lives that may involve connecting with painful memories, a bond can be created that can manifest itself in the form of a physical and emotional attraction. The client may mistake his or her appreciation for the worker's efforts as sexual feelings. The worker or the client may find that the other reminds him or her of another individual, thus triggering sexual thoughts. Regardless of the specific situation, you must, at the first hint of any sexual feelings, comments, or actions, seek consultation with your field instructor. As with other practice challenges, you should not ignore or discount such feelings. Left unattended, inappropriate client or worker thoughts can quickly dominate the relationship and result in unwise choices.

In the case of client feelings being directed toward a worker, the worker has the opportunity to address the feelings with the client and process with the client the motivations behind the feelings. Such a discussion can provide insight for the client regarding the role that sexual or seductive behaviors play in his or her life (28). An open and candid confrontation of sexual issues can be a healthy growth experience for both the worker and the client. Should this situation occur in your practicum, you may wish to role play the confrontation with your field instructor to increase your comfort and confidence levels.

In the event the worker is experiencing sexual feelings for a client, he or she also has the opportunity to examine the roots of such feelings and to gain insight and skill regarding the appropriate response to the experience. Confronting one's sexual feelings about a client can prompt feelings of guilt and discomfort but need not necessitate termination of the relationship or the practicum (28).

Suspected System Abuse of or by the Client. A particularly unfortunate challenge may emerge during your field experience in the form of client abuses of or by the social service system. Clients have been known to take advantage of the social service system through such acts as nonreport of income or information or receiving duplicated services from multiple agencies. Conversely, social service workers have been found to exploit clients through eligibility discrimination or engaging in dual relationships with clients.

Should you suspect or have evidence of such inappropriate activity, do not assume that you should not report the information just because you are a practicum student. The whistle can be blown by anyone. The NASW *Code of Ethics* (1) clearly states that social workers are responsible for recognizing and taking action in the event of unethical practice on the part of other social workers. Regardless of the specific situation in which you suspect an abuse of some kind, suggested responses include (1) informing your field instructor immediately, (2) developing clarity regarding knowledge of agency guidelines and culture regarding such situations, (3) considering the "big picture" from all perspectives (i.e., you may not have all the information or understand the particular dynamics of a situation), (4) documenting all known information (25), and (5) providing only behavioral/factual information (27). What if your field instructor does not believe you or discounts your perception? While each case will differ, consult with practicum faculty at your social work program to determine an appropriate course of action.

Developing Appropriate Expectations of Yourself and Your Clients

What are realistic expectations of yourself and your clients regarding the parameters of your relationship? Should you be available to the client 24 hours a day? How much should your client share with you regarding his or her life, and how much should you share with the client about yourself? These are just two areas in which new professionals must experiment.

Your practicum agency, field instructor, and other staff are a resource for you in developing appropriate expectations for relating to your clients. For example, based on the services provided by your practicum site, the agency may have specific guidelines for such issues as accessibility (e.g., can you be reached during office hours only or through the answering service or by beeper?). If your agency does not provide a directive, you and your field instructor can negotiate reasonable expectations based on your practicum responsibilities.

Establishing and maintaining clear parameters with your client regarding all expectations for the relationship is critical. Communicating your mutual expectations serves to build rapport and trust, clarify misassumptions, and prevent disappointments or frustrations that may occur if expectations are not met.

Use of Self in Micro Practice

As a social worker, you cannot separate your personal self entirely from your professional self. Just as the client does, you bring your attitudes, beliefs, and life experiences to the relationship. Unlike the client, however, you are responsible for

balancing the personal with the professional. Therefore, you must determine the amount and scope of integrating yourself into the client relationship.

Two issues emerge as you consider the integration of self into the professional encounter. First, sharing information with your client about your experiences can be both a positive and a negative use of self. You may feel that you have experience and insights to share with your clients that will aid them in the change process, but make sure that the encounter does not become a testimony of *your* life. A client may experience increased trust, normalization, hope, or insight regarding his or her situation if he or she learns that the two of you share similar experiences. On the other hand, the client may assume that he or she must resolve his or her situation just as you did and may experience a sense of failure if his or her outcome differs from yours.

When considering the use of self-disclosure in a social work relationship, consider following the pros and cons associated with self-disclosure (29):

Pros	*Cons*
1. therapeutic for client	**1.** burdensome for client
2. useful tool for "joining" with the client	**2.** can disrupt worker–client work and relationship
3. can normalize client's perception of the situation	**3.** can make client feel "abnormal"
4. can serve to aid client in "healing" old and new "wounds"	**4.** can serve to open old "wounds"
5. can create mutuality, hope, and attachment	**5.** can create discomfort and possible physical harm

The decision to self-disclose personal information in a professional relationship is likely to be a difficult and unclear one (29). Some information (e.g., marital status, home of origin, and schools attended) may seem benign, but you should seriously consider the implications of sharing such information with your client. Deciding whether to divulge more personal information (e.g., traumatic or life-threatening illnesses or experiences) requires considerable thought. Information that you should *not* share under any circumstances includes political views and sexual information (29).

Infusing your life experiences and beliefs into the assessment and planning process can prove inspirational for you. One step toward attaining "practice wisdom" is to combine your knowledge (which encompasses theoretical and personal data) with the information provided by your client to enable you to give meaning to the client situation (22). You must be careful, however, not to project your own experience onto your client's situation. For example, just because your parents' divorce affected you in one way does not suggest that your client experienced his or her parents' divorce in that way or that you should build your intervention around your experience. Additionally, consider that the focus must remain on the client; any disclosure must be for the benefit of the client.

In order to learn to facilitate the use of self in your helping relationships effectively, you can engage in exercises and activities that require self-exploration and assessment (30). For instance, journal daily to explore your feelings about your clients and your interactions with them (31). Delving into self-examination may elicit both elation and pain. Success comes from the outcomes that you derive from this introspective analysis. You and your clients can benefit from your continued efforts to know and understand yourself and the way in which you perceive yourself as a competent social work professional.

In sum, learning the "process" of micro-level social work practice is a complex and ongoing endeavor that changes with the client population and setting in which you work. However, you can begin to unravel this puzzle by considering and experimenting with the issues presented here.

PRACTICE APPLICATION **6.3**
How to Handle Ethical Dilemmas

As discussed throughout this text, confronting ethical dilemmas is a routine part of the social worker's life. The following scenarios bring to light a number of the issues that this unit has raised. Review each of the ten scenarios below, and discuss each with your field instructor, other staff, and fellow students to identify the challenges and potential solutions for you.

1. You are at a party, and one of your clients comes up and begins a conversation.
2. You are discussing a topic in a class that is directly related to your practicum experience. How are you supposed to discuss a case example?

(continued)

PRACTICE APPLICATION **6.3**   Continued

3. Your client happens to mention that an elderly member of his or her family is being "pushed around" by another family member. How are you supposed to address this with the client?
4. Your client states that he or she does not have the ability to pay for services from your agency.
5. Your field instructor assigns you to obtain a client's records from another agency. What is the procedure for accomplishing this task?
6. What are you supposed to tell clients *before* they begin the process of accessing the services of your practicum agency?
7. You are physically attracted to one of your clients. How are you supposed to deal with this situation?
8. What are you to tell clients about your status at the agency, including length of service and duration of remaining service, authority, and access to information and resources?
9. You hear another worker talking about a client during a lunchroom conversation.
10. You hear another worker telling a racial or ethnic "joke."

Developed by Ellen Burkemper, Ph.D., LCSW, MFT

PRACTICE APPLICATION **6.4**

Case Reenactment

Students will orally reenact a client system interaction for the class and facilitate a discussion. Students will also turn in a written description of the reenactment one week prior to the presentation. The purpose of this assignment is (1) to assist in the presenters' integration of theory and practice; (2) to assist others in integrating theory with practice; (3) to develop work group skills with students in the class; and (4) to hone presentation skills.

Oral Reenactment
- Choose a case scenario of a client system (individual, group, family, or community) from your practicum agency that either you or your field instructor found challenging. The case could have been challenging for a variety of reasons. Some suggested ideas involve challenges concerning the following:
  1. student inexperience/competence
  2. client resistance
  3. client noncompliance
  4. cultural difference
  5. values/ethics
  6. theory–practice integration
- Work with a resource group of three or four students. Members of the group will provide feedback, support, and guidance to each other. Some class time will be allowed for group work (three meetings); however, students may need to meet outside class

to prepare and rehearse/film. Each student will conduct a reenactment in addition to serving as a group member. In addition to reenacting a case for discussion, students will serve at least once in the following roles for other members of their groups:
1. member of a client system
2. to provide feedback/suggestions/discussion questions in the planning process prior to the actual reenactment

■ Develop a 5- to 10-minute reenactment of a client system interaction. The reenactment can be done live before the class or videotaped and shown to the class. It can include as many members of your resource group as needed. Introduce the reenactment by briefly discussing any background (assessment) information that may be needed to understand it. *Actors should know their parts and should avoid reading notes verbatim during the presentation.* Only information that would identify the client(s) should be changed to maintain confidentiality; otherwise, the interaction should be presented as it actually occurred.

■ Discuss the integration of theory and practice for the interaction reenacted. The presenting student shall choose at least one theory from following list and present for five minutes on the integration of theory and practice with the client system presented. The presenting student should
1. briefly summarize each theory utilized, and
2. describe the theory/practice integration with the client system presented.

■ The following list provides some examples and suggestions of theories used in social work. You may choose theories from this list as well as those not on this list.
1. Human behavior:
   a. psychodynamic personality theory (Freudian personality theory)
   b. psychoanalytic theory (Erikson's psychosocial development theory, Freud's psychosexual development theory)
   c. Piaget's theory of cognitive development
2. Social environment:
   a. social systems theory
3. Direct practice theory:
   a. psychosocial approach
   b. problem-solving approach
   c. sociobehavioral approach
   d. (small group) mezzo practice theory
   e. psychodynamic theory
   f. feminist theory
   g. reality theory
   h. cognitive-behavioral theory
   i. person-centered theory
   j. ethnic-sensitive theory
   k. crisis intervention theory

■ Facilitate a 5- to 10-minute discussion of theory–practice integration. Generate two questions about theory–practice integration that will serve to generate discussion, and be prepared to answer the questions.

Examples:
1. "I tried to use the problem-solving approach to working with this client. How might I have done it better?"

(continued)

P R A C T I C E   A P P L I C A T I O N   **6.4**   Continued

2. "How might a social worker implement a mezzo-level intervention with this client?"
3. "I had a lot of trouble using person-centered theory in this interaction. Does anyone have any suggestions?"

Written Requirement

The written description will include:

- A brief (one or two paragraph) description of the reenactment including (1) client system assessment information, (2) a summary of the interaction, and (3) a list of the participating actors and a description of their roles.
- A description of the presentation of theory–practice integration. Provide a one-paragraph summary of the theory(ies) discussed and a one-paragraph description of the interface of the theory with the case.
- List the two questions to be used to begin discussion.

P R A C T I C E   A P P L I C A T I O N   **6.5**

Learning from the Client: When Listening Is Not Enough

In a future client encounter, plan to spend five minutes at the end of the session really learning from your client. Ask your client to describe to you three pertinent details or bits of information that he or she believes you understand about the presenting situation. Without comment or editorial, write down or record (with client's permission) the client's exact statements.

Following this client encounter, but before the next time you see the client, complete the following:

- Compare your formal assessment statements (contained in the client's file) with those of the client—look for differences, particularly noting the client's language and context use.
- Discuss with your field instructor, colleagues, and classmates any words or phrases (client's, agency's, or other disciplines') that are unfamiliar to you. Clarify how the staff and agency define or understand these words or phrases.

At the beginning of the next encounter with your client,

- compliment the client on "the lesson learned" and discuss and agree to begin to use "mutual language" that ensures that your client and you are communicating clearly and effectively, and
- with your client's permission, share phrases and culturally diverse language usages with staff during staff meetings, training sessions, or your integrative practice field seminar.

Developed by Carole Price, LCSW

PRACTICE APPLICATION **6.6**

Developing the Critical Self: Taking the Pain Out of Feedback

Once you have established a working relationship with your client (possibly at the beginning of the second encounter/session), *routinely* ask the client for his or her feedback about the session you have just completed. Allow approximately five minutes for this experience during each meeting with your client. Listen carefully for the client's perception of your relationship with him or her. To grasp this critical information, you may pose the following questions:

- What happens in our sessions/meetings that you find helpful?
- What happens in our sessions/meetings that you find not helpful?

    After you have collected this information from your client, you can:

- discuss with your field instructor or colleagues the feedback provided by your client and seek constructive strategies for interacting with the client in future encounters;
- discuss with your client the feedback that you have received from your field instructor or colleague(s) and mutually agree on interactions that will enhance your worker–client relationship; and
- regularly journal your feelings about this experience and use a timeline to note your increased ability/progress in using feedback as an effective practice tool.

Developed by Carole Price, LCSW

Practice Application 6.1 Follow-Up

The documentation exercise could be efficiently rewritten as:

Ms. Jones is a 32-year-old, single, African American woman interested in adoption. She wants an African American girl or boy, age birth to five years, with mild to moderate challenges. She lives in a three-bedroom home with her eight-year-old daughter. Her annual salary is $32,000. Ms. Jones believes that she is financially and emotionally prepared to adopt.

Summary

This unit has been aimed at helping you gain insights into the "business" and "process" of micro social work practice. Consistent with the concept of generalist social work practice, the issues highlighted here are applicable across all levels of social work practice and will be discussed within the context of mezzo and macro practice in subsequent units. The foundations of practice that you establish as you develop micro-practice skills will also enable you to function competently as a mezzo- and macro-level social work professional.

STUDENT SCENARIO POSTSCRIPTS

Lauren responded to the angry client at the battered women's shelter initially by feeling defensive about the client's demeaning remarks regarding her status as a student. She was then able to acknowledge to herself and to the client the client's feelings that professionals were not helping her. Lauren offered the client the option to work with another social worker, but she assured the client that she was open to listening to the client's thoughts and feelings regarding resolution of her situation. Lauren was able to apply a strengths-based approach and encouraged the client to collaborate with her to identify the client's assets and resources and develop a plan of action. The client's frustrations were defused and the client agreed to give it a try. The situation appears to be on the way to a positive resolution, but do you have additional strategies that Lauren might have considered?

Corina became flustered when she attempted to respond to the faculty liaison's questions regarding her efforts to integrate theory with practice. She stated that theories had been discussed in some of her classes, but never in terms of actual use in her practice. She suggested that faculty who teach those courses should make sure that students really know how to use the theories, if that is what they were supposed to be teaching. She was mindful of her field instructor's presence in this meeting, so she tried not to direct the blame for her lack of knowledge to the supervisor. Corina agreed to review her theory texts and readings and engage in discussion of theory–practice integration during supervision sessions, but she continued to believe that the faculty and field instructor were responsible for this deficit in her knowledge and preparation. Corina's response is one alternative. Can you think of additional (possibly less defensive and closed) ways in which she might have handled this situation?

REFERENCES

1. National Association of Social Workers. *Code of ethics.* Washington, DC: NASW Press. 1996.
2. Council on Social Work Education. *Handbook of accreditation standards and procedures.* Alexandria, VA: Author. 1994.
3. Landon, P. Generalist and advanced generalist practice. In R. L. Edwards (Ed.), *Encyclopedia of Social Work* (19th ed.) (pp. 1101–1108). Washington, DC: NASW Press. 1995.
4. Barker, R. L. *The Social Work Dictionary* (3rd ed.) (p. 234). Washington, DC: NASW Press. 1995.
5. Vayda, E. & Bogo, M. A teaching model to unite classroom and field. *Journal of Social Work Education.* 1991, 27(3):271–278.
6. Dore, M. M., Epstein, B. N. & Herrerias, C. Evaluating students' micro practice field performance: Do universal learning objectives exist? *Journal of Social Work Education.* 1992, 28(3):353–362.
7. Urbanowski, M. L. & Dwyer, M. M. *Learning through field instruction: A guide for teachers and students.* Milwaukee: Family Service America. 1988.
8. Jarman-Rohde, L., McFall, J., Kolar, P. & Strom, G. The changing context of social work practice: Implications and recommendations for social work educators. *Journal of Social Work Education.* 1997, 33(1):29–46.
9. Raskin, M. S. & Blome, W. W. The impact of managed care on field instruction. *Journal of Social Work Education.* 1998, 34(3):365–373.

10. DiGuilio, J. F. *Back to basics: Confidentiality in the field practicum*. Paper presented at the 16th Annual Baccalaureate Social Work Directors Conference, Albuquerque, NM, October 1998.

11. Munson, C. E. *Clinical social work supervision* (2nd ed.). New York: Haworth Press. 1993.

12. Falk, D. S. & Ross, P. G. *Teaching social work writing: Empowerment through effective communication*. Paper presented at the 15th Annual Baccalaureate Program Director's Conference, Philadelphia, 1997.

13. Kagle, J. D. *Record-keeping: The good, the bad, the ugly*. Presentation at the Institute for Social Work Instruction, University of Missouri—Columbia, May 18, 1998.

14. Browning, C. H. & Browning, B. J. *How to partner with managed care*. New York: John Wiley & Sons. 1996.

15. Kagle, J. D. *Social work records* (2nd ed.). Belmont, CA: Wadsworth. 1991.

16. Sheafor, B. W., Horejsi, C. R. & Horejsi, G. A. *Techniques and guidelines for social work practice* (2nd ed.). Boston: Allyn & Bacon. 1988.

17. Salvatore, E. P. Issues in collaboration and teamwork: A sociologic perspective on the role definition of social work in primary health care. *Research in the Sociology of Health Care*. 1988, 7:119–139.

18. Abramson, J. & Mizrahi, T. Strategies for enhancing collaboration between social workers and physicians. *Social Work in Health Care*. 1986, *12*(1):1–21.

19. Gross, A. M. & Gross, J. Attitudes of physicians and nurses towards the role of social workers in primary health care: What promotes collaboration? *Family Practice*. 1987, *4*(4):266–270.

20. Rompf, E. L., Royse, D. & Dhooper, S. S. Anxiety preceding field work: What students worry about. *Journal of Teaching in Social Work*. 1993, *7*(2):81–95.

21. Goldstein, H. Toward the integration of theory and practice: A humanistic approach. *Social Work*. 1986, *31*(5):352–357.

22. Klein, W. C. & Bloom, M. Practice wisdom. *Social Work*. 1995, *40*(6):799–807.

23. Bogo, M. The student/field instructor relationship: The critical factor in field education. *The Clinical Supervisor*. 1993, *11*(2):23–36.

24. Bogo, M. & Vayda, E. *The practice of field instruction in social work: Theory and process*. Toronto: University of Toronto Press. 1987.

25. Bogo, M. & Vayda, E. Developing a process model for field instruction. *Canadian Social Work Review*. 1989, *6*:224–232.

26. DiGuilio, J. F. Concerns in the field placement. *The New Social Worker*. 1998, *5*(1):19–20.

27. Grossman, B., Levine-Jordano, N. & Shearer, P. Working with students' emotional reactions in the field: An educational framework. *The Clinical Supervisor*. 1990, *8*(1):23–39.

28. Dorfman, R. A. *Clinical social work practice*. New York: Brunner/Mazel. 1996.

29. Linsley, J. Self-disclosure: How much should I tell? *The New Social Worker*. 1998, *5*(4):4–6.

30. Dore, M. M. The practice-teaching parallel in educating the micropractitioner. *Journal of Social Work Education*. 1993, *29*(2):181–190.

31. Russo, R. *Serving and surviving as a human service worker*. Prospect Heights, IL: Waveland Press. 1993.

7 Mezzo Social Work Practice in the Field

Never doubt that a small group of thoughtful committed citizens can change the world; indeed, it's the only thing that ever has.

—Margaret Mead

Group work can be powerful, intimidating, chaotic, and immensely rewarding—all at the same time. As Margaret Mead stated, groups can change the world—whether the "world" of a group of children, the "world" of a neighborhood, or the "world" of a society of people. Groups come in various shapes, sizes, and formats and have vastly differing goals and agendas. Mezzo practice is defined as social work practice with families and small groups and requires such skills as communication, mediation, negotiation, and education (1).

Although group work has been a part of social work practice since the inception of social service delivery, its popularity has waxed and waned over the decades (2). Currently, the use of the group interventions is on the increase, in both the clinical and the nonclinical arenas. In providing services to individuals and families, managed care has embraced the use of wellness-focused group work as a more efficient and cost-effective tool for intervention, particularly in the areas of self-help and psychoeducational groups (3). In the performance of nondirect service responsibilities, the need for collaboration, coalition building, and issue-based task forces has heightened the need for well-trained group facilitators. However, even with this increase, only 0.5 percent of social workers surveyed indicate that group work is their primary area of expertise (4). This statistic suggests that, while social workers do practice group work, it is typically included in a range of other social work activities.

Although only a small minority of social workers identify their primary area of practice as group work, a significant number of social workers are engaged in administration and management—15.5 percent report these areas as their primary functions, while 9.8 percent report administration or management as a secondary function (3). Group work skills are essential if a social worker is to serve as an effective administrator or manager. Administrators are responsible for facilitation of work groups, committees, and boards and for supervising groups of employees—all tasks involving competence in group management.

Mezzo-level skills are thus an essential component of the repertoire of the social worker and, in particular, of the generalist social work practitioner. The NASW *Code of Ethics* (5) stipulates that ". . . enhancing the well-being of individuals, families, social groups, organizations and communities" is paramount to the function of social work. Although social work educators and practitioners may agree that group work skills are important to the development of a social worker, practicum students may find the actual acquisition of these skills a challenge. For instance, your agency may not offer groups as a part of its service delivery system. Or the groups in your agency may be closed and ongoing, and a "transient observer" could be disruptive to the group. Or the group in which you were going to participate may be cancelled due to lack of interest or funding. Should you find that gaining exposure to mezzo-level practice is not possible, consider seeking a group experience outside your agency in an affiliated agency or related area. Such an arrangement might be negotiated with the help and guidance of your field instructor. If group participation is not readily available, an alternative is to develop a student support group composed of students in your practicum site or social work program. Each student can assume responsibility for facilitation of one or more sessions, and the group can use itself to gain group work skills, process group dynamics, and be supported by peers.

Once they have gained experience and skills in group work, many social workers find group facilitation exhilarating. Group work provides an opportunity to build on individual group-member strengths by facilitating dialogue among the members. Through group work, members are able to see the power of the group dynamic that occurs when they share and bring new insights to the experiences of others.

Students may be reluctant to engage in group work because they may be intimidated by group facilitation, particularly if they have not been exposed to group concepts during coursework. Students may not view themselves as having enough expertise or confidence to face an entire group of people—it is much more comfortable to make a mistake with one person than with a room full of people. Even many social work professionals fear this increased level of exposure, the potential lack of control, and "group" judgments (6). Most of us have voiced (maybe not out loud) anxiety about a negative group experience: What if the members of the group do not bond with one another, reject me, or—worst case—join together to rebel against me? These fears are not uncommon among fledgling group leaders. If this describes you, you may want to begin to learn group skills by observing a group or by serving as a cofacilitator of a group.

In addition, many students wonder why they need to have group work skills—after all, they plan to work only with individuals and do not envision group work in their futures as social workers. However, students interested in clinical social work, health-related social work, or macro-level practice may not realize that facilitating a support group, chairing a quality assurance committee, or organizing a group of neighbors will almost certainly be included in a future job description. Clearly, the contemporary work of generalist social work practice encompasses considerable involvement in groups—client, interdisciplinary, community, and staff—and achieving competence in mezzo-level social work practice will serve to prepare you for that unexpected opportunity to lead a group. If you question the validity of or your interest in developing social work group skills, we encourage you to raise these issues with the other members of your practicum team, either in supervisory sessions or in integrative practice field seminar. Working through your questions and concerns with the other members of your team may enable you to gain a broader perspective on the issues.

This unit will define and operationalize mezzo practice within the context of your practicum experience. It will begin with a discussion of your exploration of the student role and expectations in mezzo work followed by a focus on the "business" and "process" of mezzo practice. The unit will close with a discussion of nondirect service group work, including facilitation of a group meeting, guidelines for presenting information to a group, and working with a task-focused group.

Expectations for Student Learning in Mezzo Practice

Mezzo social work practice is a "method of social work intervention in which small numbers of people who share similar interests or common problems convene regularly and engage in activities designed to achieve certain objectives" (7). Growth and change occur as a result of an individual's participation in the group process and are based on humans' needs for interdependence and support (2, 8). Whether the group is a therapeutic, task, or self-help group, the premise of the group intervention model is rooted in a systemic perspective that suggests that group dynamics and exchanges promote change that may not occur on an individual basis.

Mezzo practice encompasses a wide range of activities and includes considerable variation in the terms used to describe the types of group interventions employed by social work professionals (9). You may have heard of or had experience with group therapy, group counseling, support groups, work groups, task forces, or coalitions. Despite the many names attached to group work, most group interventions can be categorized within three general models of social work group practice: social goals, reciprocal goals, and remedial goals (8). Following is a brief description of each model with examples of group types and of the roles a social worker may fulfill in each area.

Social Goals Model
Based on problem-focused interests and goals. Examples include:
- neighborhood safety groups
- parent–teacher associations
- community development task forces
- coalition of professionals advocating for improved welfare legislation
    #### Social Work Role
    - initiator/convener/organizer (e.g., social worker may respond to a community need and convene a group)

♦ facilitator
♦ advocate
♦ resource (e.g., information, financial support, or access to data or people)

Reciprocal Goals Model

Based on mutual aid and self-help premise in which members support one another through sharing common experiences. Examples include:

■ 12-step programs (e.g., Alcoholics Anonymous, Overeaters Anonymous, Al-Anon, and Ala-teen)
■ grief support group
■ caregiver support group (e.g., caregivers of persons with chronic illnesses)
■ disease-specific patient support groups (e.g., leukemia support group, multiple sclerosis support group, and cancer support group)

Social Work Role:
♦ facilitator
♦ mediator
♦ educator
♦ support (e.g., resources, education, or referrals)

Remedial Goals Model

Based on the philosophy that group member interactions facilitate change. Examples include:

■ psychotherapy group composed of members with a specific diagnosis (e.g., depression, manic depression, and schizophrenia)
■ marital therapy group
■ child abuse perpetrators group
■ survivors of a trauma (e.g., child abuse, sexual abuse, rape, and criminal action)

Social Work Role:
♦ therapist/clinician
♦ educator
♦ mediator

Your style as a group leader is important to consider as you begin your role as a group facilitator or therapist. Yalom (10) provides insight into leadership style by categorizing leader behaviors as (1) emotionally stimulating—challenging, intrusive, and personal risk-taking; (2) caring—supportive, affectionate, warm, and genuine; (3) meaningful attribution—engages in interpretation, explanation, and translation of feelings; and (4) executive function—establishes rules and limits and "manages" the group. In general, the skills needed by any group leader include flexibility; awareness of client issues; insight into group process; ability to confront, clarify, interpret, and support; and ability to respond appropriately to frustration and resistance (10).

Building on the leader behaviors described here, Yalom (10) describes six leadership styles. Although the basis for the following leader types is rooted in group psychotherapy, each style may be applicable in any group type and, in some situations, one style may be more appropriate than the others. Group leader styles include:

- *The Energizer*—Charismatic, energetic, supportive, and attacking, this leader subscribes to stringent rule setting and limits. Energizers are only minimally effective because they overwhelm and "frighten" group members away.
- *The Provider*—Conveying meaning and caring to group members, the provider effects positive outcomes with minimal risks.
- *The Social Engineer*—Using group process and support, this leader type is moderately effective.
- *The Impersonal Leader*—This leader style, characterized by distance, minimal caring, rigidity of rules, and a high level of stimulation, generally results in poor outcomes.
- *The Laissez-Faire Leader*—Poor outcomes and high attrition rates result from this style, which includes attention to procedures and minimal caring.
- *The Manager*—Structured interventions with poor outcomes typify this leader style.

Effective group leaders draw behaviors and skills from multiple areas—in part, to adapt to their style, and, in part, to respond to the situation. Take a few moments and consider your previous group leader experiences. Which of the leader behaviors and styles best describe you? Consider also your group "successes" and "less than successful" experiences, and identify strengths and areas for growth related to your group skills.

Although we all utilize a mixture of different styles and behaviors depending on the needs of the situation, we typically align with one predominant style (which likely mirrors the behaviors and styles that we employ at the micro level of social work practice). As you complete your practicum experience, you will be well served by seeking out as many group work experiences as possible. Regardless of the type of group experience, you have the opportunity to apply group theory to practice, to develop group facilitation skills, and to develop group documentation skills.

PRACTICE APPLICATION 7.1

Groups, Groups, Groups

This practice application will enable you to gain familiarity with group process from the perspective of an observer. An observer is often able to perceive group dynamics and process from a different perspective because he or she does not have a vested interest in the agenda or the outcome of the group's work. To facilitate your increased awareness, follow these steps:

- Select a group that is a part of or affiliated with your practicum agency. The group may be a problem-solving group, committee, board, staff meeting, therapeutic group, or other group that meets on a regular basis. If your agency does not have such a group, consider looking outside the agency. You may consult with your field instructor or a faculty member for ideas.

- Attend the group at least two or three times.
- Journal on your group observation experiences and address the following areas:
  - purpose(s) and goals of the group (explicit and implicit)
  - summary of the group processes you observe, including reference to the stages of group development
  - summary of the contribution of each group member, including both leader(s) and participants
  - your observations of the effectiveness of the group
  - aspects of the group process or outcomes that you believe were highly successful
  - aspects of the group process or outcomes that you believe should have been addressed differently
  - summary of areas of new learning related to group processes, interpersonal communication, and the content/goals of the group
- If you have cofacilitated a group, reflect on your experiences. Were you prepared? What did you learn about your facilitation style?
- Share your observations with your field instructor, focusing on any changes in your perceptions regarding the role of mezzo social work practice in your agency and your professional development.

Developed by Suzanne LeLaurin, MSW

Learning the "Business" of Mezzo Practice

Mezzo social work practice differs significantly from individual- and family-focused micro-level practice. This section will highlight the following aspects of learning the "business" of mezzo-level practice: orientation, group work assignments, identifying yourself as a student, role transition, confidentiality, documentation, collaboration, and ongoing evaluation.

Orientation

Group activities that occur within the practicum setting may or may not be a regular, ongoing facet of the agency's operations. Clinically focused groups may be time limited, cyclical, or even one-time offerings, or they may be a regular part of the weekly, year-round schedule. The opportunity to engage in group work may be dependent on timing, client needs and interests, funding, political agendas, agency administration, and even the agency's physical space issues. Because of the uncertainty involved with group work opportunities, the group work orientation process may be included as part of your formal practicum orientation or it may be on-the-job training that occurs when a group need arises during the practicum. Whether the opportunity for group work is planned or arises spontaneously, you can assert yourself to ensure that you receive as much orientation as possible.

Practicum students are often asked to identify a need, develop a proposal for initiating a group, recruit members, and establish and facilitate the group (and make the coffee!). In this case, your preparation for your group work experience

may include reviewing information from your coursework on group interventions; observing the leadership of existing groups; interviewing coworkers regarding strategies for developing a new group; and, certainly, brainstorming with your field instructor on a plan for implementation.

Alternatively, students are often invited to join new or ongoing groups as cofacilitators. Preparation for this type of group experience will involve discussions with the current facilitator to learn about the impetus, mission, and goals of the group and to learn his or her role, and leadership style and information about the group members; observing the group you will be joining or a similar group; and gaining insight regarding your role as a practicum student in the group.

In some cases—as a result of group dynamics, group content, continuity, or billing issues or agency policy—students cannot assume the role of facilitator, or even of cofacilitator. Should you find yourself in this situation, discuss with the group's leader or your field instructor ways in which you can optimize your learning. Despite your somewhat passive role, you can observe the group interactions and process your observations with the group leader or your field instructor in order to gain an understanding of group facilitation, the application of group theory to actual practice, and the management of group conflicts. You may find it helpful to jot down process notes of statements you may have made in specific situations. Documenting the group interactions at the same time as the group leader and comparing notes may provide insights into group process as well.

Group Work Assignments

Because opportunities for group experiences may arise unplanned, you may find that organizing and leading a group is added *on top of* your current workload. If your field instructor or another staff member asks you to be involved in a new or ongoing group, be certain to discuss with your field instructor the realities of managing this new assignment along with your other responsibilities. Options for juggling this additional task may include restructuring your current workload, adding hours to your weekly schedule (and completing your practicum earlier if this is acceptable to your social work program and the agency), or not accepting any additional assignments for a period of time.

Related to workload issues in your practicum is the matter of determining the importance given to your group responsibilities. To meet your learning plan obligations, you may need to consider the type and level of group experience(s) you need to fulfill the group work requirement. Often, students cannot be involved in the inception, implementation, and termination of an entire group experience. If this is the case, will developing a group (i.e., recruiting, marketing, and selecting/forming a group, but not leading the group) or cofacilitating a group suffice, or must you facilitate a group by yourself? If you are cofacilitating a group, is there a minimum number of sessions you must cofacilitate to fulfill the group work requirement? These are questions to be addressed with your faculty liaison.

Identifying Yourself as a Student

The issue of identifying yourself as a practicum student was discussed in Unit 6, but it presents a unique challenge in mezzo-level practice. If you are joining a group that has been in existence prior to your practicum, clients, coworkers, community persons, or other professionals may view you as a disruption or "outsider." Depending on the focus of the group, adding a new member can raise issues of confidentiality, trust, bonding, and continuity. As you know from the systems perspective, a change in one part of the system stimulates change in the entire system, and your presence may effect just that outcome. Furthermore, learning that you are a student who will participate in the agency on a time-limited basis may create further challenges to your entry into the group. With the support of your field instructor and cofacilitator, you can address the issues of your participation and role as a student with the group members themselves, a strategy that may well serve to allay group members' concerns.

Role Transition

The transition you make from group observer or cofacilitator to facilitator can be made easier by anticipating the role changes. The typical initiation to group work for a practicum student is observing a group, minimally participating, and processing the experience with the group leader, focusing on group dynamics, and leadership issues. Following a period of functioning as an observer, the student may be "promoted" to the role of cofacilitator. In this scenario, the student may assume greater responsibility for the group (e.g., organizing, planning the agenda, identifying and procuring needed resources, completing group notes/documentation, and presenting information to the group). The final phase of the group indoctrination process is assuming full responsibility for facilitating a group. This opportunity may not be available in all practicum situations for a variety of reasons previously noted. However, should the opportunity for sole facilitation present itself to you, be mindful of utilizing the support available to you from the agency and your social work program. Being able to debrief concerning the group experience with your field instructor can be invaluable to honing your group skills.

Confidentiality

The issues of defining and maintaining confidentiality present several unique challenges when group interventions are employed. You are now accountable for maintaining the confidences of not just one person but an entire group of clients. Questions that may arise as you contemplate the issue of the confidentiality of your group experience include the following:

- What rules regarding confidentiality should be established for a group? How is confidentiality defined in the group setting? What (if any) information can be shared outside the group? Is confidentiality violated if group members discuss group information with one another outside the meetings or if members discuss group information with other therapists or family members?
- Do confidentiality rules differ depending on the type of group (e.g., mutual aid, task-focused, or therapy group)?
- If a group member is a client of a coworker, am I obligated to share information with that coworker? How do I respond if asked by the staff person about the client's participation in the group?
- How can I respond if a group member(s) tells me information about a fellow group member?
- Are legal implications possible if certain types of information are shared in a group?
- Do "privileged communication" laws protect me if I learn of legal violations or criminal acts?
- What is the appropriate response to a breach of confidentiality by a group member(s)?

The answers to these questions are complex, variable, and dependent on several factors: previous norms established by an existing group, the context of the specific situation, agency culture and policy, and legal mandates. Regarding agency culture, the philosophy may be that all information regarding a particular individual should be shared with all workers involved. Conversely, the agency may adhere to a stringent policy of informed consent by which the information can be shared only with the express (and, possibly, written) consent of the client.

On a related note, you must examine the issue of confidentiality within different types of groups. Although the commitment to maintain confidentiality is critical to the functioning of any client service group, the legal implications differ based on the purpose and leadership of the group. Specifically, a therapy group led by a professional protected by law may be able to maintain confidentiality (depending on the state involved). However, a self-help/mutual aid group led by a nonprofessional does not provide the protection of privileged communication and members and the leader may be subject to subpoena in a criminal/civil action (9). The issue becomes less clear if the mutual aid group leader is a professional covered by state/federal protection (11).

You must have a clear understanding of the confidentiality rules established by the particular group of which you are a member or of the rules of this type of group (if this group type is ongoing in the agency). Specifically, the group members may have pointedly discussed their preferences for the sharing of information inside and outside the group. You are responsible for obtaining this information, which is not likely to be recorded in any official agency documents.

Last, the specific details of a situation are critical to determining the parameters of confidentiality and must be considered if a violation is anticipated. For instance, if a group member informs you that another group member has expressed suicidal or homicidal ideations, you are obligated to intervene because the client may be a danger to him- or herself or others. However, if you learn from a group member that another group member is engaged in an extramarital relationship, you are not obligated to confront the client with this information but may encourage the first group member to raise the issue (assuming it is relevant) with the other group member within the group session.

In sum, the guidelines for confidentiality in group work are essentially the same as in any other area of social work practice, and similar judgments should be employed. However, the issues may be more complicated by virtue of the presence of multiple persons.

Documentation

You have learned the basics and importance of accurate and effective documentation by this point in your social work training. Just as documenting your encounters with an individual is essential for capturing and analyzing information and monitoring progress at the micro level of social work practice, so, too, is it essential for mezzo-level practice. Although documenting information obtained from an individual emphasizes facts, thoughts, feelings, and planning, the focus of group interaction recording is on group exchanges, group dynamics, and planning.

Your practicum agency may or may not have a structured format for documenting group information. The more formalized the group (i.e., therapeutic, mandated, or third-party reimbursed), the more likely there is to be a required documentation process in place. This process may involve note keeping on the group as a whole and recording in individual client files. Self-help groups, however, do not typically involve extensive record keeping. Clarity is essential regarding the "philosophy" of group documentation—are you documenting events and observations only, or are you including assessment and evaluative statements as well (12)? If your agency's practice is to include assessment in group documentation, you can report the client's behavior and provide your thoughts regarding the possible origins of or reasons for the client's comments or actions (12).

In general, documentation of client group activities should be completed immediately following the group session. A verbal debriefing with your cofacilitator, if applicable, or your field instructor is optimal. This debriefing should encompass such information as group membership, content/process, and comments regarding individual members (12). A sample form for documenting group process is provided in Figure 7.1.

FIGURE 7.1   Group Process Form

Date: Group Day:

Group Leader(s):   Group Time:

Group Members Present:

Group Content/Process _____

_____

_____

_____

_____

_____

_____

Group Members—Individual Comments

_____

_____

_____

_____

_____

_____

_____

_____

Form provided by Kids in the Middle, Inc., St. Louis, Missouri.

PRACTICE APPLICATION **7.2**

How Do Documentation Styles Compare?

The documentation sample presented in Figure 7.1 is offered as a model for recording a client-centered group experience. Compare this format with that used in your practicum agency, and answer the following questions in a journal entry:

- How do the two documentation formats compare? Do they cover similar areas? If not, how do they differ?
- Are there areas of the format that do not meet the needs of your client population?
- If your current format does not meet the needs of your client population, how might you revise your documentation system to fit the type of group that you facilitate better?

For a more detailed documentation of group process and progress, areas to address may include the following (2, 13):

- group composition (members in attendance and those absent—you may want to include a visual depiction of seating)
- session number
- issues discussed during the meeting
- group interactions/dynamics—to include individual and group exchanges (can incorporate direct quotes made by members), conflicts, and resolution of issues raised
- sociogram to depict and assess group interactions
- group leader observations regarding
  - ◆ individual issues and progress,
  - ◆ leader interaction with individual members,
  - ◆ plans for upcoming meetings,
  - ◆ issues/challenges for you as a group leader,
  - ◆ future directions, and
  - ◆ resources needed

If you are required to document group encounters in each individual client's record, a word of caution regarding confidentiality is in order. You must clarify whether your agency's policy/practice guides you to document information that relates only to that client in a client file or allows you to refer to the client's interaction with another client during the group (ensuring that the other client is not referred to by name or any other identifying information) (11). As a general rule, you should not refer to another client by name or include significant identifying information.

Documentation may also be necessary and desired for justifying the continuation of the group or the implementation of additional groups. It can help identify the costs and benefits of the group intervention (6). Individual and group out-comes, worker hours, and streamlining of services are just three areas in which the group leader can maintain records for the agency's use.

In sum, you may find that documentation of group social work practice may not be as clearly defined and structured as is documentation of practice with indi-viduals and families. However, you can attain important critical thinking and writ-ing skills by attempting to synthesize group interactions and to commit such information to a written summary.

Collaboration

By the very definition of group work, mezzo-level social work practice is collabo-ration. As a group leader, you hope to establish a collaborative relationship with the agency administration, group members, your cofacilitator, referral sources, and agency staff working with the group members outside the group. As a group member, you engage in ongoing collaboration with the other members of the group through your exchanges.

The basic knowledge and skills you have gained in the area of collaboration will serve you well in mezzo practice. Specifically, strategies for promoting effec-tive collaboration, and enhancing group process include the following:

- Ensure that your group has the support (e.g., financial and practical) of the agency's administration. Does the administration provide staff, supplies, space, budget, transportation, or child care for this endeavor? If the group is being offered on a trial basis, what is the timeframe for determining a suc-cessful outcome (6)?
- Clarify on a regular and ongoing basis *your* roles and responsibilities related to the group.
- Clarify on a regular and ongoing basis *group members'* roles and responsibilities.
- Identify issues of terms and professional/popular jargon to ensure that all parties are speaking the same "language."
- Determine mutually agreed upon goals for the group.
- Mutually establish clear and simple ground rules for group functioning, including
  - ♦ norms for attendance and participation,
  - ♦ parameters of appropriate group discussion/content,
  - ♦ logistical issues (e.g., meeting time and place, room arrangements, refresh-ments, materials, and clean-up),
  - ♦ boundaries for confidentiality.
- Commit to practicing mutual respect for all members and leaders.
- Engage in clear and effective oral and written communications with all par-ties involved in the group experience.
- Provide appropriate feedback to relevant persons on a timely basis.
- Follow up on commitments made to group members, referral sources, and other persons.

The relationship you establish with a cofacilitator should, of course, also be considered a collaboration. Building on the previous guidelines, strategies for achieving effective collaboration with your cofacilitator include the following:

- Establish clear and realistic roles and responsibilities for both facilitators.
- Routinely review facilitators' roles and responsibilities and renegotiate as needed.
- Identify and achieve consensus on group purpose, achievable goals, format, and client and worker boundaries.
- Discuss facilitators' philosophy, theoretical frameworks, and styles.
- Identify method(s) of individual, group, and facilitator evaluation.

In the event that you begin to feel that the collaborative relationship is not progressing in a positive or productive manner, you are advised to address the problems or concerns as soon as possible. Do not wait for the issues to resolve themselves! Depending on the nature of your concern, you may opt to approach the individual(s) involved or process the problem with your field instructor. Regardless of the method you choose, the important point is to assert your role as an adult learner and to take action.

Ongoing Evaluation

Routine evaluation of the group process and of your role as a group facilitator/ cofacilitator is a particularly important activity. Due to the number of persons involved in any group intervention, monitoring and understanding the interactions and dynamics are more complex tasks than evaluating a micro-level intervention. Evaluating the group's purpose and goals, dynamics, format, and outcomes is essential to the effective functioning of the group as well as to the development of your group work skills.

Evaluation of your group experiences can be conducted by using one of several different methods. You may opt to evaluate individual group member's progress and outcomes, the group process itself, your leadership style and effectiveness, or the effectiveness of the group intervention. Evaluation strategies include:

- audio- or videotaping,
- process recording,
- group member pre- and posttests (e.g., single system design analysis),
- group member feedback (e.g., satisfaction with group experience),
- facilitator debriefings (may be verbal or written), and
- program evaluation to determine whether group goals are being met, the functionality of the group, and any changes needed.

There are four important tasks that need to be completed:

1. Prior to your involvement with the group, identify the areas to be evaluated.
2. Establish how the evaluation results will be analyzed and distributed. Will you share your findings with the clients on an individual or group basis, with

the parents of the children in a group, with referral sources, or with other staff members (9)?

3. Determine the tools to be used in the evaluation.
4. Involve your field instructor or cofacilitator in the review and analysis of the evaluative data.

PRACTICE APPLICATION **7.3**

Group Facilitator Self-Assessment

This practice application will aid you in conducting an assessment of yourself as a group leader. Consider the questions below (and add any others that you think may be relevant). Follow up this exercise with a discussion with your field instructor, a staff member, and classmates about your facilitation skills.

- Was I adequately prepared to facilitate a group (theoretically and practically)?
- What were my goals for the group and have they changed?
- Do my goals match the group members' goals?
- Am I attending to members in a balanced way?
- Does the group see my role the same way I do?
- Am I comfortable in a group setting?
- Am I able to "manage" group issues (e.g., conflicts, needs, interactions, and difficult members)?
- Am I able to move the group forward, or has the group stagnated?
- Does my leadership style fit with this group?
- What do I need to change and how can I achieve this?

Evaluation is important regardless of the type of group you are facilitating/cofacilitating. Reciprocal (self-help) groups may not require as high a level of accountability as remedial (therapeutic) groups, but evaluation is important for determining the viability, dynamics, and future of the self-help group. Some types of groups lend themselves more easily to evaluation. For example, time-limited (e.g., parent education groups), goal-focused (e.g., weight loss) groups, and behavior change (e.g., smoking cessation) groups are easier to evaluate because each has tangible goals, parameters, and outcomes. On the other hand, open-ended, mutual aid groups may be more difficult to evaluate because the members at each meeting may determine the group's agenda. Moreover, the group focus may be directed not toward a specific behavior change but solely on quality-of-life issues (i.e., improving the members' life satisfaction or providing support related to an event, developmental stage, or trauma). Therefore, an appropriate tool for determining the impact of the group experience on the group member may be to assess quality of life/life satisfaction issues for the members and to obtain feedback regarding members' perceptions of needs (and whether they are being met).

Important to the evaluation process is the integration of systematic and empirical methods that identify and measure both the group's interactions and its outcomes (2). The systematic collection of evaluative data can support the need for continuing the group, initiating new groups, or disbanding the group. Further, utilizing standardized measures or measures specifically designed for your group can help identify group member issues, progress, and communication (2).

The "business" of mezzo practice has many similarities to the "business" of micro practice, but it does require specialized knowledge and skills. Specifically, social workers need to be aware of several factors that impact the group experience, including:

- the potential power of the group process, in terms of both the positive and the negative outcomes associated with a group intervention;
- the need to adhere to issues of confidentiality;
- the fact that a group experience is not the most appropriate or effective intervention for all clients;
- the fact that a group experience may be most effective when paired with individual services for some members; and
- the fact that involvement in a group intervention may not be the most efficient means of providing services.

Learning the "Process" of Mezzo Practice

Learning the "process" of mezzo-level social work practice means mastering a range of knowledge and skills. This section will highlight areas for you to consider as you develop your group social work skills, including theory–practice integration, working with "difficult" client behaviors, unique mezzo-practice challenges, developing appropriate expectations of yourself and your clients, and use of self in mezzo practice.

An important insight to gain about mezzo-level social work practice is that each group develops a "personality" of its own. Groups can be verbal or nonverbal, interactive or passive, compliant or rebellious, and bonded or fragmented. The personality assumed by the group can have a positive or a negative influence on the work of the group. A positive effect can serve as a powerful mechanism for group members to receive feedback and support and to engage in reality checking, while a negative, conflictual atmosphere can become contagious and infect the work of the group.

Theory–Practice Integration

Integration of theoretical frameworks and practice applications is an intregal part of generalist social work practice at all levels, but it presents unique challenges at the mezzo level. First, you must be knowledgeable about and able to apply theoretical concepts focused on the individual. Second, you must be equally competent in the area of theoretical concepts, focused on the interactions of group members. You can develop and hone your techniques and skills for use at the individual and group levels while exploring their overlap, and integration from both the theoretical and the implementation perspectives.

Although a number of theoretical approaches are employed in group work, the empowerment/strength-based perspective is one that epitomizes the values of the social work profession. The empowerment perspective enables you to "move beyond work with individual clients and problem situations to think of ways to engage clients together in group efforts toward both individual and community change" (2). Group intervention approaches serve as a central resource for generalist practitioners because they enable the social worker to integrate client and resource issues from the perspectives of problem identification and resolution (2). Groups, regardless of their type, can be used to empower people through social support, provision of concrete services, teaching new knowledge and skills, raising members' consciousness, and prompting social action (2).

PRACTICE APPLICATION **7.4**

Application of Theory to Group Practice: Testing Your Knowledge

Corina, Ben, Lauren, and Cameron are each responsible for facilitating or cofacilitating a group. Use the following descriptions of their group experiences to consider theoretical applications. Journal your response to the question posed.

Corina is responsible for leading a daily teen group at the detention center. The staff subscribes to a cognitive behavioral approach with this client population. Although Corina is gaining comfort with administering the token system on a one-on-one basis, she finds that she has difficulty identifying and implementing a fair, equitable, and appropriate consequence system for violations of group rules in the group setting. How can Corina apply the tenets of the cognitive behavioral approach in a just manner?

Ben facilitates an after-school group for elementary-school children. In order for Ben and the children to learn more about one another, Ben decides to have the students complete a sociogram of group interactions. What theoretical premise is Ben utilizing in this exercise?

Lauren cofacilitates a support group for battered women's shelter residents. Although the group meets daily, the number of times any one resident attends varies due to length of stay in the shelter, work schedules, and outside appointments. The shelter staff feel strongly about the need to use an empowerment perspective in working with the clients who have experienced some form(s) of domestic violence. Given the typically limited opportunities to engage with an individual client, Lauren feels challenged regarding strategies for empowering women to view options for themselves other than abuse. Within the time constraints, what strategies can Lauren employ that are consistent with the empowerment approach?

Cameron cofacilitates an after-care group in the chemical dependency treatment program. The members are struggling with reentering their worlds while adhering to a commitment of abstinence. Having grappled with the same problem in his own recovery process,

Cameron has insight into the way in which he eventually overcame his reentry problems, and he knows that he was unaware of any theoretical framework being involved. Cameron is unsure about the existence of or need for a "theory" to guide his clients in coping with recovery. When Cameron raised this issue with his field instructor, the field instructor stated that he does not use any theory. Is this possible?

The four scenarios presented here address situations frequently encountered by practicum students. Corina's problem is gaining the skills needed to translate theory into practice for individuals within a group. Lauren is frustrated because she feels that she has such limited time with her clients and questions whether she can adequately convey the value of the empowerment model. Because staff members may not verbalize their decision-making processes regarding the selection and use of theoretical frameworks, students (Ben and Cameron, for instance) are not always able to make the connections between theory and practice strategies. Do any of these situations sound familiar to you? What theoretical framework do you use in *your* group work?

In all levels of social work practice, theory is critical for guiding our work and, eventually, becomes a part of our "practice wisdom." However, until you move easily and comfortably from theoretical concepts to practice strategies, you can benefit from processing group issues as much as possible with your colleagues, faculty, and agency staff. In fact, a strategy for gaining this skill may be to routinely require yourself to identify a guiding theoretical premise as you complete your assessments, documentation, and case presentations.

Working with "Difficult" Client Behaviors in the Group Setting

Unit 6 emphasized the need to identify your definition of *dislike* and of *difficult client* as well as to individualize your response to particular "difficult" client situations as they arise in your practice. In addition to those client behaviors, attitudes, or situations that you find distasteful or challenging to address at the micro practice level, group interactions can give rise to another layer of difficult issues. Remember that any group is composed of individual members who bring their individual issues, needs, and characteristics to the group experience. For instance, individual group members can be hostile, violate professional–personal boundaries, display inappropriate behaviors, and resist your attempts to alleviate their crises. These difficult behaviors may be heightened when an individual is placed in a group, particularly if the individual perceives that his or her behavior is being supported or encouraged by the other group members (or possibly even thwarted). Moreover, a difficult behavior exhibited by one member can be contagious. If one member is angry with you, he or she may be able to convince the others in the group that they, too, should share, and act on his or her "agenda." On the other hand, a difficult behavior can be defused or ameliorated through the group's feedback to the individual. This "reality check" may let the individual know that his or her behavior is unacceptable, at least in the group.

Each group includes its own unique and interesting members, and *difficult* means different things to each worker, but group work experience provides client categories that commonly challenge group leaders. There is much to be learned from those group members who make you dread going to group!

Although each group facilitator perceives "difficult" behaviors differently, research indicates that commonalties do exist regarding member behaviors that have a negative effect on the worker. Such behaviors and attributes identified by us and others (13) include:

- irregular attendance,
- group members being at different stages regarding their problem or issue,
- premature group termination,
- varied length of membership in the group,
- disruptive members, and
- unclear goals.

The following list of difficult group member characteristics has been compiled from a variety of sources, including our own experiences (6, 9).

- *No-shows and floaters.* "No-shows" are those clients who verbally commit to regular attendance but rarely show up, while "floaters" are those individuals who attend erratically. The group leader is obligated to address such behaviors by explaining that the client's attendance is critical to the group process and establishing consequences/options for nonattendance. Of course, if floating is an accepted feature of the group, such members are not viewed as problems.
- *The obnoxious member.* Many group leaders find behaviors such as overt confrontation, constant criticism, and aggression extremely difficult to deal with, but these behaviors can actually serve a useful purpose within the group process. As a group facilitator, you can take advantage of the "obnoxious" member's willingness to participate by asking other members how they feel about an offensive comment made by this member, encouraging more reserved members to work on their assertiveness skills by responding to inappropriate remarks, and using the power of the group to let the obnoxious person know that he or she is are exhibiting offensive behaviors.
- *The nonparticipant.* "Nonparticipants" are people who regularly attend the group sessions but do not engage in the group process. Nonparticipants may not interact with the other group members or leader at all or may interact only one-on-one with the group leader. As a group leader, you may wish to explore this group member's lack of participation outside the group setting. His or her reticence may be a result of shyness, anticipated ridicule or rejection, fear that his or her problem is more severe than those of other members, or resistance related to being forced to join the group. Exploring this member's nonparticipation may also reveal that he or she benefits from the group process without making verbal contributions (6). If you and the nonparticipant deem that increased participation is desired, a direct and supportive

approach may be most effective (6). Increasing the nonparticipant's involvement with the group may be a significant intervention made at the individual level.

- *The rabble rouser.* The "rabble rouser" may be the most difficult of all difficult group members because he or she may persuasively engage the other members in mounting a rebellion against the leader or the agency. Sometimes, the rabble rouser is seeking recognition as the group's unofficial or internal leader but unfortunately chooses to gain that role through aggressive, intimidating means. As with the "obnoxious" member, the group leader can utilize the contribution of the rabble rouser to address group concerns and mobilize the group in a positive way. Channeling the rabble rouser's efforts such that he or she becomes an ally can be motivating and healthy for the group (6).

- *The phantom.* The "phantom" group member arrives late or leaves early, thus creating disruption for the group. Investigating with the phantom the reasons for his or her nonconformist behavior may reveal that he or she is overextended and could benefit from using assertiveness skills to prioritize activities and let go of activities of lesser importance. It is also possible that the phantom enjoys the attention resulting from this behavior or that he or she is placing limitations on the commitment made to the group or individual problem resolution.

- *The know-it-all.* The "know-it-all" exhibits the belief that he or she knows and has experienced more than the other group members or the facilitator. Other members (and maybe even the group leader) can perceive this person as condescending and elitist. Should you encounter a know-it-all in your group, consider the origins of such behaviors before you respond negatively. Might this individual be (over)compensating for feelings of inadequacy or staving off intimacy or exhibiting anger that he or she has to be involved in this group? Whatever the source of the know-it-all's feelings, you can allow the behaviors to be a detriment to the group's functioning (other members are likely to feel anger, intimidation, and, ultimately, disgust for the know-it-all), or you can use the group process to break down the know-it-all's interaction style. If the know-it-all's behavior is directed at educating you, monitor your feelings, and react professionally.

- *The monopolizer.* The "monopolizer" dominates the group's conversation and probably does not listen well to others (6). The monopolizer's behavior is often the result of efforts to avoid feelings, problems, or concerns, and should be addressed directly by the group leader or the group.

- *The scapegoat.* The target for the frustrations and anger of another group member(s), the "scapegoat" role can serve a function for the group (6) by enabling group members to vent and displace feelings. The scapegoat role can engender sympathy or antipathy from the group leader and other members, but the worker must confront the scapegoat and the group about the necessity for this role within the group. Once exposed, the scapegoat and the group may be able to dispense with the need for such a function as they can discuss issues more openly (6).

- *The enmesher.* The "enmesher" role can manifest itself in at least two different ways. One type of enmesher is the group member who seems to be involved in every facet of the group's experience (i.e., the "busybody"). A second type of enmesher is the member who develops an unusually close relationship with one or more other group members. In either instance, the enmesher can impact the group's functioning in an unhealthy manner. The origins of the enmeshment may stem from a need for closeness, acceptance, or intimacy. As in several of the other difficult situations, the group leader will need to address the enmesher's behavior, preferably within the group, but possibly, depending on the circumstances, outside the group setting.
- *The defender.* Group members can feel defensive for a variety of reasons. The "defender" may have been mandated or coerced into the group or may be unable to admit to having the problem/issue for which he or she is seeking help (6). The group leader can intervene with the defender by first acknowledging that defensiveness serves a purpose for that individual client and then defusing the need for continued defensiveness through supportiveness and offering alternative behaviors (6).

Although these descriptions may be useful and interesting ways to categorize group members, you are cautioned against stereotyping through either your use of labels or your responses. These behaviors can be identified as deviations from the group norm, but you should recognize that any and all behaviors can fulfill a function for the group. The behaviors and types described here should be addressed promptly and fairly by the group leader and potentially the membership, but each member deserves to be viewed as an individual who has joined this group in an effort to resolve a problem and improve the quality of his or her life.

Unique Mezzo Practice Challenges

Corina has been given the opportunity to cofacilitate a daily teen group at the detention center. During one group meeting, the issue of sexual abuse is raised by a group member. As the discussion unfolds, Corina becomes aware of the fact that the group includes both victims and perpetrators of sexual abuse. The discussion soon becomes extremely heated and emotional, and the session ends explosively with the teens being forcibly returned to their rooms. Anticipating the next day's group meeting, Corina has the following questions: (1) How does she address the previous day's exchanges—does she ignore the incident or encourage the members who are sexual abuse survivors to "confront" the members who have perpetrated sexual abuse? (2) Should the group be disbanded and reformed, ensuring that survivors and perpetrators are not assigned to the same group? (3) Should the group be broken into smaller, mixed groups? or (4) Should she ask the group members what they think should occur?

As a result of the meshing of people, issues, and group process, group work presents a variety of challenges that do not occur at other levels of social work practice. Corina's situation represents several challenges that commonly arise in the application of group interventions. First is the issue of group membership (recruitment and ongoing membership). Second, group dynamics can be a powerful force for the individuals in the group. These group practice issues will now be discussed. This discussion is intended not to replicate your previous study of group interventions but to translate the knowledge gained through your practice theory/methods coursework into actual practice skills.

Of importance when considering group dynamics is the fact that groups actually include two clients—the individual and the group. The social work role in this arena is to mediate individual–group interactions and guide the group members to relate to and support one another (6). The potential for conflict exists as a result of the need for the worker to maintain this dual focus (14). Ethical guidelines for group work are limited and provide minimal guidance for situations in which the individual's rights and needs are counter to those of the group (14). The worker's role in this situation is specific to mezzo-level social work practice and presents opportunities for skill development and intervention unmatched in other areas of social work practice.

Once you have been invited or assigned to a group or received approval to develop a group, you must begin the process of operationalizing your plans. The following discussion highlights four common issues in group development that you can anticipate as you consider your group responsibilities and raises questions that you may encounter. These issues are marketing and recruitment of group members, group membership/structure, "process" versus "content," and group dynamics. For an in-depth retrospective on these issues, we suggest you review your practice theory text(s).

Marketing and Recruitment of Group Members.   Critical to the marketing and recruitment activities of voluntary group development (regardless of the type of group) is determining that the group will meet the needs of the individual (6). Timing, location, group composition, purpose, and commitment required by the group member are all factors to consider as you promote a group and enlist participants. Questions that potential group members will raise may include the following:

- Is the group being offered in a timely manner for my particular need? For instance, will a grief support group be as helpful to me if my son died two years ago as it would be to me immediately following my loss?
- Is the location of the group convenient to my home and accessible?
- Will the other members have issues, problems, and needs similar to mine?
- Is the purpose of the group appropriate for my needs at this time? For instance, I need information about caring for my husband, who is newly diagnosed with Alzheimer's disease. Will a caregiver support group be a means of obtaining information on physical care, research findings, and available treatments?
- What is the extent of the commitment that I will be required to make to join this group? Can I attend as I feel the need, or am I expected to participate regularly?

- Will I have to stop my individual or family treatment if I join this group, and will my therapist be given information about my group participation?
- Will my insurance company pay for my group treatment?

Imagine that you are a potential group member. What additional questions emerge as you weigh the option of joining a group? What information do you need to help you determine whether group intervention is the best option for you?

Group Membership/Structure.   The majority of the knowledge and skill development in the area of group work focuses on understanding the issues of group membership and structure. If you are involved in the formation of a group during your practicum experience, you may have the opportunity to have input into determining the following:

- group purpose and goals—is the group aimed at providing support, treatment, or education?
- time limitations—will the group be open-ended (i.e., the members can attend as they desire for as long as they desire) or closed-ended (i.e., group members must commit to regular attendance for a specified period of time)?
- group membership—will the members join the group voluntarily, require a referral from a professional, require approval (if approval is required, who determines approval), or be mandated to attend by an authority?
- location—will the group be held at your agency, requiring clients to come to you for group activities, or is there a location more convenient for the majority of the members (e.g., school, workplace, or nursing home)?

Should you not have the opportunity to be involved in the formation of a group, you can still explore these issues by discussing such decisions with the person(s) responsible for making them. If the founder of the group is not available, you may wish to discuss group formation issues in your agency with your field instructor. If your field instructor is not engaged in group work, he or she may refer you to other staff who can share their experiences and insights related to group development.

"Process" versus "Content."   Related to clarifying your role as a mediator between the individual and the group is the issue of group orientation. Specifically, you are responsible for distinguishing between and balancing "content versus process" (9). *Content* is defined as the substance of the group's communication (e.g., substance abuse recovery, experiencing domestic violence, or interacting with parents), while *process* emphasizes the interactions and relationships that occur between group members (9). The purpose and goals of a group may determine that a group is solely content focused or process focused; however, in reality, most group experiences involve both content and process. Content can

occur when the group leader provides information or the members discuss issues specific to their reason for joining the group. Process-focused discussions may include members reacting to one another's statements or talking about group rules, norms, or behaviors. Combining content with process within a group intervention creates an environment in which the members can experiment with giving and receiving feedback, sharing sensitive information, and learning from one another in a safe setting (9). The fear that many new group leaders have is that process will overtake content and that they will lose credibility with the group. Monitoring the balance of process and content is key to an effective leadership style.

Group Dynamics. Developing group work skills may be considered to culminate in the actual implementation of a group intervention. You have considered the administrative and initial development aspects of the group intervention. Your efforts in this area now come together as we examine the dynamics of the group itself.

Groups typically evolve through phases of development. Ideally, a group's "life span" includes the initial, middle, and termination stages; however, depending on the purpose and structure of your group, these phases may be fluid, undistinguishable, and overlapping at times. The group's goals and needs will determine such facets of the group's makeup as longevity, personality, progress, process, and ground rules. While much of the group's development and transitions may depend on these issues as well as on the individuals who compose the group, there are a variety of basic group dynamics rules that may be helpful to consider.

- Establish mutually agreed-upon ground rules for the group that may include
  - group purpose and goals;
  - attendance;
  - boundaries;
  - sharing appropriate and sensitive information;
  - management of confrontations, conflicts, and rule violations;
  - confidentiality; and
  - leadership.
- Clarify the leader's role within the group, particularly as it concerns authority and intervening in group member disputes and problems.
- Ensure that you are culturally competent in your group work knowledge, skills, and values.

As you hone your group work skills, you can strive for competence in understanding factors that are a normal part of group process as well as those that promote effective group process (13). Moreover, knowledge of those issues that create conflict and deter group members' progress should be coupled with the ability to assess and intervene in troublesome areas (13).

Developing Appropriate Expectations of Yourself and Your Clients

How much involvement should you have in the group sessions that you facilitate? Greif and Ephross (15) suggest that a facilitator should occupy no more than 20 percent of the group's talking time. Although this is not a hard-and-fast rule, monitoring your participation in the group can serve as a mechanism for developing appropriate expectations of yourself as a group leader.

What is your responsibility if a group that you are facilitating

- does not "bond" or members do not relate well to one another?
- engages in unproductive interactions?
- includes disruptive members?
- experiences sporadic attendance by the membership?
- disbands entirely?

These are just several questions a new group leader should address with him- or herself. Just as you cannot accept credit for all your clients' successes, you cannot assume responsibility for what you may deem "nonsuccesses." As a group leader, you have an obligation to address your concerns with the group and to facilitate discussion about possible responses to these concerns. You are not responsible for the group members, individually or collectively, exercising their right to self-determination if they choose alternative courses of action.

Different expectations of yourself and your clients must be made if the group is composed of children. Because children, particularly young children, have fewer and less sophisticated social and communication skills, the group must be structured to accommodate "behavioral" communication (i.e., acting out and nonverbal communications) (16). Your expectations of yourself and your group members should be based on the children's developmental and chronological statuses.

Should any of the issues listed above occur in your group experience, you can identify your feelings about the issue, process those feelings with a colleague, and consider your response options. You can then frame the experience as a valuable learning exercise and move on.

Use of Self in Mezzo Practice

In micro-level social work practice, you and your client bring individual attitudes, beliefs, and life experiences to the relationship. In mezzo-level practice, you are presented with the challenge of incorporating into the group your own attitudes, beliefs, and life experiences along with those of *all* the group members. This can, at times, seem a daunting task for a group leader, regardless of his or her experience level. The group leader is responsible for maintaining a balanced and appropriate level of interpersonal disclosure and exposure.

Although the issues surrounding the worker's use of self are similar across all levels of social work practice, there are new and different concerns embedded within group practice. You are motivated to invest as much of yourself as possible into your role as a group leader; however, you are obligated to yourself to consider the impact of your group role on your own well-being. Issues that may arise that will affect your group-leader role include self-disclosure, boundary limitations, prior group experiences, and termination issues.

Many social workers find themselves facilitating groups based on a personal interest or experience, as in the case of Cameron, whose status as a recovering alcoholic led to his interest in substance abuse treatment. If you have personal experience or knowledge related to the group's purpose, you must consider the issue of self-disclosure. Is it appropriate to share with the group your personal experiences, and, if so, what is the purpose of sharing, when do you share, how much do you share, and how often do you relate group members' situations to your own? In determining the extent of self-disclosure, you must rely on your professional judgment, the professional judgment of others who have faced this decision, and insights about the individual group members. A rule of thumb is to consider self-disclosure only in those instances in which the group member(s) (versus you) will benefit.

Second, establishing and maintaining appropriate boundaries between you and the members of the group can be a difficult task. Group leaders may "over-succeed" in building rapport and group cohesion if the group members and the leader begin to perceive the group leader as a *member* of the group. Although an effective group leader strives for openness and expressiveness in his or her inter-actions with the group, he or she must also endeavor to demonstrate discipline, focus, and leadership (15). By clearly assuming the role of the professional, you will be better able to avoid exploitation and inappropriate interactions while pre-serving credibility and integrity with the group members.

Last, group leaders, particularly when they are practicum students, often find that they must leave their groups prior to the official or natural termination of the groups' work. On occasion, practicum students feel such a strong commitment to their groups that they continue as group leaders on a voluntary basis. Continu-ing with the group is a positive action in most cases for both the clients and the stu-dent. However, "nontermination" may mask the student's investment of self in the group and enable the student to avoid confronting his or her feelings about the group. Effectively facilitating a termination may provide you with an opportunity to reflect on your own feelings about and involvement with the group and serve as a positive model for the group members regarding appropriate endings. What do you think?

A helpful strategy for maintaining an appropriate use of self within the group experience may be to ensure that you spend adequate time in thoroughly process-ing or debriefing following each group session. If you have a cofacilitator, you can easily share individual observations and reactions. If you are a sole facilitator, you may choose to use audio/videotapes, process recordings, or your supervisory ses-sions as a method for gaining insight into your group experience.

In sum, the skills you gain in facilitation of client-focused groups have impli-cations for your social work professional development in other areas. Grasping the intricacies of establishing and facilitating a client group can aid you as you move into facilitation of nonclient groups. As you anticipate your role as the facilitator for a committee, task force, board of directors, or consortium/coalition, you will find that the knowledge and skills highlighted here also apply to this new area of work. But although the knowledge and skills required for the facilitation of client and nonclient groups overlap, leading nonclient groups does necessitate specialized attention and will be the focus of the following section.

Working with Nonclient Groups

Cameron's field instructor is the chair of an interdisciplinary agency committee. The field instructor has asked Cameron to chair a committee meeting because he will be absent due to another obligation. Cameron feels honored that his field instructor has entrusted this important committee responsibility to him. A new committee member, a female psychiatrist, joins the group at this meeting and dominates the meeting. Cameron perceives that she has her own agenda (one that is not consistent with the group mission or purpose). During the meeting, the psychiatrist interrupts other members, is verbally aggressive, and attempts to force decisions to be made that conflict with the views of other members. Cameron, mindful of his position as a student and substitute chair, does not know if he should confront her in the meeting or privately, ignore her, or attempt to gently redirect. The other committee members do not acknowledge or confront her behavior during the meeting and appear uncomfortable. What should he do?

Just as serving as the leader of a client group can be a powerful, gratifying, and challenging experience, so too can facilitating a nonclient group. Cameron is experiencing the powerful impact of one member's behavior on the group, the gratification of the leadership role, and the challenges presented by being a leader and having to contend with a difficult group member.

Nonclient group interventions take on a variety of forms, serve a myriad of purposes, and entail the use of a diverse range of micro- and mezzo-level social work practice skills. Groups charged with the mission of developing and implementing policy, making program and client decisions, ensuring quality of service delivery, or promoting intra- or interagency networking have historically been the recipients of less-than-positive reactions by human service professionals (17). "Work" groups (e.g., committees, task forces, boards, and advisory groups) are often viewed as arms of the administration that are ineffective, inefficient, political, and bureaucratically cumbersome (17). However, effective leadership of a work group can impact policy and program development, funding decisions, and client services. Gaining exposure to nonclient group dynamics, process, and leadership is therefore a valuable and necessary skill for you as a social worker. Regardless of your current or future career plans, you will inevitably find yourself a member, and possibly a leader, of such a group.

Just as gaining an understanding of the business and process of group work with clients is critical to your ability to be an effective leader, you need clarity and insight regarding the development and facilitation of work groups. Tropman, Johnson, and Tropman (17) offer the following guidelines for establishing and maintaining effective group process:

1. Understand the group purpose and goals.
2. Effective leadership is essential for success.
3. Group member selection/appointment should be based on the group's purpose.
4. Group members should generally support the other members and the leader.
5. Planning and preparation influence the outcomes produced by the group.
6. Group progress is related to preparation and follow-up.
7. Group member participation impacts the group's ability to function effectively.
8. Manipulation by group members or the leader is counterproductive.
9. Group members must feel that their participation is valued.
10. Group members must perceive evidence of group progress/productivity.
11. Communication among group members and other relevant persons or groups must be clear and appropriate.

Because work group skills are important, the remainder of this unit will focus on issues and skills relevant to your development as an effective leader of a group of this type. We will highlight group member and leader roles, techniques for group meeting facilitation, and management of difficult group dynamics.

Group Member and Leader Roles

Membership in a work group is determined through a variety of means. You may become a member of this type of group by appointment, election, or selection by a supervisor or constituency, or you may volunteer to serve as a member. Regardless of the route you take to join a group, you must be clear regarding individual member and leader roles and expectations. First, you must understand the expectations that your supervisor, agency, or group has of you in your role as a participant or leader of a work group—what are you expected to bring *back* to your primary group from the work group? Second, know also what the other group members expect of you—what are you expected to bring *to* the work group *from* your primary group?

Students completing their practica often have the opportunity to participate in nonclient groups in a variety of roles—observer, notetaker, group member, or cofacilitator/facilitator. They are often initiated by observing one or more group sessions. If you are asked to observe a group, orienting yourself to it by talking with your field instructor or other group members beforehand can provide insight into its culture and rules for group participants and observers. Specifically, is there a rule for you as an observer about where you can sit and is it acceptable or expected for you to participate by asking questions and offering input?

You may also be invited to take meeting minutes or notes and to provide a summary of the session activities. You may wish to review copies of minutes, notes, or summaries that have been completed previously to determine the style, content, and format used. Students sometimes believe that assuming this "secretarial" function is not a valid or meaningful learning experience for a new social work professional. On the contrary, taking minutes and compiling a summary of a meeting is an excellent method for observing, absorbing, and analyzing group interactions and process. Documenting meeting activities also requires you to develop and hone your professional writing skills in yet another area necessary for your future practice.

If you become a group member, you may be responsible for preparing for the meeting, participating appropriately in the group process (including volunteering for special projects or agreeing to serve when asked), representing your primary group in a professional manner, and providing adequate input and feedback (17).

Finally, if you have the opportunity to cofacilitate or facilitate a work group during your practicum, your role requires particular clarification. The leadership role may involve establishing the group's purpose, planning the agenda, coordinating the group's activities, mediating conflicts, and representing the group in other situations (17). Groups involved in developing and implementing policy may impose more formality and structure on the group leader role than do groups engaged in networking, event/program planning, or educational activities.

If you are involved in a work group from its inception, you have the opportunity to define your own participation and role within the group. In most cases, however, students are asked to join existing groups, represent staff members at meetings, or assume vacant positions for the duration of their practica. In these situations, you can prepare for your role by:

1. requesting to observe the group before you become a member;
2. observing the group's rules and roles—does the group follow parliamentary procedure (see Box 7.1), and, if so, are you familiar with this procedure?
3. interviewing current or former members regarding their experiences with the group; and
4. reviewing any documentation that pertains to the group's mission, goals, and previous accomplishments.

Techniques for Group Meeting Facilitation

You will find that the skills used for facilitation of client groups and for nonclient groups overlap. However, effective work-group facilitation can require more attention paid to preparation and detail and management of time and dynamics. The following list of techniques, compiled from the literature and our experiences, provides a helpful guide to ensuring a smooth and productive meeting (18):

- Identify appropriate group membership and ensure that you know the identity, title, and role of each member.
- Select an appropriate and acceptable meeting setting, time, and room arrangement.

BOX **7.1**

Parliamentary Procedure: What? Why? How? When?

Ben gets permission from his field instructor and the agency executive director to observe the monthly meeting of the agency's board of directors as part of the mezzo-level social work practice requirement of his learning agreement. Ben realizes almost immediately that the group meeting is facilitated using strict adherence to parliamentary procedures, with which he is unfamiliar. He finds the style of meeting facilitation using parliamentary procedure difficult to follow. He realizes that he must seek out references and resources in order to familiarize himself with it. Here are some tips that might have proved helpful to Ben.

What Is Parliamentary Procedure?

Robert's Rules of Order (19), also referred to as parliamentary procedure, establish in considerable detail a democratic (majority rules) mechanism whereby formal groups can engage in efficient and fair decision making. In general, parliamentary procedure includes:

- the use of *motions* to introduce a proposal,
- *seconds* to move a motion forward for a vote,
- *debate/discussion* to enable members to present differing perspectives and ask questions about a motion,
- *amendments* to reflect revisions to the original motions based on the debate/discussion, and
- *majority votes* (i.e., a minimum of 51 percent of members agreeing) to establish a motion as policy (18).

Why Do I Need to Know about Parliamentary Procedure?

Most formalized groups (e.g., boards of directors, committees, and policy-making bodies) subscribe to some semblance of parliamentary procedure. Many groups use portions of parliamentary procedure to maintain order within the group and enable actions to be taken expediently and consistently. They may embrace the "spirit" of the rules while not adhering religiously to each and every minute detail of them. Understanding the concepts of parliamentary procedure is a critical skill for a professional attending or facilitating a decision-making group.

How Do I Learn about and Use Parliamentary Procedure?

Consulting the definitive reference on parliamentary procedure, Robert's Rules of Order (19), is clearly the most thorough means of learning the subtleties of this process. However, given the variations in its use, you may want to consider several options for familiarizing yourself with the process. Reviewing other authors' interpretations of parliamentary procedure can be helpful. Observing as many meetings as you can in which the procedure is used can help you gain insight into the variations employed. Finally, discussing with your field instructor and other staff their experiences with parliamentary procedure can also help your learning.

When Do I Use Parliamentary Procedure?

If you join a committee, advisory group, or board that has been in existence prior to your entry, the group likely has a routine established for decision making. However, it is

(continued)

B O X **7.1** Continued

appropriate to raise questions regarding the rules for decision making: Does the group use parliamentary procedure in its literal form? If not, what liberties and deviations are acceptable? If you chair a newly founded group, you have the opportunity and responsibility to establish with the group the methods to be implemented to ensure the professional management of issues and decisions.

- ◆ The location should be noncontroversial, if possible, accessible, and an appropriate size for the number of participants expected.
- ◆ The meeting time should be as convenient as possible for all members.
- ◆ The room arrangement should be conducive to achieving group purpose— members sitting at a table is optimal for decision-making meetings, but members seated in rows of chairs may be appropriate for an informational meeting.
- Develop a clear, well-organized, and realistic agenda and give it to participants prior to the meeting. You may even want to determine an approximate timeframe for each item on the agenda.
- Have all materials, handouts, and audio/visual aids prepared and set up prior to the meeting.
- Establish the purpose and objectives of the group, in general, and of this meeting, in particular. The objectives should be concrete, realistic, and measurable.
- Begin the meeting on time and address
  - ◆ introductions;
  - ◆ announcements;
  - ◆ "housekeeping" (e.g., breaks, telephone locations, etc.);
  - ◆ role and outcome clarifications, as needed; and
  - ◆ the agenda, asking for additions or corrections.
- Establish the group rules, structure, and decision-making process.
- Ensure that the agenda is followed or amended by the group if necessary.
- Manage the group's time and discussion, being flexible in your approach.
- Periodically offer a summary of the status of discussions and decisions.
- Create an environment in which members feel comfortable participating to the degree to which they are required.
- End the meeting at the appointed time, and determine any tasks (with timeframe) to be completed outside the meeting, person(s) responsible for the outside assignments, and future meeting times, places, and agendas.

Management of Difficult Group Dynamics

As with any collaborative relationship, the work group is a compilation of different people, resources, and philosophies. Work groups create the potential for a higher quality outcome than that produced by an individual (17). Although the work group is a joining of forces and pooling of resources that can produce an outcome greater than that possible for an individual, the road to that outcome is sometimes full of potholes.

Group behaviors or events that present particular challenges for the work group leader are similar to those that plague client group leaders. Members who are disruptive, nonparticipants, consistently late or absent, or uncooperative are difficult regardless of the setting, type, or purpose of the group. In addition to these challenging behaviors, work group leaders are often faced with the need to manage and mediate conflict. Conflict is not necessarily bad: a calm meeting without disruption or conflict may seem productive when, in fact, the group's goals go unfulfilled because needs were not heard or met. When members are involved in a group as representatives of other groups, clients, or members of a professional constituency, they are often passionate and strong willed regarding their positions and goals for their group involvement; as a leader, you are required to maintain an atmosphere in which members can express their views, feel they have been heard by the other members, and leave the meeting/group experience with a sense of productivity. As a result, conflicts may emerge as a result of disagreement over interpersonal, resource, representational, or intercessional issues (18). These conflicts may be productive or unproductive. Strategies for managing productive conflict include the following (18):

- Anticipate and recognize potential conflicts.
- Attempt to reframe conflict as it relates to the group.
- Invite all members engaged in the conflict to share their views.
- Avoid "win–lose" outcomes.
- Encourage members to strive cooperatively for compromise and consensus.

An effective group leader will not take sides in a conflict, misuse his or her power as the group leader, avoid the conflict altogether, use covert means to resolve the conflict, or co-opt other members in an attempt to solve the problem (18). Have you found yourself in the role of an arbitrator of conflict? What strategies have been effective and ineffective for you?

Providing leadership for a work group is an essential component of your professional development. The NASW *Code of Ethics* (5) urges us, as social workers, to serve as leaders for our communities and our profession. In order for us to be effective advocates and representatives who can make strides for our clients and discipline, we must be able to function competently as leaders.

PRACTICE APPLICATION **7.5**

Facilitating Your Own Interdisciplinary Group Meeting

This practice application is designed to provide you with an experience in facilitating aninterdisciplinary team meeting. You and your fellow students will role play an interdisciplinary team meeting from the perspectives of multiple disciplines. To complete this application, you may use the interdisciplinary case in the Social Work from Many

(continued)

PRACTICE APPLICATION **7.5** Continued

Perspectives Practice Application 2.2 or you may create your own case. After you have identified a case that involves multiple disciplines, use the following guidelines to develop your experience:

- Develop a summary of the case situation and identify the disciplines of the players involved in the role-play.
- Identify the role and position regarding the case for each professional involved— provide a brief synopsis of each player's role and develop "scripts" for the players who will role play the team meeting (do not share the various players' parts with the other members involved in the role-play).
- Assign roles to each student.
- Role play the meeting—encourage each role player to stay in his or her character's discipline as much as possible. (You may assign the roles prior to the actual role-play to enable the players to research their disciplines' perspectives and possible positions on an issue).
- Video- or audiotape the role-played team meeting.
- Review the tape with the role players, and facilitate a discussion. You may want to address such issues as
  - group dynamics,
  - interdisciplinary issues,
  - the social work perspective, and
  - other issues that arose for individual group members.

PRACTICE APPLICATION **7.6**

Documenting Group Process: When the Obvious Isn't So Obvious

This practice application will help you further develop your group documentation skills. A group scenario will be presented. Using a documentation style/format/tool of your choice (e.g., your practicum agency's, the sample provided in this unit, or another tool), document your impressions of the described scenario in a journal entry and share them with your field instructor. Keep in mind the issues that have been raised in this unit regarding the confidentiality issues that surround documenting client/patient information in single and multiple client records.

The Scenario

You are a cofacilitator of a group of patients hospitalized in a psychiatric unit. Due to the short duration of the hospitalizations, group membership is fluid and changes frequently. Today's group includes the following members:

- Clarissa is a 27-year-old female hospitalized for a suicide attempt. She was severely depressed prior to her suicide attempt and has not responded well to medication and therapeutic interventions during the week she has been hospitalized. Clarissa's family initiated this hospitalization against her will.

- John is a 45-year-old male with a long-standing history of schizophrenia. John typically requires hospitalization when he does not comply with his medication regimen. Once he is regularly taking his medication, he is noncombative and does not experience delusions or hallucinations. John is responding well to treatment and is ready for discharge the following day.
- Jennifer is a 22-year-old female with a history of self-mutilating behaviors and anorexia. She rarely has periods in which she functions well enough to attend school or hold a job. She requires frequent hospitalizations and is considered by staff to be an extremely difficult patient because she does not respond well to treatment or relate appropriately to staff or the other patients.
- Jeffery is a 32-year-old male who was court-ordered into inpatient treatment for evaluation and treatment of his aggressive behavior. He has made numerous appearances in court for fighting with his girlfriend, family members, neighbors, and motorists who he perceives to have intentionally "cut him off." Staff report that Jeffery's aggressive behavior has continued during this hospitalization to the point that he has had to be physically restrained on several occasions.
- Gordon is a 36-year-old male, hospitalized for the first time, with a diagnosis of bipolar disorder. Gordon is currently in a manic phase and is extremely agitated most of the time. He attempts to dominate any conversation in which he participates and has incurred the wrath of his fellow group members during each group session.

Today's session begins with you asking the group to share any issues they would like to discuss. You turn to Clarissa, who is sitting next to you, and ask her to begin. Clarissa refuses to talk. She begins to cry when Jeffery makes fun of her for not talking. Jennifer attempts to come to Clarissa's aid, and Jeffery then turns his vengeance on Jennifer, demanding that she let the "crier" fend for herself (after all, what did a "kook" like her know about these issues?). John then begins to assault Jeffery verbally for picking on these "poor, helpless girls" and tells Jeffery that he does not understand what it is like to have "real problems." Jennifer begins to scream at both Jeffery and John, at which point Gordon launches into a speech about how you, the group leader, have allowed the group to get out of control. He demands to know what you are going to do to "get a handle on this bunch of loonies."

Your Turn
Document your impressions of the interactions that have occurred during this session. Prepare progress notes for both the group process and the individual client records.

PRACTICE APPLICATION 7.7
Need a Mezzo-Level Practicum Experience?
Start Your Own Group

In this practice application, you have the opportunity to consider the steps you would take to form your own group. Assume that as a component of your learning plan, you and your field instructor have agreed that, in order to gain mezzo-level practice experience, you will cofacilitate the agency's new parent education/support group. Your agency was concerned that workers spent too much time and resources individually teaching young parents basic parenting skills and supporting their efforts in the areas of parenting, nonabusive punishments, and consistency. The agency determined that a group effort

(continued)

PRACTICE APPLICATION **7.7**   **Continued**

would benefit clients and increase work efficiency. When you began your practicum, your field instructor informed you that the worker who originally intended to form this group has abruptly left the agency. Your field instructor suggested that you take this plan on and form and facilitate the group yourself.

Using your own agency context or creating a context appropriate to this scenario, develop a plan for forming such a group and share it with a member of your practicum team. Your strategy should include the following:

- developing eligibility criteria for group members
- marketing the group
- recruitment of group members
- arranging location and schedule
- obtaining needed supplies and resources
- developing group goals and objectives (including format, open versus closed group membership, frequency, timeframe, and length of group and other structural issues)
- planning the first session and beyond
- developing evaluation criteria

Summary

The group worker's a social worker too (sort of)
The group worker's a social worker too (guess so)
Why they use Scotch tape and adhesive
To make their groups cohesive. So I guess
The group worker's a social worker too.
—Excerpted from the chorus of "The Group Worker's
a Social Worker Too" (20)
Harvey Bertcher

The preceding lines describe the plight of the social worker interested in practicing mezzo-level social work. Fortunately, we have come to view mezzo-level social work practice as an integral and valuable part of the repertoire of generalist social work practitioners!

This unit has provided insights into the rewards and challenges that come with developing your mezzo-level social work practice skills. Proficiency in the implementation of group intervention is more important than at any point in social work history. In the direct practice arena, managed care's emphasis on individualized service delivery plans provides the opportunity for social workers to incorporate education, outreach, self-help, and advocacy—all of which require competency in group work (4). Critical to the nondirect service area are the emergence of (1) agency–community collaboratives and interdisciplinary service delivery teams and (2) the increasing role of social work in administrative, corporate, and nontraditional settings.

STUDENT SCENARIO POSTSCRIPTS

Despite the fact that **Corina's** initial inclination was either to avoid the issue or to disband the group, she consulted with her field instructor regarding strategies for responding to the incident. Together, they agreed that the issue could not be ignored and that Corina would open the next meeting with a brief summary of the previous day's events, establish guidelines for a discussion of the event, and ask about the group's thoughts about the future of the group. Having spent the evening processing the experience, Corina returned to the agency the next day and asked her field instructor to listen to her proposed presentation and to provide feedback from the teens' perspectives. This exercise bolstered Corina's confidence, and she was able to approach the group, regain her role as a leader, address (and learn from) an extremely difficult issue, and move the group forward.

Cameron opted to confront the psychiatrist calmly during the meeting, despite his concerns about the reactions of his field instructor and other staff, about his student role, and about the functioning of the committee. He believed very strongly that he had a right and responsibility to confront this person, regardless of her position and/or the potential implications for his practicum. Immediately following the meeting, the psychiatrist found Cameron's field instructor and demanded that he be removed from the agency. The field instructor tried to defuse the situation. The psychiatrist relented and agreed to participate in a three-way meeting with the field instructor and Cameron. The field instructor facilitated the meeting, during which Cameron and the psychiatrist agreed to work together in the future. At present, Cameron and the psychiatrist are civil and professional when they encounter each other in the agency, but they coexist with considerable discomfort.

REFERENCES

1. Barker, R. L. *The social work dictionary* (3rd ed.). Washington, DC: NASW Press. 1995.
2. Anderson, J. *Social work with groups. A process model.* New York: Longman. 1997. (p. 40).
3. Paulson, R. I. Swimming with the sharks or walking in the Garden of Eden: Two visions of managed care and mental health practice. In Raffoul, P. R. & McNeece, C. A. (eds.), *Future issues for social work practice*, pp. 85–96. Boston: Allyn and Bacon. 1996.
4. Gibelman, M. & Schervish, P. H. *Who we are. A second look.* Washington, DC: NASW Press. 1997.
5. National Association of Social Workers. *Code of ethics.* Washington, DC: NASW Press. 1996. (p. 6).
6. Shulman, L. *The skills of helping: Individuals, families and groups* (3rd ed.). Itasca, IL: F. E. Peacock. 1992.
7. Barker, R. L. *The social work dictionary.* Washington, DC: NASW Press. 1995. (p. 234).
8. Skidmore, R. A., Thackeray, M. G. & Farley, O. W. *Introduction to social work.* Boston: Allyn and Bacon. 1997.
9. Smead, R. *Skills and techniques for group work with children and adolescents.* Champaign, IL: Research Press. 1995.
10. Yalom, I. D. *The theory and practice of group psychotherapy* (2nd ed.). New York: Basic Books. 1985.
11. Dickson, D. T. *Confidentiality and privacy in social work.* New York: Free Press. 1998.
12. Sullivan, T. Personal communication, September 24, 1998.

13. Shulman, L. *The skills of helping. Individuals, families and groups* (2nd ed.). Itasca, IL: F. E. Peacock. 1984.

14. Dolgoff, R. & Skolnik, L. Ethical decision-making, the NASW Code of Ethics and group work practice: Beginning explorations. *Social Work with Groups.* 1992, *15*(4):99–112.

15. Greif, G. L. & Ephross, P. H. *Group work with populations at risk.* New York: Oxford University Press. 1997.

16. Tutty, L. M. & Wagar, J. The evolution of a group for young children who have witnessed family violence. *Social Work with Groups.* 1994, *17*(1/2):89–104.

17. Tropman, J. E., Johnson, H. R. & Tropman, E. J. *Committee management in human services. Running effective meetings, committees, and boards.* Chicago, IL: Nelson-Hall. 1992.

18. Kirst-Ashman, K. K. & Hull, G. H. *The macro skills workbook. A generalist approach.* Chicago, IL: Nelson-Hall. 1998.

19. Robert, H. M. *Robert's rules of order revised.* New York: William Morrow. 1970.

20. Bertcher, H. & Mitchell, B. *Sing a song of social work: A collection of songs, poems and stories.* Ann Arbor: University of Michigan School of Social Work. 1993.

8 Macro Social Work Practice in the Field

The good social worker doesn't go on mechanically helping people out of a ditch. Pretty soon, she begins to find out what ought to be done to get rid of the ditch.

—Mary Richmond

Although many social work practitioners focus on direct practice with individuals, families, and groups, the social work profession is also heavily involved in indirect practice at the macro level. Macro-level activities occur in organizational, community, and policy areas (1) and have the goal of benefiting large groups of clients or general society. Macro-level social work presents opportunities for practitioners to induce large-scale positive change in the lives of many clients through systemic solutions.

Given the growing complexity of client problems, becoming immersed in the practice issues that present themselves on the micro and mezzo levels is understandable. But this should not be an excuse for losing sight of the broader organizational, community, and policy issues that frame individual problems. The issues that individual clients present to social workers are often rooted in problems that affect large numbers of people in their communities. Some of these problems can, at least in part, be addressed at the micro and mezzo levels within social service agencies and neighborhoods (2), but others are best addressed at the social policy level.

Although most students focus their energies on micro and mezzo practice in their social work training, the Council on Social Work Education (CSWE) requires social work programs to provide students with the opportunity to "work toward the amelioration of environmental conditions that affect people adversely" during the undergraduate and graduate foundation practicum experience (3). By this point in your coursework, you have likely been exposed to considerable macro-level practice content. You now have the opportunity in the practicum to apply your knowledge and skills.

As you have learned, macro practice is a broad concept that covers a wide range of social work activities. Those social workers involved at the organizational level may have the job title of social planner, program developer, administrator or executive director, or organizational developer (4). Skills required for administration social work practice include (5):

- budgeting and financial management;
- working with boards;
- organizational design, development, assessment, and diagnosis;
- computer information systems;
- human resource management (selection, training/staff development, supervision, and compensation);
- management (including use of affirmative action principles);
- marketing management techniques;
- networking;
- financial resource development; and
- media relations.

Those social workers engaged in community social work may be called community developers, community organizers, social activists, or social researchers (4). Community practice skills include (5):

- program development, implementation, and evaluation;
- fundraising (grantwriting and other techniques),
- coalition formulation and maintenance;
- planned change techniques;
- macro-level advocacy;
- community analysis;
- interorganizational planning;
- leadership development and citizen participation;
- small-group decision-making techniques;
- community organizing;
- task-force membership;
- membership development and retention; and
- economic development techniques.

Finally, those involved at the social policy level may be called social policy analysts, lobbyists (4), or elected officials (6). Policy practice skills include (5):

- legislative (advocacy and lobbying skills);
- policy analysis and management;
- issue analysis techniques;

- social policy research; and
- legal (e.g., the ability to use the judicial system or draft legislation).

Although these skills are grouped under discrete headings here for illustrative purposes, the three areas of macro practice share a symbiotic relationship in practice; practitioners in one area often need skills here assigned to other areas. For example, community planners, organizers, and developers often work with boards and engage in lobbying; policy practitioners may engage in leadership development and citizen participation; and administrators of social service agencies are often involved in social policy development.

This unit will address the breadth of topics contained in macro practice, including student involvement in community planning, development, and organizing; administrative activities; and policy practice. Rather than review macro content that is covered in your practice courses, this unit will build on your knowledge of community, administrative, and policy practice to help you integrate theory and practice as well as discuss the procedural and process issues related to the integration of macro practice into your practicum.

Expectations for Student Learning in Macro Practice

Generalist practice requires a wide range of skills for helping individuals, groups, families, organizations, and communities. Therefore, in addition to micro and mezzo skills, social work practitioners must have both a clear understanding of the community and agency contexts for service delivery and the ability to intervene in order to deliver effective services. Unless you are in a practicum setting that focuses primarily on macro practice (i.e., is involved solely in administrative work, community organizing, community development, or policy practice), you will likely assume macro practice responsibilities only as you transition into the latter part of your practicum as you take on a greater quantity of and more complex work (7). Even if you consider yourself to be primarily a micro- or mezzo-level practitioner, you may find it necessary to engage in certain macro-level activities in order to meet your clients' needs effectively. Such activities may include:

1. giving a fundraising speech about your agency to a local church;
2. testifying before a local mental health funding board;
3. organizing an interagency group to develop needed services for homebound seniors;
4. working with a neighborhood group to rid the area of abandoned apartment buildings;
5. organizing a group of public housing tenants with the goal of persuading the local housing authorities to hire tenants to provide maintenance to the buildings;

6. presenting a budget to the board of directors of an agency for approval; or
7. lobbying a legislator to support a piece of social legislation.

Social work practitioners working in wide-ranging contexts must be prepared to use the various client system levels to address client needs. Micro and mezzo practice skills provide a solid foundation for and must be utilized in practice at the macro level (8). Just as you must know how to work with people as individuals to work effectively with them as a group, you must possess the ability to work with individuals and groups to work with people as members of organizations, communities, and policy-making entities (9). In your interaction with individuals, groups of clients, agency administrators, community residents, other community agencies, and politicians, you may use such micro skills as effective verbal and nonverbal behavior, warmth, empathy, genuineness, and other communication skills (such as rephrasing, reflective responding, and clarification) (2). Furthermore, the mezzo skills of networking, effectively functioning as a team member or leader, planning and conducting meetings, and group-conflict resolution are frequently utilized by macro practitioners (2, 9).

Which skills distinctive to macro practice are needed by social work students in practicum vary widely depending on the assignment and the agency context. Macro-level skills you may wish to consider learning in the field include community planning, community organizing, use of social action techniques, conducting a community needs assessment, policy analysis, coalition building, program development, lobbying, grantwriting, fundraising, public relations, staff and board of directors development and training, supervision, organizational policy development, and strategic planning (10).

The following sections will target two areas for your consideration: (1) the "business" of macro practice—administrative and task-related issues, and (2) the "process" of community, administrative, and policy practice—commonly encountered issues related to student implementation of macro assignments. Additionally, the impact of recent social policy changes on social work practice and the student role in practicum will be examined.

Learning the "Business" of Macro Practice

Although many social work practitioners engage in community practice, recent research shows that most social work practitioners define their primary practice as direct practice or define themselves as administrators, managers, planners, or program evaluators (6). Therefore, unless you are among the small percentage of students specializing in community organization, community development, social strategies, social justice, or political social work (11), your field instructor is probably a direct practitioner or an administrator. Direct practitioners are often involved, at least minimally, in some administrative-level responsibilities or may be involved in macro-level activities outside of work time. In many cases, students must be proactive if they wish to incorporate macro-learning activities into the practicum experience.

PRACTICE APPLICATION **8.1**

Gathering Information

If your agency-based field instructor engages primarily in micro- and mezzo-level service delivery, interview him or her about his or her involvement with macro-level activities. Among other questions, ask the following: With what administrative activities are you involved? With what macro-level (policy) advocacy efforts are you involved? Does the agency encourage or support these efforts? What involvement in both areas (administrative and policy advocacy) would you prefer? Do you see these type of activities as falling within your professional role within the agency? Or within your professional role outside the agency? Journal on your discussion and compare and contrast the roles of your agency-based field instructor with those of other students in practicum in your integrative practice field seminar.

Receiving a Macro Assignment

Thus far, Cameron is very pleased with his practicum experience in the substance abuse treatment center. However, he realizes that he would, at some point, like to assume some administrative duties in a social service agency. He was discouraged from pursuing this further at the interview with his field instructor, when he was told that the agency director has never worked with a student and was very "cautious" about delegating administrative responsibilities. He feels stymied and frustrated. What might he do to pursue this interest further?

Cameron is discovering institutional barriers that prevent him from becoming involved in social work within larger systems. Like Cameron, you will likely need to engage in negotiation and dialogue with your field instructor about your interests in and needs for macro practice, the types of skills you wish to develop at this point in your curriculum, and realistic possibilities for involvement in the agency. Even if your agency is eager to allow you to assume macro-practice responsibilities, planning and forethought are important to ensure that you have a meaningful and positive experience. Beyond your preference for an assignment and that of your field instructor, consider the following strategies for gaining macro-level experiences:

1. Work at the macro level in communities, in organizations, and with policy can have profound effects on the operation and the reputation of the agency. Therefore, permission from an administrator may be needed prior to launching into a macro assignment. The extent of your experience in macro practice may play a part in the assignment of activities. If you are inexperienced at macro practice (as many students are) and will need a significant additional amount of task guidance and supervision to engage in macro activities, you may find that you are offered only a modest number of choices. This may serve to conserve agency resources as well as to minimize risk to the agency.

2. You may find that your involvement in macro-level activities is highly dependent on forces outside the control of your field instructor or practicum site (e.g., lobbying may be possible only within a seasonal legislative session in your state, fundraising events may already be scheduled, or a community organizing opportunity may occur only after a "crisis").

3. Many students have a significant amount of time invested in direct practice activities and may be carrying caseloads. Your field instructor and others may be concerned that you will spread your time too thin by adding macro-level activities (12).

Despite these barriers, exposure to all three client-system levels is critical so that you can be prepared for social work practice at the conclusion of your studies. What options might you suggest to your field instructor? The following is a list of possible activities you can perform as a practicum student. Some of these activities may be possible within your practicum agency, while participation in others may entail the involvement of another agency. Involvement of another agency will require more coordination among you, your social work program, and those involved in the supervision of your practicum activities. Nevertheless, the rewards of experiencing macro practice firsthand will outweigh the extra effort that may be involved.

Administrative Practice.   Many MSW field instructors are involved in the administrative structures or procedures of their employing agencies in addition to having direct service responsibilities to clients. Therefore, you will likely find exposure through your field instructor to administrative practice to occur naturally throughout your practicum. However, taking an active, responsible role in administrative activities will offer you the greatest rewards relative to your learning goals. This may require you to make an explicit request of your field instructor. Consider requesting one or more of the following administrative tasks/responsibilities:

- assuming an active role with the board of directors (e.g., presenting a report, facilitating client representation on the board, or participating as a member of a board committee)
- preparing part or all of the agency's annual report (e.g., contributing to the preparation of the budget, developing a description of the program in which you are most heavily involved and interviewing clients to gain their perspective, or drafting the cover letter to be edited and signed by the executive director)
- working with a staff member to develop and gain approval for a new program for the agency (examples of program ideas: use of students as advocates during the grievance process for clients denied public assistance or disability benefits (13), use of students and volunteers for a summer low-income teen leadership camp or jobs programs, and use of students to train homebound seniors to participate in a peer-to-peer telephone support network)
- participating in advancing the technology/communications resources of the agency (e.g., researching and presenting information about needed computer hardware and software, participating in the creation of a Web page, or training staff in the use of a new software program)

- participating in staff recruitment and retention activities (e.g., participating in the selection of a new staff member, participating in the design and delivery of staff training on diversity issues, or supervising short-term volunteers for the agency)
- participating in media relations and marketing efforts (e.g., drafting a new brochure for a program of the agency that targets an underserved or needy population (14); drafting an op-ed piece focusing on a timely issue and, after approvals, submitting the piece to a local newspaper; or working with others to create a video about the agency to be used as a promotional piece (15))
- participating in agency networking efforts (e.g., attending a local Chamber of Commerce meeting as a representative of your agency, networking with local politicians at a legislative breakfast, or participating as a volunteer in a local United Way's allocations process)
- participating in the agency's resource development efforts (e.g., completing the literature search, needs assessment, project goals and objectives, and a portion of a grant proposal (16); researching new funding possibilities for a program; or serving as an active member of a committee planning a fundraising event for the agency)

Community Practice (Planning, Development, Organizing, and Social Action). Because a relatively small number of social work students specialize in the areas of community development, organizing, or social action (11), you may find incorporating learning experiences encompassing this area of macro practice more challenging than integrating administrative activities. Unless you are a specializing in these areas and have secured a practicum site with the goal of learning these skills, you may find that your field instructor has more difficulty offering a venue for you to observe, engage in, and receive resources needed to implement community planning, organizing, development, and social action skills. Opportunities to engage in community-practice activities in direct-service agencies may be very seasonal (i.e., prior to, during, or after the state legislative session), random (e.g., during an unexpected community crisis), or highly dependent on the orientation of the members of the board of directors or agency administrators (i.e., the board's or administration's philosophy regarding the importance of involvement in "political" activities on behalf of clients). Many community planners, organizers, and developers and those involved in social action are from disciplines other than social work. The goal of practice within these areas is to empower people affected by policy in order to effect change on a scale wider than a single agency can hope to do. In addition to the administrative activities listed above, the following activities can help you learn community practice skills:

- participating in coalition formulation and maintenance (e.g., taking responsibility for researching organizations that may be interested in working with a coalition on a particular issue, attending a coalition meeting as a representative of your practicum agency (17), or integrating technology [the Internet, databases, and fax machines] into coalition-building efforts (6))

- participating in planned change techniques and interorganizational planning (e.g., assisting in organizing community hearings to allow community input into a new employment project sponsored by local government, supporting efforts to arrange meetings of community professionals to solve problems around a communitywide public transportation issue, or working with government officials to plan a new summer employment and mentoring program for the county)
- engaging in macro-level advocacy efforts (e.g., organizing a large meeting of neighborhood residents and inviting local elected officials to the meeting to hold them accountable for their voting records on key issues in the last legislative session (17), participating in a demonstration, working with a group drafting legislation to provide case examples of discrimination in rural areas of the state against gay and lesbian clients (2), or lobbying a state legislator on a particular bill)
- participating in a community needs assessment/analysis (e.g., interviewing key members of the community using a structured interview to ascertain the most pressing community needs, engaging in community mapping, using a capacity inventory tool with individuals involved in your agency to ascertain the strengths and capacities inherent in local community members (18), or attending neighborhood public meetings to learn more about the issues most affecting the neighborhood)
- participating in leadership development and citizen participation (e.g., conducting a leadership training session on the legislative process with low-income residents emerging as community leaders, organizing a letter-writing campaign by neighborhood residents, assisting clients with voter registration efforts, or assisting in planning a conference (12))
- participating in community organizing (e.g., organizing and recruiting for a neighborhood meeting to discuss the problem of absentee landlords in the neighborhood; participating in the recruitment, training, and organizing of a group of low-income clients to testify at a county hearing on local spending priorities for federal funds; or inviting people to join in your organization's efforts to reform health care for the poor)
- participating in membership development and retention (e.g., engaging in door-to-door canvassing to recruit new members, gathering signatures for a petition drive at a central location in the community and recruiting new members, or planning a volunteer recognition event)
- engaging in economic development activities (e.g., working with low-income women to start a small business sewing infant baptismal dresses, recruiting low-income minority men to join in a worker-owned cleaning company, or providing technical assistance to teen parents in their development of a cottage industry)

Policy Practice. Social policy impacts and shapes the lives of clients. Social workers must advocate for clients within the policymaking process. Even though it may constitute a small portion of your time in practicum, seek avenues for incorporating policy practice into your field experience. Consider the following options for gaining policy practice experiences:

- participating in the legislative process (e.g., researching, preparing, and testifying in support of or in opposition to a bill during a public hearing; meeting with legislators individually to lobby for more funding for human services; or strategizing with a coalition of advocates regarding the defeat of a harmful welfare reform bill)
- participating in policy analysis and management (e.g., assisting others in providing an analysis [fiscal or human cost] of proposed legislation to a local legislator (6), assisting others in analyzing the impact on vulnerable populations of proposed regulations issued by a governmental entity, or writing an article for the agency newsletter relating the effects of new legislation on agency clients)
- participating in social policy research (e.g., participating in an evaluation of a new Medicaid outreach program and sending the results to decisionmakers (2), researching the development of government policy related to homelessness to assist in advocacy efforts, or assisting a professor in analyzing the impact of welfare reform on rural elderly caretakers of young children)
- participating in legal proceedings or issues relevant to policymaking (e.g., helping a social worker from your agency to prepare testimony as an expert witness for a legislative committee, providing testimony to a legislative committee, or communicating with an administrator of the county human service agency to request clarification on a policy negatively impacting your clients (6))

Orientation

After learning about the services your agency provides, your task is to orient yourself to the macro-level work (administrative, community practice, and policy practice) implemented by the agency. Second, you will need to be oriented to the resources needed to carry out a macro assignment. Many macro assignments entail large projects that can be time consuming. If you are considering a small project, you will likely find that you are able to work on the project at the same time that you carry out your direct practice responsibilities. You may find that your work with individuals, families, or groups provides you with an issue to approach or with case scenarios that you can (with permission) use in advocacy efforts. If, however, you would like to be involved in a large project, you may consider either (1) transferring most or all of your direct practice responsibilities to another staff member so that you can devote most of your time to the project or (2) negotiating a role within a large project under the direction of a staff member. Issues to consider concerning orientation to a macro-level project include:

- What level of access do you have to the resources needed to carry out this task (i.e., administrators or staff, financial resources, or information)?

- Do you have the permission, support, and guidance from the agency (administrators, board of directors, or staff) that you need to carry out this task?
- Does the task you are completing involve a significant risk (public relations, political, or otherwise) to the agency? Are you prepared for this risk?
- How much time and energy will the task take? Will you be able to carry out your direct practice activities and your new task effectively?
- Will other organizations with which you will be working take your role seriously and treat you as a professional?

PRACTICE APPLICATION **8.2**

Socialization into Macro Practice

Because many social work programs devote more time to direct practice skills than to indirect practice skills, many students feel unsure of their macro skills and experience anxiety contemplating a macro project. Discuss any anxieties and questions you may have with a member of your practicum team while you are arranging for task guidance to assist you throughout your macro-level work. Questions to consider include:

1. What knowledge and skills will I need for a macro assignment?
2. Do I feel that my social work program has prepared me with the knowledge and skills that I need to carry out this macro assignment?
3. What resources will I need from the agency and the social work program, and are they available?
4. What challenges do I anticipate as I engage in macro work?
5. How will I evaluate my work in this area?

Identifying Yourself as a Student

Your student status can be both a strength and a limitation in macro-level activities. As in micro- and mezzo-level activities, you can explain the limits of your experience in macro-level activities to others with whom you will be working and ask whether you can turn to them for assistance. Being forthright about your "rookie" status can allow you to question strategies, tactics, procedures, and assumptions within the framework of learning; you will not necessarily appear to be challenging the wisdom of experienced staff members. However, your student status may also limit the possibilities for tasks for which you may take responsibility. For example, you may wish to assume complete responsibility for a new marketing brochure but may be given permission only to draft certain sections.

Practice in Smaller Communities

Developing your community practice skills, particularly networking, is critical to becoming a competent generalist practitioner. However, if you are working in a nonurban or smaller community, you will likely find that these skills are of even greater importance. Smaller communities generally have fewer formal resources to which you can refer clients. As a result, many "services" are provided on an informal basis by family, friends, neighbors, or church members. As a social work professional (maybe the only social work professional in the community), you may find that you must learn about and use this informal network on a frequent basis. Moreover, you may find that you must creatively access, utilize, and develop resources to meet client needs.

In addition to understanding the dynamics of service provision in a rural setting, you must focus on developing your relationship with "key" people within the community. While knowing the elected officials, business owners, bankers, and health care providers in an urban area may enhance your ability to provide services, you will learn that such knowledge is absolutely essential in a smaller community. These groups can prove to be assets in your efforts to obtain funding, influence policy, access resources, and organize and deliver services.

PRACTICE APPLICATION **8.3**

Professional Socialization in a Smaller Community

If you are completing a practicum in a smaller community, this practice application will assist you in the process of socialization into the community, an essential aspect of macro practice.

Ask your field instructor to help you meet other human service professionals. Some possible avenues include (1) spending a few hours being introduced around the town or county, (2) attending interagency meetings, (3) participating in "Law Day" at the courthouse, (4) social lunches with professionals from other agencies/organizations/ churches, and (5) attending office openings or parties. To gain credibility as a professional, make certain to accompany another professional known by the community when being introduced.

Developed by Ellen Burkemper, Ph.D., LCSW

Role Transition

As in micro and mezzo practice, how long you will function in the observer/passive role in macro-level activities can be resolved through a negotiation with your field instructor or staff member. If you are completely inexperienced at macro-level activities, begin with identifying a small piece of a larger project for which you would like to take responsibility (see the examples earlier in the unit for ideas). Use available resources and your creativity to complete the small task to the best of your ability. You may find that, although you are not allowed to assume sole responsibility for a macro-level activity, you will be given increasing responsibility as you demonstrate increasing macro-level skills.

Confidentiality and Self-Determination

Client empowerment and involvement in macro-level activities are important elements of social work practice. An essential component of client empowerment is emphasizing the situational, environmental, political, and organizational solutions to problems in an effort to raise clients' consciousness about the limits of personal solutions and to avoid blaming the victim (6). Although encouraging clients to share their experiences with agency programs and social policies is essential to competent social work practice, equally important are the basic social work principles of confidentiality and self-determination. If you are sharing information about an individual client with other agencies or decisionmakers, you must be careful to protect his or her privacy. Unless you have received permission from the client to use identifying information outside the agency, share information only in the aggregate. Likewise, clients must never be pushed to be involved in macro-level activities inside or outside the agency. The choice to be involved must be a product of the client's free will.

Collaboration/Coalitions

Working with social work staff from other areas of the agency or staff from other disciplines, other agencies, or other sectors of society (such as public agencies, businesses, private agencies, and schools) can constitute a significant portion of macro practice, and dealing with other disciplines, perspectives, and philosophies can make reaching agreement on strategies and tactics for initiating change challenging. As noted in Unit 6, encountering different jargon, different professional socialization practices, and lack of clarity regarding roles and expertise can challenge even the most dedicated macro practitioner (19, 20). Although a diversity in the interests and backgrounds of coalition members can build strength and power (6), it can also mean that a group is together only by a fragile commitment to a single, narrow issue (21).

Facilitation of coalition or interagency meetings often requires a high level of facilitation skill. Because interdisciplinary work is central to community and policy practice and is growing in importance, try to be involved in a coalition or interdisciplinary effort if possible. Even if you are only able to observe meetings, note the facilitation style, how conflict is handled, and the methods by which consensus is built and agreements are made. Even an observation role will serve you well in the future.

Writing/Documentation Skills

Strong writing skills are as important at the macro level as at the micro and mezzo levels. CSWE requires social work programs to provide opportunities to students through the practicum to use professional oral and written communication skills of a standard consistent with those of the practicum agency and the social work profession (3). Effective writing skills are needed for such activities as grant-writing; preparation of budgets; agency annual reports; policy research, policy analysis, and developing flyers and action alerts; public relations materials (e.g., agency newsletters, press releases, press packets, and brochures); reports for the board of directors; program evaluation reports; minutes of meetings; policy position statements; and written testimony for public hearings.

Many of the rules regarding micro-level documentation presented in Unit 6 also hold true for macro practice. These include the use of accurate grammar and punctuation, focused writing, appropriate client information, and inclusion of only nonjudgmental and factual information. Macro-level writing often involves condensing and organizing a large amount of information into a useful, efficient, and easily readable document. If your project involves a written product, review previous editions or versions of similar documents. Additionally, you will need to know the completion dates for drafts of the document, the completion date for the final document, the editing process (who will need to review the document?), and the audience (who will receive or approve the final document?). Even if no review process by others is involved, ask that someone review and give critical feedback to you—you will gain a higher level of writing skills if you receive feedback.

In addition, documentation of unmet needs and needed services is an important task for advocacy for policy changes. Most agency documentation systems of direct service work with individual clients, groups, and families are designed to capture information needed for reimbursement, clinical interventions and progress, and administrative purposes (6). If the documentation system of your agency is designed to inject information into the political process, you may wish to take advantage of the opportunity to engage in this process. Ask to be involved in working with data to be used in the policymaking process. Another way to gain experience is to provide testimony at a legislative hearing. To increase the effectiveness and impact of your testimony, use the statistics, scenarios, and case illustrations that have emerged from documentation efforts.

The documentation efforts of other practitioners may also enable clients themselves to be involved in advocacy. Effective documentation can help identify clients who may be willing to share their stories for media or legislative testimony purposes. Personal stories from clients can make a dramatic and effective impact on the policymaking process, both at the administrative and legislative levels (6). It is important to note that clients often need preparation for legislative advocacy. They may benefit from rehearsing testimony and role playing the follow-up questioning process. This rehearsal can help prepare clients for the possibility of an intimidating atmosphere, questions about their personal lives, or an adversarial process.

Ongoing Evaluation

As you develop your plans for involvement in macro practice, identify points at which your work will be evaluated. Due to the lengthy process typically involved in these activities, using "benchmarks" to assess your growth and development is critical for your success in macro-level activities. For example, if you are writing an annual report for the agency, consider negotiating due dates for sections of the product so that you can receive feedback along the way. If you are working with a group of rural farmers to fight development of condominiums in the area, develop benchmarks in your plan to assess progress. Ask your field instructor to observe (either by audiotape, videotape, or live observation) your group facilitation or lobbying skills and provide feedback.

This discussion of the business of macro practice has touched several key issues commonly encountered in the process of assuming macro-level responsibilities. Once these decisions have been made and you are engaged in obtaining macro skills, the "process" of implementing macro activities raises new issues.

Learning the "Process" of Macro Practice

This discussion of the "process" of macro practice will focus on theory–practice integration, managing adverse relationships and conflicting goals, and developing reasonable expectations for completion and effectiveness of a macro practice assignment.

Theory–Practice Integration

Why should you be concerned with integrating theory with macro practice? Just as integrating theory with micro and mezzo practice is imperative for effective social

work practice (see Units 6 and 7), theory must provide the framework for social work macro practice.

As discussed earlier, macro practice entails the use of micro and mezzo practice skills; therefore, you should consider theories you have learned at both of these levels within your macro activities. Furthermore, if you have not already done so in your curriculum, you may wish to investigate community practice theories (1), management theories (4), and policy theories (6) and to discuss the theories that relate to your activities with your field instructor. In your discussions with your field instructor, consider the following questions:

1. How do the perspectives offered by the various theories in your area of macro practice help frame your work?
2. Does a particular theory help guide your work?
3. Does a combination of theories best explain the development of the organization, community, or policy with which you are working?

Managing Adverse Relationships and Conflicting Goals

Ben has been working on an assignment from his field instructor since the second week of the practicum and feels stuck. The community-based outreach program in which he works is located in a low-income community with poor-quality housing stock. A developer, with the support of the county government, wishes to purchase a significant amount of real estate in the area (displacing low-income residents in the process), rehabilitate the buildings, and sell them as owner-occupied buildings. Ben's field instructor, at the prompting of the agency administrator, has assigned him to organize a group of neighborhood residents to oppose the gentrification efforts. He is facing at least two problems: (1) the developer has a great deal of power and money and the support of the county, and Ben wonders whether he will be wasting his time fighting the development; and (2) Ben is unsure whether he is well suited to engaging in neighborhood advocacy that involves confrontation and politics. Should he ask to be released from the assignment?

Like Ben, you may experience issues that are unique to macro-level practice. You may doubt that advocacy efforts are worthwhile given your resources, the length of time you will be placed in the agency, and the influence of your opponents. You may also doubt whether you can assume the role of agitator. As a social worker, you are accustomed to seeing the various perspectives involved and working toward conflict resolution and unaccustomed to an adversarial role that may involve confrontation. The inertia, fear, and anxiety raised by these issues can be significant barriers to involvement in community practice.

Many professionals engaged in community practice have struggled with the issues of determining worthwhile efforts and doubts about their ability to engage in adversarial relationships. Social workers, however, have a professional responsibility to help "strengthen the community's capacities to solve problems through development of groups and organization, community education and community systems of governance and control over systems of social care" (22). As a social worker, you have a professional responsibility to work to strengthen the community's capacity to respond to injustices. The power of a group of concerned, organized citizens may surprise you. The right information, timing, and strategy (and a little luck!) may enable even a group of marginalized people to affect social policy (6). Additionally, you may wish to reframe relationships that you have characterized as adversarial. The U.S. governmental system was designed to "encourage and accommodate the expression of conflicting views, group conflict, negotiation, bargaining, and compromise" (6). Although conflict-resolution techniques and consensus building are important parts of social work, conflict is often the essential ingredient for social change (17). If conflict is difficult for you, you may wish to role play with and receive feedback from your field instructor on situations that involve expression of differences and tension. To learn about the important historical role conflict has played in social change efforts, you may also want to read about early unionizing efforts, the civil rights movement, the women's rights movement, and other social change efforts that used conflict techniques successfully.

PRACTICE APPLICATION **8.4**

Reflections on the Use of Conflict in Social Advocacy

Interview a social worker involved with social policy advocacy efforts about working with or promoting conflict and adversarial relationships. Among other questions, ask the following:

1. What type of techniques do you use to work toward social change?
2. Does conflict play a role in the efforts?
   a. If so, how? Do these efforts produce adversarial relationships? As a social worker, how do you come to terms with contributing to adversarial relationships? How "successful" have your efforts to promote social change been? How do you define "success"?
   b. If conflict does not play a role, why is conflict not an element of your efforts? How "successful" have your efforts been?

Discuss the results of your interview in a journal entry, and share them with a member of your practicum team or with other students in your integrative practice field seminar.

Developing Reasonable Expectations

Macro practice often entails long-term projects. Administrative tasks can be lengthy, policy practice activities can entail several months of work, and achieving community practice goals can take several years. What can you expect to achieve as a student? Setting realistic goals and objectives (achievable within a semester or two) is imperative to your sense of accomplishment and your learning. Unrealistic expectations can lead to frustration, a loss of self-confidence and perspective, as well as burn-out. As you are planning a macro-level activity, keep in mind that learning macro skills and perspectives is the primary goal. You may consider choosing several pieces of one large project if your macro-level interests lie in only one particular area. Another option is to select small portions of several projects in order to gain skills in different areas of macro practice. In the negotiation process, be clear about your interests in macro practice so that appropriate, reasonable goals and objectives can be established for your learning.

The Impact of Contemporary Social Policy on Social Work Practice and Practica

Managed care and welfare reform are two of the social policy issues currently affecting social work practice most. This section explains these issues and discusses the impact of managed care and welfare reform on social work practice and social work practica.

Managed Care

The onset of managed care in the private and public sectors has created turbulence in many sectors of society, including health care, mental health care, and the management of nonprofit and for-profit organizations. *Managed care* is a term used to describe the prepaid health sector in which care is provided under a fixed budget. It includes health maintenance organizations (HMOs), preferred provider organizations (PPOs), and forms of indemnity insurance coverage in which utilization controls are used to control costs (23). Although many social workers and other providers bemoan managed care because it represents bureaucratic control over service delivery, there is a growing consensus that managed care is here to stay (24). Managed care has a growing influence on the lives of clients as well as on the delivery of social services, and a wide diversity of opinions about managed care exists among social workers and other health providers. If you are unfamiliar with managed care terms, the guide found in Box 8.1 may be helpful.

Impact of Managed Care on Social Work Practice.   The impact of managed care on social work practice depends primarily on the type of agency, services provided to clients, and client populations. In addition to serving as mental health providers, social workers exist in a variety of roles within the framework of managed care, for instance, as case managers, executives, administrators, and utilization management staff (25). In general, social work has experienced increases in the following areas from managed care (26, 27, 28):

1. emphasis on short-term modalities of practice
2. application of technology to clinical practice

3. emphasis on documentation and evaluation of practice
4. use of less costly services
5. increased number of agency consolidations and mergers

The Advantages and Disadvantages of Managed Care.   One of the most positive effects to emerge from the advent of managed care is that mental health care

---

BOX **8.1**

Guide to Managed Care Terms

As social workers are increasingly influenced by managed care, you may encounter some of the following terms in your practice (23, 24):

Capitation—A monthly payment to a health care provider that is paid prior to service delivery. The provider agrees to provide certain services as needed for a certain length of time (usually a year) and to accept this flat fee, regardless of service usage.

Case management—The comprehensive management of a person's health care needs.

Employee assistance programs (EAPs)—Counseling and referral programs sponsored by employers that are designed to offer treatment of problems that affect workplace performance (such as chemical dependency and family issues). Employees may voluntarily consult an EAP manager or may be referred by their supervisors as a condition of their continued employment. EAP managers may offer assessment and intervention or may refer to a provider who offers specialized services.

Fee for service (FFS)—A system in which the provider of health care services is paid a fee for each service delivered.

Gatekeeper—The primary care physician whose responsibility it is to authorize all medical services and referrals for a patient in order for those services to be covered under the patient's managed care plan.

Health maintenance organizations (HMOs)—Corporations that offer health insurance and medical care. Patients in these systems can receive reimbursable care only from providers employed by the HMO organization. This model uses the capitation model, in which there is a fixed, prepaid price for health care services.

Preferred provider organizations (PPOs)—A system in which providers are included in a panel or network of "preferred providers" and provide services to patients in their own offices. Under this system, a patient may receive varying benefits depending on the provider the patient chooses. If a patient chooses to see a provider outside the preferred provider network, the patient assumes a higher cost for the services of the provider.

Utilization review—A process whereby the provider typically must provide written documentation of the need for and progress of care to a utilization reviewer employed by a managed care company. To be eligible for reimbursement, services and products provided to the patient must be authorized by the reviewer.

is now accessible to a larger number of people. Clients who may not have sought care from an independent practitioner are using their managed care benefits for short-term services (25). The disadvantages of the system are numerous. Social workers complain of increased paperwork, decreased professional autonomy, inappropriate use of short-term modalities of treatment, loss of confidentiality of client records, inappropriate interference in the therapeutic process, and problems involving ethical issues (25, 26).

Impact of Managed Care on Practicum Experiences.   The impact of managed care on the practicum experience can vary widely. Social work field offices are reporting a modest number of permanently lost placements due to managed care, creating a hardship for field offices attempting to place social work students for practicum (29). Those programs that place students in managed care organizations report that their students are not receiving support for their learning because supervisors are required to bill for all of their time and student hours are not reimbursable in most health care plans (29). Furthermore, while some organizations have opened new opportunities for students as a result of managed care (for example, utilization review and authorization of services), others have eliminated some learning experiences for students (by not allowing students to carry their own caseloads, restricting group work, and providing few opportunities for community work) (29). Changes in organizations due to managed care are a frequent occurrence, as many agencies have merged with or been purchased by other agencies, necessitating a change in the service delivery structure. In this process, programs and services may be eliminated or changed. If the effects of managed care have not been discussed in your supervision, take the opportunity to discuss this topic with your field instructor. The pace of change in managed care is rapid. You may find that the knowledge about managed care that you have gained in your coursework and any previous professional experiences is outdated very quickly. Even if your practicum site (or practicum activities) has not been directly involved or affected by managed care, you will benefit from a working knowledge of the topic as one that will continue to affect both social work practice with clients and the organizational context of practice.

Administrative Trends among Social Service Agencies

The organizational context for social work practice is also undergoing significant changes. The catalysts for change among nonprofit, for-profit, and public social service agencies include managed care and the trend toward privatization of social services. Privatization, or "the placing of public tasks in private hands" (30), involves the contracting of services formerly delivered by public agencies to outside agencies (nonprofit or for-profit). Some professionals anticipate that the role of public social services will evolve from service deliverer to administrator of services provided by outside agencies (31). Another trend of note is the increasing numbers of nonprofit agencies engaging in for-profit commercial activity. For many agencies, the development of for-profit businesses helps offset deficits that might otherwise result from their nonprofit activities (32). Although the for-profit sector of social services is still small (33), it is growing and presenting more competition for nonprofit organizations (30). Last, due to continued federal and state budget cuts for social services (34) and other factors leading to decreased revenue, many non-profit agencies are spending more resources on fundraising (35).

You may notice some evidence of these trends and their effects in your practicum. For example, your agency may be experiencing transition in the structure of the agency, resulting in increased or decreased opportunities for roles for students. You may notice staff members discussing increased workloads or that the organization is being operated more as a business than was previously experienced. In the face of budgetary constraints, some agencies may strongly encourage you to spend a significant portion of your time assisting with fundraising. In some public social service settings, services previously delivered by staff and students are now contracted out to private agencies or performed by volunteers. At times, the changes can be sudden (some students have even experienced the closing of their practicum agencies in the middle of their practica), while at other times, organizational change can occur slowly.

Welfare Reform

The federal government substantially restructured the public assistance programs (including cash assistance and food stamps) designed to assist those in poverty with the passage of the Personal Responsibility and Work Opportunity Reconciliation Act (PRWORA) of 1996. This legislation (amended in July 1997) dramatically altered the federal programs designed to provide income and food assistance to the poor as well as mandated cuts in assistance to certain populations (36). With this legislation, state and local governments now have increased control over welfare program design and resource distribution. Unfortunately, the majority of states have created welfare programs that will ultimately worsen the economic circumstances of the poor, and less than one third of all states have implemented state welfare policies that are likely to improve poor families' economic conditions (37). Although the long-term impacts of welfare reform remain to be seen, initial reports from around the country indicate that the numbers of clients receiving public cash assistance and food stamps are decreasing, poverty rates are increasing, and private social service organizations are experiencing an increase in the numbers of clients seeking assistance with basic needs (38, 39, 40, 41). Nonprofit social service agencies are concerned about the increase in numbers of clients seeking assistance with basic needs as well as whether the reimbursement rates offered by state agencies will cover the complete cost of providing services provided through a contract arrangement (36, 39).

The impact of welfare reform on social work practice is most readily seen in those agencies that serve a significant number of clients who receive or are eligible for public assistance programs. Whether you are completing your practicum in a public, nonprofit, or for-profit organization, you may observe larger numbers of your clients requesting more assistance with basic needs as a result of these changes. Even if your primary role with clients is something other than a resource to assist with basic needs, you may find that concerns with food, shelter, health care, and other related needs increasingly must be addressed prior to the exploration of other issues. Because decisionmaking has been decentralized to states and local communities, the national and local long-term impacts of welfare reform remain to be seen, and further research is needed.

PRACTICE APPLICATION **8.5**

Community Analysis through Observation

This practice application will provide a structure by which you will become familiar with the neighborhood in which your practicum site is located. Information gathered may provide insights into the issues most affecting neighborhood residents and the resources available in the community.

Walk through or sit/stand on a corner in the community in which your practicum site is located. Then drive slowly through the community. Record your answers to the following questions in a journal entry.

Community Geographic Information
1. What are the main geographical boundaries and natural barriers?
2. Is the community geographically isolated or does it border other communities?

Economic Characteristics
1. Do you see evidence of unemployed community residents?
2. What types of commercial enterprises exist in the community?
3. What type of transportation is available locally? Is it public or private? How available is public transportation?
4. What types of employment do community residents have? Is the employment mainly blue- or white-collar?
5. Do you see evidence of an "underground" economy (i.e., illegal economic activities)?

Social Characteristics
1. How would you describe community residents in terms of age, gender, ethnicity, race, family composition, sexual orientation, and social class?
2. How do community residents react to you (e.g., hostile, friendly, indifferent, curious)?
3. Does the community contain places of worship?
4. Do "public" meeting places exist in the community (e.g., meeting halls, clubs, coffee shops, bakeries, and associations)?
5. Does the community contain any parks and recreational areas/buildings? What type? What are the conditions of the recreational facilities?
6. How would you describe the housing stock? Is the stock mainly rental or family-owned? How would you describe the upkeep of the stock?
7. Is there housing for sale? Is the for-sale housing dispersed through the community or clustered?
8. Are there distinct social subcommunities within the larger community?

P R A C T I C E   A P P L I C A T I O N   **8.5**   Continued

Political Characteristics

1. Are there any signs of political activity/activism (e.g., yard signs, bumper stickers, political offices, and political meetings)?
2. What are the conditions of the roads and sidewalks? Is garbage collected regularly?

In a discussion with a member of your practicum team or in integrative practice field seminar, reflect on the information you have gathered. Additionally, discuss the following reflection questions:

1. What appear to be the most pressing needs of the community?
2. What appear to be the resources that exist in the community to address the needs?
3. How responsive do public officials appear to be to meeting the needs of the community?

Developed by Melford Ferguson, MSW, adapted from Sherraden, M. S. Community studies in the baccalaureate social work curriculum. *Journal of Teaching in Social Work.* 1993, 7(1):75–88.

P R A C T I C E   A P P L I C A T I O N   **8.6**

Community Analysis through Illustration

The completion of this practice application will provide a graphic representation of the relationships between the community in which your practicum site serves and outside entities.

Create an eco-map of the community in which your practicum site is located or serves and include the following:

1. all entities external to the community with which the community (as a whole) interfaces (e.g., governmental entities, other communities, social service agencies, businesses, and community institutions and organizations)
2. a graphic description of the relationship between the community and outside entities using different types of connections (e.g., broken lines, thin lines, thick lines, and curving lines)
3. a legend/key that explains the types of connections

Explain and discuss your eco-map with a member of your practicum team or in integrative practice field seminar.

P R A C T I C E   A P P L I C A T I O N   **8.7**

A Macro Approach to the Educational Needs of Homeless Children

Imagine that you are a social work student in a homeless shelter. When children come to the shelter, many must change schools and many miss a number of days before they are enrolled again in school. You have been directed to work with a group trying to draft state legislation to remedy the situation. The group will also try to find a sponsor of the legislation and will work to pass the bill. Answer the following questions in a journal entry and share your answers with a member of your practicum team.

1. What might be some solutions to the problem?
2. How would you begin to work on this issue within your practicum site?
3. What people or groups would you identify as important to this effort?
4. How might you go about engaging important people or groups in this effort?
5. What kinds of activities might be needed to pass this legislation?

Developed by Marian Hartung, LCSW

PRACTICE APPLICATION **8.8**
Role-Play: Social Advocacy

Choose a pressing social issue that you have encountered in your practicum. With a group of students, role-play a macro approach to the issue in integrative practice field seminar. Options include: (1) holding a press conference; (2) testifying before a legislative or funding body; (3) conducting a demonstration with picketing, songs, and slogans; (4) carrying out an act of civil disobedience; (5) holding a sit-in; and (6) staging a rally and leafleting.

PRACTICE APPLICATION **8.9**
Contact with an Influential Person

Identify an issue (political, social, policy, or legal) that is relevant for your practicum work. Identify a key player that has affected/could affect your issue. Contact this person/body through a letter, phone call, or personal visit. State your position (reasons you are concerned, who is affected, and how and what can be done to rectify/improve this situation). Be sure to recognize other perspectives on the issue and other possible means of addressing the problem. Ask the person to follow up with you regarding the action you are requesting (e.g., (co)sponsoring legislation, contacting other influential persons, or introducing an amendment to legislation) to let you know whether he or she will comply with your request. Provide documentation of your key points (e.g., a copy of a letter or a fact sheet) to a member of your practicum team and discuss your contact.

Summary

This unit discussed both the "business" and "process" of macro practice in practicum. Issues such as expectations for student learning in macro practice, receiving a macro assignment, identifying yourself as a student, role transition, confidentiality and self-determination, collaboration and coalition, writing and documentation skills, and ongoing evaluation were explored. Examples of administrative, community organizing and development, and policy practice activities students may engage in were provided. Furthermore, theory–practice integration, managing adverse relationships and conflicting goals, and developing reasonable expectations were "process"-oriented issues discussed in this unit. Last, the impact of managed care, administrative trends among social service agencies, and welfare reform on social work practice and student learning in practicum were explicated.

STUDENT SCENARIO POSTSCRIPTS

After further discussion with his field instructor about his frustrated attempts to gain some administrative responsibilities as part of his practicum, **Cameron** asked the field instructor about her administrative duties within the agency. She discussed her grantwriting, administrative reports, and coalition meetings. They agreed that Cameron will take responsibility for many of her administrative duties under close supervision and that she will sign off on all the work.

Ben, after much thought regarding his discomfort with a macro assignment that entails use of adversarial relationships with a powerful housing developer and county officials, asked his field instructor to release him from the assignment. The field instructor denied his request, stating that this assignment will be an important learning experience. They discussed Ben's feelings of discomfort that arise with situations involving conflict. The field instructor discussed the importance of the effort to stop gentrification in the area as a contribution to the empowerment of the low-income residents of the neighborhood and as a mechanism for building community between low- and moderate-income residents. The field instructor agreed to work closely with Ben and to assist him in processing his feelings of discomfort along the way.

REFERENCES

1. Netting, F. E., Kettner, P. M. & McMurtry, S. L. *Social work macro practice* (2nd ed.). New York: Longman. 1998.

2. Kirst-Ashman, K. K. & Hull, G. H. *Generalist practice with organizations and communities.* Chicago: Nelson-Hall. 1997.

3. Council on Social Work Education. *Handbook of accreditation standards and procedures.* Alexandra, VA: Author. 1994. (p. 143).

4. Brueggemann, W. G. *The practice of macro social work.* Chicago: Nelson-Hall. 1996.

5. McNutt, J. G. The macro practice curriculum in graduate social work education: Results of a national study. *Administration in Social Work.* 1995, *19*(3):59–74.

6. Haynes, K. S. & Mickelson, J. S. *Affecting change.* New York: Longman. 1997.

7. Urbanowski, M. Z. & Dwyer, M. M. *Learning through field instruction: A guide for teachers and students.* Milwaukee: Family Service America. 1988.

8. Weil, M. Community organization curriculum development in services for families and children: Bridging the micro–macro practice gap. *Social Development Issues.* 1982, *6*(3):40–54.

9. Bakalinsky, R. The small group in community organization practice. *Social Work with Groups.* 1984, 7(2):87–96.

10. Lowe, J. I. The simulation of a neighborhood family service center for teaching macro practice. *Journal of Teaching in Social Work.* 1996, 13(1/2):27–41.

11. Haynes, K. S. The future of political social work. In P. R. Raffoul and C. A. McNeece (ed.), *Future issues for social work practice* (pp. 266–278). Boston: Allyn & Bacon. 1996.

12. Siu, S-F. Providing opportunities for macro practice in direct service agencies: One undergraduate program's experience. *Areté.* 1991, 16(2):46–51.

13. Lurie, A., Pinsky, S., Rock, B. & Tuzman, L. The training and supervision of social work students for effective advocacy practice: A macro system perspective. *The Clinical Supervisor.* 1989, 7 (2/3):149–158.

14. Yankey, J. A., Lutz, C. & Koury, M. Marketing welfare services. *Public Welfare.* 1986 (Winter):41–49.

15. Center for Community Change. *How to tell and sell your story: A guide to media for community groups and other nonprofits.* Issue 18. 1997.

16. Abel, E. M. & Kazmerski, K. J. Protecting the inclusion of macro content in generalist practice. *Journal of Community Practice.* 1994, 1(3):59–72.

17. Bobo, K. A., Kendall, J. & Max, S. *Organizing for social change* (2nd ed.). Santa Ana, CA: Seven Locks Press. 1991.

18. Kretzman, J. & McKnight, J. *Building communities from the inside out: A path toward finding and mobilizing a community's assets.* Chicago: ACTA. 1993.

19. Abramson, J. & Mizrahi, R. Strategies for enhancing collaboration between social workers and physicians. *Social Work in Health Care.* 1986, 12(1):1–21.

20. Gross, A. M. & Gross, J. Attitudes of physicians and nurses toward the role of social workers in primary health care: What promotes collaboration? *Family Practice.* 1987, 4(4):266–270.

21. Richan, W. C. *Lobbying for social change.* New York: Haworth Press. 1996.

22. Specht, H. & Courtney, M. *Unfaithful angels: How social work has abandoned its mission.* New York: Free Press. 1994. (p. 26).

23. Butler-Schmitt, B. NASW/CSWE team up for managed care project. *The New Social Worker.* 1997, 4(3):12–14.

24. Browning, C. H. & Browning, B. J. *How to partner with managed care.* New York: John Wiley & Sons, Inc. 1996.

25. Dorfman, R. A. *Clinical social work: Definition, practice and vision.* New York: Brunner/Mazel. 1996.

26. Munson, C. E. Autonomy and managed care in clinical social work practice. *Smith College Studies in Social Work.* 1996, 66(3):241–260.

27. Poole, D. L. Keeping managed care in balance. *Health and Social Work.* 1996, 21(3):163–166.

28. Jarman-Rohde, L., McFall, J., Kolar, P. & Strom, G. The changing context of social work practice: Implications and recommendations for social work educators. *Journal of Social Work Education.* 1997, 33(1):29–46.

29. Raskin, M. S. & Whiting Blome, W. The impact of managed care on field instruction. *Journal of Social Work Education.* 1998, 34(3):365–374.

30. Abramovitz, M. The privatization of the welfare state: A review. *Social Work.* 1986, 31:257–264.

31. Menefee, D. Strategic administration of nonprofit human service organizations: A model for executive success in turbulent times. *Administration in Social Work.* 1997, 21(2):1–20.

32. Espy, S. *Marketing strategies for nonprofit organizations.* Chicago: Lyceum Books. 1993.

33. Ortiz, E. T. (1987). For-profit social service and social work education: Rapid change and slow response. *Journal of Independent Social Work.* 1987, 2(1):19–32.

34. Homonoff, E. & Maltz, P. Fair exchange: Collaboration between social work schools and field agencies in an environment of scarcity. In G. Rogers (ed.), *Social work field education: Views and visions* (pp. 38–50). DuBuque, IA: Kendall/Hunt. 1995.

35. Manelli, M. & McClusky, J. *Managing nonprofits in the 90s.* St. Louis, MO: KWMU radio station. August 21, 1997.

36. The Federal Funding Impact Collaborative. *Devolving responsibility: Federal welfare reform and service delivery in the St. Louis region.* St. Louis, MO: Author. 1997. [c/o the United Way of Greater St. Louis, 1111 Olive Street, St. Louis, MO 63101-1951]

37. Center on Hunger and Poverty. *Are states improving the lives of poor families? A scale measure of state welfare policies.* Medford, MA: Tufts University. 1998.

38. Brogioli, M. Declining numbers. *Charities USA.* 1998, *25*(2):14–16.

39. Kettner, P. M. & Martin, L. L. The impact of declining resources and purchase of service contracting on private nonprofit agencies. *Administration in Social Work.* 1996, *21*(3):211–238.

40. Newsome, M. Preparing for a managed care environment. *Social Work Education Reporter.* 1996, *44*(3):1,16.

41. The Federal Funding Impact Collaborative. *The status of 122 nonprofit social service agencies in the St. Louis region: Government funding support and service delivery.* St. Louis, MO: Author. 1998. [c/o the United Way of Greater St. Louis, 1111 Olive Street, St. Louis, Missouri 631011-1951]

UNIT

9 Social Work Practice and the Legal System

The time is always right to do what is right.

—Martin Luther King, Jr.

The legal system affects many aspects of social work practice. Social workers in a wide variety of roles interface with laws and the professionals who uphold them through employment in the courts, judicial or justice-related entities, probation and parole services, and victim service offices and as counselors or therapists in correctional settings. Social workers in the areas of child welfare, domestic violence, crime victim counseling, adult protection, housing, and public policy also have frequent interactions with the justice system as advocates, petitioners, and defendants (1). Social workers whose primary focus is social policy must have an intimate knowledge of federal and state legislative, administrative, and regulatory processes. However, even social workers whose roles do not involve frequent contact with the legal-judicial or legislative systems need a basic understanding of both systems to enable them to participate in social policy development and to assist clients with issues that have legal considerations (1).

Even if you are not currently involved in any aspect of the legal system in your practicum, you should be aware of the legal issues of social work practice that impact clients and practitioners. Knowledge of the legal system will undoubtedly aid you in your work with clients in the future, and knowledge of the professional legal issues will enable you to practice ethically and within the boundaries of the law. Social workers must have a working knowledge of the legal system in order to: (1) communicate and work successfully with judges and attorneys; (2) recognize the rights afforded to clients by the law; and (3) recognize certain problems of their clients as essentially legal problems (2).

Legally related activities in which social workers may engage include (1, 3):

- testifying in court on behalf of a client;
- testifying in court on their own behalfs;
- providing expert testimony;

- participating in drafting legislation;
- advocating on behalf of or in opposition to legislation;
- drafting regulations in response to legislation;
- responding to draft regulations issued by a governmental body;
- acting as an agent of a court system (i.e., enforcing the policies and mandates of the court);
- providing mediation to resolve disputes as an alternative to litigation;
- petitioning the court on behalf of an agency in guardianship hearings; and
- helping clients participate in class action lawsuits.

Your social work courses may have provided you with knowledge of the legal-judicial community. The type of agency in which you are completing a practicum, the type of work in which you are engaged with clients, and your student role will determine your opportunities to observe and participate in the legal-judicial system.

Students in clinical settings (particularly agencies that have been sued) may have the opportunity to work with professionals who are keenly aware of legal issues that impact professional practice. Up to this point in your career, you may not have been exposed to the depth of the legal considerations required for social work practice. Knowledge of the legal issues listed below is especially important in settings that involve a high level of direct client contact (4, 5).

- professional liability and malpractice
- clients' rights to confidentiality and the prevention of inappropriate disclosure
- clients' end-of-life decisions
- limits of clients' rights to confidentiality
- privileged communication
- defamation of character
- consultation with or referral to specialists
- emergency assistance and suicide prevention
- supervision of clients in residential settings
- procedures for obtaining informed consent from clients
- guidelines for appropriately terminating treatment
- limitation on intimacy with clients
- interventions with acting-out clients
- duty to protect intended victims from a client's violent acts

This unit will focus on a range of topics (e.g., professional liability and malpractice, limits of clients' right to confidentiality, and several others) that merit further discussion as you obtain more responsibility for clients in your practicum. If you feel that you do not have adequate background on any of these topics, consider reviewing your practice theory texts or including several topics in supervision discussions with your field instructor.

The idea of involvement with the legal system can produce anxiety in some and exhilaration in others. Although the aim of this unit is not to heighten your concerns about the prospect of working with the legal system, any anxiety that is produced by this discussion is best channeled into efforts to maximize your professional social work skills. The legal system is a very complex, formal system having highly intricate rules and procedures. Effective social work practice involves learning about relevant aspects of the system, utilizing the legal system for the benefit of your clients, and delivering services in a manner that minimizes your malpractice liability (6). Although the formality of the system can be intimidating at first, many professionals find their comfort levels increasing dramatically with time. If you relish working with the legal system as a new, exciting possible aspect of your practicum, you may consider the idea of shaping your employment choices after graduation so that you have ready access to the legal-judicial system. Possible sites include legal aid, public defenders' office, correctional facility, or the state or federal court systems.

Legal Terms

Just as social work has a unique set of terms, the legal-judicial system possesses an extensive, unique set of terms (or jargon) that can be difficult to learn. Some legal-judicial terms that you may encounter include those defined below (2, 3, 7, 8, 9, 10, 11, 12, 13). When in doubt about the meaning of a term, ask for assistance from an attorney affiliated with your practicum agency.

Allegation—Assertion, claim, declaration, or statement of a party to an action setting out what the party expects to prove.

Arbitration—Private decision making by one or more individuals to develop a binding decision for disputing parties.

Civil offense—Noncriminal offenses punishable by restitution or payment of a fine (e.g., violations of state fish and game laws or product liability cases).

Court process—Two phases: (1) adjudication phase—facts presented and charge determined by a judge or a jury; and (2) disposition—determination of sentence.

Criminal violations—May be a felony or a misdemeanor.

Defendant—The party against whom relief or recovery is sought in an action or suit or the accused in a criminal case.

Emancipation—A client can become emancipated through parental permission, court order, or, depending on the state, by taking certain actions (such as marriage, childbirth, independent living, or enlisting in the armed forces).

Evidence—Proof legally presented at a trial through witnesses, records, documents, exhibits, or concrete objects to convince the court or a jury. There are two types: (1) direct evidence (such as testimony of an eyewitness); and (2) circumstantial (proof of a chain of circumstances pointing to the existence or nonexistence of certain facts).

Family court—A type of court system that has jurisdiction over the following proceedings: (1) child abuse and neglect; (2) support; (3) determination of paternity and support for children born out of wedlock; (4) termination of parental rights; (5) juvenile delinquency and whether a person is in need of supervision; (6) family offenses. The court may be a division or department of a general jurisdiction.

Felony—A crime considered serious enough to be punishable by imprisonment (e.g., murder, kidnapping, first degree sexual assault).

Guardian ad litem—Under the laws of many states, all children and any adult judged legally incompetent may have a guardian ad litem appointed to represent that person's "best interests" as determined by the guardian ad litem. For example, a guardian ad litem may recommend a finding of incompetence of an elderly man to a court. In some states, the guardian must be an attorney, while in other states, the guardian may be any member of the community in good standing (including a family member, a professional, or any other citizen). The guardian may question witnesses on the stand on behalf of the client.

Informed consent—Consent provided by the client for services. The process should involve: (1) determining client competence; (2) providing complete service information; (3) ensuring client understanding; and (4) documenting the informed consent.

Jurisdiction—Authority to act (may be based on offense, age, or location).

Juvenile justice system—A separate justice system having jurisdiction over children 18 years of age or younger involved in the legal system.

Liability insurance—Insurance that transfers financial risk from the provider, agency, or school to an insurance carrier.

Malpractice—Any professional misconduct or unreasonable lack of skill resulting in harm to a client.

Mediation—Participation of an impartial third party to resolve a dispute, plan a transaction, or assist in negotiations.

Misdemeanor—A less serious crime generally punishable by a fine or imprisonment (e.g., battery, negligent operation of a vehicle, or carrying a concealed weapon).

Plaintiff—A person who brings an action or sues in a civil action and is named on the record.

Privileged communication—Communications between a social worker and a client that may be kept out of legal proceedings.

Standards of proof—The burden of proof required in a particular kind of case; the level or degree of certainty needed to prove an allegation in court. Types: (1) beyond a reasonable doubt—applies in criminal or delinquency cases; (2) fair preponderance of the evidence—applies to most civil cases.

Witness—One who is called to testify in a court proceeding. Persons may be classified as lay (factual) or expert (rendered "qualified" by the judge to give opinions in a particular area of expertise).

Grievance Procedures and Legal Resources for Clients

Advocacy on behalf of or with clients as they encounter the legal system or work with grievance procedures can be a rewarding role for social workers. Whether you work with clients interfacing with the legal or judicial system on a regular or an infrequent basis—and whether a client is a victim or a witness—you can prepare a client for court in several ways. Preparation for court proceedings can make a client more comfortable throughout the process. Clients who encounter the legal or judicial system as victims or witnesses will often prepare their testimony with an attorney. Possible roles for social workers in the preparation process include (10):

- advising clients of the formality of the proceedings (i.e., dress, titles, and process) and adversarial nature of the process;
- preparing clients for the courtroom experience by defining terms, taking them to visit the courtroom prior to the proceedings to familiarize them with the arrangement and the role of participants, procedures, and other details;
- informing clients of their rights and helping them obtain their rights (e.g., the right to be notified of all charges against them, the right to legal counsel, the right to face accusers, the right to cross-examination of all witnesses, the privilege against self-incrimination, and the right to invoke privileged communication if helping professionals are called to testify in court about clients); and
- accompanying clients to court during trials as a support and an advocate.

Another advocacy role for social workers occurs when you support clients through grievance, review, or appeal processes. Verbal support and physically accompanying clients through such processes can make a significant difference in the outcomes for clients. Providing support, encouragement, advocacy, and resources for clients enables them to pursue and persist through often complex and burdensome processes. In your micro- and mezzo-level work with clients, consider exploring issues with the clients concerning public assistance or disability benefits, housing issues, and other resources. Are your clients experiencing difficulties receiving governmental or agency-administered benefits or other assistance to which they may be entitled? Your referral to legal resources or involvement as an advocate in grievance or appeal procedures can enhance the quality of life for your clients and their families.

Increasingly, social workers are utilizing negotiation, arbitration, and mediation for resolution of their professional conflicts and for disputes between clients and others. As an alternative to often costly litigation, social workers serve in the role of mediator, performing such activities as facilitation of decisionmaking, evaluation of, and assistance in defining problems, and provision of suggestions and solutions. Mediation is widely used in child custody and divorce disputes, adoption proceedings, and special education hearings (12).

As a practicum student, you can be a catalyst for identifying civil legal issues for clients and referring them to resources for pursuing legal remedies. Resources through which they might pursue legal remedies for problems include federal, state, and local regulatory bodies for various appeal, hearing, review, grievance, and complaint procedures; community legal services (e.g., Legal Aid and other sources); the American Civil Liberties Union; public interest law groups; special interest organizations (e.g., the National Organization for Women and gay and lesbian groups); legal clinics within law schools; and private attorneys who are willing to take pro bono (free) cases (1, 2, 14). Common civil legal issues for low-income, vulnerable populations—for which you might refer clients to one of the resources listed above—include tenant–landlord/housing issues, obtaining or maintaining public assistance (such as food stamps, Temporary Assistance to Needy Families (TANF), and Supplemental Security Income (SSI) benefits), and child welfare issues.

Clients accused of criminal offenses who cannot afford private attorneys should seek representation from a public defender's office; however, the public defender's office may represent only defendants in criminal cases in which incarceration is possible. Some public defenders' offices also represent clients in civil commitments, fathers in paternity actions, parents in juvenile court actions, and clients in other types of civil cases (2).

As a practicum student, you could also work with others to produce a legal resource guide for clients on a topic pertinent to your practicum setting (e.g., laws and grievance procedures regarding divorce and child custody, mental health issues, accessing public benefits, the rights of tenants in low-income housing, and the educational rights of homeless children). Working with attorneys and translating legal jargon to produce such a resource guide could prove to be an invaluable learning experience for you and serve as your legacy to the agency.

You may also help clients identify their issues as ones that also affect others—even as issues that may merit class action lawsuits against an agency or governmental entity. Among the wide variety of issues that bring individual clients to social service agencies, difficulty meeting the basic needs (i.e., food, housing, medical care, and clothing) of a family is a common issue and may be best remedied by a systemic response. If you find many clients experiencing similar issues, consider exploring a systemic response through the legal system by contacting one of the legal resources noted above. Class action lawsuits can be an effective tool for providing resources to a targeted population. For example, in an effort to force the city to finance shelter and services for its homeless citizens, social service delivery providers joined in an effort in the mid-1980s to file a class action suit against the city of St. Louis, Missouri. The impetus for the suit was the city's lack of responsiveness to the needs of its homeless citizens for shelter and services. The settlement of this lawsuit produced city-sponsored short-term and long-term services to homeless persons that continue today (15). Although legal action can be time consuming and produce results long after the immediate need was felt, the rewards of engaging in this type of action can be felt by a large population.

Professional and Student Malpractice Issues and Liability

Due to the increase in the number of lawsuits filed against social workers, increased attention is being given to social work practice liability issues (16). The increase in litigation is due, in part, to several contemporary factors: the increase in ease with which a client can sue public employees and agencies; an expansion of the legal duties of social workers (e.g., mandatory child abuse reporting in all 50 states); and the general trend toward increasing litigation societywide (16). Although the percentage of social workers sued is small (1 to 2 percent), the number of lawsuits filed is on the increase, and the social work profession is working to increase knowledge about the legal risks social workers face in practice (16). Issues that are most prevalent for social workers and practicum students include confidentiality and documentation.

Confidentiality

A hallmark of the social work profession, the importance of worker–client confidentiality, is an area in which students are usually well versed. However, in practicum, special circumstances may leave you questioning the appropriate course of action, particularly in the areas of criminal offenses, AIDS/HIV status, and providing services to minors and (legal and illegal) immigrants.

> *Corina's confidence in facilitating the evening group in the detention facility is growing. Heading into group tonight, she requested and received permission from her field instructor to facilitate without another staff member in the room. She thinks she has built rapport with the adolescents and wants to go it alone. However, during group, one of the members reveals that, during his most recent escape from the detention facility, he took a friend's car for a joy ride and totaled the car. He states that, because of the confidentiality of the group discussions, he knows that the group will not reveal his secret to anyone in "authority." Corina thinks that this information is probably true. She feels trapped. She wants to maintain the rapport with the group that she has worked so hard to build and is tempted not to reveal the information to anyone. On the other hand, she also knows that she may have a legal responsibility to make a report. She is speechless and wonders what to say. What would you say to the group? Should Corina break the confidentiality of the group?*

As Corina discovered, even with thorough knowledge of the basics of client confidentiality, practice can present some unique challenges. The following discussion will address some difficult issues around confidentiality.

What Should I Do If a Client Discloses a Prior Criminal Offense to Me?   The above situation poses an ethical dilemma for Corina. Although the social workers' duty to protect potential victims of their clients is familiar to her, the question of whether to disclose a client's alleged past crime leaves Corina in a quandary. Although the National Association of Social Workers (NASW) *Code of Ethics* (17) provides guidance for decisionmaking ("Social workers should protect the confidentiality of all information obtained in the course of professional services, except for compelling professional reasons" [Section 1.07(c)]), no specific directions are provided on the topic of reporting past criminal activities. Most states require that a social worker report a client's past criminal or harmful act only if the victim was a child (18). Some states also require reporting past criminal or harmful activities that included elderly or vulnerable adult victims (18). Unless a client appears to pose a danger to others, most states do not require a social worker to report a past crime (18). In many cases, the issue becomes one of determining whether the client poses a danger to others as a result of past activity. The NASW *Code of Ethics* addresses this issue: "Social workers are directed to seek consultation when caught between their ethical obligation and agency policies or laws and regulations" (18). Therefore, if you are unsure whether a client could pose a danger to someone, seek consultation with your field instructor or other knowledgeable, experienced staff at your agency. Always maintain written records concerning your resolution of the issue.

What Should I Do If a Client Discloses a Positive HIV Status?   Several issues present themselves when a client discloses information about a health issue that could pose a risk for others, such as a positive HIV status. The issues include who has access to the information, what can be done with the information, and what are the liability issues for inappropriate release of the information. States are beginning to grapple with this issue, and a number of states have enacted confidentiality statutes specifically for AIDS/HIV information (8).

Due to the possible consequences of wrongful disclosure of a client's HIV-positive status (e.g., loss of family and friends, loss, or denial of employment, and social stigma), social workers must be careful to obtain written informed consent from the individual (or his or her legal guardian) prior to the release of AIDS/HIV-related information. Only after investigating the policy of your practicum agency, examining state law, and obtaining qualified legal advice (as well as consulting with your field instructor) should you consider disclosing the information without informed consent from the client.

Disclosure without informed consent is permissible under specific circumstances, depending on local and state law. For example, one exception to confidentiality restrictions is the requirement found in all states to report cases to public health agencies that may investigate and trace sexual partners for the purpose of controlling the spread of the disease. Because an HIV-positive status could pose a threat to those with whom the client is sexually intimate (e.g., spouse, partner, or acquaintances) or to those with whom the client might exchange body fluids (e.g., during needle sharing or health care provision), there are increasing pressures for notifying those persons at risk for exposure. Beyond mandatory reporting to the public health authorities, the appropriate course of action for a social worker is to encourage the client to notify those persons at risk for the disease or to gain informed consent for notification. When necessary and as a last resort, a court-ordered release of confidential information is an option for a situation in which a strong possibility of harm to another exists and the client refuses to notify those at risk. Disclosing the HIV/AIDS status of a client without consent should occur only after serious deliberation and consultation because such disclosure is illegal in many states (8). As always, careful documentation of these actions is essential.

Can I Serve a Minor without Parental Consent? Do Adolescents Possess the Same Confidentiality Rights as Adults?   Although the rights of children have increased in recent times, the Supreme Court has clarified that minors (unless emancipated) do not possess all the constitutional rights of adults and may possess rights of adults to a lesser degree (8). Although some states allow the provision of services to children without parental consent under specific circumstances, the practice is controversial (9). Because the right of decisionmaking about the welfare of nonemancipated children resides with their parents or legal guardians, the issue of confidentiality of minors can be confusing to practitioners and students. The rights of minors vary from state to state, as in the areas of contraception, abortion, and consent to chemical dependency or other health care treatment. The following issues are common areas of confusion.

School Records.   Under the federal Family Educational Rights and Privacy Act (FERPA), parents of children under the age of 18 have the right to inspect and review educational records maintained on their children. Students over the age of 18 also have a right to view their own records. Noncustodial parents have the same access to minor children's school records as custodial parents unless a court order stipulates otherwise. Furthermore, parents of minor children and students over 18 years of age have the right to a hearing to challenge the information contained in the educational record. Those schools that are not in compliance with the standards mandated by FERPA are ineligible for federal funding (8).

Social workers within a school setting may be involved in the release of student records to eligible parties. If you are in a school setting when a student or parent makes a request to view the educational record of the student with whom you have worked, consider asking to be involved in the release procedures so that you can learn the process. You may also wish to discuss with a social worker agency or school policies regarding the kind of information that can be included in a student's file.

Limits of Confidentiality with Minors.   Several situations warrant a violation of confidentiality with minors. Depending on state statute, you can disclose information regarding reasonable suspicion of child abuse or neglect and possible suicidal intentions (8). If you are working with minors, be certain to explain the limits of confidentiality to clients during the engagement process. For example, a minor should be told that you want him or her to feel comfortable sharing information with you and you will not disclose any information shared with you without his or her knowledge. You should further explain that you are required to report any information disclosed that you feel could place him or her or others at risk for harm to the appropriate authorities. Ensure that the minor understands that you will not disclose any information without cause. Additionally, explain that his or her parents or guardians may have access to school and agency records. This knowledge will allow a minor to interact with you on an informed basis.

Working with Immigrants.   Following enactment of the 1996 federal welfare reform law, social workers are struggling with questions concerning their ability to serve immigrants. This legislation eliminated eligibility for illegal and some legal immigrants for certain federal assistance programs (including TANF and food stamps) and included provisions that direct federal and state agencies to implement citizenship verification procedures with their clients over the next several years. Some agencies administering federal assistance funds must also report known illegal immigrants.

The federal government has yet to issue many definitions and specific instructions needed to implement verification and reporting procedures. Nonprofit charitable organizations are exempt from the reporting and citizenship verification mandates unless the agency receives government funds from affected programs. Those agencies that provide a service financially supported by a government program included in the legislation are restricted to serving only clients approved by the government program (19, 20).

As a practicum student, you are well advised to keep abreast of the changes affecting immigrants as a result of the 1996 welfare reform bill. Definitions and specific instructions are expected from the federal government. Buoyed by the recent victory of advocates in overturning some of the welfare law's harshest elements in the food stamp program, advocates will continue their efforts to shape the regulations and implementation of the law. However, fear invoked by citizenship reporting requirements could prevent many immigrants from receiving services from any agency. Future reporting requirements could pose ethical dilemmas for you in your efforts to maintain client confidentiality and to abide by the law. If you are completing your practicum in a federal or state agency or in an agency that receives federal support for a program, check with your field instructor regarding any restrictions to service eligibility for legal and illegal immigrants.

Documentation as a Legal Record

Documentation concepts are often taught in practice theory courses. Specific training is typically provided in the practicum agency in such areas as methods of documentation, confidentiality of records, and conditions under which the sharing of records with outside agencies is permitted. Documentation provides a record of services rendered and a tool for evaluating the effectiveness of services. Furthermore, the importance of documentation as a legal record cannot be overstated. For legal purposes, a record should contain the following elements (21):

- signed informed consents for all treatment
- signed informed consents for all transmission of confidential information

- any treatment contracts
- notation of all treatment contacts and significant information and actions regarding the contact (face-to-face and telephone)
- notations of failed or canceled appointments
- notations of supervision and consultation contacts
- all correspondence
- a complete social history including past and present evaluations and treatment, a medical history, and a record of current physical examination
- a diagnostic assessment or statement
- a record of all medications that the client is currently taking
- a record of the basis for the assessment made and treatment provided
- notations of suggestions, instructions, referrals, or directives made to the client and whether the client followed through with them

PRACTICE APPLICATION **9.1**

Agency Records as Legal Documents

This practice application will provide an opportunity to critique your practicum site's record format relative to the elements expected of a client file for legal purposes.

Obtain a copy of a client file. Compare and contrast the contents of the file with the list of elements that a file should contain for legal purposes (21), as shown in the table below. In the Agency Files column, check off those items that are contained in or are an expected part of the file. Discuss your findings with a member of your practicum team.

Expected Elements of a Client File for Legal Purposes	Agency Files
Signed informed consents for all treatment	
Signed informed consents for all transmission of confidential information	
Any treatment contracts	
Notation of all treatment contacts and significant information and actions regarding the contact (face-to-face and telephone)	
Notations of failed or canceled appointments	
Notations of supervision and consultation contacts	
All correspondence	
A complete social history including past and present evaluations and treatment, a medical history, and a record of current physical examination	
A diagnostic assessment or statement	
A record of all medications that the client is currently taking	
A record of the basis for the assessment made and treatment provided	
Notations of suggestions, instructions, referrals, or directives made to the client and whether the client followed through with them	

A practitioner's personal notes can also be used as a legal document in court proceedings. A practitioner's personal notes should contain the following for legal purposes (21):

- speculation about client dynamics
- impressions about the course of treatment
- problems resolved
- problems being worked on
- problems to be worked on in the future
- projections about termination
- summary of perceptions of significant treatment session dynamics

---

PRACTICE APPLICATION **9.2**

Personal Notes as a Legal Document

The personal notes of a practitioner can be used as a legal document in court proceedings, so it is important to review the list above with your field instructor. Ask your field instructor or another social worker at your practicum site the following questions. Take notes on the discussion and share your findings in integrative practice field seminar.

- Do you maintain personal notes on clients?
- If yes, will you share the format with me?
- If no, why do you avoid taking personal notes?
- Have your notes ever been subpoenaed?
- Will you share with me the agency procedure for subpoenaed documents?
- Will you share with me your suggestions about documentation?

Although documentation is time consuming, practitioners and students must prioritize documentation of their cases in order to optimize service delivery and minimize malpractice liability. In your practicum activities, consider using the following suggestions from the Missouri Chapter of the NASW (22):

- Maintain a log of any outgoing and incoming telephone calls (including the date, time, and content of conversation).
- When appropriate, thoroughly document assessments and development of comprehensive treatment plans (including issues to be addressed, approximate timeframes for services, and expected outcomes).
- Complete documentation as soon after the events as possible. A delay could alter your memory and result in omissions or misrepresentation of critical information.

Special Legal Issues in Practicum

Although you are a student, you are acting in the same capacity as a professional social worker in your responsibilities with clients, and, as such, are accountable for upholding the same legal, professional, and ethical standards as other social workers (23). Although you must identify yourself as a student to clients, you are held legally and ethically responsible for your actions with them. As a professional, you are held to the standards of the NASW *Code of Ethics* (17) as well as to federal and state law governing professional social work services. If you bring harm to a client during the course of your practicum, the extent to which your field supervisor, agency, and social work program could possibly be held liable is unclear (5).

Nevertheless, you are advised to ensure the existence of malpractice insurance coverage for your activities in practicum. Many social work programs either provide malpractice coverage or require students to purchase it independently. Additionally, your practicum site may provide coverage for you as it does for other staff or volunteers (24). Last, clarify the extent of all the insurance under which you are covered. Does it cover all types of activities? Would it pay for legal defense fees?

Potential liability exists in any student–client relationship, and you are well advised to follow the same guidelines as nonstudent social workers to minimize your liability. Areas of social work identified with high liability risk include group practice (potential liability for the actions of others in group), child protection and custody practice, determination of personal injury benefits, and divorce mediation (in which the client may wrongly assume that a social worker's decisions will be favorable to him or her). As social workers have developed expertise in a wider range of areas, particularly with specialized populations, the expectations for a higher standard of care requiring increased knowledge and skill have also developed in most areas of practice (9). In a society that is increasingly legalistic, clients are likely to possess knowledge about their rights and to seek damages when they incur harm as a result of professional (or student) malpractice (25).

Social Work Ethical Violations and Grievance Procedures

Along with increased recognition of the social work profession has come increased regulation of the profession. Social workers are responsible legally and ethically for their behaviors to several bodies (6).

The Employing Agency

As a professional, you are accountable to your employer for your services to clients. According to the NASW *Code of Ethics* (17), you are responsible for adhering to commitments you have made to your employer, including following agency policies and procedures. Even as a student, your employer could be held legally responsible for your actions in a lawsuit.

Profession

Various professional organizations have codes of ethics as well as grievance processes that may be utilized for ethics code violations. For example, the NASW *Code of Ethics* (17) outlines various roles and responsibilities for professional social workers. As a result of a "request for professional review" being filed with an NASW chapter, a determination will be made regarding whether a dispute meets the criteria for acceptance into the adjudication process. If designated a "complaint," a peer review process can be undertaken by a state chapter to review any alleged violation of the *Code of Ethics,* as well as an agency's personnel standards (26), by a member of NASW. If serious misconduct is found, sanctions may be imposed. Sanctions may include (9, 27):

- corrective actions (to restore or increase a social worker's competency and ethical functioning) (e.g., supervised practice, consultation, additional coursework, or an apology or restitution to a victim);
- sanction(s) (e.g., temporary or permanent revocation of NASW membership or the ACSW credential, notification of the state regulatory board, publication of action in the *NASW News* or chapter newsletter, or notification of a social worker's employer and credentialing entities); or
- a combination of any of the above.

State

In addition to the professional review discussed above, licensed social workers can also face a review by a state board of regulation and licensing (6). State regulatory boards can call practitioners before a disciplinary panel for a formal hearing. If the board finds "unprofessional conduct," a reprimand, public censure, fine, probation, or suspension or revocation of a license could result (11).

Court (Civil and Criminal)

In addition to being subject to agency, profession, and state entities, social work professionals may come under the scrutiny of federal and state civil and criminal courts. All social workers, even those who are not members of the NASW or licensed (and so do not fall under the jurisdiction of a state licensing board or the NASW), are held accountable to civil and criminal laws governing professional behavior. Civil litigation (a lawsuit) can result in monetary damages (11), while criminal charges can result in incarceration as well as loss of license or certification and sanction by the NASW.

The increase in the number of lawsuits filed against social workers may be a reflection of factors other than an increase in negligent or unethical activities, including the increased frequency with which clients seek legal recourse for malpractice. Regardless of the reasons, this trend is cause for concern. The most common categories of malpractice claim filed against individual social workers are incorrect treatment, sexual impropriety, breach of confidence/privacy, and failure to diagnose or incorrect diagnosis. Most insurance payments from the NASW-sponsored malpractice insurance policy result from claims concerning sexual impropriety and incorrect treatment (28).

If You Are Sued

What should you do if you are sued? The Missouri chapter of the NASW (22) and we suggest the following:

- Resist the urge to panic. Stay calm. Many lawsuits are frivolous, and you can continue to practice your profession during the proceedings.
- Immediately inform your field instructor and your social work program.
- Discuss your suit only with your attorney. Statements to other professionals as well as to nonprofessionals (family, friends, and fellow social work students) are generally not considered privileged information and can be admissible in court. Your communications with your personal therapist are considered privileged.
- Refrain from making any self-incriminating statements to anyone.
- Do *not* contact the suing client (plaintiff) or his or her attorney. Your professional relationship ends when the adversarial relationship inherent in a lawsuit begins.
- Assemble relevant documents (e.g., files, case notes, telephone logs, and calendars) and make them available only to your attorney and your attorney's representative.
- Follow the advice of your attorney. Your communications with your attorney are privileged.

Finally, consider this a learning process! Unless you practice social work outside the boundaries of the *Code of Ethics* (17), you are not likely to be sued more than once. As you go through the process, your involvement in a lawsuit may provide invaluable lessons that may serve you well in the future.

Professional Court Involvement

Ben had a feeling that something was very wrong with the "professional" relationship between a staff member, Harold, and a client, Regina. Staff members had been talking about Harold and the unprofessional manner in which he was working as a substance abuse counselor with Regina, but no one had been willing to go to any administrators about the situation. While Ben was conducting a home visit with Regina last week, Harold arrived and confronted her on the front porch. Ben could not help overhearing the nature of the interaction between the two, which clearly bordered on harassment. Harold felt that a rejection of his substance abuse treatment was a rejection of him and told her that "she couldn't live without my services." Ben learned today that the client is suing Harold for sexual harassment. The client has told her attorney that Ben was present during one encounter with Harold, and Ben received a subpoena today. Ben has no idea what to do and wonders whether he should call Regina to let her know that he does not wish to jeopardize his practicum by testifying against a staff member. What should he do?

Receiving a Subpoena

Receiving a subpoena can send shivers down the spine of even the most experienced practitioner. Practitioners often feel caught between a rock and a hard place: ignoring a subpoena is illegal and could result in a fine or even incarceration, yet inappropriately revealing confidential information could result in a malpractice suit and a soiled reputation that permanently damages one's career (7, 29). There are two types of subpoenas. A *subpoena ad testificandum* (commonly referred to as a subpoena) is an order compelling the attendance of a witness to provide testimony at a deposition or a trial; a *subpoena duces tecum* is an order for the production of documents or other things, such as records, notes, and files as well as electronic formats (30).

Social workers must respond to a subpoena with careful consideration. Before a social worker can make any response to a subpoena regarding work with a client, the requirements of privileged communication must be fulfilled. Privileged communication differs from the concept of confidentiality because the client, rather than the social worker, possesses the privilege to restrict the dissemination of information given in confidence in a legal action (2, 9, 31). This privilege exists in state statutes as well as within federal courts (9), although it is not absolute (and may be waived for legitimate criminal investigations and under other circumstances) (32). Currently, 45 states and the District of Columbia have enacted state statutes to protect communication between a social worker and a client as privileged (8). When a court orders disclosure of confidential or privileged information, social workers are instructed by the NASW *Code of Ethics* (17) to request that a court "withdraw or limit the order as narrowly as possible."

If you receive a subpoena (either as a student or as a practitioner), the following are suggested actions (8, 17, 30):

- Immediately inform your field instructor and the agency's legal counsel.
- Carefully read a subpoena to determine the action required, the date for a response, and the issuing court and attorney.
- Work with an attorney to prepare for your court appearance.

Both formal client records and the personal notes of a practitioner can be subpoenaed. Whether formal records or personal notes are being subpoenaed, take the following actions:

- Take all steps to ensure confidentiality. Although an attorney has power to issue a subpoena, a court has not made a decision about the validity of the subpoena. Any material requested may be protested by statutory confidentiality or privilege and should not be released without a court order or client consent.
- If you are not in an adversarial position with the client (i.e., the client is not suing you), contact the client(s) involved, discuss the material being subpoenaed, and provide them with a copy of the subpoena. With client consent, contact the client's attorney to ask questions, and provide him or her with a copy of the subpoena.
- Request a written release from a client(s) who has consented to the release of information by you to the court. If the client(s) does not consent, the material generally may not be released or discussed unless there is an appropriate reason for releasing it according to federal and state laws and the NASW *Code of Ethics*.
- Before you release any written client materials, thoroughly verify and document the legal and ethical mandates for doing so and, when possible, advise the client.
- Contact the attorney who issued the subpoena to arrange compliance after receiving the permission of your client.
- If the material requested is privileged or the subpoena is procedurally improper, consider asking your legal counsel to object to the subpoena by filing written objections, requesting a protective order, or filing a motion to quash or modify the subpoena. A court order would then be needed to receive the information.
- Attend the deposition or trial even if the claim of privilege is asserted on behalf of the client. The claim and basis for privilege must be stated for the record.
- Document all activity regarding the subpoena in the client's file.

Testifying in Court and Serving as an Expert Witness

The likelihood of being called to appear in court sometime during one's social work career is high (33). Examples of activities in which a social worker may be involved that could lead to court appearances include mandatory reporting of and involvement in a case of child or elder abuse/neglect or exploitation, involvement in a client's child custody case or worker's compensation hearings, and civil damage suits or criminal matters (including domestic violence and violation of probation orders) (29). Social workers provide testimony based on personal observations or documentation. Testimony based on personal observation may or may not involve referring to notes during the testimony, while testimony based on documents entails reading reports and possibly explaining the process of producing and storing documents during the proceedings (34).

Social workers may also be called to provide expert testimony in cases. Due to expertise and special training, expert witnesses can be asked for both facts and their opinions or conclusions about facts, as well as opinions about hypothetical situations. Examples of cases in which a social worker may be asked to testify include child custody cases, child abuse cases, and adoption placements (13).

A consultation with the attorney for whom you will be called as a witness prior to any court proceedings is essential. Meeting with the attorney will provide an opportunity to learn about questions that you are likely to be asked as well as to inform the attorney of any weaknesses in your testimony (34).

The following suggestions will serve to assist you in delivering effective testimony in court (2, 35):

- Take your time answering questions.
- Always tell the truth. Never guess, speculate, evade a question, or use humor or sarcasm.
- Never answer a question that you do not understand; rather, ask that the question be rephrased.
- Never interrupt the attorney or judge.
- Avoid professional jargon and define terms as needed.
- Offer to explain your answer if necessary.

- Cease talking if an objection is made.
- Avoid mitigating phrases such as "I think" or "I suppose" or "It seemed."
- Ensure that your nonverbal and verbal behaviors are congruent.
- If arranged prior to the trial, bring and refer to your written notes during your testimony.
- Dress formally and professionally.
- Use a demeanor that is calm, sincere, and detached even under adversarial questioning.
- Consider requesting financial compensation in exchange for expert testimony.

You are well advised to obtain as much knowledge about responding to subpoenas and providing testimony as possible. You may consider talking to your field instructor about your interest in gathering information about social work involvement in the legal system and asking whether you could accompany any agency social workers to court (if this occurs during your practicum). Consider asking whether any agency staff member has received a subpoena, and arrange an informal discussion with that person(s) to inquire about steps taken in response to the subpoena.

PRACTICE APPLICATION **9.3**
Noncustodial Parental Right to Review School Records

Imagine that you are a practicum student at a high school, assisting in a "Rainbows" after-school group for children of divorced parents. A noncustodial father arrives at school and presents a written request for the release of his daughter's complete file, to include all counseling records. The signed request is for "all documentation pertaining to enrollment, admission, student progress, counseling, and any other activity undertaken by this student while on school premises, etc." The secretary is copying the general school file but requests that you pull and copy her counseling records. The secretary informs you that the father has said that he would wait for all copies.

When you pull the counseling file, you notice that a copy of an Adult Protective Order is in the file. The order was issued last summer and is effective until next summer and orders the respondent (the father) restrained from any contact with the wife. He is granted supervised visits with his daughter. In addition to this order, you see a note that the mother will bring in a copy of their divorce decree as soon as it is available to her.

The father has not asked to see his daughter, although she is in a class just down the hall. He has asked for a copy of the complete file, including your records, which contain a complete intake form, treatment plan, and progress notes. What are your options? What would you do? (Note: For our suggested resolution, see page 223).

Developed by Dana Klar, JD, MSW

PRACTICE APPLICATION **9.4**

Reflections on the Legal System and Vulnerable Populations

Vulnerable populations often experience difficulties with the legal system. Many social workers provide assistance to clients in their dealings with the system. Knowledge of the problems encountered by a particular population can help you become a more effective advocate for clients.

1. With two or three other students, select a population and identify the point at which this population often interfaces with the legal system. Examples include
   - battered women and the police;
   - single mothers and the child support enforcement system;
   - juvenile offenders and the juvenile court system; and
   - families involved in divorce proceedings and dealing with child custody and visitation.
2. Interview at least two social workers who serve this population, and identify the body of law with which professionals working with the population need to be familiar. Research and obtain copies of significant related legislation, regulations, and any available legal resource guides for clients.
3. Interview three or four clients to learn about their experiences with the legal system. After learning more about their particular situations, ask the clients the following questions related to their experiences.
   - What do you understand about the law relevant to your issue(s)?
   - What problems did you encounter in working with the legal system?
   - What would have been beneficial for you in your involvement with the legal system?
   - What changes (if any) do you think need to be made in the legal system to promote fair treatment and justice?
4. In a journal entry, reflect on the interviews and share your entry with a member of your practicum team.
5. If a legal resource guide for clients is not available or is out of date, compile/revise a legal guide for the population and issue(s) you have selected that would help clients advocate for themselves.

Developed by Jan Wilson, LCSW

PRACTICE APPLICATION **9.5**

The Courts: How Much Do You Know?

A variety of levels (federal, state, county, and municipal) and types (civil, criminal, family, and juvenile) of court systems exist. Divide into groups of two or three and select a level and type of court system. As a group, research the organization and functions of the chosen system. Specify the jurisdiction and the types of cases the court system adjudicates. Identify which client populations are likely to be involved in the system.

As an integrative practice field seminar class, compile a table showing the variety of levels, types of court systems, jurisdictions, types of cases adjudicated, and client populations likely to be involved in the system. Each group will enter the information about its chosen level and type of court system. As a class, discuss the information your group gathered and the ways in which your particular court system relates to other courts and to clients' issues.

	Federal	State	County, Municipal
Civil a. Organization and Functions			
b. Jurisdiction			
c. Client Population			
Criminal a. Organization and Functions			
b. Jurisdiction			
c. Client Population			

Developed by Jan Wilson, LCSW

Follow-Up to Practice Application 9.3 —Authors' Suggested Resolution

In this instance, the release of records to a noncustodial parent is appropriate. However, the response in this situation must be in compliance with state law as well as school and school district policy. Given the situation, the appropriate course of action is (1) consult with the field instructor and the school (or school district's) legal counsel as quickly as possible; (2) inform the school secretary about the order of protection and your need to do some checking; and (3) inform the parent that you will need some time to determine and comply with the school's procedures regarding the release of counseling records and that you will call him within a short time period. After the parent leaves, make every effort to consult all the necessary parties as quickly as possible and respond within the timeframe you specified. You will need to conceal all address information in the student's records and inform the student and her parent(s) of the request and your duty to comply with the request.

Summary

Knowledge of legal and judicial matters is an essential part of professional social work practice. As a social work student, assume responsibility for acquainting yourself with the relevant legal aspects of your practicum setting. Familiarity with legal issues will provide you with the possibility of using the legal and judicial system to advocate for your clients on both the micro (individual) and macro (legislative and policy) levels. Furthermore, investigate potential practice liability issues within your practicum site to lessen your legal vulnerability. Knowledge of the legal and judicial system and a heightened awareness of ethical issues in your professional work will enable you to serve your clients better and to deliver your social work services with minimal liability risk (5).

STUDENT SCENARIO POSTSCRIPTS

During the group session, **Corina** asked the group for reactions to the information that the client had shared. Some members of the group lauded the client for his daring and for "getting away with it," while others talked about the importance of integrity and honesty and encouraged him to "come clean" with the friend. Corina echoed the need for integrity and the importance of sincere friendship in maintaining a support system. She also told the group that she may have to break confidentiality and explained the possible limits to confidentiality. Afterward, she checked with her field instructor and discovered that under state law, social workers are required to report criminal activity to the authorities. She did so with great trepidation and enlisted the assistance of her field instructor to make the report and to process the reporting with the clients in the next group meeting.

Ben discussed the encounter between Harold and Regina he overheard with his field instructor and his fears about jeopardizing the integrity of the practicum if he testifies against another staff member in compliance with the subpoena. The field instructor intervened with Harold and told him that Ben was present at the home visit and must testify if he is called. Harold left the agency a week before the case went to court. When the case went to trial, Ben provided testimony about what he had overheard at the home visit.

REFERENCES

1. Lynch, R. S. & Brawley, E. A. Social workers and the judicial system: Looking for a better fit. *Journal of Teaching in Social Work.* 1994, 10(1/2):65–82.

2. Saltzman, A. & Proch, K. *Law and social work practice.* Chicago: Nelson-Hall. 1994.

3. Albert, R. *Law and social work practice.* New York: Springer. 1986.

4. Kopels, S. & Kagle, J. D. Do social workers have duty to warn? *Social Service Review.* 1993, 67(1):10–26.

5. Reamer, F. G. Liability issues in social work supervision. *Social Work.* 1989, 34(5):445–448.

6. Reamer, F. G. *Social work malpractice and liability.* New York: Columbia University Press. 1995.

7. Black, H. D. *Black's law dictionary with pronunciations* (5th ed.). St. Paul, MN: West Publishing. 1979.

8. Dickson, D. T. *Confidentiality and privacy in social work*. New York: Free Press. 1998.

9. Houston-Vega, M. K. & Nuehring, E. M. *Prudent practice*. Washington, DC: NASW Press. 1997.

10. Kirst-Ashman, K. K. & Hull, G. H. *Generalist practice with organizations and communities*. Chicago: Nelson-Hall. 1997.

11. Kurzman, P. A. Professional liability and malpractice. In R. L. Edwards (Ed.), *NASW Encyclopedia of Social Work* (19th ed.) (pp. 1921–1926). Washington, DC: NASW Press. 1995.

12. National Association of Social Workers. More social workers find alternatives to litigation. *NASW News*. 1998, *43* (9):5.

13. Schroeder, L. O. *The legal environment of social work*. Washington, DC: NASW Press. 1995.

14. Brawley, E. A. Making a difference: An action-oriented approach to social policy for undergraduate social work students. *Areté*. 1985, *10*(1):50–55.

15. Johnson, A. K., Kreuger, L. W. & Stretch, J. J. A court-ordered consent decree for the homeless: Process, conflict and control. *Journal of Sociology and Social Welfare*. 1989, *16*(3):29–42.

16. Besharov, D. J. & Besharov, S. H. Teaching about liability. *Social Work*. 1987, *32*(6):517–521.

17. National Association of Social Workers. *Code of ethics*. Washington, DC: NASW Press. 1996. (p. 11).

18. Landers, S. Balancing confidences, laws and ethics. *NASW News*. 1998, *43*(5):3.

19. National Association of Social Workers. Bills tackle welfare, patients' rights. *NASW News*. 1998, *43*(8):7.

20. Levensen, D. Immigration statutes: Law, ethics collide. *NASW News*. 1998, *43*(8):3.

21. Munson, C. E. *Clinical social work supervision* (2nd ed.). New York: Haworth Press. 1993.

22. Missouri Chapter NASW. What to do if you are sued for social work malpractice. *Missouri NASW News*. 1996, *22*(1):1, 4.

23. Levy, C. S. *Social work ethics*. New York: Human Sciences Press. 1976.

24. Gelman, S. R. The crafting of fieldwork training agreements. *Journal of Social Work Education*. 1990, *26*(1):65–75.

25. Zakutansky, T. J. & Sirles, E. A. Ethical and legal issues in field education: Shared responsibility and risk. *Journal of Social Work Education*. 1993, *29*(3):338–347.

26. National Association of Social Workers. Adjudication's first step is altered. *NASW News*. 1998, *43*(10):8.

27. National Association of Social Workers. *NASW procedures for the adjudication of grievances*. Washington, DC: NASW Press. 1991.

28. Reamer, F. G. Malpractice claims against social workers: First facts. *Social Work*. 1995, *40*(5):595–601.

29. Landers, S. Subpoenas 101: Leaping a legal chasm. *NASW News*. 1997, *42*(3):3.

30. Polowy, C. I. & Gilbertson, J. *Social workers and subpoenas: Office of general counsel law notes*. Washington, DC: NASW Press. 1997.

31. Polowy, C. I. Client confidentiality and privileged communication. *Missouri NASW News*. 1998, *23*(3):1,3.

32. Schwartz, G. Confidentiality revisited. *Social Work*. 1989, *34*(3):223–226.

33. Dorfman, R. A. *Clinical social work: Definition, practice & vision*. New York: Brunner/Mazel. 1996.

34. Sheafor, B. W., Horejsi, C. R. & Horejsi, G. A. *Techniques and guidelines for social work practice* (4th ed.). Boston: Allyn & Bacon. 1997.

35. Gyurci, R. Social workers testimony in dependency and neglect cases. *Journal of Law and Social Work*. 1989, *1*(1):32–37.

10 Termination: The Beginning of an End (or the End of a Beginning?)

Ode to a Practicum Student

You began this journey with fears and excitement
as you entered your field work class.
You wondered, "can I interview a
client, write a social history,
will I have money for gas?"

You met with your field instructor on that wonderful
yet difficult first field placement day.
Somehow you knew that if you stuck with him or her
your fears about this milestone would quietly go away.

You listened carefully because you knew
independence and your caseload would come soon.
So you shadowed your field instructor on
home visits, team meetings,
whoops, even to the restroom.

Then it was time to meet your first client, you were excited,
self-conscious, your stomach sank.
You thought, "will I ask the tough questions and remember to say
you're feeling blank *because* blank *and you want* blank.*"*

Journal writing became a way of voicing "I'm stressed,
but I'm learning and growing too!"
You reflected on your personal struggles because
this work was becoming important to you.

A broker, case manager, advocate,
a social work generalist in action.
You saw complex issues, no easy answers,
the conflict, ethics, coping and satisfaction.

You worked hard learning, growing and doing,
to make this field experience go your way.
Hope that your social work career will be as productive
as you begin on this graduation day.

—Cheryl Waites, Ed.D., MSW, ACSW (1)

You are approaching the end of your current practicum experience. You may be nearing graduation from your social work program, or you may be preparing to "graduate" to your next field experience. In either case, you are faced with bringing closure to this practicum experience—a task that may entail closing cases or ending projects but also requires you to say your farewells, assess your accomplishments, and identify future learning needs. If you are continuing on for a second semester at your current practicum site, you can use this unit to anticipate issues surrounding your upcoming termination.

Throughout your social work training, you have learned about the importance of the termination process for the client. Appropriate termination and closure are essential for an effective social work intervention as the client system is allowed to plan for and participate in the ending of the relationship with you, the worker. Equally critical to the effective social work intervention is your own closure with the client systems, your supervisor, and your coworkers. Because of the importance of the termination process, this final unit will be devoted exclusively to the multiple levels and types of practicum-related terminations. To be addressed first are the issues that surround the emotional reactions you may experience as you terminate from this practicum experience. Second, you will explore the practical aspects of terminating from the agency and your field instructor. Last, working through the termination process provides an opportunity to discuss professional development issues that may now be (or soon will be) relevant to your social work career.

What Has This Practicum Experience Meant?

Terminations of any type, but particularly those related to powerful or meaningful experiences, elicit mixed feelings from most of us. On the one hand, you are probably feeling a sense of accomplishment now that you have completed yet another step in your journey to becoming a professional social worker. Completing the experiential facet of your social work education has provided you with the opportunity to experience, learn, and practice real-life social work. You have likely increased your social work knowledge, mastered many skills necessary for effective social work practice, identified and clarified more personal and professional values, and begun the process of integrating your theoretical frameworks with the actual application of the concepts. A sense of pride and competence should emerge as a result of these achievements.

On the other hand, the practicum experience may have evoked a sense of incompetence, fear, or trepidation in you. Often, putting your knowledge into practice can result in a realization of how little you feel you actually know. Further, although you have developed practice competencies for your current setting, you may question whether these skills will, in fact, transfer to a different setting. Although you may have a fear of the future and doubt your ability to be an effective social worker, the self-assessment and "reality checking" are important and

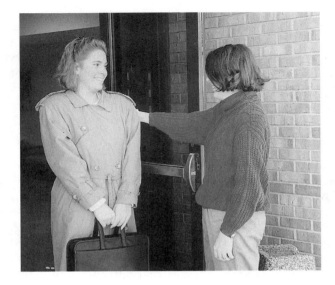

normal stages of professional development. You can utilize this period as an op-portunity to assess knowledge and skills gained and areas for future development.

A third common reaction to termination is the feelings that occur as you con-template closing or transferring client cases, wrapping up projects, and saying your good-byes to those people who have influenced your development as a social worker. You may be experiencing reluctance to leave your practicum site, the "I can't wait to get out of here" syndrome, or some combination of the two. Although not all your learning has been "pain-free," your field instructor and the staff at your practicum site have helped to shape and mold your definition of social work prac-tice and have guided you through this phase of your professional development. There may be some colleagues to whom you are ready to bid farewell, but ending your work relationship with others may be a difficult emotional event in your life.

Two important issues emerge as you enter this final phase of your practicum. First, you are encouraged to realize that your learning is far from over. In fact, effec-tive social workers are committed to being life-long learners. With the radical and rapid changes that occur in the social work profession, we must devote ourselves to staying current in the areas that affect those we serve. Second, stay in touch with your emotions and feelings regarding this experience. Being able and willing to acknowledge that you have both positive and negative feelings about the experi-ence and its termination is a normal and expected phenomenon.

An important task for you to engage in at this point in your practicum career is to consider the meaning (personal and professional) of this experience for your life. In addition to assessing the actual learning of knowledge and skills, take time to reflect on the ways in which your practicum has affected you as a person. You can use the termination of this practicum to evaluate your career choice as well as yourself as a social worker. Some students question their career choice at this stage. Although this is not unusual by any means, you should consult with a trusted person in your life (e.g., faculty, field instructor, family member, friend, or therapist) if you strongly experience such doubts (2). Your self-examination can include such questions as:

- Why did I choose to become a social worker?
- Am I gratified by being a social worker—is this profession a "fit" for me?
- Am I "burned out" on helping?
- What strengths do I have as a social work professional?
- What do I enjoy about being a social worker?
- What do I *not* enjoy about being a social worker? What can I do to change those things I do not enjoy about the social work profession? If I cannot change them, can I live with them, or might they impede my ability to practice social work?
- Was the agency and population at my practicum site one in which I enjoyed working?
- What other settings or populations would I like to explore?
- Have I identified any settings or populations that I am not well suited to serve?
- Do I want to devote myself to social work on a full-time basis?
- Where do I go from here in the short and long run (for example, administration, different population or setting, more intense involvement with clients, or less intense involvement with clients)?

PRACTICE APPLICATION **10.1**
What Is Social Work and Where Do I Fit?

The aim of this practice application is twofold: (1) to help you begin your termination process from your current practicum site and (2) to enable you to review your perception of the social work profession in general and the role of social work at your practicum site. If you have not already done so, begin by developing a written statement outlining your philosophy of social work (i.e., describing your definition and philosophy regarding the social work profession).

Develop a list of termination-related issues to discuss with your field instructor during your final supervisory session. You will include items on your list that are relevant for your situation, but we offer the following suggestions to get you started. Respond to the following questions:

- Has my perception of social work changed since the beginning of this practicum? If so, how has it changed, and what factors contributed to that change? If not, why has it not changed, and what factors contributed to that lack of change?
- Did I understand the role of social work in my practicum agency at the beginning of my practicum? Has that understanding been strengthened, clarified, or refuted as a result of my experience here?
- Regarding my learning plan, where are my strengths and areas for growth?

(continued)

PRACTICE APPLICATION **10.1**   Continued

- Do I have a better understanding of the practicum agency's policies and proce-dures? If so, what suggestions for improvement might I have? If not, why not?
- What recommendations do I have for future practicum students that will enhance their learning experiences?

Beginning the Termination: Where Do I Start?

Cameron's practicum at the substance abuse treatment program has been a powerful and significant experience for him on both the professional and the personal levels. Professionally, he has gained insights into the etiology and dynamics related to addictions, learned skills needed to work with addicts and their significant others, and become comfortable functioning as a professional in this setting (versus his previous role as a client). On the personal side, Cameron has become empowered to remain abstinent and to devote his life to helping others overcome their addictions. As a result of these profound realiza-tions, Cameron has decided that he wants to stay on at his practicum site as a volunteer following the completion of his practicum requirements. He believes that he can continue to help clients by serving as a group leader, individual therapist, or after-care worker. Cameron has not been invited to continue as a volunteer and his fellow MSW student friends voiced concerns about his "obsession" with this population. What do you think Cameron should do?

Because fieldwork can be such a powerful experience, both personally and professionally, students often have difficulty conceiving how to begin the prac-ticum termination process. Fortunately, the structure of the practicum process encompasses a definite point of termination. The following discussion will high-light issues related to initiating the termination process. A place to begin is to remember that the practicum experience is intended as a training tool and a step-ping stone for professional development. Viewing the practicum as just one com-ponent of your educational endeavor (versus the entire experience) allows you to maintain a perspective on the practicum experience. Remember that this practicum has been *one* experience, and if the practicum went extremely well, this does not mean that you have learned all there is to learn. By the same token, if your practicum was not the "success" you had hoped for, you are not doomed to be a failure in the social work profession. Framing your experiences in a realistic man-ner frees you to move on to the next chapter of your professional development.

In Cameron's case, ending his practicum is not a clear-cut issue. Practicum experiences are sometimes so intense and profound that some students feel dis-loyal, unprofessional, or uncommitted if they "abandon" their clients. Others may feel unable to separate from their settings because their practicum experiences met some personal need. Students who find it difficult to terminate from their prac-ticum sites may explore the possibility of continuing their work with their agencies as volunteers or employees. Should you find that you are experiencing difficulty moving on to your next experience, exploring your feelings about terminating may be in order. Ask yourself some hard questions related to the reasons for your reluctance to terminate:

- Do I have trouble accepting change? Why?
- Do I feel I am abandoning my clients or coworkers? Why?
- Do I feel that no one else can work with my clients as well as I do? Why?
- Can I not imagine my life without my work at this agency?
- Have I experienced an unwillingness to transition in other areas of my life?
- Am I fearful that I will not be able to get a job/another practicum?
- Did I not learn all I should have learned in this practicum and am I therefore feeling unprepared for the next chapter of my professional life?
- Have I had such a powerful learning experience that I am now so passionate about this work that I feel compelled to stay in this setting?
- Am I afraid that the skills I have learned will not be transferrable to the next setting?

Continued involvement with your practicum site as a volunteer or employee is not inappropriate and may, in fact, be a bonus for your personal, financial, and professional situation. However, you are encouraged to examine the reasons for staying as well as those applicable to terminating completely. As members of your practicum team, your field instructor or faculty members can be resources for processing these issues.

Joys and Frustrations: Taking Stock

As you begin to consider the issues related to your own termination, you have likely begun to identify the joys and frustrations associated with leaving your practicum site, your clients, your coworkers, and your field instructor. Termination provides a time for reflecting on these and other important developmental issues. Resist the temptation to romanticize or deromanticize the practicum experience. Being realistic about the practicum experience begins with an exploration of the joys and the frustrations associated with the experience.

The Joys.   Take a moment and consider those events, interactions, and activities that have brought you gratification, a sense of accomplishment, pleasure, and maybe even elation. Such a response may have occurred when you mastered a difficult skill, calmed an angry client, initiated an innovation in the agency, or received a hug from a child or elderly client. Joys are very personal experiences and important for you to recognize (even when you may have difficulty seeing your work as joyous!).

The Frustrations.   Unfortunately, the practice of social work can elicit feelings of frustration even in the educational phases. Again, we encourage you to spend a moment and recollect those experiences that created a sense of tension for you. We have compiled a list of possibilities—do any of these sound familiar to you? What would you add to the list? Most important, what thoughts do you have regarding strategies for resolving or preventing these frustrations?

- *Changing practicum sites.* You may feel that you have more to learn at your current site, that you like this population, that the agency feels comfortable and familiar, and that this is the work you want to do in your social work career. The social work program's requirement that you have to complete practica at multiple sites is an impediment to your own predesigned professional development.
- *Transferring cases or projects.* You may feel that no one else can understand your clients or projects as well as you can and you realize that you are not yet ready to part with these experiences.
- *Termination feelings.* You may be used to clients leaving you but had not anticipated the feelings associated with you leaving the clients.
- *Loyalties to the agency and clients.* Also perceived as a joy, you may have developed a strong sense of commitment and loyalty to the clients, agency, and staff, particularly your field instructor. Your loyalties may have sprung from your passion for the work in which you are engaged at your practicum and you now feel frustration that you must remove yourself from these people and the mission.

Terminating from your practicum will likely bring both joy and frustration—both of which are normal responses. The key to a successful termination is to recognize and explore your feelings and to move forward.

Lessons Learned

In order to begin to grasp the extent of learning that has occurred during your practicum experience, an essential task is the evaluation of *all* your learning experiences related to your skills and growth—even the experiences that you might deem to have been traumatic or unsuccessful. You may be inclined to believe that negative experiences cannot serve as valuable learning. However, these experiences tend to leave an indelible impression on us—you can use these to mold your approach to social work practice.

You may begin your examination of your learning by comparing your knowledge, skills, and values as you began your practicum with your current knowledge, skills, and values. Engaging in a concerted effort to examine the learning you have experienced can help you to identify those social work skills you have mastered and to develop a plan for termination (3).

A strategy for initiating this self-evaluation process is to consider the following:

- positive and negative aspects of the practicum experience
- knowledge and skills gained
- areas of personal and professional growth and change
- new or confirmed interest areas
- the realities of the experience—ascertain the ways in which you might have made different choices

- goal achievement—identify the goals met and those that remain unmet
- level of confidence
- ability to function collaboratively as a member of a service delivery team
- understanding of the value of supervision

At the point at which you are considering the termination of your practicum experience, you cannot change the way in which this experience has evolved. However, you can use the insights gained from this experience to enhance your next learning experience, whether it will be in your next practicum, as a new social work professional, or in the future as a field instructor.

As you know by now, the practicum experience can be a significant learning experience and one that is often hard to capture in words. Without a formalized plan for identifying the lessons you have learned during this practicum experience, you may find yourself unable to describe your professional growth. The following practice applications can be helpful to you in integrating your learning as you prepare for terminations and articulate your learning.

PRACTICE APPLICATION **10.2**
Termination through Journaling

If you have been maintaining a journal throughout your practicum experience, shift your focus to include specific reflections about your feelings regarding termination. If you have not journaled through your practicum, you can use this practice application to gain insight into your own termination process. Utilizing the termination process as a focal point, journal on knowledge and skills learned, positive and negative feelings about your experience, positive and negative feelings about leaving your clients, coworkers, and field instructor, and future directions for your learning. Two additional areas to include in your journal: (1) utilize your individual or group supervisory sessions or integrative practice field seminar to discuss terminations and new knowledge and skills gained, and (2) utilize the formal and informal evaluation processes available at your agency to review and assess your past, current, and future learning.

PRACTICE APPLICATION **10.3**
Termination through Presentation

Having to summarize and present information is a useful technique for identifying and gaining insight into your learning, challenges, and future learning. Ask your field instructor or seminar instructor if you can present a case/project that entails a description of your practice with a client system with which you worked from assessment through termination and evaluation.

PRACTICE APPLICATION **10.4**

Termination through Illustration

Develop an individual, group, or organizational eco-map with a future perspective—
that is, depict the client or organizational system as you envision it may be at some point
in the future after the social work intervention has been implemented and terminated. A
practice application such as this can help you identify the knowledge and skills you have
learned and mastered at each phase of the intervention as well as those of the client(s) or
project. Share and discuss your eco-map with a member of your practicum team.

PRACTICE APPLICATION **10.5**

Termination through Simulation

Role playing can be a useful exercise by simulating the dynamics involved in terminating
the range of relationships that have evolved during your practicum. Practicing the termination experience can provide you with the confidence you need and allow you to complete
the termination process in a professional and therapeutic manner. Do not be self-conscious
or uncomfortable, but consider the exercise just another aspect of your learning experience.

First, consider the following people as potential partners for rehearsing terminations:
a fellow student, field instructor, social work program faculty or staff member, or an agency
staff member. Second, specific situations that can be helpful to simulate include:

- termination session(s) with an individual client, family, or group;
- evaluation session(s) with your field instructor;
- exit interview with the dean or chair of your social work program;
- employment/graduate school interview; and
- meeting with your supervisor on the first day of your first social work position.

Identify the situation(s) that you want to simulate, select your role-play partner,
complete the role-play (carrying the situation out as far as you need or want to), and then
engage in a debriefing with your partner. You may wish to audio- or videotape the role-
play to aid you in the review process. During the debriefing discussion, both you and
your role-play partner should focus on your strengths and areas for growth.

Developed by Robert Sontag, LCSW

PRACTICE APPLICATION **10.6**

Termination through Activation

If feasible, videotape or audiotape termination encounters with clients or groups at your
practicum setting. You may then review the tape(s) with clients, colleagues, your field
instructor, and faculty members to identify your strengths and areas for growth in facilitating an effective termination.

In sum, your termination is as important for you to process as for your clients. Viewed from a strengths-based perspective, the termination phase of your social work education can be used to assess strengths, gains, and possibilities. Having examined the educational, intellectual, and emotional facets of termination, we will now shift our focus to the more pragmatic aspects of your termination from this practicum experience.

The Nuts and Bolts of Termination with Your Clients, Agency, Field Instructor, and Social Work Program

As with any social work skill, there are appropriate methods for terminating as well as inappropriate ways to achieve closure. Remember that you are terminating at least three types of relationships depending on your student status and situation. At a minimum, you are terminating from clients, coworkers/agency, and your field instructor. Additionally, you may be ending your relationship with the social work program and the school you attend. Finishing your degree may prompt transitions in your relationships with faculty, fellow students, family, friends, coworkers, or roommates. The following sections will provide a discussion of client, agency, and social work program terminations.

Terminating with Clients

Corina begins to plan for her departure from the adolescent group at her practicum. She has discussed the pending termination with her field instructor and developed a plan to transfer responsibility for the group to another practicum student, who will be continuing his practicum for the next semester. The teens had been informed at the outset that Corina was a student who would be leaving at the end of the semester. Corina implements her plan for terminating her involvement with the group by raising the issue several weeks prior to her departure. The week following this discussion, in which specific information was provided to the teens about the transition, Corina notes that Chad, a 15-year-old runaway with a history of truancy and burglary, is sullen and unresponsive and refuses to make eye contact with her. Corina had found Chad to be a challenge throughout his stay at the facility. She felt that he wanted to open up and turn his life around, but she had become frustrated by her unsuccessful (but persistent) efforts. Corina was mystified by Chad's behavior this week, and when she tried to talk with him after the group, he lashed out at her and stated that it did not matter that she was leaving. What is your assessment of this situation, and what strategies can you suggest to Corina regarding her interactions with Chad and the group?

What is appropriate client termination? How do you know you have achieved this elusive goal? When can you initiate termination, and how will you facilitate the process? How can you anticipate and handle clients' responses to your termination? These are typical and important questions for a practicum student to raise, and they will be highlighted here.

Appropriate termination in a direct practice situation should be facilitated at the point at which the mutually established goals have been achieved (4). However, you are likely aware that this ideal situation does not always occur. Terminations may arise as a result of client withdrawal or noncompliance, cessation of eligibility for benefits, or agency policy. You may have had experience throughout your practicum in terminating with clients and have learned that social workers are well within their rights and responsibilities to terminate a client relationship if a threat or injury occurs, client needs cannot be fulfilled, or the client does not meet his or her financial or treatment commitment (4). In these situations, you can attempt to employ as many as possible of the skills for facilitating an appropriate termination.

Corina's problem provides an example of a well-planned termination that becomes complicated by a client's unexpected reaction. Client reactions to termination are as varied as the clients themselves and will likely reflect the way in which the clients respond to other changes and terminations in their lives. Just as you may experience mixed feelings about your own termination, so, too, will your clients. Although most clients report positive feelings about termination, the worker must be prepared to deal with both positive and negative client responses (5). Corina's client, Chad, has presented her with a "mixed message" response to termination. On the one hand, he is saying that her departure has no relevance for him, but the intensity of his response may suggest otherwise.

Termination of the worker–client relationship can evoke similar responses for both the worker and the client. Possibilities emerge as closure is pending. For instance, when a worker announces to a client that he or she is leaving, both may experience pain, guilt, embarrassment, heightened emotions, awkwardness, or realization of an opportunity to engage in candid mutual sharing (6). Both client and worker may experience these simultaneously and may revisit these feelings on multiple occasions before the actual termination of the relationship.

Certainly, the nature and management of the termination process will influence the client's response. A planned termination may enable the client to anticipate his or her feelings, work through the transition, and view the termination as a positive experience in his or her life. However, as we see in Corina's case, even a planned termination can be troublesome. An unplanned, abrupt, or forced termination may leave the client (and you) feeling unfulfilled and lacking closure on the issues that had been the focus of the relationship.

As you know from your social work training, the topic of termination should be introduced at the outset of the professional relationship because the aim of any social work intervention is successfully to achieve the mutually established goals. Students, due primarily to lack of experience in general, often deemphasize the importance of the termination process, placing their attention disproportionately on the earlier phases of the relationship out of fear, guilt, and helplessness (7).

Raising your thoughts and feelings regarding terminating with your clients, your field instructor, and practicum faculty can serve as a "rehearsal" for the actual process (7). Although anticipating the termination phase of social work practice can result in the development of a repertoire of "termination skills," you are prudent to resist having preconceived expectations regarding a particular client's reaction when you introduce and implement the termination. Possible client responses to termination compiled from our experiences and those of others (5, 6) may include:

- a sense of accomplishment that goals have been met
- feeling pleased that he or she no longer has to be involved with you or the agency—a common reaction of involuntary clients
- denial that you are leaving the agency or that the relationship must end (clients may think that the relationship can continue even if you are no longer officially a part of the agency)
- direct and indirect acting out (e.g., anger, regression, hostility toward you or others, lateness, absences, or the introduction of new problems intended to prevent your departure)
- overreaction to the termination—clients may overemphasize the positive contributions made by the worker
- mourning—clients may experience a reaction similar to the reaction typically associated with a loss (e.g., death or divorce)

Conducting a dual-focused exploration of your feelings and your clients' feelings about termination can enable you to understand and respond to your clients' feelings better (3). Without adequate consideration of these two issues, you, as a new social work professional, may be tempted to interpret the client's reactions as rejection of you (3).

The practicum experience can prove to be a valuable arena for identifying and learning skills and strategies for appropriate termination. The following guidelines (3, 5) are helpful:

- Social workers are obligated to notify all clients of terminations (4).
- Determine in advance the best method for informing clients, staff, and community persons of termination—should you conduct home visits, write letters/memoranda, or telephone the clients?
- Determine the appropriate length of time needed to complete the termination process (will be determined by the type of caseload, type of project, and agency culture).
- Be certain to address closure issues in a forthright and timely manner—you may feel tempted to avoid talking with clients by waiting until the final encounter to address termination, particularly if the client is in denial, but you may experience unfortunate consequences of this decision later.
- Sharing experiences that both you and your client have had with terminations in general and with professional helping relationship terminations specifically can be helpful in developing a response to the termination of your current worker–client relationship—anticipating and normalizing these experiences and reactions may help the client (and you) to develop more effective coping skills.

- Identify the learning and change that has occurred and the benefits of termination. This exercise may enable the client to feel more positive about the termination and to clarify and apply the plan for maintaining the achieved change.
- Discuss with your client the areas for his or her continued growth and change—you can identify those goals that are not yet met and strategies for fulfilling those goals and discuss the client's perceived challenges to maintaining the changes he or she has experienced to date.
- Address the external factors that are responsible for or accompany the termination of your relationship with your client (e.g., fees, policies, and your departure).
- Use the termination process as an opportunity to celebrate the ending of a part of the client's life as well as the beginning of the next chapter in his or her life.

When facilitating a termination with a client under less than optimal circumstances (i.e., the relationship was stressful or unproductive, goals remain unmet, or the worker and client did not develop a viable working relationship), honesty is the best policy. Share with the client your perceptions of the problems that occurred and ask for his or her perceptions as well. You must examine your contribution to this situation, but do not allow yourself to feel responsibility for the outcome.

Terminating with clients, particularly those with whom you have established solid working relationships, is challenging even when you have facilitated an appropriate termination. You may be bolstered by adopting the perspective that "termination is a time for assessing treatment, for turning to new activities, and for savoring a sense of accomplishment and independence, not for mourning" (5).

Terminating with Your Field Instructor and Agency Staff

As Ben is preparing for the completion of his foundation practicum at the community center, he is offered a position made possible by a three-year grant awarded to the agency. Ben provided input into this project, so he feels very committed to seeing it come to fruition. If he accepts the position, he will have the opportunity to continue working with clients with whom he has established positive working relationships. The position is well funded, full-time with benefits, and would provide Ben with additional social work experience and could mean a future for him with this agency and in this community. However, two outcomes result if Ben accepts the position: (1) he will be unable to complete his MSW degree in the two-year period he had planned, and (2) he must delay his plans to develop more advanced clinical skills to enable him to realize his goal of becoming a family therapist. He is experiencing a dilemma because he could use the money and the experience, but he feels that he has learned all he can learn at this agency. What would you do if you were Ben?

Termination skills learned for your practice can be a useful strategy for engaging in the termination process with your field instructor and agency staff.

Just as you address your clients' feelings about change and loss, you, too, will benefit from tackling those issues regarding your own change and loss related to leaving the practicum site. Termination from your field instructor and agency staff encompasses dual issues: (1) formal termination—which includes disposition of practicum responsibilities and the evaluation process; and (2) informal termination—which involves the personal farewells. An important aspect of a successful and gratifying termination is to achieve a balance between the attention and resources devoted to each of the areas involved in the termination process (i.e., emotional, educational, and practical tasks).

Formal Termination.   Formal termination from your practicum site involves two primary tasks. First, you and your field instructor must review the status of your practicum assignments and determine the future of each of these cases or projects. Next comes the formal evaluation of your performance as well as of your perception of your practicum experience.

Regarding the disposition of your practicum work assignments, you and your field instructor must address each individual activity in which you have been involved to determine if continued attention is required and, if so, the way in which this will be facilitated. You can and should begin this discussion well in advance (four to eight weeks, at least) of your actual completion date because planning and transitions can be timely and complicated. Specific issues to address during your supervisory sessions may include the following:

- *Closure or transfer of client cases.* You and your field instructor must review each case to evaluate whether the goals have been met and to determine whether the case should be closed or continued. If the case is to be kept open, you and your field instructor can identify the worker/program who will assume responsibility and then facilitate the transfer process.
- *Projects.* Informing your field instructor of the status of any practicum-related projects is the first step in terminating your involvement in such projects as grant proposals, research projects, educational materials, and program evaluations. Ideally, these projects will be completed as you are finishing your practicum. Realistically, this may not be the case—projects, particularly those that involve collaborating with others, often have a way of taking longer than expected. Should you find yourself in the midst of a project, present your suggestions for handling the remainder of the project requirements to your field instructor. Can you, for instance, ask another worker or practicum student to assume responsibility for the project's completion? Might your field instructor take over the remainder of the project? Is this a situation in which you may consider continuing your relationship with the organization? These are all possibilities and should be considered carefully based on the needs of the project and available resources.
- *Group activities.* If you have been involved with a group at your practicum site, you will want to develop a plan for transitioning out of the group. If you have served as a cofacilitator, your departure from the group may not create

a disruption or a need for disposition because your cofacilitator can carry on the group leadership responsibilities in your absence. However, if you have been the sole group leader, you must determine whether the group will continue following your termination and, if so, who will become the new group leader. A transition task such as a change in group leadership may require additional time for planning because a new facilitator must be identified and introduced to the group for at least one to two sessions prior to your departure.

- *Administrative issues related to termination.* "End of practicum" duties that you may be required to complete include physically transferring cases/projects, completing final documentation, notifying agency staff and relevant community persons (including clients), and returning identification badges, parking permits, keys, and other agency supplies.

The final activity required for your completion of your practicum experience is the twofold formal evaluation process: the field instructor's evaluation of the student and the student's evaluation of the field instructor. The field instructor's evaluation of your performance is used as the basis for your official grade, while the evaluation that you complete regarding your practicum perspective is typically used by the practicum faculty to evaluate the quality of field instruction at your site. Both documents are of critical importance to your and other students' social work education and should be given serious attention by all involved in their completion.

Being Evaluated.   The formal and informal evaluation of your performance during this practicum is a significant task that culminates in your termination (and, of course, your grade). "An educational evaluation is a teaching-learning process which qualitatively identifies strengths and weaknesses so as to enable and motivate the student to improve performance" (8). The evaluation of your social work practice competence may and should be achieved using a variety of methods. Your field instructor's evaluation of you is likely to serve as the formal and official evaluation that is submitted to the social work program to serve as the basis for the grade you will receive. However, you may also be evaluated by your peers, agency staff members, or through the use of simulated examinations or informal feedback (8). Regardless of the type or extent of your evaluation, you are encouraged to focus not on the grade that is assigned but on the feedback provided and identify ways in which you can incorporate that information into your growth as a social work professional (8).

Being open to hearing feedback about your performance is essential to being able actually to utilize the information you receive. Munson (9) offers these suggestions for receiving evaluative information.

- Make an effort to hear the details that are being provided without becoming immediately defensive about your performance or person.
- Be open to the possibility that the information is, in fact, valid, and consider ways in which you can incorporate the information in a change of behavior.

- Ask questions to clarify your understanding of the feedback being provided—if specific behavioral information is not provided upon repeated requests, the feedback may not be valid.
- Keep the encounter professional—do not assume that your field instructor is being critical of you as a person;
- Resist the temptation (no matter how emotional you may become) to display anger, to personalize (internally or externally) responsibility, to refuse to listen to criticisms, to deflect the attention to another issue, to justify your behavior, to blame the field instructor, to trivialize the situation by using humor, or to bargain for a revised evaluation.
- Acknowledge that you have *heard* the information provided to you by your field instructor.
- Initiate discussion regarding strategies for changing or improving your performance.
- Reframe feedback that seems negative and critical into opportunities for future growth.

Even a glowing and exemplary evaluation requires you to engage in critical listening skills. We have a tendency to assume that no change is needed if we are positively evaluated by supervisors and peers. In order to continue to grow and develop as a social work professional, change is essential. In fact, some field instructors may have difficulty delivering feedback that they perceive as negative or harsh. If you have not received feedback regarding your areas for growth—and you may not welcome the receipt of such information—you may want to encourage your field instructor to provide such feedback for you to enable you to grow further.

Being the Evaluator.   Your field instructor's evaluation of your practice skills and knowledge is but one aspect of the evaluation and termination process. You will, in all likelihood, be asked to provide feedback to your social work program regarding your perspective of the experience you are completing. In fact, approximately 90 percent of social work programs ask students to complete an evaluation of their field experiences (10). This evaluation may be in the form of a standardized quantitative evaluation form (anonymity may or may not be an option), an interview with your practicum liaison, or some combination of the two methods.

Information provided by students regarding their practicum experiences may be used for several purposes. First, your feedback may be made available to other students to aid them in selecting their practicum sites. Second, practicum faculty may use the information to determine the quality of field instruction provided by a site or field instructor. Last, some social work programs provide copies of students' evaluative feedback to field instructors for their use in improving their field instruction skills.

Consider and be able to articulate your feelings about the practicum experience. Do you believe that the environment was amenable to student learning? In evaluating their practica, students report that satisfaction with the practicum setting is based on agency and field instructor factors that include (1) a healthy work setting (i.e., high morale, activity, and staff commitment), (2) innovation in practicum tasks and activities, (3) clarity regarding roles and responsibilities, (4) field instructor support, and (5) orientation to the practicum (11).

Just as students may experience anxiety and defensiveness about being evaluated (9), they naturally experience anxiety when required to provide evaluative feedback to their field instructors, particularly for the first time (10). Ideally, you and your field instructor have been providing each other with feedback from the outset of your practicum, thus making a formal feedback process simply a summarization of previous feedback sessions. However, if you have not had the opportunity to provide feedback to this or any other supervisor, you may begin by asking for clarification regarding the evaluation's purpose, process, and format and the ways in which the information will be used. Obtaining this information may serve to ameliorate your concerns about evaluating your supervisor (10). Placing an emphasis on giving your field instructor balanced feedback is important; balanced feedback means informing your field instructor of the positive and negative aspects of your learning experience in a professional manner without directing your comments to the field instructor's personal qualities.

Equally important, however, is your recognition of your lack of objectivity regarding your experience. You do possess biased feelings (possibly positive *and* negative) about the practicum you are just about to complete. These feelings may involve the quality of the relationship you have established with your field instructor and other staff, your emotional state, and expectations regarding your grade. Simply acknowledge these and any other reactions and share them with your field instructor if you determine that he or she will benefit from having this information (10). If you do have negative feelings about the experience or your field instructor, consider ways in which you can frame this feedback so that your field instructor can "hear" and use the information. Moreover, you must be cautious so that, even if your experience was not ideal, you do not burn your bridges with your field instructor, other staff, or the agency. You may want your field instructor or another staff member to serve as a reference for you, or you may find yourself working with one of these professionals in the future.

When you are delivering evaluative feedback, there are several additional guidelines that may enhance the quality of the experience for both you and the recipient of the information. The following list is compiled from our experience as well as from suggestions from others (9):

- Take an active and invested role in the evaluation process.
- Provide detailed, specific feedback.
- Keep the focus of your feedback on the individual's professional behavior(s) as they relate to the practicum supervisory role.
- Avoid offering personalized feedback regarding the field instructor or other staff.
- View your feedback as a valuable and necessary facet of the practicum experience for both you and your field instructor.

Providing feedback to your field instructor can be a valuable learning experience for both you and your field instructor. You can each gain insights into your own styles and behaviors as well as learn skills related to evaluation.

Informal Termination.   Although the formal aspects of completing your practicum are important and necessary, so, too, are the informal aspects. Initiation of or participation in the "ritualization" of termination is an important component in your learning process. Informally, termination rituals might include such activities as saying good-bye and thank you to agency staff, writing notes of appreciation to all those who have been important parts of your learning experience; attending the event commemorating your farewell from the agency; and accepting gifts from staff or clients (check agency policy regarding accepting gifts from clients).

Having the experience of acknowledging your departure accomplishes several important milestones in your professional development. First, we all enjoy the opportunity to bring closure to a situation when closure is warranted. Should you leave the agency without recognition, both you and the staff may feel as though you have "unfinished business." Just as clients may distance themselves from you emotionally and physically, you, your field instructor, and the staff may experience similar feelings. Being able to say your farewells may enable all of you to process feelings about your leaving the agency or program. Second, your field instructor and the agency staff have the opportunity to acknowledge your contributions and engage in an informal review of the work that you have completed during the practicum. Last, a ritual activity (e.g., a farewell party, a gift, or a card) that celebrates the completion of this phase of your professional training enables agency staff to begin to view you as a professional and a colleague.

A last piece of the informal termination process is to discuss with your field instructor and agency staff the issue of letters of reference. You may opt to obtain letters of recommendation (although generic letters are not as helpful as letters written for your application to a specific position) or at least verify with your field instructor and other staff members that they are willing to provide references for you. Ensure that the reference they will write will be a positive one—you obviously do not want any surprises.

Terminating with the Social Work Program

If you will be graduating from the social work program following the completion of your current practicum, you have an additional termination issue to address. You have spent considerable hours with the faculty and students who compose your social work program. This group of people may have become a "family" for you as you have grown, learned, commiserated, and struggled with both your fellow students and faculty. Despite the fact that you may be more than eager to move on from this phase of your life, the faculty and student relationships that you have established have served to shape and guide you as you enter your social work career.

Just as we have discussed the merits of attending to appropriate termination with clients, your field instructor, and agency staff, you can use the occasion of your graduation from the social work program to reflect on your classroom terminations as well. The chaos of completing coursework and practicum and preparing for graduation (which may involve relocation or an employment search) may not leave you the time or resources needed to explore your feelings about separating from your social work program.

Graduation (or maybe the period after graduation) provides an opportunity to think about the knowledge and skills that you have gained, the relationships that you have forged, the personal changes that you have undergone, and your visions for your personal and professional futures. You may, however, need some time and emotional distance from the school experience in order to delve into your feelings. Whenever you feel you can, we encourage you to consider the contributions you have made and received through your social work education. Let the faculty and your student peers know you valued the impact they made on your education, and provide balanced feedback regarding your experience with the social work curriculum.

Professional Development: Where Does It Begin and Where Does It End?

You may have just begun to consider yourself a social work professional, and we are already introducing the concept of ongoing professional development! Professional development begins with the first social work course you completed and, one hopes, does not end for the duration of your life. This segment of the unit will highlight such professional development issues as the search for employment, strategies for succeeding in your first social work position, becoming involved in the professional social work community, and obtaining professional credentials.

Employment Search: A Needle in a Haystack?

Social workers learn in their training to establish goals and develop plans to achieve those goals. As a social work student, you established a goal to graduate, obtain a social work position, and become a social work professional. The search for employment is but one step in that march toward your goal. Numerous resources are available to aid you in your search for employment as a social worker. Your university or college probably offers career planning and placement services—take advantage of them early and often! Career counselors are invaluable resources for developing your resume, identifying the availability of positions, designing job search strategies, and preparing for interviews.

The Preparation.   As you anticipate your social work employment search, consider developing a professional portfolio. The professional social work portfolio is a compilation of materials and products that you have completed during your social work training that can now be used to depict and document your social work achievements (12). You may find that assembling examples of your accomplishments will help you articulate and demonstrate your social work competence to potential employers. Additionally, your self-confidence may receive a boost when you are able to see examples of your work collected and organized in one place. Increased confidence in your abilities and assets can serve to enhance the impression you make during an interview. Examples of items to consider including in your portfolio are (12):

- reports, papers, and projects from your practica or coursework;
- grant proposals;
- case documentation (with agency permission and identifying client information disguised);
- correspondence (e.g., letters to politicians, editors, or other professionals and memoranda written to staff within your agency);
- "toolbox"—a list of social work skills, or "tools," that you have gained;
- resume (including a list of social work–related activities) and cover letter;
- self-assessment; and
- practicum evaluations.

The Search.   Networking with other social workers is also an excellent means to securing employment. You can let people know that you are "on the market." You may find networking with students and faculty in your social work program, staff at your practicum site(s), and members of professional social work organizations a particularly useful strategy to consider. Because organizations that employ social workers often do not participate in on-campus recruiting and hiring activities, you cannot rely on the employer to seek you out. Alumni surveys suggest that many graduates find employment at the agencies where their practica were completed. With this thought in mind, maintaining your ties with faculty, your former field instructor(s), and the staff at your practicum site(s) may be a professionally astute and meaningful endeavor.

If you do, in fact, receive an offer of employment from your practicum site, treat it just as you would any other offer. You may feel tempted or obligated to accept such an offer because it is flattering or convenient or because you feel a sense of loyalty, but (like Ben in the earlier student scenario) you should weigh all the issues and options carefully.

While working with your career service office and professional networking will likely yield the best results for your job search, we would like to suggest some additional strategies for securing a social work position.

- *Informational interviewing.* There are two types of informational interviewing that you may wish to consider:
    - ◆ Meeting with agency personnel (who may be social work supervisors or human resource personnel) to discuss the types of social work positions for

which they hire can provide you with insights regarding agency mission and culture, position type and scope, salary ranges, and frequency of openings. Although not all agencies are interested in conducting informational interviews when they do not have position vacancies, you should find that many agencies are willing to meet you. Even if the agency does not have an opening at the time of the informational interview, you may be considered should an opening occur as a result of the initiative you have shown.

   ♦ Interviewing social work practitioners who are employed in the type of position, agency, or setting in which you may be interested can provide you with a more realistic portrayal of employment options.

■ *Internet resources.* Position vacancies are routinely posted on the Website locations for federal and state governmental agencies; some social service agencies; college/university career service centers or schools of social work; local, regional, and national newspapers; and professional social work organizations;

■ *Resources in other areas.* If you are thinking of relocating following completion of your social work degree, consider obtaining a subscription to the local newspaper (or checking out the newspaper's Website), contacting United Way for a listing of local social service agencies, or connecting with your school's alumni or the NASW chapter in that area for networking and job listings.

To form your mindset about the employment search process, we have compiled the following list of suggested strategies (13, 14, 15, 16):

■ Identify an area (population, setting, type of organization, location, and type of social work) in which you are interested. Consider working social work temporary positions rather than committing to a job that you do not want.

■ Consider the realities associated with your employment search—minimum salary expected/required, relocation options, commuting options, and other life obligations.

■ Be true to yourself and know your strengths and preferences—do not take a job that you know you do not want.

■ Develop or finalize your resume, which should include heading (name and contact information), professional objectives, educational history and professional experience (include volunteer and practicum information), awards and honors, memberships, and reference information.

■ Compose a generic cover letter that can be amended to adapt to a specific position vacancy. Provide ample information about yourself and your social work skills and interests.

■ Obtain information regarding the application process.

■ Prepare for interviews by researching your potential employer and the community in which the agency is located and in which services are delivered.

■ Rehearse for the interview—your anxiety will be lessened through mock interviewing with social work professionals, friends, or family members.

■ Plan to dress appropriately—if you are unsure of the "culture" of the organization, you are well advised to dress professionally and somewhat conservatively (e.g., suit/dress, necktie, and minimal jewelry/makeup).

Application Process.   Be certain to adapt and personalize the cover letter and resume for each position for which you apply. Following are tips for managing the interview process:

■ Be on time—being a few minutes early is even better!
■ Greet the interviewer openly with a smile and a firm handshake.
■ Smile frequently, but always appropriately.
■ Listen and speak with interest, enthusiasm, and intelligence.
■ Allow the interviewer to assume and maintain control of the interview—try to determine whether he or she wants to do most of the talking or expects that you will do most of the talking.
■ Maintain a high level of enthusiasm, but do not convey "overeagerness" or desperation.
■ Devote more time to the "significant" questions (e.g., practice approaches and experiences) that you are asked and less time to the "insignificant" questions (e.g., coursework and non–social work positions).
■ Take notes so that you may refer to them later in the interview or following the interview.
■ Remember the interviewer's name and use his or her title.
■ Do not speak negatively about your social work program, previous employers, former field instructor(s) or practicum site(s), social work agencies, or social workers.
■ Make and maintain eye contact with all persons you meet during the interview. Attend to your posture, but appear relaxed (do not sit on the edge of your seat).
■ Ask for clarification if you are unsure about the meaning of the question you have been asked.
■ Observe (or ask about) the pace and the "feel" of the agency and the work. (Do people seem frantically busy? Are staff idling at their desks? What is the appearance of the physical space? How do staff interact with one another and the clients?
■ Develop a list of questions that you can ask during the "down" times of the interview.
■ Although you may not have an opportunity to present such a statement, have a summary statement to offer regarding your understanding of the position, timeframe, and your interests.
■ Most of all, be honest and be yourself!

Follow up the interview with a letter or note thanking the staff at the agency for the interview. Reiterate your interest in the position and your availability.

The Negotiation.   An area you may not yet have considered is your response to an actual offer of employment. Depending on when the offer is made, you may want to delay your response in order to allow yourself time to consider the offer, discuss it with others, or weigh it against other offers. A delay of 48 hours is a reasonable request to make of a potential employer (15).

As you begin a new career, you will tend to focus your attention and energy on completing your degree and landing that first job. In this process, you may neglect to consider the way in which you can and will negotiate the details of the job being offered. As a social worker, you are by now well trained in the area of advocating for others. Social workers are not always the best advocates for themselves, however. One area in which you are well advised to assert your advocacy skills is in the discussions that surround employment arrangements, including salary, benefits, and "tangibles" (e.g., job description, schedules, flexibility, and work-space issues).

Regarding salary, you will want to have conducted a thorough examination of several related issues prior to entering into any negotiation with a potential employer. Salaries are often an issue about which beginning professionals feel (and should feel) curious. The National Association of Social Workers has tracked salary trends since the early 1960s (when MSWs' average salaries were $7,350/year) (17). First, NASW, in 1990, recommended beginning minimum salaries as follows: BSW—$20,000; MSW—$25,000; MSW with two years of social work experience—$30,000; and MSW with special administrative expertise—$45,000 (17). Additionally, using data from 1995, NASW reports the following as the actual salary ranges for social workers based on type of social work degree: BSW—$20,000 to $29,000; MSW—$30,000 to $39,000; and Ph.D/DSW—$40,000 and over (17). Further, median salaries for NASW members surveyed have steadily risen during the 1990s but have not kept up with the rate of inflation (17). Of interest is the fact that social workers employed in aging, children, and family services and occupational social work typically earn less than their counterparts who work in mental health settings, administration, research, or teaching positions, private solo or group practice, and governmental agencies (17).

Knowing the average range of salaries for your degree and experience and the type of agency, position, and geographic area will provide you with a distinct advantage in discussing a job offer. You can obtain this information from several sources, including the career center at your college or university, your state's NASW chapter office, and informational interviewing with faculty, student colleagues, and practitioners. Once you are well informed about the realities of salaries given your situation, determine a salary range that you find acceptable and be prepared to state it during the discussions that follow an offer of employment (18).

The benefits being offered to you may account for 25 percent to 30 percent of the total "package" being presented to you (18). Be certain that you are clear about the benefits that your potential employer is offering you. Inquire about the following benefits typically included with a professional social work position (18):

- health/dental insurance (ask for specific information regarding the type and extent of coverage)

- professional insurance, life insurance, and retirement programs (again, ask for specific details)
- leave policies (e.g., sick, family, vacation, and personal)
- educational benefits (e.g., payments and time allocated for pursuit of a professional degree or credential [to include supervision] and continuing education)

Last, but certainly not least, is the negotiation concerning the "tangibles." These may be the issues that make a job attractive or not to an interviewee. Gaining insight into the specific expectations and options related to the job you are being offered is critical to your future quality of life and professional development. Be willing to ask questions and make requests regarding such issues as the following:

- *Job description.* How specifically defined is the current description, and is there room for current or future negotiation of job duties?
- *Work schedule.* Are the hours you work rigidly determined, or are there options for flexibility (i.e., permanent or intermittent "flex" time or compensatory time)?
- *Dress code.* What are you expected to wear in various work situations (and will this involve a major expenditure for a new wardrobe before you begin the new job)?
- *Flexibility.* Will you be able to determine your daily agenda/calendar, or will the position/agency dictate that for you?
- *Supervision.* Who will provide your supervision, and is that person a licensed or certified social worker in the event that you want to pursue licensure or certification? If not, is there a qualified social worker available to provide supervision, or will the agency fund you to seek supervision outside the agency?
- *Work space.* Will you be required to share an office, telephone, or computer and, if so, is there space available for private interviews with clients?
- *Travel requirements.* If your potential position involves travel, will an agency vehicle be provided for your use (and if so, what is the availability of that vehicle), or will you be reimbursed for using your own vehicle (and if so, what is the rate of reimbursement)? If the position requires considerable travel, you must determine if your vehicle is adequate for that task and, if not, you must decide whether you can afford to purchase a new vehicle at this time.
- *Safety issues.* Does the agency provide training on safety issues? If you will be seeing clients outside the office, what safety precautions (e.g., cellular telephones, pagers, or escorts in certain situations) are available?

Landing that first job is obviously an exciting end to your long journey toward becoming a social worker, but we urge you to use the social work skills of communication and advocacy to secure a gratifying employment arrangement. Negotiating a mutually agreed-upon employment situation can mean the difference between a positive first experience and an unsatisfactory one for both you and your new employer.

Succeeding in Your First Social Work Position

As you anticipate your first postdegree social work position, you may be bombarded by a mixture of feelings—excitement, trepidation, eagerness, and downright fear! A helpful place to begin sorting out these emotions and preparing for your first social work position may be to review Unit 1, on getting started in your practicum. Remember that you have been functioning as a social work professional since you began your first field experience (even if you did not feel that you were!), and you can benefit from recalling the strategies you used to become familiar with that setting. In addition to reviewing your practicum orientation and socialization experience, here are some general guidelines that you may find useful as you begin this next chapter of your social work life (13, 14, 16).

- Get to know the organizational norms of your new employment site, both the formal and informal practices, rules, and traditions.
- Identify any potential or actual conflicts you may have with the organization (e.g., mission, organizational norms). If you perceive any possible conflicts, you must decide whether you think they will inhibit your ability to provide effective services. You may also be able to use these challenges as a strategy for your own professional and personal growth.
- Stay in touch with colleagues from school, practica, or previous employment and establish a formal or informal peer support group if you can.
- Use a peer support group as a supplement to your supervision, and prepare for a licensure or credentialing examination. If supervision is not available or adequate, obtain outside supervision (the NASW chapter office and your alma mater are resources).
- Take the initiative in your new job to meet people and get involved in the agency. Although you are not required to take your new coworkers into your personal life, becoming active in formal and informal office activities can be a way to integrate yourself into the agency.
- Do not be afraid to ask questions! Just because you now have a social work degree does not mean that your learning has ended and that everyone assumes that you have all the answers. Your learning curve has just steepened again, and you are encouraged to take advantage of the opportunities available to learn from your new colleagues.
- Maintain your physical, emotional, and social health to prevent burn-out.

Involvement with the Professional Social Work Community

Your socialization as a social worker does not end with graduation or even with your first social work position. Your career as a social worker evolves as you move from student to practitioner and possibly on to supervisor or administrator. Many of the suggestions offered here to guide you through your student career have merit for the entirety of your professional life. To keep your passion and to avoid stagnation and burn-out, you can use the following strategies:

- Regularly revisit and modify your professional goals, interests, and needs—you may find that you prefer to change positions more frequently than others you know, or you may find gratification in long-term employment with one organization. You may choose to relocate, work part-time, return to school, or move into administration or private practice.
- Regardless of your career choices and directions, you will benefit from ongoing evaluation completed with your significant others, professional mentor, or a career counseling service.
- Assess your interest in pursuing supervisory/administrative positions, private practice, consulting, or any one of the many opportunities available to social workers.
- Based on your ongoing evaluation, develop a multiyear plan for keeping your social work career exciting. This may involve planning for additional training, requesting a change of job duties, or taking a leave.
- Keep in mind the realities of the profession you have chosen and your life issues.
- Avoid reacting drastically to the myriad changes that confront the social work profession.
- Actively engage in self-care on a regular and frequent basis.

Inherent in the successful movement from one phase of your professional life to the next is continued attention to your thoughts and feelings about your growth. As we have emphasized throughout this text, a significant facet of your development as a social worker is your ability to take responsibility for your learning. Your willingness to challenge yourself, ask the difficult questions, and confront the answers will help you to establish your professional social work identity and respond to each new transition that comes your way.

The transition into your life as a professional social worker is an important developmental milestone. Because the profession you have chosen is an intense and sometimes stressful endeavor, it is extremely important that you seek out and receive support from others in the profession. Joining professional social work organizations is one strategy for becoming and staying "connected" to your profession. If your social work position is located in an agency that does not employ any other social workers, having professional ties is even more critical to decreasing your sense of isolation and increasing your feelings of connectedness to other social work professionals.

The National Association of Social Workers is the primary professional social work organization, and you may have taken the opportunity to join this organization as a student. Being an NASW member provides you with access to information through its journals and newspaper. However, you can be a member of a large national organization such as NASW and still not "be involved." We encourage you to begin your involvement with such organizations by attending local or state chapter meetings and volunteering to serve on committees, recruit new members, and present information to others at meetings.

Additionally, you will find as you immerse yourself in your new profession that there are many specialized international, national, regional, or local organizations that embrace social workers. For example, you may learn that social workers in your community with specialized interests (e.g., gerontology, home health, and volunteer management) have organized and meet regularly. Similarly, you may find that the area of service delivery in which you are involved has an affiliation to a larger professional organization that has a subgroup for social workers (e.g., elementary education associations with social work sections). Take the initiative and explore what is out there. Or create something! You will be glad you did.

A final area of professional involvement to consider once you have become an established practitioner is that of giving back to the social work profession by becoming a field instructor. As you know, being a field instructor is an important contribution to the learning of a new professional. Serving in this capacity is a way you can share your knowledge and skills and see the impact that mentorship can have on another social work professional. Additionally, you may choose to volunteer your time and service to the local social work program(s) (which may or may not be your alma mater) through serving on committees or guest lecturing in social work classes. Practitioners are able to provide linkages to social work programs from the social service community and are invaluable in identifying directions for curriculum and school policy.

Social Work Credentials: To Get or Not to Get?

Over the past several decades, the social work discipline has become more professionalized with the advent of national-level certifications, state-level licensures, and certifications, and areas of specialization credentials. As a new professional, you may feel overwhelmed and confused by this plethora of options. More important, you may be uncertain which of these credentials is most critical for you to pursue. Once you determine the credential(s) that you wish to obtain, the next step is understanding the various criteria for being awarded the credential, the benefits of being credentialed in that area, and the requirements for maintaining the credential once you have received it. Presented here is a brief summary of available credentials that you may want to consider at some point in your career.

National Credentials

1) **Academy of Certified Social Workers (ACSW)**
   National Association of Social Workers
   750 First Street, NE, Suite 700
   Washington, DC 20002-4241
   1-800-638-8799
   Website: http://www.naswdc.org

- Criteria for certification:
  - MSW from a CSWE-accredited social work program
  - NASW membership
  - two years of full-time (or equivalent), paid, supervised post-MSW/Ph.D. social work experience accumulated prior to completion of the examination
  - successful completion of examination, which includes content on:
    - assessment and service planning
    - intervention
    - professional development
    - ethical standards
    - administration
  - three professional references

2) **Board Certified Diplomate in Clinical Social Work (BCD)**
   American Board of Examiners in Clinical Social Work
   8484 Georgia Avenue #700
   Silver Springs, MD 20910
   301-587-8783
   - Criteria for certification:
     - graduate social work degree from a CSWE-accredited social work program including at least minimum clinical course content in human growth and development, psychopathology, and clinical methods
     - minimum of one year clinical practicum experience with individuals, couples, families, or groups
     - minimum of 3,000 hours supervised (by a BCD) social work experience
     - successful completion of examination

State Licensure/Certifications.   All states in the United States now have some form of legal regulation (i.e., licensure, certification, or registration) available for professional social workers. To obtain information on the requirements in the state in which you seek the social work credential, we suggest contacting at least one of the following:

1. National Association of Social Workers
   750 First Street, NE, Suite 700
   Washington, DC 20002-4241
   1-800-638-8799
   Website: http://www.naswdc.org
2. Your state chapter office of the National Association of Social Workers
3. American Association of State Social Work Boards (AASSWB)
   400 South Ridge Parkway, Suite B
   Culpepper, VA 22701
   1-800-225-6880 or 540-829-6880

4. Social Work Examination Services
   132 Naples Road
   Brookline, MA 02146
   1-800-933-8802 or 617-277-0161 or 212-473-3239
   Website: http://www.tiac.net/users/swes
   e-mail: swes@tiac.net

Applications for state licensure examinations must be obtained from the state licensure board office. Each office can provide information regarding the criteria for making application, the application process, testing sites and times, passing rates, notification procedures, reexamination requirements, and cost. Ensure that you clarify your understanding of the following issues when making inquiries about licensure credentials or preparing for an examination (19):

- Determine the type and level of licensure you seek—most states grant multiple levels (e.g., baccalaureate, master, advanced, and clinical).
- Confirm your understanding of the requirements for obtaining the credential. In some states, you can sit for the examination immediately upon completion of your degree, while in other states, you cannot take the examination until you have fulfilled the professional experience and supervision requirements.
- Inquire about options for taking the examination—computer-delivered, available accommodations for special needs, and frequency of retakes if you fail to pass the examination.
- Inquire about examination preparation materials, workshops, and study groups.

Specialized Credentials. If you find yourself interested in obtaining a credential in a specialized area, consult with colleagues, the state chapter of the NASW, or your alma mater regarding criteria and contact information. Although not typically required for receiving third-party reimbursements or obtaining employment, specialized credentials verify that you have developed expertise in a particular area and that your knowledge and expertise are sanctioned by an accrediting body. Use caution, however, in seeking specialized credentials until you determine that the accrediting body is a credible entity that is recognized by social workers and the NASW or CSWE. Additionally, obtaining specialized credentials may entail significant costs in the application, examination, and renewal processes.

An exercise that you and your integrative practice field seminar colleagues may want to consider is an investigation of available social work credentials, in general, with an emphasis on the specialized credentials, in particular. You and your fellow students may wish to divide credentials by area of interest, gather and compile the information, and then share it with one another.

Summary

This unit has discussed termination with clients; your field instructor; the practicum site; and your social work program, school, and fellow students. Termination and evaluation have educational, emotional, and logistical components. Suggestions for evaluation of both the student and the field instructor were highlighted. Also discussed was professional development in the areas of employment searching, strategies for success in your first social work position, involvement with the professional social work community, and social work credentials for you to consider.

As you approach the termination of this practicum experience, take a moment and congratulate yourself on the completion of the beginning phases of becoming a professional social worker. Consider also the legacy that you leave at your practicum—what have you contributed to the agency that will live on after you are gone? There have been many high points and some low points, but they have all resulted in learning and mark the beginning of your social work career. As a student of both authors wrote in her final journal entry, "There is always something to learn" (20).

STUDENT SCENARIO POSTSCRIPTS

Cameron was able to "hear" the feedback from his fellow students regarding his "obsession" with working with addicted persons and consulted with his field instructor and a favorite faculty person. Admittedly, he did not want to consider the possibility that he was overly invested in his practicum and this area of his professional development. However, after considerable soul searching, he came to the conclusion that he had possibly crossed a boundary in terms of his professionalism and that he had lost the "detached concern" that is necessary for effective social work practice. Although painful, this process enabled Cameron to realize that he should broaden his experience base and from here, he opted to complete a practicum in a different setting. He had not lost his enthusiasm or commitment for working in substance abuse treatment, but he realized that he could benefit from shifting his focus to include a wider range of skill areas.

Corina immediately shared her concerns with her field instructor. The field instructor, having seen this type of reaction from adolescents before, helped Corina to process her feelings about Chad and her work with him. From there, the two went on to discuss ways in which Corina could help Chad acknowledge his feelings, terminate appropriately with her, and feel positive about someone "leaving" him. As with her initial efforts to facilitate an effective termination, Corina mapped out her strategies and even rehearsed with her field instructor how she would approach Chad. Again, Chad provided Corina with an unexpected turn of events—he escaped from the facility! Corina was able to learn new skills even if she did not have the opportunity to apply them.

Ben struggled for several weeks with the dilemma of either staying on at the agency as an employee or moving on to other things. He processed this dilemma with everyone he knew, but ultimately, he alone had to make the decision. Although he knew that his day-to-day life would be made easier by having a full-time paid position with benefits, he weighed that against having to delay his goals of becoming a family therapist. In the end, he opted to leave the agency in pursuit of his original aspirations.

REFERENCES

1. Waites, C. Ode to a practicum student. *The New Social Worker.* 1998, *5*(2):23.
2. Bergel, V. Social worker heal thyself. *The New Social Worker.* 1998, *5*(4):28.
3. McRoy, R. G., Freeman, E. M. & Logan, S. Strategies for teaching students about termination. *The Clinical Supervisor.* 1986, *4*(4):45–56.
4. Landers, S. Terminating, when it's over, is it? *NASW News.* 1994, *39*(9):3.
5. Fortune, A. E., Pearling, B. & Rochelle, C. D. Reactions to termination of individual treatment. *Social Work.* 1992, *37*(2):171–178.
6. Shulman, L. *The skills of helping individuals, families, groups, and communities.* Itasca, IL: F. E. Peacock Publishers, Inc. 1999.
7. Fair, S. M. & Bressler, J. M. Therapist-initiated termination of psychotherapy. *The Clinical Supervisor.* 1992, *10*(1):171–189.
8. Lazar, A. & Mosek, A. The influence of the field instructor-student relationship on evaluation of students' practice. *The Clinical Supervisor.* 1993, *11*(1):111–120.
9. Munson, C. E. *Clinical Social Work Supervision* (2nd ed.). New York: Haworth Press. 1993.
10. Floyd, C. Evaluating your field instructor. *The New Social Worker.* 1997, *4*(2):18–19.
11. Giddings, M. M., Thompson, K. H. & Holland, T. P. The relationship between student assessments of agency work climate and satisfaction with practicum. *Areté.* 1997, *21*(2):25–35.
12. Coconis, M. A. *Using coursefolios and program portfolios in professional self-development.* Paper presented at the 18th Baccalaureate Program Directors' Meeting, Albuquerque, NM. October 1998.
13. Russo, R. *Serving and surviving as a human service worker.* Prospect Heights, IL: Waveland Press. 1993.
14. Baldino, R. G. The importance of peer support for the new social worker. *The New Social Worker.* 1998, *5*(2):18–19, 29.
15. Lafikes, G. Common sense for the job interview. *St. Louis Post-Dispatch.* 1998, September 20: p. G19.
16. Ginsberg, L. H. *Careers in social work.* Boston: Allyn & Bacon. 1998.
17. Gibelman, M. & Schervish, P. *Who we are. A second look.* Washington, DC: NASW Press. 1997.
18. Doelling, C. N. *Social work career development. A handbook for job hunting and career planning.* Washington, DC: NASW Press. 1997.
19. Social Work Examination Services. *License exam notes.* 1998.
20. Knapp, Lisa. Personal communication. 1998.

APPENDIX A

Criteria for Determining the Best Graduate Social Work Program for You

Developed by Gary Behrman, LCSW

The following checklist includes items important to consider when making your MSW program selection.

- **Accreditation**
  - ☐ MSW program is accredited by the Council on Social Work Education— graduating from a nonaccredited program may limit professional opportunities and income and prohibit eligibility for certain professional credentials.

- **School/Program Mission**
  - ☐ I have reviewed the school/program literature and understand the mission.
  - ☐ The school/program mission is congruent with my values and career goals.
  - ☐ I have explored the way in which the school/program mission is integrated into the curriculum and field experiences.
  - ☐ The school/program mission enjoys a strong reputation in the community.

- **Flexibility**
  - ☐ I have inquired about the school/program's flexibility, particularly regarding:
    - ➤ full- or part-time student status
    - ➤ course offerings
    - ➤ transferring hours
    - ➤ field experience (e.g., point in my program at which I undertake practica, selection process, and scheduling of hours)
    - ➤ leave of absence policy

- **Faculty**
  - ☐ Faculty mentoring and advising are considered important by the school/ program's administrative team and the faculty.

☐ Faculty are adequately available to meet with students outside of class times.

☐ I have reviewed the information and have a thorough understanding of the faculty's research and teaching interests.

☐ Teaching assistants are used to teach/coteach graduate courses and, if so, the percentage of courses that are taught/cotaught by teaching assistants.

- **Curriculum**
  ☐ I have received a course offerings list for the upcoming academic year.

  ☐ The number and scope of curricular concentrations provided will meet my career goals.

  ☐ The course offerings will meet my career goals.

  ☐ I have reviewed the course offerings and believe that the number and range of elective courses offered are adequate for my career goals and interests.

  ☐ The typical class size is appropriate (maximum size should not exceed 20–25 students).

  ☐ Attending and observing a class are options for a prospective student.

- **Practicum/Field Experience**
  ☐ Meeting with a representative of the practicum faculty is an option for a prospective student.

  ☐ I have reviewed the information on practicum and understand the following:
  - ➤ practicum site development and design
  - ➤ number and type of sites available
  - ➤ selection or placement process
  - ➤ opportunities for local, regional, national, and international practicum opportunities
  - ➤ possibilities for sites that offer practicum stipends
  - ➤ option for completing a practicum at my place of employment
  - ➤ criteria used for selecting, approving, and training field instructors
  - ➤ criteria used for developing and evaluating practicum opportunities
  - ➤ specific requirements for completing the practica (e.g., contact hours, schedules, integrative practice field seminar requirements, and grading system)

- **School/Program Demographic Profile**
  ☐ I have received the following information regarding student body:
  - ➤ number and type of ethnic minorities represented
  - ➤ average age
  - ➤ gender split
  - ➤ undergraduate degrees represented
  - ➤ domicile of students (i.e., are most students local or commuting, or do most students move to this area to attend the school?)

- **Resources**
  - ☐ I have reviewed information about or toured the following school/program's available resources:
    - ➤ financial aid options throughout the school/program
    - ➤ library
    - ➤ computer labs
    - ➤ writing assistance programs
    - ➤ health care services
    - ➤ disability support services
    - ➤ student organizations
    - ➤ student government opportunities

- **Alumni**
  - ☐ I have reviewed the following information concerning alumni:
    - ➤ rate of employment following graduation
    - ➤ location, type, and salaries of employment
    - ➤ notable graduates
  - ☐ Meeting with alumni to discuss the school/program is an option.

- **Location**
  - ☐ If I am considering a school/program that will involve relocating, I have inquired about the following concerning the community I would be joining:
    - ➤ cost of living
    - ➤ available and affordable housing (i.e., where do current students live?)
    - ➤ cultural opportunities
    - ➤ recreational/social opportunities
    - ➤ sports/athletic opportunities
    - ➤ safety and security issues
    - ➤ public and private transportation options

- **Students**
  - ☐ Meeting with students currently attending the school/program is an option.

APPENDIX B

Sample BSW Review Questions

The following review questions address various areas of the generalist practice or foundation social work courses. The questions may help you prepare for a cumulative licensure/certification exam. For each question, choose the one best answer. Correct answers may be found immediately following the questions.

Human Development—*Contributions Made by Carole Price, LCSW*

1. The adaptive and problem-solving aspect of mental functioning is the
   a. Superego
   b. Id
   c. Ego
   d. Equifinity

2. According to Erikson's theory of psychosocial development, basic mistrust can develop in the _____ to _____ year of life. People with mistrust can exhibit _____ and experience dependence on powerful players in their lives.
   a. First to third, time perspective
   b. Birth to first, time confusion
   c. First to third, time confusion
   d. None of the above

3. Someone who is overly concerned with others' opinions of him or her, painfully self-conscious, and afraid to be seen has a weak sense of
   a. Autonomy
   b. Identity
   c. Initiative
   d. Guilt

4. Sally is beginning to expand her social radius to include her peers, the culture, and mentors within the community. She is beginning to make adult choices. She is experiencing
   a. Industry vs. inferiority
   b. Intimacy vs. isolation
   c. Identity vs. role confusion
   d. Generativity vs. stagnation

5. In the _____ stage of cognitive development, the capacity to think about abstract events, metacognition, and experimental thinking are present.
   a. Sensorimotor period
   b. Preoperational period

    c. Concrete operations

    d. Formal operations

6. You are working with a six-year-old client who is unable to understand another child's perspective in a disagreement. This child is demonstrating
    a. Centering
    b. Perceptual dominance
    c. Egocentrism
    d. Intuition

7. The Oedipus complex occurs in the phallic stage and
    a. Features the development of castration anxiety
    b. Is related to the Electra complex
    c. Leads to identification with the father and introjection of the father's morals, values, and attitudes
    d. All of the above

Systems Theory—*Contributions Made by Donald Linhorst, Ph.D.*

Define terms by matching.

1. ____ Energy

2. ____ Energy transformation

3. ____ Boundaries

4. ____ Boundary maintenance

5. ____ Linkages

6. ____ Hierarchy

7. ____ Entropy

8. ____ Synergy

9. ____ Homeostasis

a. ranking of system members according to their relative access to energy
b. system function that differentiates a system from its environment
c. an unattended system's tendency toward disorder and decreasing usable energy
d. points at which a system is distinguished from environment
e. the capacity for action in a system
f. tendency of a living system to work toward greater organization and increase in usable energy
g. prime function of all social systems
h. an open system's state of dynamic balance
i. energy exchanges that occur across boundaries of two or more systems

10. True or False? Two or more members within a system who have a higher intensity of energy exchanges between themselves than they have with other system members may be considered a subsystem.

11. True or False? Integration refers to the action by which a system brings about harmonious interaction of members in service of both a system's goals and each member's self-determination.

12. True or False? Examples of pattern maintenance include training, opportunities for advancement, demotion, and expulsion.

13. The goal of a social system is
    a. The initial interests that bring members together
    b. Whatever purpose the system expends energy to accomplish
    c. To assist members in the accommodation and assimilation process
    d. To achieve consensus among the members

Research—*Contributions Made by Stephen Wernet, Ph.D.*

The following information applies to questions 1 and 2:

A social worker began working with 10 students identified by their teachers as experiencing difficulties developing and maintaining friendships with their peers. The social worker gave a social skills pretest to the students, met weekly with them for two years, and engaged their family members to role play at home with them. After two years, the students scored significantly higher on the posttest compared to the pretest.

1. If the social worker claimed that the improvement was due solely to the intervention, the social worker would not have taken into account the possible influence of
    a. Practice effect
    b. History
    c. Statistical regression
    d. Maturation

2. The social worker's research design is known as
    a. Static group comparison
    b. Solomon four group design
    c. Pretest posttest control group design
    d. None of the above

3. The social worker could control for alternative explanations to the hypothesis by
    a. Use of a control group and randomly assigning participants
    b. Testing more often
    c. Working only with voluntary clients
    d. None of the above

4. The "Hawthorne Effect" can occur
   a. When the independent variable appears to be effective solely due to its part in an experiment
   b. When the subject selection process leads the independent variable to cause the dependent variable
   c. Both of the above
   d. None of the above

5. During a research study on the difficulties couples experience with infertility problems, a much-publicized television show on coping strategies for infertile coupled aired. The study results could be affected due to
   a. History
   b. Experimental mortality
   c. Random matching
   d. One-time group study

6. Statistical regression occurs with subjects because
   a. People who love statistics tend to regress
   b. Progress tends to occur more quickly with these subjects
   c. Clients who are extreme in some manner will likely become less extreme over time
   d. None of the above

7. In order for a research design to be a true experimental design, it must
   a. Be projected in time (occur in the future)
   b. Involve a directional hypothesis
   c. Exercise control over the independent variable
   d. Match the experimental and control groups
   e. All of the above

8. A social worker in a rural county of a southwestern state would like to study the use of the public health system by various groups of minority populations in the area. To ensure an adequate sample of each of the minority populations, _____ of the general population should be used.
   a. Simple random sampling
   b. Stratified random sampling
   c. Systematic random sampling
   d. None of the above

9. Accidental sampling entails
   a. The use of subjects that are readily available
   b. A highly structured process of subject selection
   c. Sampling after an accident in an experiment
   d. All of the above

10. A social worker submits a research proposal to an institutional review board (IRB) for approval. The research hypothesis is that female gymnasts suffer from anorexia and bulimia at a rate higher than the general population. The

social worker wishes to send a survey to all gymnasts in the local area. Questions from the board center around whether the survey instrument is clear and will measure the anorexic and bulimic behavior. Their concerns relate to the instrument's
a. Reliability
b. Validity
c. Error rate
d. None of the above

11. The level of significance at which the null hypothesis is usually rejected is
   a. $p < .95$
   b. $p < .05$
   c. $p < .50$

12. An important focus of the single system design is
   a. Ensuring a representative sample
   b. Random assignment
   c. Using a baseline for comparison purposes

13. Descriptive statistics allows one to
   a. Portray a picture of a data set
   b. Decide whether to reject or accept the null hypothesis
   c. Provide statistical significance

14. "How effective is Medicaid coverage in reducing the incidence of childhood death?" In this research question, the dependent variable is
   a. Medicaid coverage
   b. Childhood death
   c. Both
   d. Neither

15. Studies that examine social phenomena by obtaining data at a single point in time are called
   a. Longitudinal
   b. Static
   c. Dynamic
   d. Cross-sectional

Diversity and Practice Theory—*Contributions Made by Carole Price, LCSW, and Susan Tebb, Ph.D.*

1. A common history and a common language are involved in a special form of culture generally referred to as
   a. Family culture
   b. Social work culture
   c. Ethnic culture
   d. None of the above

2. A sense of connectedness to persons and the environment and a strong sense of relationship between oneself and one's forebears, family, community, and the land characterizes
   a. Latino culture
   b. Asian and Pacific Island culture
   c. Anglo culture
   d. Native American culture

3. Strong familial ties are characteristic of many cultures, including
   a. Asian
   b. Latino
   c. African American
   d. All of the above

4. Avoidance of eye contact by a client of Asian ancestry may be an expression of
   a. Personality
   b. Cultural norms
   c. Immediate social circumstances
   d. Either a or b, but not c
   e. a, b, and/or c

5. Ethnic culture is defined as a unique form of culture entailing
   a. A common religious heritage
   b. Experiences of racism and discrimination
   c. Shared ancestry or history
   d. Common beliefs, values, and behaviors

6. A client begins to discuss her anxiety, problems with her sleep, and her desire to gain a broader perspective on her life. Using the problem-solving approach, the first issue on which to focus would be
   a. The anxiety
   b. The life perspective
   c. The problem of becoming a client
   d. The problems with her sleep

7. The phases of group development, in order, are
   a. Norming, forming, storming, performing
   b. Forming, norming, storming, performing
   c. Forming, norming, performing, storming
   d. None of the above

8. In the _____ stage of group development, the group members engage in more active exploration and testing of the group situation, explore the interpersonal potential in the group, and begin to develop relationship patterns and differentiate roles.
   a. Storming
   b. Norming
   c. Performing
   d. All of the above

9. The following are core ethical principles of social work practice *except*
   a. Pursuit of social justice
   b. Respect for individual self-determination, regardless of the effect on others
   c. Nonjudgmental acceptance of the client, regardless of the effects on others
   d. All are ethical principles

10. Partializing and prioritizing a client's problem helps the client to
    a. Explore the root of the problem
    b. Decrease client dependency on the social worker
    c. Gain insight into the crisis and the stressful event that caused the crisis
    d. Gain a cognitive grasp of the situation

11. Social workers should NOT do the following when making referrals
    a. Relate the resource to the client's perceived needs
    b. Provide information about the community resource options available to the client
    c. Expedite the process by selecting only the best resources based on your experience and feedback from clients
    d. Provide the opportunity for the client to ventilate about the process of pursuing resources

12. Advice and suggestion are appropriately used under the following circumstances *except*
    a. To assist the client to formulate personal goals
    b. When using crisis intervention techniques
    c. To help the client decide the best means to accomplish his or her personal goals
    d. When a client, severely impaired by an organic impairment or decompensation, is unable to determine a goal

13. A _____ group is an example of a reciprocal group.
    a. Treatment
    b. Self-help
    c. Children's arts and crafts after-school group
    d. None of the above

14. Communities are different from organizations in that organizations
    a. Are goal driven
    b. Contain a formal authority structure
    c. Are social systems
    d. None of the above

15. All of the following are necessary elements of informed consent *except*
    a. The consent must be documented
    b. The client must have accurate information about the treatment to which he or she is consenting
    c. Consent must be given without coercion
    d. The client must be of sound mind and have the ability to understand and reason about the decision

16. A 12-year-old girl drops into your office to talk about her decision to get an abortion. She is most concerned about her stepfather's reaction to her pregnancy and states that he "is always bugging her." You should
    a. Report to children's protective services only if she reveals child sexual abuse
    b. Make a report to the children's protective services if, after talking to her further, you have reasonable suspicion of child abuse
    c. Make a report to children's protective services regardless of further information the child provides
    d. None of the above

17. A parent tells you that she wants to teach her child to do his homework without her prompting and that she wants the behavior to last throughout his academic career. Using learning theory (behavioral approach), the first step would be to
    a. Discuss methods of reinforcing the behavior
    b. Ask how often she must prompt the child to do the homework
    c. Discuss possible reasons the child may have for avoiding her homework
    d. None of the above

18. True or False? A governing board of an agency has no legal authority or responsibility for the operation of the organization; rather, members provide input and advice.

19. True or False? Class advocacy seeks change to benefit only a specific individual client.

20. True or False? The generalist perspective ensures that a social worker will focus on several levels of intervention.

21. True or False? The use of person-centered theory is appropriate for clients who are experiencing problems caused by external or environmental factors.

22. True or False? Reality therapy applies the use of unconscious motivations and nonorganic mental illness.

23. True or False? The crisis intervention model is applicable when the functioning of a client has been suddenly impacted by a loss or tragedy and is to be used during a four- to six-week period following the precipitating event.

24. The following were characteristics of the charity organization movement *except*
    a. The focus of the work was on the social causes of dependency
    b. Modeling and mentoring of the poor were emphasized
    c. Professional training was unnecessary
    d. a and c

25. The four elements that make up the social work profession DO NOT include
    a. Networking
    b. Values and ethics
    c. Methods
    d. Evaluation

Social Policy—*Contributions Made by William Padberg, DSW*

1. Social welfare
   a. Promotes the well-being of the individual and of society as a whole
   b. Includes provisions concerned with treatment as well as prevention of social problems
   c. Involves services to individuals as well as efforts to modify social institutions
   d. All of the above
   e. None of the above

2. Social Darwinism
   a. Held that the human species was involved in a struggle for survival in which only the fittest would survive
   b. Was a scientific breakthrough in the field of botany
   c. Was a school of social thought developed and proclaimed by Charles Darwin
   d. Is the conceptual framework for Social Security

3. Values
   a. Differ from ethics
   b. Are beliefs concerning desirable modes of conduct or desirable end states of existence
   c. Underlie social policies
   d. None of the above
   e. All of the above

4. _____ is stressed in the "process approach" to policy analysis.
   a. The exploration of the steps or stages in the formulation of policy
   b. The cost-benefit value of policy
   c. The examination of success or failure of policy
   d. The inclusion of a variety of disciplines in the analysis of policy

5. _____ is stressed in the "performance approach" to policy analysis.
   a. The exploration of the steps or stages in the formulation of policy
   b. The cost-benefit value of policy
   c. The examination of success or failure of policy
   d. The inclusion of a variety of disciplines in the analysis of policy

6. An example of a universal benefit is
   a. WIC benefits
   b. Public schooling
   c. Temporary Assistance to Needy Families (TANF)

7. Social Security enjoys wide popularity because
   a. It is a progressive tax
   b. States can set payment amounts as they see fit
   c. Nearly all U.S. citizens expect to receive some benefits from the program
   d. None of the above

8. Unemployment compensation
   a. Provides income for unavoidable expenses during times of involuntary unemployment
   b. Prevents workers from being employed
   c. Provides income for job-related expenses
   d. None of the above
   e. All of the above

9. The Food Stamp Program is funded and administered by the
   a. U.S. Department of Health and Human Services
   b. U.S. Department of Agriculture
   c. U.S. Department of the Interior
   d. None of the above

10. True or False? The Earned Income Tax Credit provides benefits for the working poor.

11. True or False? The Supplemental Social Security Income program is funded and administered entirely by states.

12. True or False? A Diagnostic Related Group system (DRG) is an effort by the federal government to contain health costs.

13. True or False? A person must be eligible for TANF to be eligible for Medicaid coverage in every state.

14. True or False? The Head Start program is part of the federal TANF program.

15. True or False? The development of the U.S. system of social welfare was greatly influenced by the Elizabethan Poor Law.

Answers

Human Development
1. C; 2. B; 3. A; 4. A; 5. D; 6. C; 7. D

Systems Theory
1. E; 2. G; 3. D; 4. B; 5. I; 6. A; 7. C; 8. F; 9. H; 10. T; 11. F; 12. T; 13. B

Research
1. D; 2. A; 3. A; 4. A; 5. A; 6. C; 7. E; 8. B; 9. A; 10. B; 11. B; 12. C; 13. A; 14. A; 15. D

Diversity and Practice Theory
1. C; 2. D; 3. D; 4. E; 5. C; 6. D; 7. B; 8. A; 9. B; 10. D; 11. C; 12. A; 13. B; 14. B; 15. A; 16. B; 17. B; 18. F; 19. F; 20. T; 21. F; 22. F; 23. T; 24. A; 25. A

Social Policy
1. D; 2. A; 3. E; 4. A; 5. C; 6. B; 7. C; 8. A; 9. B; 10. T; 11. F; 12. T; 13. F; 14. F; 15. T

APPENDIX C

Social Work: The Puzzling Profession

Adapted from original work by Pamela Huggins, LCSW

Across

1. Practice at community/administrative level
7. The lens we bring to practice
9. Primary theory of social work
11. Social work used to be a hobby but is now considered a _____
14. One of the goals of social work (or what a body builder might want)
17. Social workers often work with people who have committed or been victims of _____
20. Another name for public assistance
22. Consumer of social work services
23. A set of statements to explain factual data

Down

2. One of the roles a social worker might play to obtain needed services for a client group
3. Simulated or rehearsed client interaction can be completed with the use of a _____ play
4. Public assistance health care coverage
5. Generalist social work degree
6. Federal agency that makes policy for immigrant clients
8. Tool for assessment of individual's environment and relationships (or an atlas of one's life)
9. A perspective that social workers espouse (or what you strive for at the gym)
10. Practice with groups
12. Type of social work a BSW practices
13. Guide for social work agency or government practice
15. Practice with individuals and families
16. Advanced social work degree
17. Professional organization for social workers
18. Often creates dilemmas for social workers but also guides us in how to practice social work
19. The object of a self-care campaign
21. Social workers seek empirical knowledge through _____

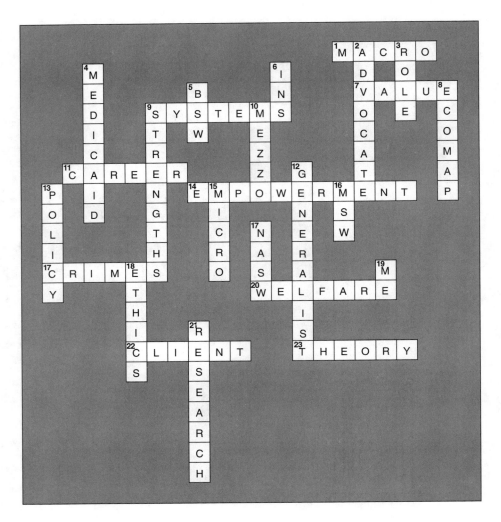

APPENDIX D

NASW Social Work *Code of Ethics*

Preamble

The primary mission of the social work profession is to enhance human well-being and help meet the basic human needs of all people, with particular attention to the needs and empowerment of people who are vulnerable, oppressed, and living in poverty. A historic and defining feature of social work is the profession's focus on individual well-being in a social context and the well-being of society. Fundamental to social work is attention to the environmental forces that create, contribute to, and address problems in living.

Social workers promote social justice and social change with and on behalf of clients. "Clients" is used inclusively to refer to individuals, families, groups, organizations, and communities. Social workers are sensitive to cultural and ethnic diversity and strive to end discrimination, oppression, poverty, and other forms of social injustice. These activities may be in the form of direct practice, community organizing, supervision, consultation, administration, advocacy, social and political action, policy development and implementation, education, and research and evaluation. Social workers seek to enhance the capacity of people to address their own needs. Social workers also seek to promote the responsiveness of organizations, communities, and other social institutions to individual's needs and social problems.

The mission of the social work profession is rooted in a set of core values. These core values, embraced by social workers throughout the profession's history, are the foundation of social work's unique purpose and perspective:

- service
- social justice
- dignity and worth of the person
- importance of human relationships
- integrity
- competence.

This constellation of core values reflects what is unique to the social work profession. Core values, and the principles that flow from them, must be balanced within the context and complexity of the human experience.

Purpose of the NASW Code of Ethics

Professional ethics are at the core of social work. The profession has an obligation to articulate its basic values, ethical principles, and ethical standards. The *NASW Code of Ethics* sets forth these values, principles, and standards to guide social workers' conduct. The *Code* is relevant to all social workers and social work students, regardless of their professional functions, the settings in which they work, or the populations they serve.

The *NASW Code of Ethics* serves six purposes:

1. The *Code* identifies core values on which social work's mission is based.
2. The *Code* summarizes broad ethical principles that reflect the profession's core values and establishes a set of specific ethical standards that should be used to guide social work practice.
3. The *Code* is designed to help social workers identify relevant considerations when professional obligations conflict or ethical uncertainties arise.
4. The *Code* provides ethical standards to which the general public can hold the social work profession accountable.
5. The *Code* socializes practitioners new to the field to social work's mission, values, ethical principles, and ethical standards.
6. The *Code* articulates standards that the social work profession itself can use to assess whether social workers have engaged in unethical conduct. NASW has formal procedures to adjudicate ethics complaints filed against its members.[1] In subscribing to this *Code,* social workers are required to cooperate in its implementation, participate in NASW adjudication proceedings, and abide by any NASW disciplinary rulings or sanctions based on it.

The *Code* offers a set of values, principles, and standards to guide decision making and conduct when ethical issues arise. It does not provide a set of rules that prescribe how social workers should act in all situations. Specific applications of the *Code* must take into account the context in which it is being considered and the possibility of conflicts among the *Code*'s values, principles, and standards. Ethical responsibilities flow from all human relationships, from the personal and familial to the social and professional.

Further, the *NASW Code of Ethics* does not specify which values, principles, and standards are most important and ought to outweigh others in instances when they conflict. Reasonable differences of opinion can and do exist among social workers with respect to the ways in which values, ethical principles, and ethical standards should be rank ordered when they conflict. Ethical decision making in a given situation must apply the informed judgment of the individual social worker and should also consider how the issues would be judged in a peer review process where the ethical standards of the profession would be applied.

[1]For information on NASW adjudication procedures, see *NASW Procedures for the Adjudication of Grievances.*

Ethical decision making is a process. There are many instances in social work where simple answers are not available to resolve complex ethical issues. Social workers should take into consideration all the values, principles, and standards in this *Code* that are relevant to any situation in which ethical judgment is warranted. Social workers' decisions and actions should be consistent with the spirit as well as the letter of this *Code*.

In addition to this *Code*, there are many other sources of information about ethical thinking that may be useful. Social workers should consider ethical theory and principles generally, social work theory and research, laws, regulations, agency policies, and other relevant codes of ethics, recognizing that among codes of ethics social workers should consider the *NASW Code of Ethics* as their primary source. Social workers also should be aware of the impact on ethical decision making of their clients' and their own personal values and cultural and religious beliefs and practices. They should be aware of any conflicts between personal and professional values and deal with them responsibly. For additional guidance social workers should consult the relevant literature on professional ethics and ethical decision making and seek appropriate consultation when faced with ethical dilemmas. This may involve consultation with an agency-based or social work organization's ethics committee, a regulatory body, knowledgeable colleagues, supervisors, or legal counsel.

Instances may arise when social workers' ethical obligations conflict with agency policies or relevant laws or regulations. When such conflicts occur, social workers must make a responsible effort to resolve the conflict in a manner that is consistent with the values, principles, and standards expressed in this *Code*. If a reasonable resolution of the conflict does not appear possible, social workers should seek proper consultation before making a decision.

The *NASW Code of Ethics* is to be used by NASW and by individuals, agencies, organizations, and bodies (such as licensing and regulatory boards, professional liability insurance providers, courts of law, agency boards of directors, government agencies, and other professional groups) that choose to adopt it or use it as a frame of reference. Violation of standards in this *Code* does not automatically imply legal liability or violation of the law. Such determination can only be made in the context of legal and judicial proceedings. Alleged violations of the *Code* would be subject to a peer review process. Such processes are generally separate from legal or administrative procedures and insulated from legal review or proceedings to allow the profession to counsel and discipline its own members.

A code of ethics cannot guarantee ethical behavior. Moreover, a code of ethics cannot resolve all ethical issues or disputes or capture the richness and complexity involved in striving to make responsible choices within a moral community. Rather, a code of ethics sets forth values, ethical principles, and ethical standards to which professionals aspire and by which their actions can be judged. Social workers' ethical behavior should result from their personal commitment to engage in ethical practice. The *NASW Code of Ethics* reflects the commitment of all social workers to uphold the profession's values and to act ethically. Principles and standards must be applied by individuals of good character who discern moral questions and, in good faith, seek to make reliable ethical judgments.

Ethical Principles

The following broad ethical principles are based on social work's core values of service, social justice, dignity and worth of the person, importance of human relationships, integrity, and competence. These principles set forth ideals to which all social workers should aspire.

Value: *Service*

Ethical Principle: *Social workers' primary goal is to help people in need and to address social problems.*

Social workers elevate service to others above self-interest. Social workers draw on their knowledge, values, and skills to help people in need and to address social problems. Social workers are encouraged to volunteer some portion of their professional skills with no expectation of significant financial return (pro bono service).

Value: *Social Justice*

Ethical Principle: *Social workers challenge social injustice.*

Social workers pursue social change, particularly with and on behalf of vulnerable and oppressed individuals and groups of people. Social workers' social change efforts are focused primarily on issues of poverty, unemployment, discrimination, and other forms of social injustice. These activities seek to promote sensitivity to and knowledge about oppression and cultural and ethnic diversity. Social workers strive to ensure access to needed information, services, and resources; equality of opportunity; and meaningful participation in decision making for all people.

Value: *Dignity and Worth of the Person*

Ethical Principle: *Social workers respect the inherent dignity and worth of the person.*

Social workers treat each person in a caring and respectful fashion, mindful of individual differences and cultural and ethnic diversity. Social workers promote clients' socially responsible self-determination. Social workers seek to enhance clients' capacity and opportunity to change and to address their own needs. Social workers are cognizant of their dual responsibility to clients and to the broader society. They seek to resolve conflicts between clients' interests and the broader society's interests in a socially responsible manner consistent with the values, ethical principles, and ethical standards of the profession.

Value: *Importance of Human Relationships*

Ethical Principle: *Social workers recognize the central importance of human relationships.*

Social workers understand that relationships between and among people are an important vehicle for change. Social workers engage people as partners in the helping process. Social workers seek to strengthen relationships among people in a purposeful effort to promote, restore, maintain, and enhance the well-being of individuals, families, social groups, organizations, and communities.

Value: *Integrity*

Ethical Principle: *Social workers behave in a trustworthy manner.*

Social workers are continually aware of the profession's mission, values, ethical principles, and ethical standards and practice in a manner consistent with them. Social workers act honestly and responsibly and promote ethical practices on the part of the organizations with which they are affiliated.

Value: *Competence*

Ethical Principle: *Social workers practice within their areas of competence and develop and enhance their professional expertise.*

Social workers continually strive to increase their professional knowledge and skills and to apply them in practice. Social workers should aspire to contribute to the knowledge base of the profession.

Ethical Standards

The following ethical standards are relevant to the professional activities of all social workers. These standards concern (1) social workers' ethical responsibilities to clients, (2) social workers' ethical responsibilities to colleagues, (3) social workers' ethical responsibilities in practice settings, (4) social workers' ethical responsibilities as professionals, (5) social workers' ethical responsibilities to the social work profession, and (6) social workers' ethical responsibilities to the broader society.

Some of the standards that follow are enforceable guidelines for professional conduct, and some are aspirational. The extent to which each standard is enforceable is a matter of professional judgment to be exercised by those responsible for reviewing alleged violations of ethical standards.

1. Social Workers' Ethical Responsibilities to Clients
   1.01 Commitment to Clients

   Social workers' primary responsibility is to promote the well-being of clients. In general, clients' interests are primary. However, social workers' responsibility to the larger society or specific legal obligations may on limited occasions supersede the loyalty owed clients, and clients should be so advised. (Examples include when a social worker is required by law to report that a client has abused a child or has threatened to harm self or others.)

   1.02 Self-Determination

   Social workers respect and promote the right of clients to self-determination and assist clients in their efforts to identify and clarify their goals. Social workers may limit clients' right to self-determination when, in the social workers' professional judgment, clients' actions or potential actions pose a serious, foreseeable, and imminent risk to themselves or others.

1.03   Informed Consent

(a) Social workers should provide services to clients only in the context of a professional relationship based, when appropriate, on valid informed consent. Social workers should use clear and understandable language to inform clients of the purpose of the services, risks related to the services, limits to services because of the requirements of a third-party payer, relevant costs, reasonable alternatives, clients' right to refuse or withdraw consent, and the time frame covered by the consent. Social workers should provide clients with an opportunity to ask questions.

(b) In instances when clients are not literate or have difficulty understanding the primary language used in the practice setting, social workers should take steps to ensure clients' comprehension. This may include providing clients with a detailed verbal explanation or arranging for a qualified interpreter or translator whenever possible.

(c) In instances when clients lack the capacity to provide informed consent, social workers should protect clients' interests by seeking permission from an appropriate third party, informing clients consistent with the clients' level of understanding. In such instances social workers should seek to ensure that the third party acts in a manner consistent with clients' wishes and interests. Social workers should take reasonable steps to enhance such clients' ability to give informed consent.

(d) In instances when clients are receiving services involuntarily, social workers should provide information about the nature and extent of services and about the extent of clients' right to refuse service.

(e) Social workers who provide services via electronic media (such as computer, telephone, radio, and television) should inform recipients of the limitations and risks associated with such services.

(f) Social workers should obtain clients' informed consent before audiotaping or videotaping clients or permitting observation of services to clients by a third party.

1.04   Competence

(a) Social workers should provide services and represent themselves as competent only within the boundaries of their education, training, license, certification, consultation received, supervised experience, or other relevant professional experience.

(b) Social workers should provide services in substantive areas or use intervention techniques or approaches that are new to them only after engaging in appropriate study, training, consultation, and supervision from people who are competent in those interventions or techniques.

(c) When generally recognized standards do not exist with respect to an emerging area of practice, social workers should exercise careful judgment and take responsible steps (including appropriate education, research, training, consultation, and supervision) to ensure the competence of their work and to protect clients from harm.

1.05 Cultural Competence and Social Diversity

(a) Social workers should understand culture and its function in human behavior and society, recognizing the strengths that exist in all cultures.

(b) Social workers should have a knowledge base of their clients' cultures and be able to demonstrate competence in the provision of services that are sensitive to clients' cultures and to differences among people and cultural groups.

(c) Social workers should obtain education about and seek to understand the nature of social diversity and oppression with respect to race, ethnicity, national origin, color, sex, sexual orientation, age, marital status, political belief, religion, and mental or physical disability.

1.06 Conflicts of Interest

(a) Social workers should be alert to and avoid conflicts of interest that interfere with the exercise of professional discretion and impartial judgment. Social workers should inform clients when a real or potential conflict of interest arises and take reasonable steps to resolve the issue in a manner that makes the clients' interests primary and protects clients' interests to the greatest extent possible. In some cases, protecting clients' interests may require termination of the professional relationship with proper referral of the client.

(b) Social workers should not take unfair advantage of any professional relationship or exploit others to further their personal, religious, political, or business interests.

(c) Social workers should not engage in dual or multiple relationships with clients or former clients in which there is a risk of exploitation or potential harm to the client. In instances when dual or multiple relationships are unavoidable, social workers should take steps to protect clients and are responsible for setting clear, appropriate, and culturally sensitive boundaries. (Dual or multiple relationships occur when social workers relate to clients in more than one relationship, whether professional, social, or business. Dual or multiple relationships can occur simultaneously or consecutively.)

(d) When social workers provide services to two or more people who have a relationship with each other (for example, couples, family members), social workers should clarify with all parties which individuals will be considered clients and the nature of social workers' professional obligations to the various individuals who are receiving services. Social workers who anticipate a conflict of interest among the individuals receiving services or who anticipate having to perform in potentially conflicting roles (for example, when a social worker is asked to testify in a child custody dispute or divorce proceedings involving clients) should clarify their role with the parties involved and take appropriate action to minimize any conflict of interest.

1.07 Privacy and Confidentiality

(a) Social workers should respect clients' right to privacy. Social workers should not solicit private information from clients unless it is essential to providing services or conducting social work evaluation or research. Once private information is shared, standards of confidentiality apply.

(b) Social workers may disclose confidential information when appropriate with valid consent from a client or a person legally authorized to consent on behalf of a client.

(c) Social workers should protect the confidentiality of all information obtained in the course of professional service, except for compelling professional reasons. The general expectation that social workers will keep information confidential does not apply when disclosure is necessary to prevent serious, foreseeable, and imminent harm to a client or other identifiable person or when laws or regulations require disclosure without a client's consent. In all instances, social workers should disclose the least amount of confidential information necessary to achieve the desired purpose; only information that is directly relevant to the purpose for which the disclosure is made should be revealed.

(d) Social workers should inform clients, to the extent possible, about the disclosure of confidential information and the potential consequences, when feasible before the disclosure is made. This applies whether social workers disclose confidential information on the basis of a legal requirement or client consent.

(e) Social workers should discuss with clients and other interested parties the nature of confidentiality and limitations of clients' right to confidentiality. Social workers should review with clients circumstances where confidential information may be requested and where disclosure of confidential information may be legally required. This discussion should occur as soon as possible in the social worker–client relationship and as needed throughout the course of the relationship.

(f) When social workers provide counseling services to families, couples, or groups, social workers should seek agreement among the parties involved concerning each individuals' right to confidentiality and obligation to preserve the confidentiality of information shared by others. Social workers should inform participants in family, couples, or group counseling that social workers cannot guarantee that all participants will honor such agreements.

(g) Social workers should inform clients involved in family, couples, marital, or group counseling of the social worker's, employer's, and agency's policy concerning the social worker's disclosure of confidential information among the parties involved in the counseling.

(h) Social workers should not disclose confidential information to third-party payers unless clients have authorized such disclosure.

(i) Social workers should not discuss confidential information in any setting unless privacy can be ensured. Social workers should not discuss confidential information in public or semipublic areas such as hallways, waiting rooms, elevators, and restaurants.

(j) Social workers should protect the confidentiality of clients during legal proceedings to the extent permitted by law. When a court of law or other legally authorized body orders social workers to disclose confidential or privileged information without a client's consent and such disclosure could cause harm to the client, social workers should request that the court withdraw the order or limit the order as narrowly as possible or maintain the records under seal, unavailable for public inspection.

(k) Social workers should protect the confidentiality of clients when responding to requests from members of the media.

(l) Social workers should protect the confidentiality of clients' written and electronic records and other sensitive information. Social workers should take reasonable steps to ensure that clients' records are stored in a secure location and that clients' records are not available to others who are not authorized to have access.

(m) Social workers should take precautions to ensure and maintain the confidentiality of information transmitted to other parties through the use of computers, electronic mail, facsimile machines, telephones and telephone answering machines, and other electronic or computer technology. Disclosure of identifying information should be avoided whenever possible.

(n) Social workers should transfer or dispose of clients' records in a manner that protects clients' confidentiality and is consistent with state statutes governing records and social work licensure.

(o) Social workers should take reasonable precautions to protect client confidentiality in the event of the social worker's termination of practice, incapacitation, or death.

(p) Social workers should not disclose identifying information when discussing clients for teaching or training purposes unless the client has consented to disclosure of confidential information.

(q) Social workers should not disclose identifying information when discussing clients with consultants unless the client has consented to disclosure of confidential information or there is a compelling need for such disclosure.

(r) Social workers should protect the confidentiality of deceased clients consistent with the preceding standards.

1.08   Access to Records

(a) Social workers should provide clients with reasonable access to records concerning the clients. Social workers who are concerned that clients' access to their records could cause serious misunderstanding or harm to the client should provide assistance in interpreting the records and consultation with the client regarding the records. Social workers should limit clients' access to their records, or portions of their records, only in exceptional circumstances when there is compelling evidence that such access would cause serious harm to the client. Both clients' requests and the rationale for withholding some or all of the record should be documented in clients' files.

(b) When providing clients with access to their records, social workers should take steps to protect the confidentiality of other individuals identified or discussed in such records.

1.09   Sexual Relationships

(a) Social workers should under no circumstances engage in sexual activities or sexual contact with current clients, whether such contact is consensual or forced.

(b) Social workers should not engage in sexual activities or sexual contact with clients' relatives or other individuals with whom clients maintain a close personal relationship when there is a risk of exploitation or potential harm to the client. Sexual activity or sexual contact with clients' relatives or other individuals with whom clients maintain a personal relationship has the potential to be harmful to the client and may make it difficult for the social worker and client to maintain appropriate professional boundaries. Social workers—not their clients, their clients' relatives, or other individuals with whom the client maintains a personal relationship—assume the full burden for setting clear, appropriate, and culturally sensitive boundaries.

(c) Social workers should not engage in sexual activities or sexual contact with former clients because of the potential for harm to the client. If social workers engage in conduct contrary to this prohibition or claim that an exception to this prohibition is warranted because of extraordinary circumstances, it is social workers—not their clients—who assume the full burden of demonstrating that the former client has not been exploited, coerced, or manipulated, intentionally or unintentionally.

(d) Social workers should not provide clinical services to individuals with whom they have had a prior sexual relationship. Providing clinical services to a former sexual partner has the potential to be harmful to the individual and is likely to make it difficult for the social worker and individual to maintain appropriate professional boundaries.

1.10 Physical Contact

Social workers should not engage in physical contact with clients when there is a possibility of psychological harm to the client as a result of the contact (such as cradling or caressing clients). Social workers who engage in appropriate physical contact with clients are responsible for setting clear, appropriate, and culturally sensitive boundaries that govern such physical contact.

1.11 Sexual Harassment

Social workers should not sexually harass clients. Sexual harassment includes sexual advances, sexual solicitation, requests for sexual favors, and other verbal or physical conduct of a sexual nature.

1.12 Derogatory Language

Social workers should not use derogatory language in their written or verbal communications to or about clients. Social workers should use accurate and respectful language in all communications to and about clients.

1.13 Payment for Services

(a) When setting fees, social workers should ensure that the fees are fair, reasonable, and commensurate with the services performed. Consideration should be given to clients' ability to pay.

(b) Social workers should avoid accepting goods or services from clients as payment for professional services. Bartering arrangements, particularly involving services, create the potential for conflicts of interest, exploitation, and inappropriate boundaries in social workers' relationships with clients. Social workers should explore and may participate in bartering only in very limited circumstances when it can be demonstrated that such arrangements are an accepted practice among professionals in the local community, considered to be essential for the provision of services, negotiated without coercion, and entered into at the client's initiative and with the client's informed consent. Social workers who accept goods or services from clients as payment for professional services assume the full burden of demonstrating that this arrangement will not be detrimental to the client or the professional relationship.

(c) Social workers should not solicit a private fee or other remuneration for providing services to clients who are entitled to such available services through the social workers' employer or agency.

1.14 Clients Who Lack Decision-Making Capacity

When social workers act on behalf of clients who lack the capacity to make informed decisions, social workers should take reasonable steps to safeguard the interests and rights of those clients.

1.15 Interruption of Services

Social workers should make reasonable efforts to ensure continuity of services in the event that services are interrupted by factors such as unavailability, relocation, illness, disability, or death.

1.16 Termination of Services

(a) Social workers should terminate services to clients and professional relationships with them when such services and relationships are no longer required or no longer serve the clients' needs or interests.

(b) Social workers should take reasonable steps to avoid abandoning clients who are still in need of services. Social workers should withdraw services precipitously only under unusual circumstances, giving careful consideration to all factors in the situation and taking care to minimize possible adverse effects. Social workers should assist in making appropriate arrangements for continuation of services when necessary.

(c) Social workers in fee-for-service settings may terminate services to clients who are not paying an overdue balance if the financial contractual arrangements have been made clear to the client, if the client does not pose an imminent danger to self or others, and if the clinical and other consequences of the current nonpayment have been addressed and discussed with the client.

(d) Social workers should not terminate services to pursue a social, financial, or sexual relationship with a client.

(e) Social workers who anticipate the termination or interruption of services to clients should notify clients promptly and seek the transfer, referral, or continuation of services in relation to the clients' needs and preferences.

(f) Social workers who are leaving an employment setting should inform clients of appropriate options for the continuation of services and of the benefits and risks of the options.

2. Social Workers' Ethical Responsibilities to Colleagues

2.01 Respect

(a) Social workers should treat colleagues with respect and should represent accurately and fairly the qualifications, views, and obligations of colleagues.

(b) Social workers should avoid unwarranted negative criticism of colleagues in communications with clients or with other professionals. Unwarranted negative criticism may include demeaning comments that refer to colleagues' level of competence or to individuals' attributes such as race, ethnicity, national origin, color, sex, sexual orientation, age, marital status, political belief, religion, and mental or physical disability.

(c) Social workers should cooperate with social work colleagues and with colleagues of other professions when such cooperation serves the well-being of clients.

2.02 Confidentiality

Social workers should respect confidential information shared by colleagues in the course of their professional relationships and transactions. Social workers should ensure that such colleagues understand social workers' obligation to respect confidentiality and any exceptions related to it.

2.03 Interdisciplinary Collaboration

(a) Social workers who are members of an interdisciplinary team should participate in and contribute to decisions that affect the well-being of clients by drawing on the perspectives, values, and experiences of the social work profession. Professional and ethical obligations of the interdisciplinary team as a whole and of its individual members should be clearly established.

(b) Social workers for whom a team decision raises ethical concerns should attempt to resolve the disagreement through appropriate channels. If the disagreement cannot be resolved, social workers should pursue other avenues to address their concerns consistent with client well-being.

2.04 Disputes Involving Colleagues

(a) Social workers should not take advantage of a dispute between a colleague and an employer to obtain a position or otherwise advance the social workers' own interests.

(b) Social workers should not exploit clients in disputes with colleagues or engage clients in any inappropriate discussion of conflicts between social workers and their colleagues.

2.05 Consultation

(a) Social workers should seek the advice and counsel of colleagues whenever such consultation is in the best interests of clients.

(b) Social workers should keep themselves informed about colleagues' areas of expertise and competencies. Social workers should seek consultation only from colleagues who have demonstrated knowledge, expertise, and competence related to the subject of the consultation.

(c) When consulting with colleagues about clients, social workers should disclose the least amount of information necessary to achieve the purposes of the consultation.

2.06 Referral for Services

(a) Social workers should refer clients to other professionals when the other professionals' specialized knowledge or expertise is needed to serve clients fully or when social workers believe that they are not being effective or making reasonable progress with clients and that additional service is required.

(b) Social workers who refer clients to other professionals should take appropriate steps to facilitate an orderly transfer of responsibility. Social workers who refer clients to other professionals should disclose, with clients' consent, all pertinent information to the new service providers.

(c) Social workers are prohibited from giving or receiving payment for a referral when no professional service is provided by the referring social worker.

2.07 Sexual Relationships

(a) Social workers who function as supervisors or educators should not engage in sexual activities or contact with supervisees, students, trainees, or other colleagues over whom they exercise professional authority.

(b) Social workers should avoid engaging in sexual relationships with colleagues when there is potential for a conflict of interest. Social workers who become involved in, or anticipate becoming involved in, a sexual relationship with a colleague have a duty to transfer professional responsibilities, when necessary, to avoid a conflict of interest.

2.08 Sexual Harassment

Social workers should not sexually harass supervisees, students, trainees, or colleagues. Sexual harassment includes sexual advances, sexual solicitation, requests for sexual favors, and other verbal or physical conduct of a sexual nature.

2.09 Impairment of Colleagues

(a) Social workers who have direct knowledge of a social work colleague's impairment that is due to personal problems, psychosocial distress, substance abuse, or mental health difficulties and that interferes with practice effectiveness should consult with that colleague when feasible and assist the colleague in taking remedial action.

(b) Social workers who believe that a social work colleague's impairment interferes with practice effectiveness and that the colleague has not taken adequate steps to address the impairment should take action through appropriate channels established by employers, agencies, NASW, licensing and regulatory bodies, and other professional organizations.

2.10 Incompetence of Colleagues

(a) Social workers who have direct knowledge of a social work colleague's incompetence should consult with that colleague when feasible and assist the colleague in taking remedial action.

(b) Social workers who believe that a social work colleague is incompetent and has not taken adequate steps to address the incompetence should take action through appropriate channels established by employers, agencies, NASW, licensing and regulatory bodies, and other professional organizations.

2.11 Unethical Conduct of Colleagues

(a) Social workers should take adequate measures to discourage, prevent, expose, and correct the unethical conduct of colleagues.

(b) Social workers should be knowledgeable about established policies and procedures for handling concerns about colleagues' unethical behavior. Social workers should be familiar with national, state, and local procedures for handling ethics complaints. These include policies and procedures created by NASW, licensing and regulatory bodies, employers, agencies, and other professional organizations.

(c) Social workers who believe that a colleague has acted unethically should seek resolution by discussing their concerns with the colleague when feasible and when such discussion is likely to be productive.

(d) When necessary, social workers who believe that a colleague has acted unethically should take action through appropriate formal channels (such as contacting a state licensing board or regulatory body, an NASW committee on inquiry, or other professional ethics committees).

(e) Social workers should defend and assist colleagues who are unjustly charged with unethical conduct.

3. Social Workers' Ethical Responsibilities in Practice Settings

3.01 Supervision and Consultation

(a) Social workers who provide supervision or consultation should have the necessary knowledge and skill to supervise or consult appropriately and should do so only within their areas of knowledge and competence.

(b) Social workers who provide supervision or consultation are responsible for setting clear, appropriate, and culturally sensitive boundaries.

(c) Social workers should not engage in any dual or multiple relationships with supervisees in which there is a risk of exploitation of or potential harm to the supervisee.

(d) Social workers who provide supervision should evaluate supervisees' performance in a manner that is fair and respectful.

3.02 Education and Training

(a) Social workers who function as educators, field instructors for students, or trainers should provide instruction only within their areas of knowledge and competence and should provide instruction based on the most current information and knowledge available in the profession.

(b) Social workers who function as educators or field instructors for students should evaluate students' performance in a manner that is fair and respectful.

(c) Social workers who function as educators or field instructors for students should take reasonable steps to ensure that clients are routinely informed when services are being provided by students.

(d) Social workers who function as educators or field instructors for students should not engage in any dual or multiple relationships with students in which there is a risk of exploitation or potential harm to the student. Social work educators and field instructors are responsible for setting clear, appropriate, and culturally sensitive boundaries.

3.03 Performance Evaluation

Social workers who have responsibility for evaluating the performance of others should fulfill such responsibility in a fair and considerate manner and on the basis of clearly stated criteria.

3.04 Client Records

(a) Social workers should take reasonable steps to ensure that documentation in records is accurate and reflects the services provided.

(b) Social workers should include sufficient and timely documentation in records to facilitate the delivery of services and to ensure continuity of services provided to clients in the future.

(c) Social workers' documentation should protect clients' privacy to the extent that is possible and appropriate and should include only information that is directly relevant to the delivery of services.

(d) Social workers should store records following the termination of services to ensure reasonable future access. Records should be maintained for the number of years required by state statutes or relevant contracts.

3.05 Billing

Social workers should establish and maintain billing practices that accurately reflect the nature and extent of services provided and that identify who provided the service in the practice setting.

3.06 Client Transfer

(a) When an individual who is receiving services from another agency or colleague contacts a social worker for services, the social worker should carefully consider the client's needs before agreeing to provide services. To minimize possible confusion and conflict, social workers should discuss with potential clients the nature of the clients' current relationship with other service providers and the implications, including possible benefits or risks, of entering into a relationship with a new service provider.

(b) If a new client has been served by another agency or colleague, social workers should discuss with the client whether consultation with the previous service provider is in the client's best interest.

3.07 Administration

(a) Social work administrators should advocate within and outside their agencies for adequate resources to meet clients' needs.

(b) Social workers should advocate for resource allocation procedures that are open and fair. When not all clients' needs can be met, an allocation procedure should be developed that is nondiscriminatory and based on appropriate and consistently applied principles.

(c) Social workers who are administrators should take reasonable steps to ensure that adequate agency or organizational resources are available to provide appropriate staff supervision.

(d) Social work administrators should take reasonable steps to ensure that the working environment for which they are responsible is consistent with and encourages compliance with the *NASW Code of Ethics*. Social work administrators should take reasonable steps to eliminate any conditions in their organizations that violate, interfere with, or discourage compliance with the *Code*.

3.08 Continuing Education and Staff Development

Social work administrators and supervisors should take reasonable steps to provide or arrange for continuing education and staff development for all staff for whom they are responsible. Continuing education and staff development should address current knowledge and emerging developments related to social work practice and ethics.

3.09 Commitments to Employers

(a) Social workers generally should adhere to commitments made to employers and employing organizations.

(b) Social workers should work to improve employing agencies' policies and procedures and the efficiency and effectiveness of their services.

(c) Social workers should take reasonable steps to ensure that employers are aware of social workers' ethical obligations as set forth in the *NASW Code of Ethics* and of the implications of those obligations for social work practice.

(d) Social workers should not allow an employing organization's policies, procedures, regulations, or administrative orders to interfere with their ethical practice of social work. Social workers should take reasonable steps to ensure that their employing organizations' practices are consistent with the *NASW Code of Ethics*.

(e) Social workers should act to prevent and eliminate discrimination in the employing organization's work assignments and in its employment policies and practices.

(f) Social workers should accept employment or arrange student field placements only in organizations that exercise fair personnel practices.

(g) Social workers should be diligent stewards of the resources of their employing organizations, wisely conserving funds where appropriate and never misappropriating funds or using them for unintended purposes.

3.10 Labor–Management Disputes

(a) Social workers may engage in organized action, including the formation of and participation in labor unions, to improve services to clients and working conditions.

(b) The actions of social workers who are involved in labor–management disputes, job actions, or labor strikes should be guided by the profession's values, ethical principles, and ethical standards. Reasonable differences of opinion exist among social workers concerning their primary obligation as professionals during an actual or threatened labor strike or job action. Social workers should carefully examine relevant issues and their possible impact on clients before deciding on a course of action.

4. Social Workers' Ethical Responsibilities as Professionals

4.01 Competence

(a) Social workers should accept responsibility or employment only on the basis of existing competence or the intention to acquire the necessary competence.

(b) Social workers should strive to become and remain proficient in professional practice and the performance of professional functions. Social workers should critically examine and keep current with emerging knowledge relevant to social work. Social workers should routinely review the professional literature and participate in continuing education relevant to social work practice and social work ethics.

(c) Social workers should base practice on recognized knowledge, including empirically based knowledge, relevant to social work and social work ethics.

4.02 Discrimination

Social workers should not practice, condone, facilitate, or collaborate with any form of discrimination on the basis of race, ethnicity, national origin, color, sex, sexual orientation, age, marital status, political belief, religion, or mental or physical disability.

4.03 Private Conduct

Social workers should not permit their private conduct to interfere with their ability to fulfill their professional responsibilities.

4.04 Dishonesty, Fraud, and Deception

Social workers should not participate in, condone, or be associated with dishonesty, fraud, or deception.

4.05 Impairment

(a) Social workers should not allow their own personal problems, psychosocial distress, legal problems, substance abuse, or mental health difficulties to interfere with their professional judgment and performance or to jeopardize the best interests of people for whom they have a professional responsibility.

(b) Social workers whose personal problems, psychosocial distress, legal problems, substance abuse, or mental health difficulties interfere with their professional judgment and performance should immediately seek consultation and take appropriate remedial action by seeking professional help, making adjustments in workload, terminating practice, or taking any other steps necessary to protect clients and others.

4.06 Misrepresentation

(a) Social workers should make clear distinctions between statements made and actions engaged in as a private individual and as a representative of the social work profession, a professional social work organization, or the social worker's employing agency.

(b) Social workers who speak on behalf of professional social work organizations should accurately represent the official and authorized positions of the organizations.

(c) Social workers should ensure that their representations to clients, agencies, and the public of professional qualifications, credentials, education, competence, affiliations, services provided, or results to be achieved are accurate. Social workers should claim only those relevant professional credentials they actually possess and take steps to correct any inaccuracies or misrepresentations of their credentials by others.

4.07 Solicitations

(a) Social workers should not engage in uninvited solicitation of potential clients who, because of their circumstances, are vulnerable to undue influence, manipulation, or coercion.

(b) Social workers should not engage in solicitation of testimonial endorsements (including solicitation of consent to use a client's prior statement as a testimonial endorsement) from current clients or from other people who, because of their particular circumstances, are vulnerable to undue influence.

4.08 Acknowledging Credit

(a) Social workers should take responsibility and credit, including authorship credit, only for work they have actually performed and to which they have contributed.

(b) Social workers should honestly acknowledge the work of and the contributions made by others.

5. Social Workers' Ethical Responsibilities to the Social Work Profession

   5.01 Integrity of the Profession

      (a) Social workers should work toward the maintenance and promotion of high standards of practice.

      (b) Social workers should uphold and advance the values, ethics, knowledge, and mission of the profession. Social workers should protect, enhance, and improve the integrity of the profession through appropriate study and research, active discussion, and responsible criticism of the profession.

      (c) Social workers should contribute time and professional expertise to activities that promote respect for the value, integrity, and competence of the social work profession. These activities may include teaching, research, consultation, service, legislative testimony, presentations in the community, and participation in their professional organizations.

      (d) Social workers should contribute to the knowledge base of social work and share with colleagues their knowledge related to practice, research, and ethics. Social workers should seek to contribute to the profession's literature and to share their knowledge at professional meetings and conferences.

      (e) Social workers should act to prevent the unauthorized and unqualified practice of social work.

   5.02 Evaluation and Research

      (a) Social workers should monitor and evaluate policies, the implementation of programs, and practice interventions.

      (b) Social workers should promote and facilitate evaluation and research to contribute to the development of knowledge.

      (c) Social workers should critically examine and keep current with emerging knowledge relevant to social work and fully use evaluation and research evidence in their professional practice.

      (d) Social workers engaged in evaluation or research should carefully consider possible consequences and should follow guidelines developed for the protection of evaluation and research participants. Appropriate institutional review boards should be consulted.

      (e) Social workers engaged in evaluation or research should obtain voluntary and written informed consent from participants, when appropriate, without any implied or actual deprivation or penalty for refusal to participate; without undue inducement to participate; and with due regard for participants' well-being, privacy, and dignity. Informed consent should include information about the nature, extent, and duration of the participation requested and disclosure of the risks and benefits of participation in the research.

(f) When evaluation or research participants are incapable of giving informed consent, social workers should provide an appropriate explanation to the participants, obtain the participants' assent to the extent they are able, and obtain written consent from an appropriate proxy.

(g) Social workers should never design or conduct evaluation or research that does not use consent procedures, such as certain forms of naturalistic observation and archival research, unless rigorous and responsible review of the research has found it to be justified because of its prospective scientific, educational, or applied value and unless equally effective alternative procedures that do not involve waiver of consent are not feasible.

(h) Social workers should inform participants of their right to withdraw from evaluation and research at any time without penalty.

(i) Social workers should take appropriate steps to ensure that participants in evaluation and research have access to appropriate supportive services.

(j) Social workers engaged in evaluation or research should protect participants from unwarranted physical or mental distress, harm, danger, or deprivation.

(k) Social workers engaged in the evaluation of services should discuss collected information only for professional purposes and only with people professionally concerned with this information.

(l) Social workers engaged in evaluation or research should ensure the anonymity or confidentiality of participants and of the data obtained from them. Social workers should inform participants of any limits of confidentiality, the measures that will be taken to ensure confidentiality, and when any records containing research data will be destroyed.

(m) Social workers who report evaluation and research results should protect participants' confidentiality by omitting identifying information unless proper consent has been obtained authorizing disclosure.

(n) Social workers should report evaluation and research findings accurately. They should not fabricate or falsify results and should take steps to correct any errors later found in published data using standard publication methods.

(o) Social workers engaged in evaluation or research should be alert to and avoid conflicts of interest and dual relationships with participants, should inform participants when a real or potential conflict of interest arises, and should take steps to resolve the issue in a manner that makes participants' interests primary.

(p) Social workers should educate themselves, their students, and their colleagues about responsible research practices.

6. Social Workers' Ethical Responsibilities to the Broader Society

   6.01 Social Welfare

   Social workers should promote the general welfare of society, from local to global levels, and the development of people, their communities, and their environments. Social workers should advocate for living conditions conducive to the fulfillment of basic human needs and should promote social, economic, political, and cultural values and institutions that are compatible with the realization of social justice.

   6.02 Public Participation

   Social workers should facilitate informed participation by the public in shaping social policies and institutions.

   6.03 Public Emergencies

   Social workers should provide appropriate professional services in public emergencies to the greatest extent possible.

   6.04 Social and Political Action

   (a) Social workers should engage in social and political action that seeks to ensure that all people have equal access to the resources, employment, services, and opportunities they require to meet their basic human needs and to develop fully. Social workers should be aware of the impact of the political arena on practice and should advocate for changes in policy and legislation to improve social conditions in order to meet basic human needs and promote social justice.

   (b) Social workers should act to expand choice and opportunity for all people, with special regard for vulnerable, disadvantaged, oppressed, and exploited people and groups.

   (c) Social workers should promote conditions that encourage respect for cultural and social diversity within the United States and globally. Social workers should promote policies and practices that demonstrate respect for difference, support the expansion of cultural knowledge and resources, advocate for programs and institutions that demonstrate cultural competence, and promote policies that safeguard the rights of and confirm equity and social justice for all people.

   (d) Social workers should act to prevent and eliminate domination of, exploitation of, and discrimination against any person, group, or class on the basis of race, ethnicity, national origin, color, sex, sexual orientation, age, marital status, political belief, religion, or mental or physical disability.

APPENDIX E

The Social Work Covenant

Sister M. Vincentia Joseph

I promise to fulfill the obligations established by the social work profession, to help those in need, and to build a more just society.

My obligations rest in the vulnerability of those in need, and the trust they place in my professional competence to help them adjust to the complex demands of life.

I, therefore, bind myself to the good of my clients and the good of society as the first principle of my professional ethic.

In recognition of this bond of charity and justice, I accept the following obligations:

- To honor the fiduciary relationship between client and self, and to promote the general welfare of all clients throughout all aspects of my professional practice.
- To care for all who need my help with equal concern and dedication, but with special regard to serve the poor, the weak, and the victims of discrimination and oppression.
- To maintain my professional competence through continued educational development, and to promote and share collaborative endeavors throughout the profession.
- To foster self-determination for all clients by clearly informing and involving them in all decisions that affect their lives, and to help each client choose directions consistent with their values and beliefs without coercion or deception.
- To hold in confidence what I hear, learn, and see as an essential component of my practice except when conditions present a clear potential for serious and immediate harm to self and others.
- To promote equitably the general welfare of society through prevention and elimination of discriminatory policies and through active participation as an advocate for improved social conditions and social justice.
- To treat colleagues and employers with respect, fairness, and good faith, and to uphold and advance the values, ethics, knowledge, and mission of the social work profession.

Through these words and subsequent actions, I pledge and commit myself to the ethical principles established by the social work profession and our collective concern to help those in need.

INDEX